THE ARCHITECT OF GENOCIDE

RICHARD BREITMAN

THE ARCHITECT OF GENOCIDE

HIMMLER AND THE FINAL SOLUTION

THE BODLEY HEAD
LONDON

First published in Great Britain 1991
© Richard Breitman 1991
The Bodley Head, 20 Vauxhall Bridge Road, London SW1V 2SA

Richard Breitman has asserted his right to be
identified as the author of this work

A CIP catalogue record for this book
is available from the British Library

ISBN 0 370 31352 6

Printed in Great Britain by Mackays of Chatham PLC,
Chatham, Kent

To Carol, David, and Marc

CONTENTS

ACKNOWLEDGMENTS

ALTHOUGH Heinrich Himmler's activities were not well covered in earlier studies, the literature on the Holocaust is immense. Working in this richly mined field, I have become aware of how much my own work builds upon a foundation laid by others. I have also been lucky to stumble into a number of friendships that began with discussion of common interests.

Robert Wolfe encouraged me to enter the intimidating labyrinth of the captured German records in the National Archives (Record Group 242), and, once I had done so, helped me find new routes when I thought I had reached a dead end. Wolfe called my attention again and again to the American Historical Association–National Archives Guides to the Captured German Records, which represented almost an index to the mountain of material. Before each visit to the National Archives, I spent many hours poring over the relevant guide or guides so that I could inspect a relatively small number of rolls of film once I got there. When I could not find what I was seeking, I would simply go up to Wolfe's office and ask if he knew where there might be additional material on Göring or Rosenberg or a particular event. Often he gave me specific citations off the top of his head; sometimes he checked comments he had scribbled on the front of his own guide.

As I focused more and more on Himmler and the mysteries of the "Final Solution of the Jewish Question," my exploration and Wolfe's intersected more and more, for he had been working for years on his own study of the Final Solution. In spite of the fact that I represented a competitor as well as a "customer," he continued to be unfailingly generous with his time as well as with suggestions. My trips to the National Archives became not merely research expeditions but also short

ix

tutorials in which I learned some things about the archives and particular documents, and a good deal more about the Final Solution. When I found something new and important, I would show it to Wolfe first and await his reaction. He was always pleased, but he usually told me as well that there was more to be found, that I should keep looking. He was an ideal mentor.

Also at the National Archives, John E. Taylor gave me the benefit of his decades of experience. Also helpful were Timothy Mulligan, Larry McDonald, Richard Boylan, Jo Ann Williamson, David Langbart, Amy Schmidt, Kathy Nicastro, Les Wappen, and George Loukides.

Robert J. Walsh at the U.S. Army Intelligence and Security Command, Fort Meade, Maryland, complied promptly and cooperatively with my Freedom of Information Act requests.

Hermann Weiss at the Institut für Zeitgeschichte in Munich guided me to sources not to be found elsewhere, and Daniel Simon and David Marwell both proved unfailingly helpful at the Berlin Document Center. Agnes Peterson provided assistance with relevant collections, particularly the Himmler Diaries, at the Hoover Institution at Stanford University, and I benefited from her own experience in working on Himmler.

Larisa Vassilievna Yakovleva, director of the Central Archive of the October Revolution in Kiev, extended courtesies and cooperation to me during my research there. I am deeply grateful to her for giving me permission to look at captured German records there. Stanislav Kostetsky translated for me, assisted me, and made my stay in Kiev both possible and pleasant. Alf Erlandsson gave me access to United Nations War Crimes Commission Records.

Walter Laqueur seemed to know instinctively what I was likely to find in the archives; he also put me in touch with a number of people who provided useful information from their personal experiences. Gerhard L. Weinberg used his vast knowledge of the records and the field to point me in the right direction on a number of occasions. Henry Friedlander helped me obtain a number of West German trial records and saved me from errors about the Nazi euthanasia policy and practices; I look forward to his forthcoming book on the subject. Sybil Milton provided excellent information about archival holdings, and I will benefit from her future research on Nazi policies toward gypsies. Heinrich Rosenlehner and Peter Mende took time out from their official duties to decipher some German shorthand notes for me; they helped me in less tangible ways as well.

Charles W. Sydnor, Jr., gave me the benefit of his knowledge of Heydrich the man and of the SS generally. His future biography of Heydrich should be an important work. Sydnor also unselfishly sent me copies of documents that he had obtained from not generally available sources. Karl Schleunes provided copies of documents he had obtained at Yad Vashem in Israel, and Shlomo Aronson obtained some information for me from Yad Vashem.

Hannu Rautkallio and I exchanged information about Himmler's travels to Finland. He also sent me photographs, as did Christelle Pluciennik and Karen Gallagher. Walter Stoll obtained some material for me in the Soviet Union. Bent Blüdnikow sent me some documents from Danish archives. Dr. Hans Deichmann gave me detailed information about his experiences at I. G. Farben, and Mrs. R. C. Prawdin satisfied my curiosity about her late husband's books on Genghis Khan. Others who prefer to remain nameless helped me find new sources as well.

I held long and fruitful discussions of war crimes with Peter Black, Barry White, Michael MacQueen, Robert Waite, Michael Wolf, Betty Shave, and especially Konrad Kwiet. Shlomo Aronson allowed me to read his unpublished manuscript on Allied dilemmas during the Holocaust and the impact of the Holocaust on Israel. Geoff Eley sent me a then unpublished analysis of the *Historikerstreit*. I benefited greatly from stimulating contacts with Yehuda Bauer, Hans Mommsen, Leni Yahil, and Christopher Browning, even—or especially—when they did not share or accept my views.

Others who read one or more chapters and provided advice and suggestions include: my American University colleagues Allan Lichtman, James Malloy, and Arnost Lustig; also Margaret Lavinia Anderson, Gerhard Weinberg, Peter Black, Henry Friedlander, Bradley F. Smith, and Stephen Lofgren.

James F. Harris undertook the Herculean task of reading the entire manuscript at a late stage and persuading me to make numerous substantial changes to sharpen the argument and make it more comprehensible. My editor at Alfred A. Knopf, Ashbel Green, spared me the difficulties that usually result from an attempt to write simultaneously for academic and general audiences. His guidelines and criticism served to improve the book for both. Of course, I alone am responsible for the problems that remain.

The American University provided financial support for my research on a number of occasions, and Department Chair Robert Beisner, Dean Betty Bennett of the College of Arts and Sciences, and Dean of Faculties Fred Jacobs were extremely helpful in this regard. Ann Ferren encouraged this project as she has done with some of my past ones. It would have been difficult to complete this book without such help.

The Western European Program at the Woodrow Wilson Center, Smithsonian Institution, awarded me a fellowship in 1987 that allowed me to spend more than my normal time for research and writing. I am indebted to Michael Haltzel at the Wilson Center, my office neighbor Jeffrey Diefendorf, and Carole Fink, for their reactions and suggestions during that time. Kevin Murphy performed research assignments for me during my time at the Wilson Center, and Monica Cousins checked some files for me at the National Archives.

My greatest debt is to my wife, Carol, and my sons, David and Marc, who did more than put up with my frequent absences and late-night hours. Carol read and criticized my chapters, and my family all reminded me constantly of the joys of humanity, which made it possible for me to cope with the darkness of Himmler and the Final Solution.

THE ARCHITECT OF
GENOCIDE

INTRODUCTION

THE MASS MURDER of some six million Jews, usually called the Holocaust, has placed an indelible stamp upon the twentieth century and upon our consciousness. Adolf Hitler's Third Reich exploited all the ingenious advantages of modern technology to transport Jews from most parts of Europe to various killing sites, including specially constructed extermination camps, where they were executed in gas chambers as quickly, smoothly, and quietly as possible. This combination of sophisticated technology and barbaric mass murder raises serious questions whether there has really been progress in history, and it is a stark commentary on the human capacity for evil. The fact that some of the murderers were well-educated citizens in a highly industrialized society only adds to the incomprehensibility of the events. The Holocaust is of the utmost importance for historians, philosophers, psychologists, for the modern world.

In various ways the fields of history, political science, literature, philosophy, jurisprudence, and cinema already reflect its importance. Some of the historical works about the Nazi bureaucracy of mass murder—for example, Raul Hilberg's *The Destruction of the European Jews*—are modern classics.[1] Other scholarly studies, personal accounts, and novels have examined life and death in Nazi concentration camps and in the ghettos—and the moral choices faced by those who were persecuted but kept alive. Holocaust survivor and writer Elie Wiesel won a Nobel Peace Prize for his ability to apply the lessons of the Holocaust to moral and political problems in the contemporary world. The Nuremberg trial of the major war criminals immediately after World War II defined a new crime—crime against humanity—and made it clear that simply following orders was not an adequate defense for those who had murdered and tortured. The trials of Adolf Eichmann and, more recently, John (Ivan) Demjanjuk, as well as movies such as Claude Lanzmann's *Shoah*, have conveyed to a broad public a sense of what the Nazi regime tried to accomplish, as well as what some of the men who made and carried out the arrangements were like. There is no lack of information about the Holocaust.

In spite of this at times overwhelming attention to the subject, some of the key individuals who ordered or arranged the killings remain mysterious figures, whose personalities are difficult to fathom and whose exact roles in these events is unclear. Among them, remarkably, is Heinrich Himmler, more directly associated with Nazi programs of mass murder than anyone else. As it turns out, this gap in our knowledge is more significant than it might at first seem.

The commandant of Auschwitz once said: "Our system is so terrible that no one in the world will believe it to be possible. . . . If someone should succeed in escaping from Auschwitz and in telling the world, the world will brand him as a fantastic liar. . . ."[2] That was nearly true during part of the war, and there is a danger that it may become true again. Those who are prejudiced or naïve may not try to absorb the events of the Holocaust at all; it seems to them common sense to be skeptical about the accounts of gas chambers and crematoria and millions of murdered Jews.

Time usually gives people (and historians) perspective on events, but time may be an enemy of the Holocaust. The number of survivors diminishes each day; those who lived through the Nazi era as adults will disappear within decades. Historians and archivists will have to provide the concrete evidence to convince future generations of what happened. But it is usually easier to see history through the lens of the individual, and there is no better vantage point overlooking the Holocaust than the life of Heinrich Himmler.

Like his Führer, Himmler was an easy man to underestimate. Part of the reason lay simply in his physique: short, pudgy, unathletic. He was very nearsighted, and the pince-nez or the thick glasses he wore did little for his appearance. Contemporaries who looked at this flabby, balding man could see nothing of the Nordic ideal to which he was so devoted. One of the Nazi Party Gauleiter, the regional bosses who frequently created difficulties for him, once wisecracked: "If I looked like him, I would not speak of race at all."[3] Heinrich Himmler got little respect from outsiders until he built his beloved order, the Schutzstaffel or SS, into the most powerful single organization in Nazi Germany. And even then his competitors mocked him.

There were dashing performers on the political stage of his day. Adolf

Hitler was perhaps the ultimate charismatic leader, Joseph Goebbels also was a brilliant speaker, and Hermann Göring, a former World War I ace, knew how to plunder, consume, and entertain in a style comparable to that of the Roman emperors. Himmler's own deputy, Reinhard Heydrich, was an accomplished fencer, musician, and pilot, talents that Himmler could only admire. In the upper ranks of the Nazi movement were other swaggering buccaneers who attracted attention, envy, admiration, or disgust, passion of one kind or another. By contrast, Himmler came across as dull, pedantic, and humorless—totally without flair. His speeches were carefully organized, and on occasion he could be emotional and impulsive, but he did not inspire. Seemingly the very antithesis of the raving madman, some called him the "gentle Heinrich." ✗

Himmler did not seek to overwhelm others with his life-style. Even at the peak of his power he remained more the private than the public figure. He had a villa in Berlin-Dahlem, away from the bustle of the capital, and a small estate on the Tegernsee in Bavaria, where his wife and daughter lived. His only extravagant "residence" was his castle Wewelsburg near Paderborn in Westphalia, which he regarded as a retreat for himself and the cream of the SS. No outsiders were permitted at Wewelsburg, and there was, of course, no publicity about the top-secret SS gatherings there.

A man who knew Himmler intimately and who saw him almost daily during much of World War II described Himmler's personality as opaque, with something of the Japanese (inscrutability), rather than the European. Himmler appeared to be easygoing, jovial, at peace with himself. On social occasions, but also with his staff or in business meetings, he made himself seem the average middle-class, paternalistic Bavarian, using dialect to enhance the impression. But, according to Himmler's associate, there were signs of another Himmler within. ⅄

His eyes were extraordinarily small, and the distance between them narrow, rodent-like. If you spoke to him, these eyes would never leave your face; they would rove over your countenance, fix your eyes; and in them would be an expression of waiting, watching, stealth. His manner of reacting to things which did not meet with his approval was also not quite that expected from the jovial bourgeois. Sometimes his disagreement was clothed in the form of a fatherly admonition, but this could suddenly change and his speech and actions would become ironic, caustic, cynical. But never, even in these expressions of disagreement and dislike, did the man himself seem to appear. . . . Never any indication of directness . . . Himmler[,] when fighting[,] intrigued[;] when battling for his so-called ideas used subterfuge, deceit—not dueling swords, but daggers in his opponent's back. His ways were the ophidian ways of the coward, weak, insincere and immeasurably cruel. . . . Himmler's mind . . . was not a twentieth century mind. His character was medieval, feudalistic, machiavellian, evil.[4]

Himmler's personal traits manifested themselves often during the Holocaust, in the preparation of secret plans, in measures designed to mislead the victims, and in curious documentation of what he had done.

The story that follows is not simply about what happened, but about the men who planned genocide. It is of the utmost importance that the chief planner was a master of deceit. His deceitfulness, which will surface again and again in the chapters that follow, helps to explain events and documents that might otherwise seem inconsistent.

Himmler's general rule was not to refer explicitly in writing to mass killings of Jews, and he employed circumlocutions even when it was not strictly necessary for security. One good example came in November 1942, by which time Nazi executions of Jews in the extermination camps —Belzec, Sobibor, Treblinka, Maidanek, Chełmno, and Auschwitz— were well under way. Although the gassing was supposed to be a tightly held secret, the information had already leaked out to the West through various channels in Switzerland. One of the reports that reached Rabbi Stephen Wise, president of the American Jewish Congress, told of Nazis who were making soap from the flesh of the Jews gassed, and artificial fertilizer from their bones. In September 1942 Wise gave this information to Undersecretary of State Sumner Welles, who asked the American special envoy at the Vatican, Myron Taylor, to find out whether the Vatican could confirm it and could do anything about Nazi barbarities. It was hard to keep a secret in Rome. News of Wise's information and the American inquiry leaked back to the Reich Security Main Office and to Himmler,[5] possibly from sources inside the Vatican or, more likely, from sources contacted by the Vatican.

Himmler knew that no one was supposed to be manufacturing fats or artificial fertilizers from corpses (in fact, it turned out that this part of the report was erroneous). He wrote to Heinrich Müller, head of the most important division of the Reich Security Main Office, demanding a guarantee that the bodies were not being misused. Even in this letter, however, Himmler was unwilling to state the facts baldly. He wrote of the "large emigration movement" of Jews and added: "We both know that there is an increased mortality rate with those Jews put to work."[6] Himmler admitted that there were a large number of bodies to dispose of, but not that there was an extermination program. There cannot have been many people in Nazi Europe better informed about what was actually happening to the Jews than Heinrich Müller. Himmler's letter was not designed to conceal anything from his trusted subordinate; it simply followed his internalized rules about how to refer to the deportations of Jews to the death camps, or how not to refer to them—especially on paper. Even while in the process of murdering millions of human beings, Himmler maintained his own sense of what was proper behavior—in the camps and in written communications.

His efforts to use disguise continued almost right down to the end. In the last phase of the war, when defeat was becoming obvious, Himmler attempted to pass himself off as a "responsible" leader with whom the Allies might do business. The effort not only failed, but alienated Hitler, who, learning of his attempts to conduct negotiations with the Allies, dismissed Himmler from his offices.

Just before the end of the war, and just after Hitler had committed suicide, Himmler's longtime secretary, Erika Lorenz, went from Salzburg to an SS castle in the town of Fischhorn, near Hitler's mountain headquarters at Obersalzburg. Frau Lorenz had a special assignment: to destroy the contents of a steel file cabinet in the castle. Two SS officers let her into the castle and showed her the file cabinet. She took everything out, laid the contents on the floor, then packed them into a laundry basket, which she and an officer carried to the furnace. Before she burned the load, Frau Lorenz noticed that there were some personal letters from Himmler's family there, but that most of the contents were official files.[7] Her job was to help her boss destroy his own record of what he had done.

Himmler's last resort was a literal disguise. He and his immediate staff clothed themselves as simple soldiers and set off by car, trying to escape notice in the British zone of occupation, first near Flensburg in Schleswig-Holstein, on the Danish border; then they headed south, left their cars behind to cross the Elbe on a fishing boat, and walked south through Neuhaus to Bremervörde, north of the city Bremen and east of Bremerhaven.

On May 20, 1945, Himmler and two adjutants left the main party and took off for the south. Himmler was now wearing civilian clothes and a black patch over one eye, having discarded his customary pince-nez. They ran into a squad of Russian soldiers, who failed to recognize them but turned them over to a group of British soldiers. Himmler undoubtedly preferred to be in British hands; he considered the Anglo-Saxons part of the Nordic family of races. It is also hard to imagine what fate the Russians would have devised for him. The three were then driven to a British POW camp at Seelos-bei-Bremervörde, where they were interrogated. Himmler gave his name as Hitzinger; he actually carried the papers of a Heinrich Hitzinger, one of the many Germans condemned to death by a people's court. He had kept the papers in case they might prove useful. The British authorities suspected the three of being deserters from the Wehrmacht. They were shipped around for a couple of days, ending up at 031 Interrogation Camp at Barnstedt, near Lüneburg, on May 23.[8]

Himmler decided to make one last effort to communicate seriously with this racially kindred foe. Perhaps, in spite of all he had done, he still hoped to be given a position of substance in a new German regime. The three men insisted on seeing the officer in charge, and they were brought before Captain Tom Selvester. After Himmler was left alone with Captain Selvester, he removed the patch over his eye and put on his spectacles. In a soft voice he said, "Heinrich Himmler."

Selvester sent for intelligence officers from the British Second Army, he had Himmler searched, and he waited. He later described Himmler's behavior:

> . . . he behaved perfectly correctly, and gave me the impression that he realized things had caught up with him. He was quite prepared to talk, and indeed at times appeared almost jovial. He looked ill when I first saw him, but improved tremendously after a meal and a wash. . . . He was in my custody for approximately eight hours, and during that time, whilst not being interrogated, asked repeatedly about the whereabouts of his "Adjutants," appearing genuinely worried over their welfare. I found it impossible to believe that he could be the arrogant man portrayed by the press before and during the war.[9]

He was to receive a more thorough search and harsher treatment that evening at an interrogation center in Lüneburg. When Sergeant Major Edwin Austin ordered him to undress, Himmler could only assume that the man didn't know who he was. Austin made it clear that he did. Himmler was stripped and searched, with the aid of army doctor C. J. Wells. When they got to his mouth, Himmler clamped down on the doctor's fingers and then bit open a cyanide capsule carefully lodged in a gap between his teeth on the right side of his jaw. (It was not a last-minute improvisation; Himmler had been carrying the capsule, he had told his wife, since early in the war.) In spite of efforts to prevent Himmler from swallowing and to pump out the poison, he died after fifteen minutes. One of the British officers exclaimed: "The bastard's beat us!"[10] He certainly cheated Allied authorities as well as historians

and psychologists of the opportunity to demand answers to a great many
questions.

Three days later, after British army surgeons had taken casts of his
features and removed parts of his brain and skull, four soldiers from
the Second Army Defence Company, a guard unit, buried Heinrich
Himmler in a secret grave on Lüneburg Heath. British authorities did
not want the site to become a rallying point for Nazi enthusiasts.[11] But
his grave was not to be Himmler's last secret; Frau Lorenz and others
had helped him to preserve others from the light of history.

A HISTORIAN or a biographer is tempted to look for some extraordinary, crippling experience in the youth of the man who became the
Reich Führer SS. The problem is that Himmler's childhood circumstances were relatively normal, even privileged. There is no simple en- ✗
vironmental or psychological explanation as to why Himmler became a
mass murderer on an unprecedented scale.

Born in 1900, the second of three sons of a Bavarian secondary-school
teacher (later deputy principal) and a very pious Catholic homemaker,
the young Heinrich Himmler grew up in quite comfortable conditions.
The family had a full-time maid to help Anna Maria Himmler (née
Heyder), daughter of a businessman, but she was said to be a diligent
mother who made sure her three children were well cared for. His father,
Gebhard Himmler, was not the aloof and distant authority often regarded as typical of that generation of Germans but, rather, an active
if strict parent who took considerable interest in the upbringing and
activities of Heinrich and his brothers, Gebhard (two years older) and
Ernst (five years younger). The family had a reading circle, emphasizing
classical literature, and Gebhard Senior carefully supervised the boys'
educational and cultural progress.[12]

Gebhard Himmler, who bore the title of professor, had tutored Prince
Heinrich of Wittelsbach, the royal family of Bavaria, and Heinrich
Himmler was named after the prince, who graciously consented to become his godfather. This connection with the court was not only highly
useful; it was also indicative of a family trait. The Himmlers were much
concerned with maintaining and enhancing status, and Heinrich's activities and friends had to pass muster socially.[13] Throughout his life he
remained sensitive to the importance of rank.

Both Gebhard Junior and Heinrich were bright, consistently ranking
at or near the top of their respective classes.[14] Heinrich was not quite so
successful as his easygoing older brother, and it appears that he had to
work a bit harder. During his career in elite, classics-oriented secondary

schools (*Gymnasia*) in Munich and Landshut, Gebhard Himmler consistently exploited his contacts at school, at court, and in society to smooth the way for his sons and to prepare them for professional careers.[15] On the surface, the Himmlers were all devoted to one another and successful. Unlike those of many other early Nazis, Himmler's background and standing were solidly middle-class. Given his family's connection to the Bavarian court and the traditional weight that Germans placed on educational distinction, it would be possible to place him in the upper middle class. But such ranking takes little account of the circumstances of the era, or of more elusive psychological factors unique to the individual.

There is a fair amount of information available about Himmler's childhood and youth because of a practice that his father initiated. During the summer of 1910, when Heinrich was ten years old and about to enter the *Gymnasium*, his father instructed him to keep a diary, as a way of symbolizing that a new and more important stage of life was beginning. Gebhard actually wrote the first entry for Heinrich, providing a model. During that summer and for some years thereafter, Gebhard checked over the diaries, making corrections and additions when he thought it necessary.[16] Heinrich continued to record his activities sporadically in his diaries through age twenty-four.

The boy who registered his mundane daily undertakings grew into a man who had his staff keep an appointment book for him, listing everyone who came in to see him, as well as an office log, detailing even incoming and outgoing phone calls, and a log of incoming and outgoing correspondence. He carefully kept records of personal expenses, reimbursing his office accounts from his private funds.[17] One can see in Himmler's childhood the beginnings of the adult's methodical nature and his attempts to impose order and structure.

Two well-known studies of Heinrich Himmler's youth have drawn heavily on the diaries, which were uncovered in 1945 and then all but forgotten until 1957. Although these analyses are superior to anything written about Himmler's adult personality, they do not resolve the mystery of how this mild-mannered boy turned into the man who used the police state and the war machine to destroy millions of innocent civilians. Bradley F. Smith's *Heinrich Himmler: A Nazi in the Making, 1900–1926* described the evolution of a political bureaucrat with an elitist racial ideology, but not a pathological killer: "the twentieth century cannot escape from its monstrosities by uncovering a mark of Cain or a Mephistophelean pact with the devil."[18] Using psychoanalytic theory to explore the diaries, Peter Loewenberg, in contrast, found the young Himmler to be lacking an inner emotional core and possessing a weak ego that allowed him to identify with whomever he was with. Loewenberg diagnosed Himmler as schizoid, severely disturbed. His hostility toward his father and his fear of loss of control (including loss of control of sexual desire) were displaced into desire for war and romantic conquest: "He was . . . precisely what one should expect of the subordinate of a dictator and the head of a vast police network."[19] Perhaps so, but there is little evidence in the diaries of abnormal conflict between child and father (or mother), and much evidence of genuine affection. From age nineteen on (no diary survives from when he was seventeen or eighteen), Himmler was also more expressive and emotional in his diary than Loewenberg's psychoanalytic model would predict.

Other factors can account for some of what Loewenberg ascribes to Himmler's repressed hostility toward his father. First, he had recurring health problems—a severe lung infection as a toddler, the usual childhood illnesses more draining in a boy who was far from robust, a serious case of typhoid fever at age nineteen, and chronic stomach disorders that were to plague him throughout his life. Loewenberg is on stronger ground when he points out that gastrointestinal problems are often partly the result of psychological pressures, and that Himmler seems to be a typical case of this kind.[20]

It is not hard to find major causes of tension in Himmler's youth. Although he mastered his schoolwork through careful attention to his duties, he could only struggle through the sports so crucial to adolescent status. His lowest grades were always in gymnastics. With his schoolwork and his outside interests—reading, gardening, harpsichord, chess, and stamp collecting—he did not want for things to do. He did not possess, however, the self-confidence of the boy who was good at soccer or gymnastics—or, later, at impressing girls. Even as an adult, according to one observer, Himmler was uneasy in the company of women. He never quite outgrew the social supervision of his parents. He worked with weights to increase his strength, but he never succeeded in overcoming his physical deficiencies. In comparable ways, he chastised himself for his failings of personality—for example, his tendency to talk too much—in the hope that he would learn, improve, and become better liked.[21] The results were about the same as with his body-building, but he persisted. It was almost as if the striving mattered more than the goal.

A vulnerable boy may withdraw into the family and himself for prolonged periods, disciplining himself to absorb the injuries that the outside world has inflicted. This retreat works only if he can block out or reduce the self-doubts raised by lack of acceptance. Often withdrawal leads to a second strategy: deprecation of the worth of those who deny him respect and acceptance. A third and more advanced method is to build a view of the world that allows the person to define for himself and to perform a particular role, and thereby to maintain self-esteem, in spite of difficulties with peers. That self-esteem then becomes the foundation for a renewed effort to obtain influence. Himmler chose a system of beliefs and values based on military virtues—valor, obedience and self-discipline, careful training, and self-sacrifice.

Himmler was fourteen when World War I began. He followed the events closely, as his diary entries indicate, and he and his friend Falk Zipperer also frequently played war games.[22] The drama of the war and the personal involvement in bloodless games stimulated his imagination and molded his aspirations. He pushed his parents to use their connections to help him gain a spot among the officer candidates even before he had finished at the *Gymnasium*. His parents were not enthusiastic, all the more because Heinrich wanted to do more than serve in the war— he wanted to become a professional army officer. Military training as an officer candidate was not easy for him physically or emotionally, but he stuck it out. The war ended, however, before he had an opportunity to reach the front.[23]

Like so many other conservative Germans, Heinrich Himmler was mortified by Germany's sudden defeat in 1918, by the socialist revolutions that swept across the country, and by the humiliating peace settlement that the new republic received in 1919. Himmler did not keep a diary during the revolution itself, but his attitude emerges clearly from subsequent comments: the accursed revolution and revolutionary governments had destroyed everything.[24] He did not acknowledge that the revolution and the peace settlement were the consequences of Germany's military defeat.

The Treaty of Versailles, which Germany had been forced to sign, had stipulated a limit of a hundred thousand men for its army, terminating Himmler's prospects of becoming an army officer. The old methods and social standards no longer meant so much, as inflation wracked the country and weak coalition governments in Berlin avoided hard decisions. Bavaria became a stronghold of right-wing discontent with the new republic, which went by the name of Weimar, after the city where the Constituent Assembly first met. Returning World War I veterans, and those, like Himmler, who had missed the fighting but were entering the real world after the war, found themselves adrift in terms of both career and politics.

Himmler completed the rites of passage. He finished school, and tried to serve an apprenticeship on a farm until illness forced his withdrawal. So he turned to the Munich Technische Hochschule, an institute of technology, where he began to study agriculture (again not suiting his parents' status aspirations). He soon became a passionate advocate of farming. One SS official later saw Himmler's agricultural background as the stimulus for his subsequent interest in racial breeding and even his desire to destroy what he considered to be human vermin. He thought he could apply the principles and methods of agriculture to human society.[25]

At the time he began his studies, in the fall of 1919, he suffered an identity crisis produced partly by career frustrations and partly by personal anxieties. Himmler had sworn to remain chaste, but he now ran into other people with different intentions and life-styles, and he envied them. When he became interested in the younger daughter of a widow who ran a boarding house where he ate, his first reaction was: "I think I have found a sister." That defense worked when she already had a boyfriend, but after she became available, he confessed his love to his diary. Maja Loritz, however, did not feel the same way toward him. Through his own self-restraint and through his lack of success with women, Heinrich Himmler seems to have remained a virgin until age twenty-six.[26]

A woman criticized young Himmler for not valuing women enough. He tried to deny the charge, but in explaining himself he made it clear that he believed there were places where women did not belong. Then he set out his image of the ideal woman—except that he was really discussing male attitudes and needs.

A proper man loves a woman on three levels: as a dear child who has to be chided, perhaps even punished on account of her unreasonableness, and who is protected and taken care of because she is delicate and weak and because one loves her. Then as wife and as a loyal, understanding comrade who fights through life with one, who stands faithfully at one's side without hemming in or chaining the man and his spirit. And as a goddess whose feet one must kiss, who gives one strength through her feminine wisdom and childlike, pure sanctity that does not weaken in the hardest struggles and in the ideal hours gives one heavenly peace.[27]

Throughout his life, Himmler continued to view women in terms of stereotypes.

His wife was no exception. Dashing into a hotel to escape a storm in 1926, he bumped into a not-very-attractive blonde and blue-eyed former nurse who seemed to fit his requirements. That she was eight years older than he, Protestant, and divorced caused some problems with his parents, but two years later Heinrich and Margarete Boden, daughter of a German landowner in West Prussia, were married.[28] The image, however, suited him better than the reality, and the two spent little time together after Heinrich became absorbed in politics full-time.

Around the time of his unsuccessful romance with Maja Loritz, Himmler also began to experience problems with his religion. He had entered a dueling fraternity, whose activities he feared might violate the teachings of the church. Then, he objected to priests' mixing politics into their sermons. His religious faith was extremely important to him—he once wrote that he would always love God, remain a Catholic, and defend the church even if he were excluded from it. Yet his complaints and doubts always returned to plague him, sometimes even while he was in church.[29] Although he did not state it explicitly in his diary, he may also have felt a more general contradiction between his unrestrained glorification of military action and the Christian precept of turning the other cheek.

The strain of frustrated love and religious torment put him in a miserable condition, from which he sought to escape. Heinrich Himmler had sought war partly because he had patterned himself a soldier, whose code was clear and simple; now he also sought war because it would resolve his conflicting impulses and emotions. "If I only had to undergo battle," he wrote, "to put my life on the line . . . Man with his . . . longing for battle . . . is a miserable creature. And yet I am proud to fight this struggle. I will not submit."[30]

One of Himmler's subordinates in the Final Solution later described him as a person divided. He had a positive side, an affinity for plants and nature, and a negative side that resulted in inhumanity to humans; a weak side and a brutal side as counterweight; sensitivity to some human feelings combined with complete heartlessness on many occasions; a strong side and weakness that approached cowardice.[31]

The nature of the battle, or of the challenge he would undertake in the early 1920s, was still open. If he could not find war in Germany, he could at least emigrate and find real challenges elsewhere—Spain, Russia, Turkey, Peru, and the Baltic were all under consideration. In 1921 he predicted that either there would be war in Germany, or within two years he would no longer be in the country. In 1923 he participated in Hitler's Beer Hall Putsch as a follower of Captain Ernst Röhm.[32] It was his initiation into political war.

Somewhere along the way, probably because of his awkwardness with his peers, he became determined to find a different path for himself and his country. He was educated and in certain ways intellectually curious, but he was too young and self-absorbed to handle the complexities of the world, so he simplified them. Then he adapted his reading and learning to his self-defined standards, accepting what fit in neatly and rejecting whatever contradicted his views. He did not seek intellectual synthesis; he sought reinforcement and additional information to help him define and achieve his goals.

The irony was that his fascination with the military and his pronounced German nationalism made him receptive to a racial ideology that glorified what he was not: the blond, blue-eyed, athletic, Nordic type. He had to delve back into German history to find an uncontaminated German race, but in later years he thought he could reverse the effects of centuries of racial intermarriage. His own inadequacy did not prevent him from pursuing this Nordic ideal. No one ever maintained that Heinrich Himmler was weak of will. Hitler's first biographer came quite close to the mark in assessing Himmler: his passion for race and race-building arose from a deep contempt for the individual, including himself.[33]

Himmler's anti-Semitism was initially conventional. Like some conservative Bavarian Catholics, he was suspicious of Jews, but he was capable of distinguishing among those he liked and those he disliked. His own emotional and intellectual quest, however, drove him to literature in which Jews and Freemasons were presented as arch-conspirators against Germany, and this demonic enemy came to fixate him more and more. Once he had abandoned Catholicism—his last recorded visit to church was in February 1924—the next logical step was to reject the ethics that accompanied his religion. Then he would add Jesuits to the unholy alliance of enemies of the German race, and turn against the Catholic faith generally. A boy who had once attended church almost daily became, by the 1930s, a militant anti-Catholic. In 1937 Himmler told the SS-Gruppenführer, the elite of the organization, that he firmly believed that the predominant element of the priesthood was a homosexual association serving a form of Bolshevism that was two thousand years old.[34]

He did not entirely abandon ethics—quite the contrary. He retained a sense of what was proper behavior in one's private life and career, and he was rigorous with himself about financial matters. Even after he had spent years in power, he was determined to pay for his lunchtime and dinnertime cigars out of his own funds, not from his office account, and he instructed his staff accordingly.[35] But his sense of morality did not intrude into political or racial matters; these superseded all else. His men had to do what was necessary to preserve and secure the German race, even if they found the required measures repugnant, inhuman, immoral, or "un-German"—as he himself normally might. The times and the enemies were not normal, he felt.

Before he lost his faith, Himmler was already looking for a new secular cause that he could blend with his military aspirations. In 1921 he heard a lecture in the Löwenbräukeller, Munich's most famous beer hall, given by Count von der Goltz, a general who had continued to fight in the East after World War I ended. His reaction was extremely enthusiastic, and he added: "Now I know more definitely: if there is a campaign in the East again, I will go along. The East is the most important thing for us. The West dies out easily. We must fight and settle in the East."[36] Anti-Semitism and German conquest of land in the East were to remain two of his great lifelong causes.

Heinrich Himmler's attraction to the East represented both an extension of, and a rebellion against, his father's attitudes. One of Gebhard Himmler's pupils later recalled that their teacher used to have them visualize the geography of Europe as a triangle, with the Ural Mountains from the Arctic Sea to near the Caspian Sea as the base and Gibraltar as the apex; all of Europe fell within the confines of the connecting lines. Then he had personalized the geography lesson for his students by recounting his own trip several years earlier with Prince Heinrich of Bavaria to the northern regions of Russia. He had described peasant houses of rough logs of wood, clothing of sheepskin fastened with a girdle, and long beards to defend against the cold. So Gebhard Himmler's tales about his experiences in Russia undoubtedly stimulated Heinrich's initial interest.

Beyond the Urals was Asia. Professor Himmler also used to tell his students that Asia was the cradle of mankind, and that all peoples and all history moved from east to west. Attempts to reverse this historical law, such as Swedish King Charles XII's battle at Poltava in 1709 or Napoleon's famous expedition in 1812, were doomed to futility. The immensity of Russian territory and the harshness of its winters made a foreign occupation of Russia virtually impossible. Here Heinrich, with his dreams of military conquest, obviously refused to follow his father's lessons.[37]

Himmler's membership in an extremist paramilitary organization and his dedication to conquest in the East prepared him to become a Nazi before he ran into Adolf Hitler or was exposed to Hitler's own ideology. When, in 1924, Nazi official Gregor Strasser offered him a position as assistant and secretary,[38] Himmler's ideology melded with his career ambitions. He began as a bureaucrat, a role for which his upbringing and his talents had prepared him well, and he developed into a Nazi leader with a bureaucratic style.

What developed more slowly and mysteriously was his talent for intrigue and deception. There are a few signs of a young Himmler who was aware that full candor was disadvantageous, and who knew that there were circumstances in which one did not write too much. While he kept his diary at home, his parents could and did inspect it; not coincidentally, the entries contain no reference to sex. During the chaotic month of November 1918, after Germany had experienced the sudden loss of the war, revolution, and a socialist takeover of power in both Berlin and Munich, Himmler warned his father to be careful what he put into his letters: "you can't be sure." He also reassured his father not to worry about him, for "I am sly as a fox."[39] This may well have been Himmler's goal, rather than the reality, but in any case it showed the direction he was to take.

Through his reading, Himmler came to believe that the enemies— the Jews foremost among them—were incredibly devious and vicious, and that he would have to learn the same skills to defeat them. In 1926, for example, after reading a new book entitled *Torture*, Himmler commented: "A gruesome book on the beast in men that comes out also through the state in all centuries in history. One notices in some places that the book is hostile to the Jews." Still another source of learning would have been his experiences in the internal struggles within the Nazi movement during the still-cloudy period before he became Reich Führer SS in 1929, and even there he could look for hidden Jewish influences. In 1929 his Nazi comrade Albert Krebs described the fixation of the Himmler he had just met:

> What concerned him were the "secret factors." Did the former naval lieutenant actually have a Jewish or a half-Jewish wife? How did SA officer Conn come to have his remarkable name? Was it perhaps a camouflage for Cohn? In which bank did Gauleiter Lohse formerly work? Could he have fallen thereby into some kind of dependency on Jews?
> ... Of course, the leadership of the army was also of Jewish descent, related by marriage to Freemasonry, trained by Jesuits.[40]

There was no way to disprove the conclusions drawn by someone who was determined to see hidden enemies wherever he looked.

Himmler's search for secrets and conspiracies was in actuality a projection onto others of his own tendencies. Nazi Party Foreign Press chief "Putzi" Hanfstaengel described him as someone who quickly and easily jumped onto a bandwagon in order to lull others into a false sense of security "while he unobtrusively and imperturbably works at the realization of his secret plans. He kills—with all the neatness of the toreador, but without any of the show."[41]

. . .

ν H E N I have told people that I was working on a book about Himmler, the characteristic responses were surprise, repulsion, and disdain. People know who Himmler was and at least some of what he did. They don't necessarily understand, however, why someone might want to learn more about this man. Getting close to my subject involved more than a little psychological strain. To limit one's interest only to the uplifting and aesthetically satisfying, however, would be a recipe for future disasters.

ϗ   I have chosen to focus here on Himmler's role in the decision-making of what the Nazis formally called the "Final Solution of the Jewish question" (*die Endlösung der Judenfrage*). In spite of all we have learned about this program for genocide, many questions remain. Some concern the meaning, significance, or comparability of events already explored; others involve discussions of original motives or causes; and still others revolve around specific episodes not yet clearly illuminated in the historical record. Finally, there are disputes among scholars who have drawn contradictory messages from the same set of events or evidence. An outsider may at first get the impression that the experts are splitting hairs, that the disputes are arcane. Nothing could be further from the truth. There are weighty battles regarding the causes of the Holocaust and the moral and political lessons we draw from it. Some of the disputes also raise serious questions about how we do research and write history.

ϗ   To clarify Himmler's role and motives, particularly concerning the fundamental decision to proceed with the mass murder of the Jews, is to supply answers to several controversial general questions. And because of the difficulties in obtaining evidence, a historian interested in broad questions and controversies about the Holocaust needs some of the techniques of the biographer. He or she has to follow one individual over a long enough period of time to be able to isolate consistencies of personality and of method and use them to interpret or augment fragmentary evidence. In this way, a scholar can penetrate beyond the limitations of the historical record and still end up with a picture of the whole. So I am interested here in both Himmler and the Holocaust.

Even the term "Holocaust" is controversial. The word is derived from an ancient Greek translation of the Old Testament term signifying a burnt offering or sacrifice exclusively to God.[42] At best, the literal meaning may convey the sense that millions of Jews died because of their religion. At worst, the term may imply that the victims were somehow sacrificed to God. In any case, the Nazis considered Jews a "race," not a religious group. Nonbelievers and Jews who had converted to Christianity were not exempted from the transports to the death camps.

⌈Jewish communities and spokesmen in Israel, the United States, and elsewhere have seized upon the term "Holocaust" to summarize the fate of Jews under the Nazis, but there is also a debate over whether Nazi mass killings of other victims—Poles, Russians, gypsies, Jehovah's Witnesses, homosexuals, and political prisoners, among others—constitute part of the Holocaust. Is the Holocaust restricted to Jews?⌋

⌈Historians prefer to avoid moral or theological judgments and to find useful analytical concepts. In the journal *Holocaust and Genocide Studies* and elsewhere, Yehuda Bauer of the Hebrew University of Jerusalem has distinguished the Jewish experience from that of the other groups on empirical grounds.[43] The Nazis did try to wipe out virtually all Jews, whereas their murderous policies for other groups were more selective. In some cases—for example, with the gypsies—further research is needed to show what distinctions were made, why some were killed and others spared.⌋

Bauer's "holocaust" is, however, not exclusively Jewish. He uses "holocaust" for any case where the ruling power tries to kill off a designated enemy people entirely—men, women, and children. He employs the word "genocide" not as a synonym for "holocaust," but for an attempt to wipe out the national identity and culture of a people by methods including (but not limited to) mass murder, but falling short of total annihilation. So in this view the Nazis practiced genocide against Poles and gypsies, but "holocaust" may still apply elsewhere. Bauer argues, for example, that Turkish policies toward the Armenians in 1915 resulted in a near holocaust; this was more than a case of genocide. His definition of genocide, however, runs counter to the more common meaning (and the literal meaning of the Greek and Latin roots)—killing of a people—and is unlikely to win complete acceptance.

"Holocaust" was not used, of course, during the Third Reich. The phrase "Final Solution of the Jewish question" allowed Nazi officials to avoid dirtying their lips with words like "mass murder" or "extermination." The program known as the Final Solution was an attempt to eliminate the Jewish "race" from the earth. This was to be accomplished by means of mass murder, though working people to death and allowing some privileged categories of elderly Jews to die out were also significant parts of the process. But the exceptions only highlighted the general practices of executions and gassings.

Historians who use "Final Solution" implicitly emphasize the experience of the perpetrators, rather than the victims, and that is indeed the main thrust of this book. I am conscious that some readers may find such a study incomplete, or may even take it as granting a sort of undue recognition to a number of the worst criminals in history. I do not see, however, how we can comprehend the causes and lessons of the Holocaust without a clear understanding of the motives and actions of those most responsible for it. Whatever its weaknesses, "Final Solution" at least applies to a single, specific group defined by descent. The Nazis are not known to have spoken of the Final Solution of the Polish problem or of the gypsy problem.

⑥ Another dispute, which Germans call the "historians' controversy," exploded onto the pages of the West German press in the 1980s. This battle erupted after a number of prominent West German scholars and writers complained that too much weight was placed on the Nazi era, as compared with prior German history and with postwar West German success. If the Nazi era became a standard for absolute evil overshadowing all else, how would it be possible for Germans to recognize political, social, and economic continuities without simultaneously poisoning all German history? And if all German traditions and achievements were tainted, how could West German citizens develop a healthy sense of national consciousness and political allegiance?[44]

The most outspoken advocates of a new approach, the Berlin historian-philosopher Ernst Nolte and Joachim Fest, biographer of Hitler and publisher of the *Frankfurter Allgemeine Zeitung*, specifically questioned whether the Nazi effort at genocide was unique in the context of the twentieth century. In this view, the Turkish massacre of Armenians during World War I, the bloodshed of the Russian Civil War, the Bolshevik rhetoric about extermination of the bourgeoisie, and the Stalinist purges and violence against the peasantry and suspected political opponents, helped to pave the way for the Holocaust—and were more original. The Khmer Rouge massacres in Cambodia were also cited as evidence that genocide did not end with World War II. In the context of this debate, such comparisons were meant to demonstrate that other nations had committed horrible crimes without losing faith in their entire history, without being forced to surrender their national consciousness. Nolte and Fest raised further controversy by speculating that reports of communist mass killings in the Soviet Union might have provoked Hitler to act against what he saw as a Jewish-communist conspiracy: the Final Solution might have been, at least in Hitler's mind, they suggested, an act of preventive warfare.[45] This hypothesis is also, quite obviously, an attempt to shift some moral opprobrium from Nazi Germany to the Soviet Union.

Opponents such as the German philosopher-sociologist Jürgen Habermas denounced such genocide analogies as an effort to diminish the magnitude of German crimes (and as an attempt to clear the way for a more assertive and nationalistic German role in world affairs). Other scholars have strongly asserted the originality and uniqueness of the Holocaust. In the words of University of Stuttgart historian and Hitler expert Eberhard Jäckel:

> ... never before had a state with the authority of its responsible leader decided and announced that a specific human group, including its aged, its women, its children and infants, would be killed as quickly as possible, and then carried through this resolution using every possible means of state power.[46]

It is possible to draw comparisons between the Holocaust and other instances of genocide, but in many ways the Final Solution remains *sui generis*. The question of Nazi motivation for the Final Solution, however, requires a more careful, scholarly analysis than is possible in the pages of the popular press. With such an important and sensitive subject, it is dangerous to toss out "possible" Nazi motives unsupported by detailed research. It is also contradictory to defend an argument containing a political agenda by rejecting criticism as politically motivated.

Not coincidentally, academic experts are no longer in agreement regarding Hitler's exact role in the Final Solution—something that would not have been questioned decades ago. The traditional view, which dates back at least to the Nuremberg trial of the major war criminals, was clear. Hitler's implacable and virulent anti-Semitism developed at an early age and formed the kernel of his political ideology and his program as chancellor, and it was hard to view the escalating Nazi persecution of German Jews after 1933 and the Final Solution as anything but the gradual implementation of his preconceived notions. Hitler did not react to outside events so much as impose his will upon reality. This conclusion was a deduction from his own writings, speeches, and private conversations, as well as from the course of events; there is no known surviving document in which Hitler himself ordered the extermination of the Jewish race.

The earliest historian of the Final Solution nonetheless concluded from Hitler's pre-eminent position in the Third Reich, and from his anti-Semitism (as well as from testimony by Nazi officials), that he and only he could have authorized such a program.[47] Scholars who analyzed Hitler's early political career supplied supporting evidence. In *Mein Kampf*, for example, Hitler had claimed that the killing of twelve to fifteen thousand Jews in Germany during World War I by means of poison gas (!) might have saved the lives of hundreds of thousands of German soldiers.[48] The belief that the Jews had been responsible for Germany's defeat in World War I must have exerted a powerful influence upon

Hitler when World War II was approaching. As the war began, so did killings of Jews, albeit on a small scale at first. By the middle of 1941 the stage was set for a massive escalation, under the cover of the war in the East. Some scholars still emphasize the logical unfolding over time of a preconceived idea,[49] but they are probably now in the minority.

In 1970 Karl Schleunes of the University of North Carolina, Greensboro, argued that the road to Auschwitz was not straight, but twisted. During the years 1933–39, Schleunes demonstrated, the Nazi regime had employed a number of different methods to persecute Jews, at times permitting private or party violence against Jews, but more often restraining it, while introducing one piece of legislation after another against Jews. In agreement with Raul Hilberg's earlier study, Schleunes pointed out that a number of party and government agencies took initiatives to "resolve" the Jewish question, but he emphasized the contradictions among them. For whatever reasons, Hitler sometimes reined in the radical anti-Semites, who wanted to escalate persecution. Meanwhile, the regime had encouraged, even forced, Jewish emigration from Germany during the entire period. These zigzag policies reflected Nazi hostility toward Jews, and even a desire to be "rid" of Jews, but they did not lead inevitably to the conclusion that Hitler had a preconceived plan to wipe out all the Jews of Europe. In fact, they suggested that, if he did have a Final Solution in mind, no one else knew about it. Schleunes, however, ended his study with early 1939, suggesting that Hitler turned Jewish matters over to the SS at that point.[50]

Other historians who expressly rejected the "great-man approach" to history and emphasized the influence of structural conditions, then took a longer journey on Schleunes's "twisted road" to Auschwitz. West German scholars such as Uwe Dietrich Adam, Martin Broszat, and Hans Mommsen extended into World War II the pattern of stops and starts, trial and error, bureaucratic competition as well as cooperation to resolve the fate of the Jews.[51] In spite of differences of opinion among them, the scholars in this school all concluded from the sequence of events that the Nazi regime had no preordained plan for the mass murder of the Jews. After emigration became impossible for all but a limited number of Jews, the Nazis supposedly turned to the idea of a Jewish "reservation" in Poland. In 1940 there was a Nazi plan to ship millions of Jews to Madagascar, which, however, the continuation of the war against Britain precluded. After the German invasion of the Soviet Union, some saw a possibility of expelling Jews farther to the east. Meanwhile, wartime shortages of food and housing intensified the pressures to get rid of the Jews. Then the unexpected continuation of the war in the East blocked the idea of deporting Jews deep into the U.S.S.R.[52] In short, according to this school, the Final Solution was improvised after other Nazi efforts to resolve the Jewish question failed. It was a last resort—the only option remaining consistent with the Nazi belief that Jews represented a mortal danger to the Third Reich.

Princeton University historian Arno Mayer has very recently developed a related interpretation. For Mayer, the Nazis turned against the Jews out of frustration over the failure of the *Blitzkrieg* against the Soviet Union, and out of a desire for revenge, with the Wehrmacht generals playing at least as important a role as Hitler, Himmler, and the SS.[53] Mayer set the date of this perceived military frustration in December 1941. In terms of chronology, his interpretation is the polar opposite of Nolte's argument that the Final Solution may have been, in Hitler's eyes, a kind of *preventive* warfare against a Jewish-communist foe, but there is one strong similarity between them: Nazi fears of, and hostility toward, the Soviet Union were translated into the Final Solution because of the perceived link between Jews and communism. Genocide became, in this view, a byproduct of the war in the East. There is also an indirect link between the theory of an improvised Final Solution and Nolte's argument; both versions have the Nazi regime responding to outside pressures, not unilaterally initiating mass murder.

There were also reassessments of Hitler's role during the war. Broszat believed that Hitler shaped the climate and context of decision-making but did not personally plan genocide and did not approve it until the end of 1941 or early 1942, after the killing was well under way.[54] Mommsen revised the received picture of Hitler even more radically. His Hitler could not cope with the measures implied by his own anti-Semitic rhetoric; he was a charismatic figurehead—Mommsen regarded him as a weak dictator—who left the hard decisions for others. Mommsen pointed out the absence of evidence that anyone in Hitler's headquarters even discussed the extermination of the Jews—and took this to mean that it was not discussed. The most important figure behind the escalating persecution of the Jews, Mommsen stated, was Heinrich Himmler, whose ambition made him determined to outbid the other officials seeking a role in Jewish policy, and whose organization gave him the means to carry out mass murder.[55]

Christopher Browning, professor at Pacific Lutheran University, dissented from others' efforts to devalue Hitler's influence and, in conformance with Hilberg's view, still saw the key decision coming out of the Führer's headquarters in the late summer of 1941, before the military campaign in Russia ran into serious problems. Browning, however, retained the notion that Hitler had no original plan for genocide; there was, rather, a Nazi policy of resettling Jews. Nor did he think the Jewish question was high on Hitler's and Himmler's agendas early in the war.[56] And he too emphasized the process of trial and error, and the initiatives from below.

If the Final Solution was improvised during the midst of the war, there is reason for scholars studying it to stress the conditions and atmosphere engendered by the war itself, the role of bureaucrats, the reasons for the failure of other attempted "solutions of the Jewish question," and the initiatives in the field as essential causes of genocide. On the other hand, the earlier the existence of high-level plans for mass murder, or actions that could only stem from such plans, the greater the importance of Nazi ideology and the less the importance of mid-war imperatives and of improvisation from below. Determining the chronology of planning becomes essential in the debate.

In a way, this controversy is a model for the field of history. It is concerned not only with collecting and interpreting evidence, but in setting particular events in order and understanding the logic or illogic of that order. A political scientist or a sociologist might concentrate more on the overall patterns of genocide during the entire war; a lawyer or a philosopher might look at the crimes committed and the legal or moral implications. But for them it might not matter whether the Nazis planned and carried out killings in 1940 or 1943. No one would be as sensitive as the historian to the chronology itself.

The historian's job is important. Until we know when leading Nazis devised plans for genocide, when they began to take specific actions leading to genocide, all assessments of the causes of genocide can only be rough approximations. One of the reasons for tracking Himmler's movements and methods in this book is precisely to help determine the chronology of planning and decisions, and thereby narrow the disagreements over the causes of the Final Solution.

A planned Final Solution and an improvised one carry quite different moral and philosophical implications. Those who regard it as planned still regard bureaucrats who made arrangements to transport Jews to the death camps and soldiers who complied with orders to shoot Jews as murderers, but they make Hitler the prime cause or agent in a calculated process. Some who favor improvisation may suspect that the emphasis of Hitler's role in the planned-solution interpretation is meant to diminish that of other Germans, to ease Germany's moral burdens and moral responsibility.

The moral argument can cut both ways, however. From another standpoint, planned mass murder is worse than murder perceived as a last resort. Some who believe the solution was planned may regard those who believe in improvisation as looking for excusable causes of genocide. Historian Charles Sydnor, Jr., has likened the difference between a planned Final Solution and an improvised one to that between first-degree murder and manslaughter.[57]

Like Schleunes's twisted road to Auschwitz, historical scholarship often follows a zigzag pattern of provocative hypothesis and criticism, detailed studies and contradictory studies, cacophony rather than harmony. Eventually someone may provide a synthesis that does justice to all the evidence and satisfies many, if not all, of the combatants or their successors. In the meantime, however, the plethora of disagreements can be confusing or even alarming to an outsider who looks to the experts for "the truth."

In this case, perhaps more than most, there is good reason for concern. The Holocaust was probably the worst chapter in the history of the modern world, possibly the worst in all human history. It is hard to see how, some forty-five years after the end of World War II, we can have absorbed all of its lessons if we still do not know the answers to basic questions such as how, when, and why the Final Solution came about, or who was primarily responsible. It may be difficult to get answers to these questions, because there are gaps in the documentary record and legitimate differences of opinion over the facts. Even so, scholars on both sides of this debate have made serious errors.

Some of those who believe that Hitler planned and ordered the Final Solution have found it sufficient to analyze his political ideology in the 1920s and to quote later speeches in which he prophesied the destruction of the Jews; then they shift to the Nazi preparations for mass murder. They have overlooked the significance of Nazi proemigration policies during the 1930s and dismissed Hitler's occasional comments about relocating Jews in Madagascar or in the Soviet Union. They have assumed that everyone would accept their selection of Hitler's rhetoric as evidence—not only of his consistent and serious intent, but also of his direct role in events. What is more, they have not provided enough connecting links between Hitler's views and the preparations for, or decisions on, the Final Solution.[58]

Scholars who stress the improvisation interpretation have exhibited other weaknesses. Discounting Hitler's rhetoric and in some cases his influence as well, they have studied records of mid-level officials, field operations, and ghettos. Some have uncovered evidence that Nazi officials at these levels had no inkling of a master plan for the Jews: bureaucrats, party and SS authorities, and the police fought among themselves regarding the best way to handle the Jews. They have found that some underlings proposed mass murder and that others opposed it. These discoveries have demonstrated that mid-level officials could often influence the course of events and the fate of many thousands of Jews for a considerable length of time. Not content with the importance of this finding, the proponents of improvisation argued either that there was no master plan or that it was approved quite late, after the critical initiatives had come from below.

Arno Mayer's rejection of a planned Final Solution rests on the most slender grounds of all. Although he ranged far and wide throughout history in *Why Did the Heavens Not Darken?: The "Final Solution" in History* to seek parallels to the Final Solution, his description of Nazi orders and killings in 1941 is quite thin. He omitted discussion of earlier events that might undercut his theory that difficulties in the war in the East caused the Nazi forces to lash out against the Jews in frustration and anxiety. The book contains no references to sources whatsoever—no listing of archival records, no footnotes even for direct quotations. There is only a bibliography of other published works on the subject.

Perhaps interpretive works resting on widely known and noncontroversial events and sources do not need documentation. With the Final Solution, however, the basic sequence of orders and actions is in dispute. Mayer has argued that he has written carefully documented works before; he no longer has the need to "prove his manhood."[59] Even apart from its gender implications, this statement sounds peculiar coming from a highly visible academic historian.

Footnotes help other researchers find archives and documents where they may obtain additional details and pursue other subjects. And they allow others to check the accuracy of information an author puts forward. But, most important, footnotes give some sense of the quality of the sources on which the author's information is based. Readers need as much information as possible to find their way through the difficulties of comprehension and the competing interpretations of the Final Solution.

There are limitations on even the most important contemporary documents. An original document is a wonderful thing, but it is not an objective piece of reality. Officials can create documents for all sorts of reasons. Minutes or summaries of meetings can provide a record of decisions or discussions useful for later reference. But the authorities or authors can inflate their own roles or seek to influence the outcome of decisions elsewhere through the way they write. They can also seek to protect themselves with memos for the file, written after the event, more to conceal or cloud the issue than to illuminate it. More important, they can choose to omit sensitive episodes or not record decisions at all—particularly if they sense that written evidence may come back to haunt them. And, of course, where records are kept more or less automatically and accurately, they can be destroyed after the fact.

Even if all documents are basically accurate, they may reflect only a limited portion of the decision-making. The proponents of improvisation have overlooked the possibility that Hitler and Himmler may have concealed their intentions for the Jews, withheld them from subordinates in the ministries and in the field, until the opportune moment, and avoided direct documentation of their own plans and decisions. It is not really possible to determine Hitler's policies or role by drawing inferences from the policies or the records of ghetto administrators.

In short, surviving documents may not reflect the full reality. If anything, we must suspect that the records of the decisions to proceed with the Final Solution are less complete than records of noncriminal policies. Other cases of genocide in history have not left much evidence of advance plans either. If the Final Solution was planned in advance, then Hitler's secretive nature and Himmler's tactics of deception have misled a prominent school of historians. A cover-up still needs to be exposed. A detailed study of the men at the top of the Nazi hierarchy during the critical years, however old-fashioned this may seem to the proponents of history from below, is a necessary part of any explanation of the origins of the Final Solution. Surprisingly, this has not yet been done.

Some years ago British scholar Gerald Fleming wrote a short, provocative study entitled *Hitler and the Final Solution*.[60] His book was designed to rebut David Irving's foolish argument that Hitler was not involved in the Final Solution and was not even aware of it until perhaps 1943.[61] Fleming did not take care to demonstrate *when* Hitler committed his crimes, only that he *did*, which is a weakness in the book. But he gave no quarter to those favoring improvisation, arguing that Hitler's mind was set on mass murder of the Jews from the early 1920s on. After 1933, Fleming implied, the Führer was simply waiting for the proper moment to strike.

Fleming added new evidence to the case his predecessors had made that the idea of murdering large numbers of Jews had occurred early to Hitler. Could one really say that Hitler had already decided upon genocide? A lot depends on what constitutes a decision. Is it a decision if a person keeps an idea firmly in mind but tells no one about it and does nothing about it? Or is the decision made only when the individual begins to commit himself—not necessarily to start the executions, but at least to commit time and resources to the preparations? It is doubtful whether any human being is as rigid as Fleming's Hitler. In any case, Fleming's interpretation can be neither proved nor disproved; it will never convince those who do not share the same view of Hitler.

In spite of these weaknesses, Fleming's book made progress in two areas. First, he demonstrated that Hitler frequently kept his cards close to his vest and even boasted of his refusal to confide in others, of his willingness to lie to them and surprise them later.[62] Fleming constructed a psychological profile of the man, partly based on independent evidence, and then used it to explain Hitler's *modus operandi* for the Final Solution. Other Nazi officials pursued different policies for years, simply because Hitler kept them in the dark. There was no signed Hitler order for the mass extermination of the Jews, because this kind of man would never have written one. He instead expressed his "wish" to Himmler, who set in motion the machinery of death, according to Fleming. As a skillful, deceptive politician, Hitler kept himself insulated from the worst crimes.

Fleming also discovered or recapitulated a substantial number of statements by officials from Himmler on down that Hitler had initiated the Final Solution. These statements were not perfect evidence: subordinates sometimes invoke the authority of the person at the top to justify some action even when he or she has not specifically ordered it. Nonetheless, there were enough independent sources to convince some of the skeptics that Hitler did assert his authority at some point.

Fleming's book reinforced my view that more research might well turn up crucial evidence about the Nazi leaders. It also suggested that a historian who knew the subject well enough could manage to fill in at least some gaps in the documentary record by using his or her knowledge of the individuals involved in the decisions. A person may change his mind on an issue, but does not easily change his personality, methods, and values. In short, it suggested that the historian of the Final Solution had to use biographical techniques too.

In the course of my research on a previous Holocaust-related book, *Breaking the Silence*,[63] which I wrote with Walter Laqueur, I became familiar with some of the archival collections in which the papers of Heinrich Himmler and Himmler's various offices are found. The bulk of the records were in the United States National Archives and in the West German Federal Archives at Koblenz, but there were other important papers at the Hoover Institution at Stanford University, at the Berlin Document Center, and elsewhere. I was astounded by how much paperwork Himmler had generated; his father must have been proud of him. In this sense, Himmler was a far better subject for a historian or biographer than Hitler, who was notoriously averse to writing memos and keeping records. It might be possible to demonstrate how Himmler's programs for the Jews were related to his other concerns and priorities.

There was another excellent reason to focus on Himmler, rather than Hitler. Fleming, who was the most radical adherent of a planned Final Solution, and Mommsen, perhaps the most radical exponent of an improvised one, both regarded Himmler as a critical figure in the process. According to Fleming, Himmler heard Hitler's wish, then made it come true. According to Mommsen, Himmler won the competition for jurisdiction over Jewish policy by eventually outbidding and outworking all his rivals. Surely there were enough surviving records on Himmler to determine which version was closer to the truth.

To be sure, there were plenty of problems. By the time Himmler's records entered the captured German collection of the United States National Archives, they were incredibly disorganized. Even with the aid of guides prepared by National Archives experts, it was a massive task to locate most of the relevant information. There were also obvious gaps. Some files had apparently been removed for war-crimes purposes and had never found their way back home. In a few cases I ran across these files in their new locations. The more I studied Himmler's record-keeping, however, the more I realized that what had reached Washington (and Koblenz) was only a part of the whole. Some of Himmler's records had been lost during the last phase of the war, and other documents were intentionally destroyed by Nazi officials—as Frau Lorenz had done with the contents of the file cabinet at Fischhorn.[64]

Another problem was fragmentary documentation, of which perhaps the best example is Himmler's handwritten notes on a good number (but by no means all) of his private meetings with Hitler.[65] Himmler took into some of these meetings lists of agenda items—issues about which he wanted to consult his Führer, decisions that the Führer had to make. In most cases Himmler used single words or brief phrases to remind himself what questions to raise, and during these meetings he recorded Hitler's responses in simplified form: "yes" (or a check mark), "no," "decision reserved," item crossed off (probably indicating that it was not discussed). Hitler was notorious for long harangues about every conceivable subject, yet Himmler's notes are laconic. They are not so much a record of the course of the discussion as of the minimum agenda that Himmler had planned and the decisions he was able to extract during the meetings. But they cannot be taken as evidence that he and Hitler did not discuss other matters in these meetings.

Even more frustrating, at first, was my discovery of seemingly critical but completely unrecorded meetings or discussions. I knew that they had taken place, because I found passing references to them, or notations in Himmler's appointment books. But I could not find out anything directly about their substance, because it seemed that no record had ever been kept. Gradually, and with the aid of other documents, I realized that the absence of documentation, which must on one level have bothered Himmler, was nonetheless a significant part of the story. Sherlock Holmes once found it highly significant that a dog did not bark at an intruder in the night. Exceptions to Himmler's habit of recording suggested that there were matters to be concealed. His pattern of recording and concealing—the two ingrained habits locked in combat—shaped the events that unfold in this book.

Concealment is rarely perfect, and it was not perfect in this case. There were deductions one could draw about undocumented meetings, hypothetical conclusions that became good probabilities if events directly followed the meetings. There were also people who survived the war who might have testified about these meetings and related events.

To follow up on various clues and to get a better sense of some of the individuals, I turned first to the voluminous war-crimes interrogations in the National Archives. Conducted between 1945 and 1949, the pretrial interrogations of surviving Nazis, government officials and military men, victims of persecution, members of the German resistance, and witnesses of Nazi crimes contained a vast array of material about a wide range of subjects.[66] Much of this material was more detailed and more valuable than the actual testimony in the war-crimes trials themselves. The interrogations also came quickly enough after the war so that memories, particularly of dates of events and discussions, were of some use, even if they required corroboration. By way of the Zentrale Stelle der Landesverwaltungen zur Aufklärung von NS-Verbrechen, Ludwigsburg, and also with the assistance of Henry Friedlander, I gained access to even more detailed interrogations, witness testimony, and expert analysis in later West German war-crimes proceedings.

I quickly learned that, except in very rare cases, those accused or suspected of crimes did not willingly testify candidly about their own activities during the Nazi era, even though they were threatened with further charges of perjury. Sometimes skillful war-crimes investigators broke their subjects down, on occasion by exposing lies with documents just pulled from the captured files. In other cases the suspects continued to lie about themselves but, to demonstrate their cooperativeness, provided incriminating information about others, particularly about higher authorities. Relatively few—Himmler's chief of staff, Karl Wolff, unfortunately was one—lied consistently. There was much information about Himmler and his subordinates here, even if I had to be selective about whom to believe.

Another set of sources offering valuable information but requiring judgment and discretion was contemporary American reporting about developments in Nazi Germany—particularly confidential diplomatic reports and intelligence reports. As it happened, in my previous research I had delved extensively into these records. I knew not only when American officials sent choice and reliable information back to Washington, but sometimes even who their German informants were.

I was aware that some of the inside information about Himmler or about Nazi policies toward the Jews came from men close to Hermann Göring, from officials in the Jewish section of the Gestapo, from Hjalmar Schacht, from prominent German industrialists, and from high officials in German military intelligence. The reliability of these sources had sometimes been proved: they had given certain Americans advance warning of actual events. They spoke about intentions, even when nothing was yet written down. Sometimes even well-placed sources were misinformed, and there were plenty of people who habitually passed on garbage. In other words, I had to sift out the good intelligence from the bad, but intelligence analysts do this job regularly under the pressure of current events. I had the luxury of doing it at my own pace, more than four decades after the reports and the events.

All in all, there was plenty of evidence about Himmler, the man and his ideas. There were also enough details of his appointments, correspondence, phone calls, travels, and reading prior to and during the war to reconstruct most of his activities and movements during the formulative years of the Final Solution. For whatever reasons, Himmler's previous biographers had not made use of his appointment books and the office log kept by the manager of his personal staff, Rudolf Brandt. Himmler's appointment book for 1941, which would itself have confirmed or denied the reliability of postwar testimony about the timing of particular meetings, is lost, though the corresponding books for 1938, 1939, 1940, and 1942 survive. As it turned out, there were more leads in 1939 and 1940 regarding Jewish policy than I had a right to expect. For the rest, I tried to build bridges among the known facts, using the knowledge of Himmler that I had acquired during my research. It is easier to follow and document Himmler's role in this process than to ascertain Hitler's participation, but Hitler too emerges more clearly than in previous historical accounts.

Because the chronology is so crucial to the historians' debates, I have taken care to lay out and to document even events that may not seem directly related to the Final Solution, particularly in chapters two through eight. I have tried, at least to a degree, to re-create the flow of events as Himmler experienced them, with the ultimate goal of establishing the landmarks of the Final Solution and the relationship between the Final Solution and the other events and Nazi programs.

I cannot claim to have done a perfect job. No doubt I have left out some important subjects or events and underplayed others. Not everyone will agree with all my deductions—which are identified as deductions, not as incontestable facts. The reader may judge how sensibly I have handled the problems posed by the concealment of events and evidence. And the specialists will find plenty of references to the relevant surviving documents in my endnotes.

My method of approximating what took place, of filling in the gaps left by the bearers of secrets, will yield better results—if not in my hands, then in someone else's—than blindly following a carefully marked trail of neatly filed documents. The best-kept, most organized files are not necessarily the key to historical reality, particularly when we are concerned with mass murder on an unprecedented scale.

What follows is the account of how Himmler and the SS gained control of Nazi Germany's Jewish policy and other related activities during World War II—and how they planned a war against Jews and certain other perceived enemies. The SS's plans did expand over time as Germany's war prospects brightened. Nonetheless, the idea of executing Jews was an essential element from the beginning, although a comprehensive program—the Final Solution—came later. The evolution of planning had more to do with the geography, scope, and methods of killing than with any change from a moderate to a radical goal.

CHAPTER 1

▼▼▼▼▼▼▼▼▼▼▼▼▼▼▼▼▼

HITLER, HIMMLER,
AND THE SS

IN SOME WAYS Hitler and Himmler were opposites who attracted—
and then complemented—each other. Hitler was the ultimate charismatic leader, whereas Himmler had no charisma whatsoever. Hitler was
a would-be artist and architect; Himmler lacked all artistic skill. Hitler
usually had little concern for details and paperwork, and he hated bureaucracy; Himmler was painstaking and methodical in carrying out his
tasks. Hitler was garrulous, emotional, and domineering; Himmler,
often courteous, knew how to appear modest and gave the appearance
of being a good listener. When he interrogated a subordinate, he asked
questions and made few comments on the answers. One of Heydrich's
key intelligence officials described his first serious encounter with Himmler as an examination by a finicky schoolmaster.[1]

Himmler did not come into direct contact with Hitler until 1926,[2] by
which time his basic ideology was in place. He already believed in German
racial superiority, the menace of the Jews, and the need for military
expansion to the east. He already wanted a strong leader to accomplish
revolutionary changes for Germany, and it had become clear to him that
Hitler was that Führer. The actual person of Adolf Hitler was blended
into Himmler's ideal.

Hitler needed Himmler for more practical and less emotional reasons.
Once Hitler decided to pursue a semilegal path to power, he had to
make the Nazi Party more respectable and efficient. He required men
who could build up a political organization, and Himmler had a record
of being a hardworking, dedicated bureaucrat. As Hitler struggled to
bring both the unruly storm troopers of the Sturmabteilung (SA), the
first Nazi paramilitary force, and the tiny SS under control, he apparently
decided to pick someone both capable and unlikely to cause trouble. In

January 1929 Himmler was appointed Reich Führer SS. At the time the SS supposedly had only 280 men, but Himmler quickly began to expand it.[3]

Their joint belief in the need for a disciplined elite force within the Nazi movement tightened the bond between Hitler and Himmler. Hitler himself on one occasion described the difference between the SA men and the SS:

> The SA attracts the militant natures among the Germanic breed, the men who think democratically, unified only by a common allegiance. Those who throng to the SS are men inclined to the authoritarian state, who wish to serve and obey, who respond less to an idea than to a man.[4]

(This comment came just after Hitler had noticed that the SA membership was concentrated in Protestant areas and the SS in Catholic areas.) Himmler had ended up with the right organization; it suited his own nature.

In the summer of 1931 Hitler laid out two functions for the SS: a police force and an elite troop. This assignment not only fed Himmler's growing ambitions; it also fit into what he had learned from history. "We are not wiser than the men of two thousand years ago," Himmler told the SS leaders. "Persians, Greeks, Romans and Prussians all had their guards. The guards of the new Germany will be the SS." Himmler projected his guards as a force that would secure the home front and ensure victory during war. Never again would Germany experience another 1918, another revolution stabbing the German army in the back, he predicted in 1931.[5]

The SS under Himmler also became a racial-ideological elite. One of Himmler's early ideological mentors, Richard Walther Darré, author of the Nazi "blood-and-soil" doctrine, helped to convince Himmler of the need for a new racial-German aristocracy. Darré, like Himmler, had studied agronomy, and the two men knew all about the breeding of livestock. Darré projected a new Nordic German aristocracy achieved through selective breeding on a voluntary basis.[6] Himmler had appointed Darré as head of the SS Race and Settlement Office, and until they quarreled in the late 1930s the two men both tried to turn the SS into their new stock. But there is also evidence that Himmler had arrived at similar ideas of a racial aristocracy himself, in the 1920s, through reading the racist writer Hans F. K. Günther.[7]

Himmler imposed racial entrance requirements for members—pure Aryan descent back to the year 1750 for SS officers and 1800 for enlisted men, minimum height, and proper bone structure, no Slavic or Mongolian characteristics. Applicants were placed into one of five categories —pure Nordic; predominately Nordic or Phalic; harmonic mixed blood with light Alpine, Dinaric, or Mediterranean features; mixed blood with predominately eastern-Baltic or Alpine origin; or mixed blood of non-European descent—and only the first three were acceptable.[8]

Himmler also insisted on approving the prospective brides of SS men. Even in later years, when he was at the height of his power, he personally handled the applications in cases where there was some doubt. After all, the women too had to be racially suitable and capable of bearing children. Himmler instilled into his select membership an antireligious, antihumanitarian ideology that defined history as a constant, merciless struggle among races for survival, and which ranked the German and Nordic races above all others. Then he imposed a code of honor that raised loyalty and discipline to paramount virtues.[9]

Himmler's religious childhood must have left him with the impression that ideology and elitism would not suffice. The SS became an "order" with rites and symbols borrowed—or imagined—from the ancient Germanic tribes. Many SS officers wore silver Death's Head rings and carried SS daggers; the Gruppenführer all had coats of arms, which hung on a wall in Himmler's castle at Wewelsburg, where they meditated. Beneath the dining hall was a crypt for the SS elite.[10] Himmler undoubtedly had a mystical streak, but he may also have believed some spiritualism necessary for the organization.

Resting on this racial-ideological-mystical foundation, the SS was a peculiar amalgam. Since Himmler's ideal was the primeval German peasant warrior and farmer, army veterans, farmers, and police with suitable physical characteristics were eagerly recruited. Though Himmler, like Hitler, detested lawyers, a great deal depended on how loyal and useful lawyers could make themselves. Intellectuals too had roles to play in the new elite. Himmler needed trained personnel to run the specialized branches and functions of the SS.[11] Alongside the irrational cult of the order was a quite rational, functional apparatus.

The SS gradually became a quasi-governmental conglomerate whose scope and range increased along with Himmler's own political influence after the Nazi takeover. It carried out police functions and ran concentration camps, developed military units, took over or founded agricultural and industrial enterprises, even engaged in medical, archeological, and academic research.[12] The SS reflected Himmler's own ideology and range of pursuits, and in some cases he controlled its functions personally. It was commonly believed that Himmler assigned personnel to the concentration camps down to the last washerwoman.[13]

Before Hitler came to power, Himmler was not one of the better-known or most visible Nazi leaders. Yet there were some signs of Hitler's trust in him and of his growing importance. He, Rudolf Hess, and businessman Wilhelm Keppler, one of Hitler's early economic advisers and liaison to the business community, accompanied Hitler to the secret negotiations with former Chancellor Franz von Papen in January 1933 that led to a coalition agreement and Hitler's appointment as chancellor.[14]

After Hitler became chancellor, Himmler was at first apparently left behind among the scavengers in the race for government offices and spoils. He started out with only the minor position of police chief of Munich, but he was still Reich Führer SS, head of a party organization, which gave him a power base. Hermann Rauschning, who knew Himmler personally, later commented that Himmler took advantage of the fact that other Nazis looked down upon him and regarded him as incompetent. He acquired not the trappings of power but the reality. Surveying Himmler's maneuvers in the first month of his new police post, historian Shlomo Aronson concluded that the "schoolmaster" was also a clever and coldly calculating tactician who knew how to deceive, intimidate, and outmaneuver even experienced businessmen with good contacts among the Nazis.[15]

Himmler took over the Bavarian Political Police and, one after another, the police forces of the other German states. Hitler formally named him chief of the German police in June 1936. After Reich Interior Minister Wilhelm Frick had complained to Hitler that Himmler was operating the police independently, the Führer had responded that Frick need not worry—the police were in good hands.[16] Free of his nominal government superior, Himmler was also increasingly free of the Nazi Party's own bureaucracy. His own dual status—head of the SS and chief of all police—became the symbol of a melding of SS and police organizations and personnel.

By this time Himmler had made a considerable effort to recruit members of the old German elite to the SS through a combination of flattery and pressure. According to Rauschning, Himmler specialized in exploiting their human weaknesses. First one collected information about a person's bad habits—about alcohol, gambling, debts, women, or boys. Then, at the appropriate moment, one sent a friendly invitation to the subject and asked for compliance—or else. Once the aristocrats were in the SS, they would be tamed and controlled—one way or another.[17]

Himmler also went out of his way to recruit prominent industrialists to his "circle of friends," which was organized by Wilhelm Keppler.[18] Some prominent businessmen inside and outside this circle became ei-

ther formal or honorary members of
porate executives added a certain luste
could be extremely useful in solving tec

Keppler himself undertook even more d
foreign policy for both Hitler and Himmle
aware that Hitler wanted to reduce German
ported raw materials and foodstuffs. So he ha
produce synthetic fats and oils and had turned
Imhausen, founder and owner of a chemical fir
who conducted experiments with one of German
—coal. Imhausen had eventually succeeded in der
from coal. Since no one could quite gauge the effec   taste
and health, Keppler had decided to conduct tests on t   nan "guinea
pigs" available in the SS's concentration camps. Over a three-year period,
according to Keppler, Imhausen's synthetic-fat compound was tested on
some twelve thousand prisoners at Sachsenhausen, "without anyone
there raising objections." The exact effects of the coal-based fat on the
health of the prisoners is unknown.[19] The length of time involved in the
testing, however, suggests that the early versions must have been faulty.

Eventually, in December 1939, Keppler notified Himmler that he now
had a suitable fat for cooking and frying. Himmler was apparently impressed and ordered his manager of SS economic enterprises, Oswald
Pohl, to get in touch with Keppler. According to postwar testimony by
Himmler's chief of staff, Karl Wolff, Himmler intended to construct an
SS-owned synthetic-fat factory in a location safe from Allied bombers.
He hit upon Auschwitz as the best spot for the plant. The product tested
at Sachsenhausen would then be produced by camp labor from Auschwitz. Himmler obviously understood the principle of synergy. But Hermann Göring blocked the plan, because he was worried about the
expanding number of SS economic enterprises, which posed competition
for his own state-owned economic conglomerate.[20] Instead, chemical
giant I. G. Farben ended up with the choice Auschwitz location and with
concentration-camp laborers for its synthetic-rubber (Buna) plant. The
Imhausen firm avoided obvious identification with the SS. (In a strange
instance of corporate and family tradition, however, Imhausen's son,
Jürgen Imhausen-Hippenstiel, would be arrested fifty years later for
supplying Libya with equipment and plans to build a poison-gas plant.[21])

Hitler generally approved of the SS's expansion and diversification,
sometimes overriding opposition by government agencies.[22] He also oversaw one unusual SS creation. In November 1938 Himmler announced
that he and Hitler alone would determine the policies for the use of the
SS Death's Head units, units of concentration-camp guards who had

ideological and military training.[23] Himmler also lobbied with Hitler during 1938 to expand, equip, and militarize Death's Head formations. By the onset of war they included nearly twenty-four thousand men. They were not quite the military equivalent of the real SS soldiers, soon to be given the name Waffen-SS (Armed SS), but the three Death's Head regiments would not have to fight against the regular Polish army.[24]

Himmler consulted Hitler about major and minor matters—from the basic laws for the SS to appointments and promotions. He became, in the identical words of two quite knowledgeable contemporaries, Hitler's "voluntary tool."[25] Those who saw him with the Führer described him as almost hanging on Hitler's every word. Himmler's own personal-staff office manager, who saw him virtually every day, described his attitude toward Hitler as reverence and love. Rudolf Höss, commandant of Auschwitz, described Himmler as probably the truest, most unselfish follower of Adolf Hitler.[26]

After the war a onetime staff member of Himmler's was asked who the evil spirit behind Himmler had been. The questioner implied that it must have been some subordinate, but the staff member replied: "the evil spirit behind Himmler was Hitler."[27] Another intelligent observer, a historian who regularly attended Hitler's military conferences, testified that until he met Hitler he had the impression that Himmler and Bormann were great and important men. After he came to know Hitler, he said, he realized that they were merely Hitler's handymen.[28]

Hitler must have appreciated the devotion, discretion, and reliability of the man. On one occasion, even with Göring, Hess, and Bormann present, he spoke softly and at length to Himmler alone.[29] Hitler also took Himmler with him on such triumphal occasions as the takeover of Czechoslovakia in mid-March 1939 and revealed something of his innermost feelings. After the Führer entered the Hradčany Palace in Prague, the seat of Czechoslovakian kings since the eleventh century, he was beside himself with joy over winning Bohemia and Moravia for the German people. He took Himmler into a private room and embraced him: "Himmler, is it not wonderful that we stand here, here we are now, and we will never again leave. . . . I have done this elegantly."[30] These incidents are vignettes, but they typify the general pattern.

Himmler did have a certain degree of latitude. Anyone with regular access to the Führer had the opportunity to take up Hitler's pronouncements and do something with them—or to leave them alone. Himmler was loyal to the Führer but not to Göring, Bormann, or others. Within the scope of the Führer's directives, he did as much as he could to advance himself and his own organizations. Himmler was also clever enough to stimulate the Führer's interest in certain subjects or policies. He even recommended books for Hitler to read, and he was pleased when Hitler liked them.[31] Both men, it seems, found one book singularly useful.

IN 1934 the highly respected Stuttgart publisher Deutsche Verlags-Anstalt came out with a new and quite readable book on Genghis Khan and the Mongols. *Genghis Khan: The Storm Out of Asia* was followed the next year by a sequel, *The Legacy of Genghis Khan.* The author was a Russian émigré who wrote under the pen name Michael Prawdin. Michael Charol had come with his family to Germany not long after the Russian Revolution. Still young, he became fluent in German and wrote in that tongue. His first book dealt with the Romanovs in the years before the revolution. Because of his historical interest and his Russian background, he then turned to Genghis Khan.[32]

Professional historians would not regard these two volumes on Genghis Khan as pure historical works; too many novelistic devices were employed, too many conversations repeated verbatim, too many undocumented probes made of Genghis Khan's thoughts. Despite the lack of archival research, however, the author had read widely in the existing historical literature in many languages and had apparently reflected astutely on the reasons for Genghis Khan's successes. All in all, the books contained some historical value even for the purists—and Himmler was hardly a purist. What mattered above all about the past, for Himmler, was how the Nazis, and particularly the SS, could learn from it to advance their cause and strengthen their organization. In December 1932 Himmler had written regarding another work: "A perfect book of ancient German peasant law for us, for one can extract much for the future."[33]

Prawdin's *Genghis Khan* must have seemed equally useful. So the SS Training Office, headed by Himmler's protégé and friend Gottlob Berger, ordered a special revised and expanded one-volume edition of Prawdin's two books on Genghis Khan, which appeared in 1938. For similar educational purposes, Berger also made use of a number of other historical novels, one on Himmler's hero, the Saxon ruler Heinrich I,[34] but Prawdin's book struck so many of the right chords that it apparently became one of Himmler's own favorites. Himmler frequently gave it as a Christmas present to his subordinates, and every SS leader got a copy. The book was also distributed, according to one account, in hospitals (to soldiers) during the war.[35]

Prawdin's Genghis Khan generally conformed with what is known of the real historical figure. Born around 1162 (the scholars prefer 1167)

39

into the one of the leading families of the nomadic Mongols, Temuchin, as he was originally named, had to overcome great adversity early in his life. A neighboring tribe poisoned his father, who had been more a military leader chosen by the various semi-independent Mongol clans than a real monarch. The clans quickly abandoned the young Temuchin, who was left to the mercy of his father's Tatar enemies. His daring escape from captivity established his reputation for bravery and cleverness, and slowly he was able to recruit new followers and rebuild the Mongols' military strength. After demonstrating astute diplomacy and military prowess against the local enemies of the Mongols (he originated the use of war games and of massed squadrons of cavalry), Temuchin was elected ruler (khan). His Mongol hordes covered long distances faster than the world had ever seen, and they were often able to surprise and outflank their foes. He expanded his sway in all directions against far more sizable peoples until he dominated much of Russia, China, Korea, Persia, Asia Minor, and even Eastern Europe. He became known as the ruler of rulers, the man who subjected most of the known world and who planned for the conquest of the rest.

Along the way, Genghis Khan shed even more blood than was customary in those places and those times. Beginning with the murder of his half-brother and the execution of other nomadic leaders whom he defeated in battle, Genghis Khan proceeded in stages to the destruction of cities and the extermination of entire enemy populations—men, women, and children. According to Prawdin, Genghis Khan was not senselessly cruel or barbaric. He simply regarded human life as worth very little, and when he saw some purpose in taking it—military necessity, vengeance, or the need to terrorize his enemies—he did so "as we destroy rats when we regard them as noxious." During one campaign in Afghanistan he asked a captured Afghan prince whether people would forever remember the bloodshed, and the prince replied that, if the campaign continued, no one would be left alive to remember. Predictably, Genghis Khan concluded that his fame would still live on with other races and countries.[36]

How did Himmler react to these descriptions of mass carnage? He would have recognized that the Mongolian leaders came very close to conquering all Europe and conducting a war of extermination against his beloved thirteenth-century Germans. (According to Prawdin, only the untimely death of Genghis Khan's son and successor, and the need to elect a new khan, forced the withdrawal of the Mongol armies from Europe—after they had destroyed their major military opponents.[37])

The Mongols exemplified the tough, brutal, Eastern races of lesser culture that had threatened Europe for centuries and would continue to threaten for centuries more unless Nazi Germany solved the problem. On one level, this book (and others like it) must have confirmed Himmler's deepest fears. Hitler apparently felt the same way. In one of his midday monologues during the war he described Asia as a disquieting reservoir of men. Whether the tsars or the Bolsheviks ruled did not make that much difference; the danger would be even greater, Hitler said, if the Mongols were to take over. A permanent state of war on the Eastern front would help Germany and Europe to form a sound race that could protect itself, Hitler concluded.[38]

Still, Prawdin's Genghis Khan and the Mongols possessed so many qualities and policies that Himmler regarded as admirable that he could not have regarded these historical figures simply as the ancient enemy of the German race. Genghis Khan was, of course, a military genius who had trained and commanded an elite force always ready to fight and ever devoted to its leader. Himmler had established SS military units that were more dedicated to the Führer and to Nazi ideology than the regular armed forces were. The whole Mongolian people had also mobilized for war, and peacetime for them was but a period of preparation for war. Nazi Germany had begun to prepare for war almost from the moment Hitler had taken power.

Genghis Khan had achieved his greatest successes through mobility and surprise against foes of superior numbers. He had lived to conquer, regarding it (according to Prawdin) as man's greatest joy—to ride one's enemies' horses, to take away their possessions, to clasp in his arms their wives and daughters. Yet he did not gorge himself on the spoils. He had personally remained attached to the simple nomadic life and resisted the softening effects of urban civilization. All of this conformed to the image that Hitler had fashioned for himself.

Genghis Khan regarded his race as superior to all others, and he promoted this consciousness among his subjects. His warriors did not tire of fighting, and they did not long for peace and a life of ease. Moreover, they did not die out, for "each victory, each conquest, had brought new wives and new children. Every man fallen in battle had left a dozen offspring or more." (Prawdin claimed that one of Genghis Khan's sons had forty, one of his nephews a hundred.) And because the bravest and most distinguished men acquired the most beautiful women, the physical appearance of the Mongols continually improved over generations. Genghis Khan used prisoners of war as forced laborers, but when their numbers and presence became inherently threatening (they might be "carriers of pestilence"), he did not hesitate to execute them.[39] Himmler must have perceived so many parallels here to Nazi Germany's own specific needs that he could not but have been impressed.

41

On the other hand, the idea of racial intermingling clearly struck him as the wrong way to go about increasing the population, and as one cause of the Mongol Empire's decline. A Himmler subordinate noted that Himmler drew conclusions from this book about the need to maintain the purity of the race.[40] And a study of the historical expansion of Germans to the east put out by the SS Educational Office observed that racial intermingling of the German rulers with the native populations in other parts of the continent had weakened German blood and German influence: "in all parts of Europe German blood became diluted and turned into cultural fertilizer for foreign peoples."[41] Himmler did not intend to make the same mistake.

Prawdin also assessed the long-term effects of Genghis Khan's empire in favorable terms, rejecting the contemporary image of the Mongol leader as a bloodthirsty monster. He was said to have initiated a fertilization among great national cultures, established unity and order in China that lasted six centuries, stimulated nationalism in the rubbish heap of Western Asia and thereby created modern Persia, and ruled Russia for two centuries and stamped it with an ineradicable Mongolian die. Even the decomposition of the Mongol Empire held obvious lessons for the present. Prawdin singled out pacific Buddhism as a major cause of the decay and decline, and Himmler and Hitler shared the view that Christianity had similarly softened and wrongly influenced the German people. All these elements in the rise and fall of the Mongol Empire help to explain why Hitler's and Himmler's frequent wartime references to Genghis Khan were usually favorable.[42] Another fact that must have colored their attitude was that Genghis Khan had conquered and dominated Russia.

Himmler resolved the problem of Mongol racial inferiority in an ingenious if most unlikely way. He told a prominent German naturalist and anthropologist who specialized in Central Asia that emigrants from the lost continent of Atlantis had founded a great civilization in Central Asia and had established themselves as the ruling elite of native races in Asia. Himmler cited as his authority an "expert" author who called himself Karl Weisthor and who believed himself to be a direct descendant of the god Thor.[43] Himmler admired certain Asian leaders and institutions at the same time as he regarded Asiatic races as inferior; the blood that coursed through the veins of a Genghis Khan, an Attila the Hun, and a Stalin, he said in a speech in September 1942, was German.[44]

There are echoes of Prawdin's Genghis Khan in many of Himmler's wartime policies.[45] And whether or not Hitler actually read this book,[46] he clearly got something out of it. Just before the outbreak of World

War II, in a secret speech on August 22, 1939, to the commanders of the armed services, Hitler proclaimed:

Our strength is in our quickness and our brutality. Genghis Khan had millions of women and children killed by his own will and with a gay heart. History sees only in him a great state builder. . . . Thus for the time being I have sent to the East only my "Death's Head Units" with the order to kill without pity or mercy all men, women, and children of Polish race or language. Only in such a way will we win the vital space that we need. Who still talks nowadays of the extermination of the Armenians?[47]

According to one of Himmler's closest friends, Karl Gebhardt, Hitler borrowed something beyond a favorable view of Genghis Khan's reputation from the book—the idea that bloodshed bound warriors together and tied them permanently to their leader. Hitler apparently invented a new term for this concept—*Blutkitt* ("blood cement"). The best English equivalent might be "blood that serves as a bond." Gebhardt believed that Hitler had taken the term from the book on Genghis Khan. Actually, the word itself does not appear in Prawdin, but the idea is expressed in at least two places. Genghis Khan was said to have welded a people together through common battles and victories, through the shedding of blood.[48] A second passage is even more revealing. One of the nomadic tribes took the most binding oath known to them.

. . . with a sword they sacrificed a white stallion, a bull, a ram, and a hound, and then solemnly repeated after Jamuga the sentences of the pledge.

"Oh God, O heaven, O Earth, creators of these beasts, hearken to our oaths. May that happen to us which has happened to these animals if we break our vow, and are false to the holy alliance we have now sworn."[49]

The collective killing of highly prized animals, a crime by normal standards, here served as a means to prevent any of the warriors from abandoning their leader. Hitler and Himmler were to use a similar technique. Subordinates with bloodstained hands were most unlikely to desert their Führer and their cause. Except this time the blood was not that of animals.

Karl Wolff once testified that Himmler used to dislike an SS officer and Economics Ministry official named Otto Ohlendorf because he was too respectable, because he acted as if "he alone carried the Holy Grail in his pure hands."[50] The solution: Himmler appointed Ohlendorf as head of one of the *Einsatzgruppen* that carried out hundreds of thousands of executions of Jews and other enemies during the campaign against Russia.

Hitler and Himmler were mostly able to conceal their technique of implicating others in their crimes, but as the war began to slip away, so did Hitler's self-control. By November 1943 Soviet forces had retaken Kiev, American and British troops were pushing up the Italian peninsula, and the Americans were driving the Japanese out of the Solomon Islands in the Pacific. The climate was far from ideal for Hitler's speech on the twentieth anniversary of the Beer Hall Putsch, which was being recorded and then broadcast by radio. During the speech Hitler became furious and announced that the German people had inflicted such suffering and destruction on the peoples of Europe that they could expect no mercy in case of defeat. If Germany were defeated, he, Adolf Hitler, would not shed a single tear, even if all the cities of Germany were laid waste, and every German man, woman, and child put to the sword. The German people would only have themselves to blame. The censors deleted this outburst, but a Turkish press official was there to witness the rhetorical explosion.[51]

There is no doubt that Hitler sometimes selected enemies of Germany for punishment.[52] Less clear is which enemies he selected, when, and how many he wanted destroyed. Many charges against him cannot be proved, partly because Hitler was not the sort of person to put things on paper, but also partly because he did not always involve himself in the details. Others brought plans to him for his approval, which he gave orally. On the Jewish question, it is easier to follow what Himmler and Reinhard Heydrich planned and did than to track Hitler's continuing role. But one thing is clear from the general relationship between Hitler and Himmler: in spite of his own ambition for himself and for the SS, Himmler would not have acted against Hitler's orders or wishes in 1939—or for a great while thereafter. Only impending military defeat, Hitler's declining health, and his disengagement from reality allowed Himmler to separate himself from the Führer's will toward the end of the war.

Hitler was close enough to Himmler personally and politically to have given the Reich Führer SS special and confidential instructions for the SS regarding a forthcoming racial war against the Jews and other racial enemies. On the other hand, Himmler could well have taken it upon himself to prepare for the day when it would be possible to carry out Hitler's public threats against international Jewry or statements about the Jews that Hitler made in private. When the Führer wanted something, Himmler was usually eager to bring it about—even without express instructions. Himmler not only wanted to please his Führer; he knew that, if he did not take charge, someone else might well do so and get the credit. That was one of the lessons of Kristallnacht.

CHAPTER 2

PLANS FOR
GERMAN JEWS

HERSCHL GRYNSZPAN had a grievance against Nazi Germany. Grynszpan, a seventeen-year-old Polish Jew living in Paris, had just learned that his parents, along with some seventeen thousand other Jews of Polish citizenship living in Germany (in many cases for a generation or more), had been forcibly deported to Poland. The Polish government had helped to precipitate this action by taking steps to block the automatic right of Polish citizens living abroad to "return" to the country. But the man most responsible for the deportation was Heinrich Himmler, who decided to act before a new Polish regulation on passports took effect on October 30, 1938. On October 26 he ordered the police to put aside other tasks, collect all Polish Jews with valid passports, and get rid of them before October 29. Without any notice, police seized them, transported them to the east, and brutally dumped them over the border into Poland. Now they were Poland's problem.[1]

As it turned out, Himmler had created a serious new problem for himself. Young Grynszpan wanted to act against Germany. So, on the morning of November 7, 1938, he walked into the German Embassy in Paris, pulled out a gun, and seriously wounded Secretary of Legation Ernst vom Rath.[2] Grynszpan faded from the spotlight, even though he later ended up in Nazi hands; the shooting, however, did not fade. It gave Nazi officials a convenient ground for punishing German Jews throughout the country.

Grynszpan was the second Jew in the last few years to shoot a representative of Nazi Germany. A Jewish rabbinical student named David Frankfurter had assassinated a Nazi Party Foreign Section official in Switzerland in early 1936. Nazi reaction was muted at the time, probably because of the impending Olympic Games to be held in Berlin; the leadership did not want to do anything that might force a boycott or cancellation of the games. But after the shooting of vom Rath, the German press was instructed to point out that this was the second such Jewish attack—and that it was a part of the international Jewish conspiracy against Germany.[3] The intelligence section (SD) of the SS had already reached this conclusion about the assassination in Switzerland.[4]

In 1935 Reinhard Heydrich, head of the SD, described the police as the state's defensive force that could act against the legally identifiable enemy, whereas the SS was the offensive force that could initiate the final battle against the Jews.[5] Heydrich too was a personal symbol of the organizational link between the police and the SS, for he also ran the Prussian Gestapo, technically a political police force for the largest state, and then what was called the Security Police, the fusion of the nation's political and criminal police forces.

Heydrich was a real find for Himmler—someone he had come across by mistake, but whom he had sized up correctly. In 1931 Himmler was trying to form an intelligence service to get a better picture of the enemies—communists, Jews, Freemasons, and reactionaries. A high SA officer recommended a retired naval lieutenant who had been a Nachrichtenoffizier, a term that could mean "intelligence officer" or "communications officer." At the time Himmler had assumed that a Nachrichtenoffizier was someone who obtained intelligence, but Heydrich had been a signals officer, someone who transmitted information.[6]

There were plenty of reasons for Heydrich to try for the SS job anyway. His career was in ruins. A Naval Court of Honor had ousted him from the navy because of conduct unbecoming an officer. He had abruptly terminated a relationship with a young Berlin woman, whose father was well connected in the navy, in order to marry Lina von Osten. At his disciplinary hearing Heydrich accused the first woman, who had since suffered a nervous breakdown, of improper behavior, which he said had led him to break off with her. The Naval Court of Honor found his conduct at the trial reprehensible.[7] So, in spite of his lack of involvement in the Nazi movement or in politics generally, in July 1931 Heydrich came to Himmler's chicken farm at Waldrudering, in Bavaria.

As Himmler later recounted the story, Heydrich simply admitted that he had been a radio officer. Himmler stared at the tall, blond, impressive figure and told him not to be concerned about lack of experience. He then asked Heydrich to sketch out his vision of a Nazi Party intelligence service. Heydrich wrote for fifteen minutes: Himmler returned, read it, and hired him on the spot to run what became the SD.[8] Himmler had found a clever and energetic right-hand man who also fit the physical standards of his own Nordic ideal.

During the 1930s Himmler spent many hours talking with Heydrich about the goals and functions of the SS and the SD.[9] At that time Himmler often spoke of the law of history that pitted the German people against their eternal enemies.[10] Heydrich had learned and passed on to his subordinates that behind every threat to Germany—communist, socialist, capitalist, or even Catholic—lurked the cunning Jew, extending his connections to other groups, masterfully organized throughout the world. So the SD was in the process of building up an index-card file of all Jews in Germany, of Jews who had emigrated from Germany, and of the most important foreign Jews, a supervisory measure it had borrowed from a clever young academic named Fritz Arlt, who had done an ethnic-biological investigation of the population of Leipzig.[11]

The enemy within would be even more dangerous in time of war, and it was becoming clear that Germany was approaching another war. Hitler was convinced that the German people needed much more land to feed themselves and to "breathe." By the fall of 1937 he had decided to take over Austria and Czechoslovakia, but they were only the first small steps. The bigger expansion would have to follow: no later than 1943–45, he had told the foreign minister, the war minister, and the heads of the armed services in November 1937. Hitler was not at all sure that his successors would be able to acquire the necessary *Lebensraum* (living space) for Germany. Concerned about his own health, he worried that the early deaths of his parents foreshadowed his own.[12] He had to act soon to accomplish his historical mission.

Precisely when war came and which countries would be involved depended, however, not only on Hitler's own decisions—and in the realm of foreign policy he did make his own decisions—but also upon the other major powers. The Anschluss, the quick German takeover of Austria in March 1938, did not particularly ruffle the Western powers. Austria was, after all, a German country, an artificial product of the peace settlement of World War I, which had actually sought union with Germany in 1919. Even though the German army marched in uninvited and against the wishes of the Austrian government, the Anschluss could be passed off as national self-determination.

Czechoslovakia was quite a different case. The evidence is now persuasive that Hitler wanted to provoke a war with Czechoslovakia during the fall of 1938. British Prime Minister Neville Chamberlain offered to satisfy so many of Hitler's outrageous demands for Czech territory in which ethnic Germans lived, however, that the Führer reluctantly had to accept the fruits of appeasement—the Sudetenland, a sizable chunk of Czech territory—at the Munich Conference at the end of September. It looked very doubtful whether Britain and France could make further concessions after Munich. Even if they had, Hitler would not have been satisfied. After Munich he swore that he would never again allow some *Schweinehund*, the German equivalent of "SOB," to cheat him out of a war. This was a remarkable reaction to a treaty settlement that most of the world considered a great German victory.[13] Nor was he willing to wait much longer. Even before Munich, he had stated that if there was a diplomatic settlement, he would complete the destruction of Czechoslovakia the next spring. The day after the Munich Agreement was signed, Hitler said he would annex the remainder of the country at the first opportunity. And at the end of 1938 he told his close associates that the events of 1939 would far overshadow those of 1938.[14]

Since he had perceived the Jews as the source of Germany's World War I defeat, Hitler must have been determined to neutralize them this time. One method of disposing of Jews was to have the police literally force them out of the country before the war started—push them across borders, give them deadlines by which they had to leave the country, throw thousands into concentration camps, where they were beaten and abused and then released with a warning to leave the country soon or else. During the last few years, but particularly during 1938, Nazi Germany and Himmler's police had used these devices liberally.[15]

This policy of forced emigration served a dual purpose—removing Jews, and weakening Germany's neighbors and opponents, as Nazi officials themselves had explained in advance. In a 1935 brochure composed out of a series of articles for the SS newspaper *Das Schwarze Korps*, Heydrich had explained that any people weak enough to let Jews into their country would suffer from racial mixing, loss of racial consciousness, and inevitable decline. He accused the Jews of maintaining their goals of ruling the world and destroying the Nordic peoples.[16] Nazi pressure and abuse created panic among the Jews; the expulsions and the flow of refugees created near chaos and anti-Semitic reactions abroad.

Yet fewer than half of the German and Austrian Jews had left the country, even under such persecution. They simply could not do so. Some three hundred thousand more had applied for American immigration visas, but the annual American quota for Germany and Austria combined was only a little more than twenty-seven thousand.[17] Few countries in the world were willing to take in substantial numbers of Jews at this time.

Some foreign observers were able not only to discern the logic behind

Nazi persecution of the Jews, but also to peer toward the future. The American consul general in Vienna, the veteran diplomat John Wiley, wrote to Washington in mid-1938 that Nazi Germany's policy toward the Jews might be "inspired by the possibility of war and the desire to eliminate a hostile element in the population. If there is war, Heaven alone knows what will happen to these unhappy and wretched people."[18] The events of November 1938 gave the world a small sample of what was to come.

On the day the shooting of vom Rath took place, the SS elite were heading toward Munich for the big festivities that occurred every year on November 8–9—the anniversary of the 1923 Beer Hall Putsch. Although Hitler's plan to seize power in Munich and then to march on Berlin had failed badly in 1923, the Nazis had transformed the anniversary into a heroic historical pageant in which the early party members played the leading role. Himmler had had the good fortune to have participated in the putsch, though at the time he was a follower not of Hitler but of Ernst Röhm, later the head of the brownshirted SA.[19]

Himmler had scheduled in Munich a meeting of the thirty or so top-ranking SS officers, the Gruppenführer and Obergruppenführer. On the afternoon of November 8 the select audience of SS chiefs may have listened with particular care to their leader and mentor for signs of the SS's future course on the Jewish question, for that morning the Nazi Party newspaper *Völkischer Beobachter* had indicated that the shooting of vom Rath would lead to a new German attitude toward the Jews.[20]

Himmler did not present a short-term program to deal with German Jews or with Jews elsewhere. He did not mention the Grynszpan–vom Rath case. Instead he offered a vision of the next decade in which the Jewish question played a critical role. Within ten years, he proclaimed, there would be unprecedented clashes—not only a struggle among nations but also an ideological struggle against the Jews, Freemasons, Marxists, and Catholics worldwide. The Jews dominated this alliance, Himmler claimed; they were the source of everything negative. They had come to realize that, if Germany and Italy were not destroyed, the Jews themselves would be. As Hitler often did, Himmler thus linked the ideological-racial struggle against the Jews with Germany's foreign policy and military needs.

Himmler then explained how Nazi Germany's policy of expelling Jews was creating the precondition for a worldwide battle against the Jews. Germany would continue to drive Jews out mercilessly, and Italy and Poland were moving in the same direction. Other European states, such as Sweden, Norway, Denmark, Holland, and Belgium, were not yet anti-Semitic, but they would become anti-Semitic as Germany sent them more and more Jews. Czechoslovakia was already anti-Semitic, Himmler stated, as was the entire Balkan Peninsula. In Palestine, he argued, there was a desperate struggle against the Jews. (He did not specify whether he meant the Arabs alone, or the Arabs and the British.) There would come a time, he concluded, when the world would have no more place for the Jews.

So the Jews had drawn the natural conclusion, Himmler explained. They thought they could eliminate the danger to themselves by destroying the source of anti-Semitism, Germany. If Germany lost this struggle, Himmler warned, there would be nothing left for the Germans—no Indian-style reservation; all Germans would be starved and butchered, whether or not they had supported the Nazis. Having conjured up a powerful Jewish race fearful for its own survival, he found it easy to suspect a planned Jewish offensive against Germany. Then he used the Jewish threat to Germany he had portrayed as justification for future radical measures against the Jews.

Himmler did not buttress his argument with evidence. He began with the notion that group heredity determined behavior, and a kind of logic carried him the rest of the way. The Jewish reaction Himmler simply deduced from what he regarded as the essence of Jewishness: the fanatical drive to sustain themselves at the expense of others. It was an example of a not incapable mind following false premises to extreme and absurd conclusions. But no external authority and no internal voice of conscience induced him to reconsider, to question his premises or his conclusions, and his loyal audience undoubtedly agreed with him.

All Germans had to rally to the cause in this battle, Himmler declared to the group. German blood created warriors, and wherever German blood existed throughout the world, there were potential recruits for the Nazis. He stated bluntly that he intended quite sincerely to collect, to steal, German blood wherever he could. He implied that Germans outside the country who refused to join Nazi Germany could become the most dangerous enemies of all. In later years Himmler would describe the task of gathering up Germanic and Nordic people as the positive side of racial policy, whereas the measures designed for racial enemies were the negative side. The positive balanced with the negative; they were equally necessary.

All of these considerations led Himmler to stress the hard tasks that lay ahead. The SS would have to carry out orders without pity if they were to save the German *Volk*. He told the Gruppenführer that they might even be astounded when he, acting against his own feelings and conscience, again and again ordered them to eliminate and punish harshly. But it was necessary. Finally, he contrasted the two possible outcomes: what lay ahead was either the Greater German Empire or nothingness. If the SS carried out its duty, then the Führer would create the greatest empire the world had ever seen. "In this sense," he concluded, "go to your duty and work."[21]

Himmler linked the Jewish question with German foreign policy in two different respects. In the long run, Nazi anti-Semitism would help to unite Europe behind Germany. In the short run, however, Jewish influence elsewhere might cause problems for Germany. If Himmler did not announce any specific program for dealing with the Jews, it was likely because he perceived Nazi Jewish policy to have major diplomatic repercussions and because he was looking toward war. Only two days later, in a speech to hundreds of German journalists, Hitler discounted the prospects for peace and urged the press to help convince the public to support the regime in any future war.[22] But in between Himmler's speech and Hitler's speech, a major action against the Jews took place —contrary to Himmler's wishes.

On the late afternoon of November 9, vom Rath died. A messenger brought the unhappy news to the Führer about 9:00 p.m. that evening, while he was attending the reception for the old party veterans. Goebbels was sitting next to Hitler, and the two men carried on a long private conversation. Somewhat out of favor because of his open affair with the actress Lida Baarova, Goebbels seized the opportunity to urge action against the Jews and regain the Führer's good graces.[23] Then Hitler left, nominally dissociating himself from what was to come. Goebbels soon gave a vitriolic anti-Semitic speech, noting that some popular disturbances directed against synagogues had already occurred. He stated that the Führer had decided the party was neither to prepare nor to organize demonstrations, but that it would not oppose spontaneous outbreaks. The party and SA men present got the intended message; no one should be able to tell that Hitler had arranged for attacks on Jews and Jewish buildings. The evening gathering quickly broke up; the Gauleiter sent word back to their districts, and SA leader Viktor Lutze explained the situation to his men in Munich. The word went out that synagogues and Jewish businesses were to be a particular target.[24] For the SA men, it was a most welcome message; it had been a long time since they had had a chance to vent their anger. Busy elsewhere, Himmler knew nothing of all this.

As a tornado of violence began to spread across Germany, the SS leadership staying at the Four Seasons Hotel in Munich received a phone call from Gestapo headquarters in Berlin reporting on events and asking for instructions. Heydrich, Rudolf Brandt, and Karl Wolff were at the hotel. Heydrich sent Wolff and his assistant to find Himmler and decide what was to be done. Himmler, as it turned out, was then with Hitler who ordered the SS to keep out of the way—neither participate in nor oppose the violence. In the recollection of Wolff's assistant Schallermeier, Hitler had said: "They should remain neutral." The first directives went from Munich to Berlin just before midnight. The police were instructed not to interfere with actions against Jews and particularly against synagogues, but they were to prevent plundering and special excesses and to secure archival material kept in synagogues. Furthermore, the police were to prepare for the arrest of twenty to thirty thousand Jews. Again demonstrating fear of Jewish intentions, the telegram (signed by Heinrich Müller) authorized the sharpest measures against any Jews in possession of arms.[25]

Later Heydrich had a chance to issue more detailed instructions to the police that reflected Himmler's unmistakable concern for detail and propriety. Whatever actions occurred should not endanger German lives or property; synagogues could be burned only if there was no danger to the surrounding buildings. Healthy, nonelderly adult Jewish males were to be seized first, and concentration camps notified. As he often did, Himmler had a subordinate (Schallermeier) write a memo for the files about the whole episode. As Schallermeier remembered it, the memo read, almost verbatim: "I suspect that this airhead Goebbels got us into this untenable situation in this most difficult period."[26]

Over the next twenty-four hours more than one thousand synagogues all across the country were destroyed. Approximately a hundred Jews were killed, and thirty thousand Jews were seized and sent to concentration camps. In spite of official attempts to call a halt to the violence on November 10, sporadic incidents continued in some areas until November 13. It was a pogrom the likes of which Central Europe had not seen for five centuries. The destruction of windows in shops owned by Jews gave the event its name—Night of Broken Glass. The shopwindow glass was all imported from Belgium, and replacement would require half the annual production of the Belgian glass industry, as Göring would soon complain.[27]

This orgy of destruction might have gladdened the hearts of some anti-Semites. To Himmler, it was a disaster and a humiliation. First, there was the damage Kristallnacht inflicted on Germany's image abroad and upon German foreign relations. If one was going to punish Jews, it had to be done quietly—not out in the open, in front of foreigners and reporters. Second, Germany could hardly afford to allow such widespread destruction of property, even if there were ways to try to shift the burden upon the Jews themselves. Himmler did not even want to believe that the Führer knew all about Goebbels's initiative, let alone that he authorized it, but Göring later found out just what had happened. When someone insisted to him that the guilty parties had to be punished, Göring replied: "You want to punish Hitler?"[28]

✗ Two factors probably weighed even more heavily upon Himmler than the damage to foreign policy: the involvement of Goebbels and the SA. In spite of his talent and his ideology, Goebbels was an intellectual with a taste for modern culture, a brilliant speaker with a caustic tongue, a *bon vivant* with a sense of humor that usually came out at the expense of others, and an individualist. He was a modern man of the city, and in this sense has even been described as the "most Jewish" of the Nazi leaders.[29] Himmler romanticized the German past and the German farmer. He could not match Goebbels's flights of rhetoric; he plodded through his speeches. Himmler needed firm ideological grounding, and ✗ as head of the SS he became a chief executive, thinking constantly of his organization. The two men were poles apart—and they both knew it.

Goebbels was also a compulsive philanderer. As minister of propaganda, he controlled the German film industry, which gave him access to a good many actresses who were financially dependent upon his decisions. A few months after Kristallnacht, Himmler told Alfred Rosen- ✗ berg that Goebbels used precisely the kind of financial pressure on female employees that the Nazis had cursed Jews for. Himmler called him the most hated man in Germany.[30]

✗ The involvement of the SA must have sickened Himmler. The SA was a throwback to the early years of the Nazi movement, when the state police forces were unfriendly and the Social Democratic and communist opposition powerful. Gaining control of the beer halls and the streets was politically necessary, and the use of violence against unpopular targets, particularly in Bavaria, hardly hurt the Nazi movement with much of the electorate. The SA had recruited a good many thugs to do its work in the early years. Under the former army captain Ernst Röhm, who had envisioned himself as a military commander-in-chief after the Nazis came to power, the SA grew into a huge force. Röhm, however, was a notorious homosexual, and the SA had a disreputable and undisciplined past, which had made them both unacceptable to most of Germany's professional military officers. By 1934 Hitler had been forced to choose between satisfying Röhm or satisfying the regular army.

Himmler and Hermann Göring had found a way out of this dilemma. After a conversation between the two "old party comrades,"[31] Göring (who held the title of minister-president of Prussia) appointed Heydrich to run the Gestapo, the huge Prussian political police, which gave Himmler the last and most important link in the German state police empire. Himmler and Göring then "uncovered" evidence that Röhm was conspiring to overthrow Hitler. The Führer authorized the SS and the Gestapo to execute the SA traitors and other assorted enemies on June 30, 1934, in a wave of bloodshed that became known as the Night of the Long Knives. Suddenly the SA was virtually leaderless and powerless, and the path was free for Himmler's SS to become far more powerful than the SA had ever been. In spite of his own role in emasculating the SA—or because of it—Himmler preserved the animosity between the SS and the SA, and regarded any possibility of reviving the influence of the SA as an insult. When the commander-in-chief of the army said, in January 1939, that he wanted to use the SA as a training-and-reserve force for the army, Himmler flew into a rage. Well into the war he tried to block the appointment of SA men to positions of influence, and he told one SA officer that the officer had apparently not forgotten the 30th of June—which was (and was perceived as) a direct threat.[32]

The very last thing Himmler wanted was for the SA to find a way back to political influence in Nazi Germany. Himmler had tried to make himself and Heydrich the primary authorities (after Hitler) over Jewish policy.[33] Kristallnacht was an irresponsible outburst arranged and carried out by two arch-rivals encroaching on the SS's domain.

Under the circumstances, one can almost believe the story that Karl Wolff told (Swiss) High Commissioner for the Free City of Danzig Carl J. Burckhardt two weeks later: the events of the past weeks (Kristallnacht) had made Himmler ill, and he had put himself in a sanatorium to recover. The smooth, handsome Wolff, however, was not above gilding the situation, particularly when it made his boss look better in the eyes of a foreign diplomat. In an internal memorandum around the same time, Wolff wrote only that Himmler had gone on vacation until early December. Later Wolff would specify that Himmler was in Italy. At any rate, Himmler's appointment book contains no entries between November 8 and December 8.[34] But the SS was ably represented in the late-1938 deliberations over how Germany should resolve its "Jewish problem."

FOLLOWING Goebbels's suggestion, Hitler decided to make the Jews pay a huge fine of a billion marks to compensate for the damage "they" had caused the previous night. He also decided to press to exclude the Jews rapidly from the German economy. Goebbels immediately banned further demonstrations, indicating to the public that new laws would provide the final response to the assassination.[35] On November 11 Hitler gave Göring a mandate to resolve the Jewish question "one way or another" and to coordinate the necessary steps by various agencies. Göring summoned a large number of officials from various agencies to a meeting at the Air Ministry in Berlin on November 12 to deal with the economic consequences of Kristallnacht and the ways to remove Jews from the German economy.[36]

✗ Göring, a famous World War I ace, now commander-in-chief of Germany's air force, was also head of the Office of the Four-Year Plan—a kind of economic tsar who was responsible for preparing the economy for war. In this capacity he was interested in safeguarding the economy against damage and in preventing the loss of foreign exchange; he had to calculate the costs and benefits of measures designed to persecute the Jews further.

Some foreign diplomats regarded Göring as a moderate among the Nazi leaders on the Jewish question,[37] and their impression was partly correct. He was not so rigid a racist as Himmler, and was more inclined to except individual "good" Jews from persecution, especially if he himself could benefit financially.[38] Nonetheless, Göring too saw the Jews as a destructive element within the Reich and elsewhere. In the summer of 1938 he had told an astonished American diplomat that within ten years the United States would become the most anti-Semitic country in the world, and that the combination of Jews and blacks raised grave questions about America's future. Around the same time, Martin Bormann had informed the Nazi Party Gauleiter that Göring intended to bring about a "fundamental cleaning up" of the Jewish question that would "satisfy the demands of the party to the fullest measure."[39]

✗ Göring dominated much of the meeting on November 12, but Heydrich got in some good shots toward the end. He warned that the measures they were considering—to fine, identify, and restrict the Jews within Germany—would prove inadequate; the only solution was to get rid of them. He explained how his men (including Adolf Eichmann) had streamlined the process of forcing Jews out of newly annexed Austria. Heydrich called for the creation of a central emigration authority in Germany, and Göring threw his support behind that idea almost immediately. At the same time, Heydrich made it clear that very strong measures would have to be taken against Jews who remained in the country, though he opposed the establishment of closed ghettos because of the difficulty of police supervision. Göring also announced that, if Germany went to war in the foreseeable future, there would be a great reckoning with the Jews.[40] Whether there was more behind this statement than Göring's customary bravado remained to be seen.

On the surface, Göring and Heydrich disagreed simply over whether it was worth the loss of foreign exchange to let Jews leave the country. Those countries willing to admit some Jews required them to have means of support or their own capital. On November 12 Heydrich had explained that he had forced the rich Jews to supply the poor Jews with funds, so that more of them could get visas. Göring, however, was still concerned about the departure of any Jewish funds.[41] His own approach was to make foreign Jews come up with the capital and to negotiate an agreement for a mass exodus of German Jews. The result would have been more profitable for Nazi Germany, which would take over or hold on to all German Jewish assets, and it might have cleared out more Jews.

A Danish Jew named Hugo Rothenberg who had earned Göring's gratitude over two decades earlier met with Göring privately on November 29 and condemned the Nazi violence and the concentration camps. Göring admitted that Kristallnacht had damaged Germany's economic position and foreign trade, which was his foremost concern. But he insisted that under all circumstances the Jews would have to leave Germany and recommended a foreign loan to finance emigration. When Rothenberg pointed out that in the present climate it would be very difficult to get foreigners, and particularly foreign Jews, to implement such a plan, Göring warned that Germany naturally had other ideas in case emigration did not work.[42] He did not spell out their nature.

The idea of an international agreement to remove Jews from Germany had been floating around for years, but it had become slightly more realistic after President Franklin Roosevelt had invited nearly forty nations to an international meeting in Évian, France, in July 1938. This Évian Conference had created a body called the Intergovernmental Committee on Refugees, which was supposed to negotiate with Nazi Germany, to find places throughout the world where substantial numbers of Jews could settle, and to help finance and arrange mass resettlement. None of the Nazi powers, however, showed any desire to meet with representatives of the committee until Göring displayed signs of interest.[43]

By late 1938 Göring seemed increasingly troubled. Observers noted that he had lost a lot of weight and that he seemed depressed. During the Munich crisis he had perhaps come to realize that the Führer's foreign-policy objectives were far more radical than he had believed. Now Göring was facing a very uncomfortable choice: to follow the Führer loyally against his better judgment and see Germany enter a war he did not think Germany could win, or to drag his heels and lose his position of eminence in the Third Reich.[44] A negotiated settlement of the Jewish problem might reduce some of the tension between the Western nations and Germany and lessen the chance of a war. So, even apart from the profitability of the deal for Germany and for himself, there was reason for Göring to support the idea, and he did.[45]

Göring, however, faced an array of opponents of a negotiated settlement of the Jewish question, a strange coalition of Nazi radicals who, in spite of bitter quarrels with one another, approved of forced emigration and policies even more extreme. Goebbels had re-entered the picture with the SA at Kristallnacht; Foreign Minister Joachim von Ribbentrop remained steadfastly opposed to negotiations with the Intergovernmental Committee on Refugees;[46] and there was always Himmler and the SS. In late November *Das Schwarze Korps*, edited by Günter d'Alquen, who was a member of Heydrich's SD,[47] elaborated on the framework that Heydrich had laid down at the meeting on November 12:

> The Jews must be driven from our residential districts and segregated where they will be among themselves, having as little contact with Germans as possible. . . . Confined to themselves, these parasites will be . . . reduced to poverty. . . . Let no one fancy, however, that we shall then stand idly by, merely watching the process. The German people are not in the least inclined to tolerate in their country hundreds of thousands of criminals, who not only secure their existence through crime, but also want to exact revenge. . . . These hundreds of thousands of impoverished Jews [would create] a breeding ground for Bolshevism and a collection of the politically criminal subhuman elements. . . . In such a situation we would be faced with the hard necessity of exterminating the Jewish underworld in the same way as, under our government of law and order, we are accustomed to exterminating any other criminals—that is, by fire and sword. The result would be the actual and final end of Jewry in Germany, its absolute annihilation.

Das Schwarze Korps raised the possibility that other nations might still take in Germany's Jews. It even claimed that it would welcome the founding of a Jewish state. Barring that, however, it stated, Germany would certainly go ahead and resolve its Jewish problem.[48]

Shortly afterward, the American consul general in Berlin, Raymond Geist, who had excellent contacts within the Gestapo, analyzed the situation even more explicitly. In a personal and confidential letter to his former superior George Messersmith, now assistant secretary of state, Geist warned that the Nazis had embarked on a program of "annihilation" of the Jews; the West would be allowed to save the remnants, if they chose to do so, but there was little chance of getting any cooperation from the Third Reich. There were already signs that Nazi objectives extended beyond German Jews. Reich Health Leader Leonardo Conti told government physicians in mid-December that the government intended to find a "final solution" to the Jewish problem in Europe.[49]

On January 24 or 25, 1939, in an address to high-ranking SS officers, Heydrich concentrated on the danger from the Jews—"the eternal subhumans," he called them. This term "subhumans" was not at all common usage in 1939, but it was to become quite common after 1941, when the Nazis had adopted what they considered to be appropriate measures to deal with subhumans. Heydrich noted that Jews had frequently, throughout history, been expelled, which had been an error—presumably because it had not resolved the problem. Himmler's last cryptic note on Heydrich's speech was "inner martial spirit." The SS men had to steel themselves to deal with the task.[50]

A number of contemporary sources indicate that there were only two possibilities for German Jews: emigration or death. In this situation, Göring was a moderate, because he was willing to bargain with the Intergovernmental Committee on Refugees over a large-scale emigration, whereas Goebbels, Ribbentrop, Heydrich, and Himmler were not. Well-informed diplomats perceived this alignment among the Nazi leaders.[51]

Göring certainly knew that the Führer would have to approve any deal. He could not have wanted to take further political risks when he was already in difficulty. One German official, after a frank conversation with Göring in December 1938, commented to a friend that Göring was not only dependent upon Hitler but actually afraid of Himmler and Heydrich.[52] So Hjalmar Horace Greeley Schacht, the well-known German financier, not Göring, became the point man for a negotiated settlement of Nazi Germany's Jewish problem. President of the Reichsbank and former minister of economics, Schacht asked Hitler for permission to explore confidential negotiations with the intergovernmental committee. Hitler agreed, but did not further explain his objectives. Göring too gave his approval—they discussed the subject thoroughly, Schacht claimed.

In December 1938 Schacht surfaced in London and presented a plan to George Rublee, the American lawyer who was director of the intergovernmental committee. Schacht explained that 150,000 German Jews between the ages of fifteen and forty-five could leave the country over a three-year period, to be followed later by their dependents. Some two hundred thousand Jews would have to remain in the country, apparently as hostages for the good behavior of international Jewry. Meanwhile, German authorities would create a trust fund from seized Jewish assets, and the emigrants could use up to one-quarter of the fund to make purchases of supplies, equipment, and transportation arrangements from German companies. Outside sources—foreign Jewish interests—would have to bear the bulk of the resettlement costs through a bond; the German trust fund, though in the government's hands, was supposed to serve as collateral.[53] The Schacht plan would have meant the virtual confiscation of most German Jewish property and would have given a boost to German exports.

Even if the deal was one-sided, Schacht was sincere about arranging the release of German Jews. Later in December he warned a delegation of American Quakers, also interested in speeding the exodus of Jewish refugees: "Be quick, for nobody knows what happens in this country tomorrow." Göring, Schacht said, was not interested in charity work, but in getting Jews out quickly. Other agencies, however, made life difficult for Schacht. Even after Hitler gave him permission to meet with Rublee, the Foreign Office tried to prevent the initialing of agreements and any promises about the future treatment of Jews in Germany.[54]

Rublee came to Berlin, and he began negotiations with Schacht in January 1939. At their final meeting, on January 19, Schacht appeared quite distressed. The next day Hitler dismissed him as head of the Reichsbank. The general explanation was that longstanding disagreements about the currency had finally done Schacht in. Göring, for example, said that Schacht had been unwilling to carry out some of Hitler's wishes, implying that he had refused to reflate the currency. It seems, however, that Himmler also had a role in the dismissal. He had long considered Schacht an enemy, and he did not approve of Schacht's efforts to negotiate with the refugee committee. So, by one diplomat's account, Himmler submitted a secret report to Hitler that Schacht had been disloyal to Nazi interests during the negotiations. Schacht's ouster followed immediately.[55]

Göring then stepped in and quickly appointed one of his own economic experts, Helmut Wohlthat, to continue the negotiations with Rublee.[56] Wohlthat reached an agreement in which the German government and the international committee would each take certain steps independently. That device precluded a formal contract and avoided implicating the Western nations in Nazi extortion. Before he initialed the memoranda, Wohlthat got approval not only from representatives of various government ministries, but also from Göring personally.[57]

Göring's support did not clear away all the obstacles. Himmler was opposed to the terms Wohlthat had worked out.[58] Those who were satisfied with the progress and the results of forced emigration had little reason to want an orderly transfer of Jews elsewhere. Besides, an agreement would be too easy on the Jews themselves. At the first meeting of the Reich Central Office for Jewish Emigration, on February 11, Heydrich told other officials to proceed as if an agreement with the international committee did not exist.[59]

Hitler himself gave out mixed signals. On November 9, 1938, for example, he had supposedly told Göring that he was interested in sending German Jews to Madagascar, and that he would make an initiative to the West. No one did much about Madagascar until 1940, however, after the German conquest of France, when there was talk of transferring the island to German control. Yet Hitler also understood the benefits of forced emigration. Toward the end of November he told the South African minister of defense that he did not intend to export Nazism, but that he was exporting anti-Semitism (by sending German Jews elsewhere). World Jewry, he claimed, did not want the Jews to disappear from Europe, for the Jews were an outpost for the Bolshevization of the world. He added that the Jews would one day disappear, not just from Germany, but from Europe.[60] The comment was reminiscent of Himmler's November 8 statement that one day the world would have no place left for the Jews.

In mid-January Göring presented a number of specific proposals to Hitler regarding the Aryanization of Jewish property, the banishing of Jews from sleeping cars and dining cars on trains, mixed marriages, and the like.[61] It was probably during this conversation that Hitler made known his intention to launch a major rhetorical attack against international Jewry and the West in his forthcoming speech on January 30, the anniversary of the Nazi seizure of power. (This information leaked from members of Göring's staff to American diplomat Geist, who reported what was coming eight days before the speech.) Yet, in spite of his planned verbal assault, the Führer did not disapprove of the Wohlthat-Rublee agreement negotiated in late January and initialed in early February. Göring implied to representatives of the Intergovernmental Committee on Refugees that, for the time being, Hitler would go along with a deal; he said that he had six months to reach an agreement with international Jewry; if no agreement came about, Nazi authorities would chart another course.[62]

Göring may have assessed Hitler correctly, but the course of events reveals a Führer closer to the radicals. In the spring of 1939 Göring and Wohlthat sent the Führer measures to implement their emigration agreement. Wohlthat drew up draft decrees establishing a Jewish trust fund within Germany, providing for state aid to train Jews to prepare them for emigration, and even giving legal guarantees to Jewish education. Hitler, however, did not sign them, allegedly because the Intergovernmental Committee on Refugees and the Jewish-organized Coordinating Foundation abroad had not done enough to raise outside funds and find places of settlement. One German Jew who participated in the negotiations with representatives of the committee reported that Wohlthat and Göring were sincere but were fighting a losing battle in the face of Hitler's actual intentions.[63]

In the meantime, in his speech to the Reichstag on January 30, Hitler had already pointed in the direction of the future Nazi policy of mass murder. Historians have interpreted his remarks as everything from a clear announcement of the forthcoming Final Solution to a typical outburst of anti-Semitic rhetoric without substantive meaning. Actually, the speech, planned in advance, fit into the context of Hitler's foreign policy.[64] It was too calculated to be without importance.

Czechoslovakia was Hitler's next target, but he still had to decide whether to launch his long-planned expansion to the East, or to delay until the Western powers were neutralized. One front at a time—that was the lesson he had learned from World War I. His original strategy had been to head east, but that rested on the presumption that the Western powers would not attack Germany, which had begun to look more and more questionable. So he had begun to plan for attacks on France and Britain in the not-too-distant future. Air-force and naval construction efforts were adjusted accordingly. A month after the takeover of Czechoslovakia, the new chief of the German general staff, Franz Halder, told Raymond Geist privately that Hitler had hoped that the Western democracies would not interfere in Germany's Eastern aims— to acquire *Lebensraum*—but since Western diplomacy was directed against Germany, Hitler was looking again to act against the West.[65]

On January 30, 1939, Hitler wanted to issue a strong warning to his adversaries in the West, whom he of course associated with the Jews. He singled out his British critics Churchill and Anthony Eden and American Secretary of the Interior Harold Ickes as apostles of a war sought by international Jewry. Again he challenged the hypocrisy of the Western democracies for criticizing recent German expansion, and he warned that Germany knew how to resist all pressure. He also urged the Western nations to take Germany's Jews off his hands. Europe would not find rest, he proclaimed, until the Jewish question was cleaned up.

> In my life I have often been a prophet and was often ridiculed [for it]. In the time of my struggle for power it was primarily the Jewish people who received with laughter my prophecies that I would sometime take over leadership of the state and with it the entire people in Germany and then, among many other things, bring the Jewish problem to a solution. . . .
> Today I want to be a prophet again: if international finance Jewry

in and outside Europe should succeed in thrusting the nations once again into a world war, then the result will not be the Bolshevization of the earth and with it the victory of Jewry, but the destruction of the Jewish race in Europe.[66]

When Hitler warned international Jewry against forcing another world war, he was warning the Western powers not to obstruct his own objectives in the East with all-out war. He assumed a link between the Western democracies and the Jews, and he knew there was going to be war—the question was whether the West would jump in. If they committed all their resources to war, not only would they regret it militarily, but the Jews would suffer the results of genocide. Or so he said.

Neither the forced emigration policy nor the Schacht-Göring plan for a negotiated removal of German Jews aimed to clear all Jews from German territory, because Hitler had to have Jews to remain as hostages in the hope of controlling the behavior of the Western powers. If a world war broke out, however, the value of Jews as hostages would diminish sharply, and they would become a far greater threat to German security, leading Nazis believed. Inherent in his January 30 speech was Hitler's obvious appreciation that such a war would radically alter the Nazis' need and ability to act against the Jews—at least those within Germany's reach. Hitler had long associated war with the complete abandonment of all humanitarian restraints; "the most cruel weapons are humane if they lead to a quicker victory," he had written in *Mein Kampf*.[67]

One way to test the seriousness of Hitler's threats on January 30 is to look for other evidence of the coordination of his foreign policy and racial goals. On February 10 the Führer gave another speech, a very private one, to high-ranking officers in the three armed services. After claiming that all his prior foreign-policy moves were steps in the execution of a plan, Hitler described the German *Volk* as the strongest people in the world. He then predicted that the next war would be an ideological and racial war that would determine the fate of the German race. According to one witness, Hitler made it clear that he intended to establish German domination of Europe and the world for centuries. Another exponent of a wartime program to kill Jews was Goebbels. On one occasion in March 1939, he pressed for a total elimination of the Jews: "we cannot allow Jewry, as a seat of infection, to exist any longer." Goebbels said that this elimination might be done in more humane fashion in time of peace and in more inhumane fashion if there were war.[68]

With mass murder or even genocide, however, there is a huge gulf between talk and action. For the historian to take Hitler's threat as something that, even in 1939, was likely to happen, there need to be some signs—if not hard evidence—of a general strategy or a preliminary plan. It need not have been Hitler who provided the evidence; he was not in the habit of drawing up detailed plans personally anyway. But those who would have to respond to Hitler's desire and carry it out required some advance preparation.

As far as is known, neither Himmler nor Heydrich wrote or talked much in 1939 about plans for the Jews. Himmler did tell his lunch companions in January 1939 that he would use the next ten years to thrash people, since good nature alone could not accomplish anything.[69] A revealing statement about his disposition and philosophy, the remark was too general, however, to be taken as more than a hint of plans for the Jews. Other SS and police officials could at times be more specific —and indiscreet.

In this connection, Raymond Geist's April 1939 letter to Washington is of extraordinary interest and importance. Geist had dealt personally with both Himmler and Heydrich, and he was friendly with Himmler's press secretary. He had a good feel for the Nazis involved in Jewish policy, and he had inside sources of information. In April 1939 Geist predicted the future course of Nazi Germany's Jewish policy as a sequence: placing all the able-bodied Jews in work camps, confiscating the wealth of the entire Jewish population, isolating the Jews, putting additional pressure on the whole community, and getting rid of as many as possible by force.[70] It was roughly what Heydrich and *Das Schwarze Korps* had indicated in November 1938,[71] and it was what the Gestapo and the SS later proceeded to do. In broad outlines, this was the first SS plan for the mass murder of Jews.

After the war Geist testified that in 1938 he had learned from Gestapo official Karl Hasselbacher, who was in charge of the section dealing with Jews and Freemasons, that Nazi Germany intended to exterminate those Jews who remained in the country.[72] Hasselbacher's superior was Heinrich Müller, and Müller's superior was Heydrich. In short, Geist's source was excellent, even if we do not have an original German document spelling out Heydrich's exact plan. The first step toward the Final Solution was a strategy consisting of phases leading toward mass murder.

Geist's information, however, was not about a plan for the elimination of all Jews. In fact, it was not even a plan for the murder of all German Jews; the Himmler-Heydrich policy of forced emigration remained in full swing in April 1939. They still found it desirable to force Jews out, create trouble abroad, and (allegedly) enhance German security. If and when a real world war came, there would be plenty of German, Austrian, and Czech Jews within reach. They would kill as many as possible—not

by men with higher professional standing, that would overlap the functions of the Death's Head units in Poland.

Sometime in July 1939 Heydrich had reached an agreement with an officer of the army general staff, according to which special units of the Security Police and SD would accompany the army into foreign territory and combat elements hostile to Germany behind the lines of the regular troops. The seven German mobile-police formations known as *Einsatzgruppen* formed during the next months each consisted of two to four companies (*Einsatzkommandos*). The bulk of the commanders and officers came from Heydrich's own SD, which was richly stocked with intellectuals; the manpower came from the police (both the Security Police and the Order Police) and the SS. The total strength of the *Einsatzgruppen* in Poland was about twenty-seven hundred men. Technically these *Einsatzgruppen* were subordinated to the army—this the result of pressure from the military[4]—but their only real responsibility was to the men who assigned them their functions: Himmler and Heydrich.

Because of their past experiences with the not always bellicose army leadership, and because of their desire to crush potential political and racial opponents ruthlessly, Hitler and Himmler wanted to keep the army out of the campaign behind the front lines. In the end this strategy worked, but there was some friction. On August 25, for example, Admiral Wilhelm Canaris expressed concern about the anticipated use of the SS Death's Head units in Poland—even before any action had started. After Heydrich and his legal adviser in the SD, Werner Best, informed army officials on August 29 that at least thirty thousand dangerous Poles (in two installments) would be sent to concentration camps, the chief of the general staff, Franz Halder, sent a message to Göring regarding his "reservations" about Himmler's measures.[5] Once the arrests and killings started, there were some stronger protests and stronger language.

Partly because of the German military's sensitivity about international law, Himmler was cautious about unveiling SS policies and setting down orders in writing. He apparently gave Eicke and Heydrich nothing but oral instructions for the Death's Head regiments and the *Einsatzgruppen*. When necessary, he alluded in writing only to the "known tasks." Such restraint was in keeping with his general view that as few people as possible should know his objectives. As a result, we can reconstruct Himmler's initial directives to the Death's Head regiments and the *Einsatzgruppen* only from contemporary statements and/or recollections by others.[6]

On September 3, for example, Himmler orally informed the just-formed *Einsatzgruppe* under commander Udo von Woyrsch that its mission was to suppress the Polish uprisings with all available means. One high-ranking police official also recalled that an army colonel had quoted Woyrsch as saying that he had a special mission given by the Führer through Himmler: to spread fear and terror among the people in order to forestall violent resistance.[7]

The planned operations of the *Einsatzgruppen* received the cover name "Tannenberg." It was a name that virtually all Germans knew. Himmler had been thirteen years old when the great German victory over the Russian forces took place at Tannenberg, in East Prussia, in 1914. The battle had liberated East Prussia from the Russian invaders and destroyed an entire Russian army. It had given Germany an edge in the East that it maintained throughout World War I. It had enhanced the reputation of two generals, Paul von Hindenburg and Erich Ludendorff, to the point where they were later able to gain virtual control of the government, and even after Germany's military defeat in 1918, Hindenburg had enough glitter left to be elected president of the republic in 1925. Tannenberg was Germany's greatest single victory of the war. When he was twenty-one, Himmler had studied this battle carefully to glean whatever military lessons he could.[8]

Himmler may have chosen to use the name simply because of the coincidence of dates. The Nazi attack on Poland was originally scheduled for August 26, the anniversary of the World War I battle. When the outbreak of war was postponed, Himmler had the opportunity to attend a state ceremony commemorating Hindenburg's victory.[9] But there was another famous battle at Tannenberg. In the year 1410 a Polish army had inflicted a crushing defeat on the Teutonic Knights at Tannenberg, a fact that a romantic medievalist and would-be German warrior certainly would have known.

The first battle had the right opponent but the wrong outcome. The second battle had a different (though still Slavic) opponent, but the right outcome. There was, however, a third Tannenberg—not a battle, but a man. Otto Richard Tannenberg was a well-known writer of the Pan-German school popular in Himmler's youth and teenage years. In 1911 he published a book urging his countrymen to create a great European empire by uniting all Germans and German-related peoples. Although not so extreme a racist as Himmler was to become, Tannenberg made some interesting comments about relations between Germans and Slavs:

> Peace [in the East] is a dirty word; peace between Germans and Slavs is like a paper treaty between fire and water. . . . Since we have power, we hardly need to look for justification [to conquer and settle land with peasants and future warriors], any more than the British made the effort to do so in South Africa.

In the good old times . . . a stronger people forced a weaker people out of its native territory through powerful battles of annihilation. Today such acts of force no longer occur. . . . The smaller nationalities and ethnic groups have discovered a new term: international law [*Völkerrecht*]. In actuality, this is nothing more than their calculation of our good-natured stupidity. . . . Space must be created. The western and southern Slavs or us. Since we are the stronger, the choice will not be difficult.[10]

Tannenberg's views certainly approached those of Himmler, who was about to carry them out.

On the evening of September 3 Himmler joined the Führer's entourage on a quick ride to the Stettin railway station in Berlin, where three special trains were ready. Hermann Göring's train stopped off along the way, but Hitler's train and Himmler's, the last appropriately named "Heinrich," proceeded southeast into Silesia and close to the German-Polish border. From there it was easy to travel into Poland by car or jeep (and soon by plane) and to inspect the battlefronts.

Himmler shared his train with Foreign Minister Ribbentrop, and Hans Heinrich Lammers, state secretary in the Reich Chancellery, and he had brought along businessman Fritz Kranefuss as a guest. According to Himmler's first biographer, "Heinrich" had fourteen cars, including a mobile Gestapo and SS headquarters, anti-aircraft coaches, sleepers, food-storage and luggage coaches, and space for the secretaries and staffs. Also aboard was Walter Schellenberg of the SD, a specialist in foreign intelligence, who acted as liaison between Himmler and Heydrich back in Berlin. The underlings included Himmler's office manager, Dr. Rudolf Brandt; his military adjutant, Werner Grothmann; his bodyguard, Police Sergeant Kiermeier; and his Estonian-Finnish masseur, Felix Kersten.[11] Traveling with Hitler were the top military authorities; Hitler's personal and military adjutants; Major General Bodenschatz as liaison to Göring; Walter Hewel as liaison to Foreign Minister Ribbentrop; Himmler's chief of staff, Karl Wolff, who served as liaison to the Reich Führer SS; Martin Bormann's younger brother Albert; and Reich Press Chief Otto Dietrich, who was soon to write a short book about the journey. Later Theodor Eicke also operated his command headquarters for the Death's Head regiments from the Führer's train.[12]

Himmler's trip into Poland gave him the opportunity to take part in the German conquest and observe military strategy. In World War I he had missed out on the fighting. Now he got a firsthand view of war, and it hardly dampened his enthusiasm or his advocacy of ruthless measures. Himmler authorized the execution of civilians who resisted German authority by guerrilla warfare—or who were captured possessing arms. He insisted on deciding personally the fate of large groups of captured insurgents. He also approved the taking of prominent Poles as hostages as a response to insurgency. Wherever Poles had spilled German blood, Himmler ordered ruthless retaliation. After panic-stricken and angry Poles attacked and killed four to six thousand German inhabitants in the city of Bromberg (Bydgoszcz) during the early days of the German invasion, Himmler ordered the execution of more than one thousand hostages as retaliation and the incarceration of many thousands more.[13]

Himmler's mission went further than doling out harsh punishment to deter anti-German activity. The *Einsatzgruppen* had lists of people who were considered to be especially hostile to Germany, including leaders and members of Polish patriotic organizations, communists, and clergymen. On September 7 Heydrich told his division heads that the Polish leadership had to be "neutralized." The next day Canaris learned that Heydrich had talked of sparing the common people but killing the nobility, priests, and Jews (this in the context of measures to suppress guerrilla warfare), and the following day General Halder informed the Abwehr's liaison man of Hitler's and Göring's intention to destroy the Polish people; more than that, he said, should not even be hinted at in writing.[14]

At a conference on September 12 aboard the Führer's train, which had stopped at the Silesian border town of Ilnau, Canaris protested to General Wilhelm Keitel, chief of the High Command of the Armed Services (OKW), that extensive shootings were planned in Poland, and that the nobility and the intelligentsia were to be exterminated. Canaris warned that the world would hold the armed services responsible for such methods. Keitel responded that the Führer and Göring (sic) had worked these things out between themselves.[15] At some point in the discussion, probably while the men were discussing the situation on the Western front, Hitler walked in and proceeded to launch a monologue. After discarding the possibility of a French attack, Hitler went on to consider aloud various possibilities for dealing with Poland. According to the recollections of Lieutenant Colonel Lahousen, an eyewitness, Hitler said that it was

imperative to break all elements of the Polish will to resist, and . . . it was especially necessary to eliminate the clergy, the aristocracy, the intelligentsia, and the Jews. Now, I don't remember the exact term that he used, but it was not ambiguous and it meant "kill."

There is one expression that he used in this connection, which I am
sure of . . . : "Political Housecleaning."[16]

One week later, having returned from his own inspection tour of the
Einsatzkommandos, Heydrich forecast a "political housecleaning" in Poland directed against the same four groups. Army authorities insisted
that any such housecleaning be postponed until civilian authorities took
over from the military administration.[17] In spite of gaps and slight in-
consistencies in recollections and documents, the bulk of the evidence
points toward planning and authorization—at the highest level—of an
SS campaign to murder and incarcerate perceived Polish and Jewish
enemies that extended beyond the length of the military campaign.[18]

Some army officers created problems for Himmler by opposing or
restricting measures ordered against Polish Jews. On September 18 Field
Marshal Wilhelm List, commander of the Fourteenth Army, issued orders to stop plunderings, rapes, burnings of synagogues, and summary
executions. After the burning of synagogues and violence against Jews
in Cracow, the Fourteenth Army command sought to court-martial the
police who had executed eighteen Jews without due process on September 21.[19] Woyrsch's *Einsatzgruppe* went about torching synagogues and
beating and killing Jews so openly that Field Marshal August von Mack-
ensen slammed his fist on a table and insisted that Woyrsch's formation
be withdrawn from his area. And it was. Somewhat later, just after the
Polish war had ended, German troops near Przemyśl encountered two
trains full of Jews from Germany that were being forced across to the
Russian-occupied zone of Poland. Field Marshal List took charge of the
trains and arranged for the Jews to be sent back to Germany.[20]

These instances were atypical. Knowing how committed Hitler himself
was to the punishment of Jews, Keitel and Army Commander-in-Chief
Walther von Brauchitsch seemed more interested in insulating the military from the crimes of the SS than in preventing them. In some instances regular soldiers joined the SS formations in killing and looting.
Concessions from the top and spontaneous cooperation from below,
however, did not eliminate all of Himmler's problems with the military.
A number of strong-minded officers still refused to bend to political
realities.[21] Himmler and Heydrich again had to confront the fact that
the army was not a reliable supporter of the kind of ideological and
racial warfare that Hitler had ordered in Poland. Some officers threatened to undermine Himmler's hold over the *Einsatzgruppen* by raising
doubts in the minds of the men about their activities, by weakening the
"blood cement" that Hitler had counted on. On October 3 Heydrich

pointed out that the old problem of relations between the SS and the military had arisen once again with full gravity.[22]

AS HITLER unleashed a wave of terror in Poland, there were some signs that Himmler was cutting his risks in other areas. On September 3, before setting out for Poland, he met with Heydrich and two other SS-Gruppenführer to warn them not to undertake actions against the Catholic and Protestant churches in Germany for the duration of the war. Himmler even wanted to stop some expropriations of church property already under way. The reason he gave was that he wanted to avoid disturbing the political situation at home and abroad.[23]

Also revealing of Himmler's methods was a September run-in with Ernst Schaefer, a prominent naturalist and anthropologist who had specialized in Central Asia and had spent considerable time in Tibet. Himmler loved to cultivate suitable intellectuals, and Schaefer's knowledge nurtured Himmler's fantasies about Asia. Himmler had eagerly arranged for the SS to sponsor Schaefer's successful 1938 expedition to the mountain land often closed to outsiders, and Schaefer had been granted a substantial rank in the SS.[24] Although Schaefer had never been a soldier, he now had visions of Lawrence of Arabia. He thought about a new expedition to Tibet, through which he might bring the monarchy over to the German side.

After Germany attacked Poland, and the British and French declared war, Himmler summoned Schaefer for another talk.[25] The SS chief said that the war with England and France still might not be a serious one. If it became real, he wanted Schaefer to proceed to Moscow and prepare a joint move with Germany's new ally Russia against Tibet, Kashmir, and Afghanistan, to arm and incite various tribes and peoples against the British and threaten their position in India. Typically, Himmler did not lay out the full extent of his plan for Schaefer.

Himmler had gleaned little from the large map spread out in his office. He brushed aside Schaefer's concerns about the geographical difficulties of traveling from Russia to Tibet (through the Himalayas). The naturalist was also worried that Himmler wanted him to undergo two months of military training. Himmler said that, as soon as Schaefer's group had left, he would announce that Schaefer had died. By this time Schaefer began to think that the death announcement would be a prophecy.[26]

So Schaefer tried to work with one of Himmler's rivals in the intelligence sphere. He had already had some contact with Wilhelm Canaris of the Abwehr through a business representative of his father; now he went back to the admiral in the hope of working out a more realistic plan, beginning, for example, with flying into Tibet. Canaris noted that the Abwehr was preparing expeditions to Persia and Afghanistan, and that all such efforts should be coordinated, which he tried to do. Then he apparently raised the matter with Himmler.[27]

After writing a scathing letter to Schaefer, Himmler summoned the scholar to his special train near the Polish border. Himmler screamed at him as he had never been screamed at in his life, Schaefer said later. Schaefer was informed that his loose talk might already have ruined his mission. Himmler lectured: "Never tell a person something earlier than is absolutely necessary, never tell a person more than he has to know to carry out his task, never tell more people than necessary. . . ."[28] (Several months later these precepts were incorporated into what became known as Hitler's fundamental command.[29]) This was not just an outburst; it was the real Himmler lecturing on the proper technique for administering and implementing sensitive policies. It very well defined how Himmler himself would handle his plans for the Jews.

Himmler forbade Schaefer to discuss the matter with anyone other than Himmler himself or his chief of staff, Karl Wolff. He ordered Schaefer to go off for military training (and some discipline). It turned out that the Russians wanted no part of a military operation, but were willing to allow Schaefer's camouflaged group to pass through Russian territory. As late as May 1940 this trip was still a possibility. Meanwhile, after Schaefer delivered a satisfactory report on preparations for his trip, Himmler forgave the naturalist and invited him to come along on another visit to Poland.[30]

During his September 1939 trip Himmler got the opportunity to observe Polish Jews in the countryside and in small towns—quite possibly his first experience with the *Ostjuden* in their native habitat. Prewar Poland had the densest Jewish population in the world—3.3 million. There is no contemporary record of Himmler's reaction. But we do have the near-contemporary reactions of Reich Press Chief Otto Dietrich, one of the officials on Hitler's train, to seeing the Jewish section of Kielce, which Hitler toured on September 10:

> If we had once believed we knew the Jews, we were quickly taught otherwise here. . . . The appearance of these human beings is unimaginable. . . . Physical repulsion hindered us from carrying out our journalistic research. . . . The Jews in Poland are in no way poor, but they live in such inconceivable dirt, in huts in which no hobo [*Landstreicher*] in Germany would spend the night.[31]

Himmler's first biographer, who interviewed a number of Himmler's close associates, writes that during this trip Himmler ordered some of the "criminal specimens" to be brought before him. He pointed to trembling old men with a stick, demonstrated to his entourage the construction of their bones, and ridiculed their earlocks. He called them "vermin."[32]

Himmler must have realized that the Jewish question in Poland was of such magnitude that it could be resolved only in conjunction with the new German scheme for Poland itself. To be sure, the Jews raised certain problems that the Poles did not. Poland was a defeated country, whose only allies had been lukewarm. Nazi Germany could work its will in Poland without great concern. But Hitler and Himmler insisted on regarding the Jews as a tightly knit race, and they mistakenly judged Jews to have great influence in the corridors of power in London, Paris, and Washington. So Heydrich reported on September 14 that Himmler was presenting all suggestions on the Jewish question directly to the Führer, for only Hitler could make decisions with potentially far-reaching foreign-policy repercussions.[33]

After some consideration of other possibilities, during the second half of September Hitler decided to divide Poland into a zone annexed by Germany, a rump territory administered by Germany, and the zone more or less left to the Russians by the Molotov-Ribbentrop pact of August 23, but modified in the course of subsequent negotiations. Hitler wanted Germany to build defensive fortifications on the Vistula River, but resettlement of vast numbers of people would also provide "protection" for Germany. Western Poland was to be Germanized through colonization, the central section (the Government General of Poland) would remain Polish at least for some time, and within the Government General there would be a special area as far away from Germany as possible, near Lublin, between the Vistula and Bug rivers, for Jews (including Jews from Germany) and other unreliable elements. The whole scheme for the partition of Poland and racial stratification was haphazard and improvised, not the result of long-held convictions about the shape of the German empire in the East. At the same time, it clearly reflected Hitler's and Himmler's racial hierarchy.[34]

Hitler's decision to remove Polish and German Jews to the Lublin "reservation" was a new element in Jewish policy, but it was consistent with the earlier SS plan for German Jews, with stages involving the separation of adult male laborers, and the isolation, pauperization, and killing of as many as possible.[35] It was logical to use the same approach in Poland; the only complications were the numbers involved. And it is plain to see why Himmler and Heydrich thought such decisions might have far-reaching repercussions upon foreign policy. Lublin apparently represented an extension of the first SS plan for mass murder, with Polish Jews added to the list of victims.

On September 21 Heydrich sent an express letter to his *Einsatzgruppen* commanders in which he alluded to the "final goal" of Jewish policy, which he said had to be held strictly secret. This (unspecified) final goal, he continued, could not be accomplished immediately, but only by stages. The use of stages leading toward a radical goal replicated the approach already mapped out for German Jews. The most far-reaching goal he specifically mentioned later in the letter was the deportation of Jews to the Lublin area. Heydrich's letter also called for the removal of Jews from rural areas of western Poland and for the establishment of ghettos in the Polish cities, so that Jews could be more strictly observed and controlled.[36]

To anyone who had risen into the upper ranks of the Nazi elite, and particularly into the leadership of the SS, Heydrich's term *Endziel* had an apocalyptic resonance. Heydrich would not have wanted to be too explicit in any official letter, let alone a letter that was copied to the High Command of the Army, the Reich Interior Ministry, the Food Ministry, and civil administrators in the occupied territories. But the "final goal" alluded to something discussed previously within the SD and the Gestapo. The *Einsatzgruppen* had already killed some twenty thousand Poles and Jews; they would not have been surprised to learn that more killing was intended.[37]

Both Adolf Eichmann and Erich von dem Bach-Zelewski were shown this document in the course of postwar interrogations; neither had seen it before. Although both were of the opinion that the overall plan known as the Final Solution came about later, both testified that the term *Endziel* could only mean physical extermination.[38] Heydrich's reference to a final goal was not definite evidence of a clear decision about all Polish Jews, but it did point in one direction.

During October Hitler is supposed to have expressed the hope that within twenty years hard work, hunger, and pestilence would complete their devil's work in Poland.[39] In November Arthur Seyss-Inquart, making an inspection trip in the Government General, reported that one of the district officials thought his area suitable for a Jewish reservation because of its swampy character, "which would lead to a strong decimation of the Jews." And in December one of the district officials in charge of Lodz, making preparations for the establishment of a ghetto, declared that the ghetto was only temporary: "In the end, at any rate, we must burn out this bubonic [Jewish] plague."[40] In the eyes of a number of Nazi officials from Hitler on down, elimination of Jews and many

Poles from the Government General would be a positive development, however it came about.

Himmler wanted to take charge of the whole process of Germanizing Poland, but there were obstacles. Hitler had begun to select Nazi officials for administrative positions in the East as early as September 8.[41] Albert Forster, named civil commissar in Poland and soon Gauleiter of Danzig–West Prussia, was no friend of Himmler's.[42] (The Gauleiter were technically directly subordinate to Hitler. A Gauleiter did not necessarily have to bow to the wishes of the head of the SS.) Hitler's appointment of Hans Frank as governor in the Government General became an even more serious problem for Himmler, but Frank's deputy, Seyss-Inquart, was Himmler's friend, and conferred frequently with the Reich Führer SS.[43]

In spite of the advancement of others, Himmler quickly made progress, taking advantage of his proximity to Hitler. During the fourth week in September, when Hitler and Himmler were both relaxing at the Kasino Hotel in the Polish shoreline resort town of Zoppot, Himmler persuaded Hitler to entrust him with the resettlement of Germans from Estonia, Latvia, Lithuania, and eastern Poland, which were now all caught in the Russian zone of influence. He also announced a reorganization of the Gestapo and the SD, creating an umbrella security organization called the Reich Security Main Office (*Reichssicherheitshauptamt* or RSHA), within which the SD and the Security Police were supposed to cooperate. Under Heydrich's leadership, the RSHA was to be heavily involved in what might be called the positive and negative dimensions of the resettlement program in Poland: settlement of Germans and expulsions or elimination of non-Germans.[44]

Toward the end of September Hitler instructed Reich Chancellery State Secretary Hans Heinrich Lammers to prepare a new and secret decree placing Himmler in charge of the resettlement of ethnic Germans into the newly conquered Polish territory and the elimination of harmful elements from the area. Lammers suggested that resettlement was something that Germany might want to postpone until the end of the war, but Hitler saw no reason to delay. Moreover, he instructed Lammers not to discuss the policy with anyone.[45] Lammers, however, had to secure funding from Reich Finance Minister Count Lutz Schwerin von Krosigk, which meant that he had to explain at least one of Himmler's new functions. Without referring to the elimination of "harmful" elements, Lammers passed on the Führer's request for initial funding of ten million marks for the resettlement of Germans in the East. Lammers also cleared the text of the proposed decree with Himmler, who found the wording exactly to his liking.[46]

Some hint of these developments reached Reich Agriculture Minister Darré, who became irate. Darré was hoping to play a major role in the development of Poland; now his former "student" Himmler was shutting him out. On October 4, in a long, hostile letter, he criticized Himmler's secrecy and his lack of expertise in dealing with settlement issues. Darré argued that only the state (not the SS) could manage the population, agricultural, and security problems involved in the introduction of German farmers into Poland. He denounced Himmler's apparent intention of establishing SS settlements on the German-Russian border. Himmler had a notion that farmers could not only provide the basis for a new, Germanized agriculture but also serve as a military outpost against the East. Darré derided this romantic idea of "peasant defense" as neither fish nor fowl: neither a modern, effective defense force, nor a good way to go about agricultural reorganization in Poland.

Hitler quickly got angry—at Darré—and took Himmler's side. When Darré offered to resign, Hitler declared that under wartime conditions only he could decide when an official could leave his post. He would let Darré know soon enough. And he forbade Darré to enter Poland; the minister was not to bother Himmler at all.[47] Himmler was able to issue the new decree that gave him a new title—Reich Commissar for the Strengthening of the German people (RFV)—on his birthday, October 7.[48]

Although the decree itself remained secret, Hitler had announced the broad outlines of the new policy in the East in his speech to the Reichstag on October 6. Germany would retract the "splinters of Germandom" from Eastern and Southern Europe to remove the basis for conflict with the Soviet Union, and it would create a clear line of division between Germans and Slavs.[49] This seemingly clear pronouncement passed blithely over the immense practical difficulties of any such resettlement: moving millions of ethnic Germans into Poland, expelling millions of Slavs, Jews, and gypsies from areas to be Germanized and into some new location, and deciding precisely which Poles were suitable for Germanization or for use as laborers. Intermarriage of ethnic Germans and Poles and assimilation of some of those with German ancestry into Polish culture meant that there was no neat dividing line. Responding to Hitler's declaration, Himmler soon decided upon a national census that would place Poles into four categories, ranging from those suitable for Germanization to those to be treated as intractable enemies. Hitler also announced that Germany would have to use strict measures to adapt and regulate the Jewish question in the East.[50]

In guidelines to his new RFV deputy Ulrich Greifelt, Himmler laid out the first phase of activity: the removal from the Danzig–West Prussian region of about 550,000 Jews and the leading Poles who were hostile to Germany into the Government General, the seizure of land owned by the Polish state or Poles who had been executed or expelled, and the temporary quartering of the ethnic Germans from the Baltic, who were expected within weeks. Himmler had to admit that the whole process of Germanization, including the planned resettlement of cities and the countryside, would take many years, perhaps decades.[51]

During October several resettlement operations in Poland began almost simultaneously. Himmler established an Immigration Center, headed by Heydrich's Security Police, to deal with the incoming ethnic Germans, and shortly thereafter he ordered evacuations from Danzig, Gdynia, and Posen to create room for these Germans. He also went off to the South Tyrol to conclude the negotiations with the Italian government regarding the removal of ethnic Germans there.[52] Meanwhile, Adolf Eichmann had begun to arrange the first deportations of Jews from formerly Polish Upper Silesia, the Reich Protectorate (Bohemia-Moravia), and Vienna to a town named Nisko on the line of demarcation between German Poland and Russian Poland. Eichmann quickly tried to expand the first operation into a much larger deportation plan including even the Jews from the Reich.[53]

After his return from Italy, Himmler conferred with Heydrich, and on the afternoon of October 17 he reported to Hitler.[54] There is no surviving record of this meeting. Later that evening, however, Hitler spoke to General Wilhelm Keitel, chief of OKW. It is a safe assumption that whatever Hitler may have told Himmler would have been more candid and specific than he revealed to Keitel.

Hitler told the general that the armed forces ought to be happy to be relieved of administrative matters in Poland, which would now be handled by civilian authorities independent of the German government. The new administration would not try to make Poland into a model province or state, or to put the place in order economically and financially. Germany would maintain a lower standard of living there and exploit Polish labor. But it could not permit the Polish intelligentsia to become the nucleus of a nationalist movement. Implementation of German policy required a harsh racial struggle without legal restrictions, with methods irreconcilable with "our other principles." Presumably Hitler meant the military's principles. He noted that German officers had visited a Polish bishop in Cracow and Prince Radziwill on his estate—one could not solve Germany's problems in Poland by following social conventions, he said pointedly. Germany needed Poland as a military outpost and as a dumping ground for Jews and Poles, and Hitler here referred specifically to Himmler's new task of Germanization and resettlement of the annexed areas. He declared that through cleverness and harshness Germany could avoid having to meet Poland again on the battlefield.[55] This discussion—or monologue—was a warning to the military to stay out of matters that no longer concerned it. The establishment of a civilian government over Poland left Himmler freer to carry out his mission as he and Hitler saw fit.

Himmler still needed to define the relationship between the various SS agencies and government agencies involved in the resettlement programs. During the next few days Himmler conferred again with Heydrich and with Werner Lorenz of the Volksdeutsche Mittelstelle, a liaison office for programs for ethnic Germans in Europe. Himmler had usurped some of the functions of the Volksdeutsche Mittelstelle with the creation of the RFV, and Lorenz probably had to be placated and given something to do. One of the problems for Himmler was that Lorenz's agency was nominally a Nazi Party organization (under Rudolf Hess) rather than of the SS. So, around this time, Himmler redrafted the lines of authority for the Volksdeutsche Mittelstelle, retaining the party as superior authority for "party policy," putting in the foreign minister as authority for "foreign policy," and making the Volksdeutsche Mittelstelle an executive organ of his own RFV on ethnic German matters. Lorenz retained some responsibility for the handling of the arrangements for the Baltic Germans, expected to arrive shortly.[56]

There were other, more serious problems of competition. On October 19 Göring announced that his Office of the Four-Year Plan would take over all Polish and Jewish territory in the annexed sections of Poland. After a slight delay, Göring in effect delegated jurisdiction over agricultural property in Poland to Himmler's RFV but installed his own Main Trusteeship Office to manage the urban and industrial property. Himmler accepted the arrangement for the time being.[57]

Finally, the RSHA's deportations of Jews from the former Czechoslovakia, Austria, and Silesia were not going smoothly. At least one of the problems was that the areas convenient to "cleanse" and the areas suitable for German colonization were by no means identical. Another difficulty was that Nazi officials were trying to persuade Jewish organizations to participate willingly in this program and share the administrative burden of preparing people for the transports. But the early reports on the results were so horrendous—hundreds of deaths, thousands pushed over the demarcation line into Russian territory—that it was hard to maintain the façade of a resettlement program. Calling for a more coordinated and centralized approach, RSHA Division IV chief Heinrich Müller instructed Eichmann to stop the transports temporarily. In early November, when Eichmann protested the halt in the deportations of

Jews to Nisko, Himmler made it known that he personally had made the decision, for "technical reasons."[58] Himmler apparently approved a temporary substitute. An official representing the Gauleiter of Vienna wrote that deportations of Viennese Jews to Poland had been postponed until the end of February, and that until then Eichmann had obtained permission from Berlin to "force" normal emigration of Jews at least to the level of some twenty-five hundred per month.[59]

Eichmann's operation, however, was only part of a broader process of cleansing German territory of Jews. In accordance with Heydrich's express letter of September 21, the RSHA was already driving Polish Jews from the western-Polish countryside into cities and beginning to deport some from the cities to the Lublin region. Himmler decided to take another look at the situation in Poland. Together with Karl Wolff and a substantial SS entourage including a key subordinate, Higher SS and Police Leader for the Government General Friedrich-Wilhelm Krüger, Himmler made a whirlwind tour of some of the major Polish cities. In Bromberg, for instance, he heard a report from the head of one of the killing squads, which had been liquidating Polish intellectuals and Jews. (By mid-November Bromberg was pronounced free of Jews.) Himmler also stopped to witness the execution of some twenty alleged Polish saboteurs and murderers of ethnic Germans, carried out by the head of the German self-defense force, Himmler's friend and former staff member, Oberführer Ludolf von Alvensleben. One of the victims was only wounded, and Alvensleben pulled out his own pistol to complete the job.[60]

Alvensleben was a man who understood the policy of the mailed fist and would not allow sentimental considerations to interfere with ideological concerns. For example, a relative of his who owned an estate in Poland, Count von Alvensleben-Schöneborn, had allegedly married a Pole against the wishes of the family, made friends with Polish nationalists such as Prince Radziwill, and had dealings with Poles, Russians, foreign diplomats, and Germans friendly to Jews. He had hired Polish and Jewish tutors for his two sons, and he was said to have contributed money to Polish nationalist organizations. That the count was a Polish citizen did not matter to Alvensleben: Germans who betrayed their race should be executed. So he shot his own relative.[61]

Such ruthlessness appears to have enhanced Alvensleben's reputation. After a soldier complained to his superiors about a particularly gruesome execution of Jews in Schwetz, the protest reached General von Brauchitsch, who passed it on to Hitler. The Führer entrusted Alvensleben with investigating the incident. Alvensleben concluded that the victims, twenty-eight women and ten children, had been "members" of the Polish nationalist organization, the Westmarkverein, which supposedly had been involved in anti-German activity.[62] He found that this political involvement justified the sentences.

Himmler went from Bromberg to Lodz, Warsaw, and Lublin.[63] Lodz, which German authorities were about to rename Litzmannstadt (after General Litzmann, conqueror of Lodz in World War I), was the second-largest city in Poland, and its nearly 250,000 Jews constituted one-third of the population as well as a large segment of the business community. Before the war, if there was any place in Poland where a Jew could feel safe and at home, it was Lodz. Now thousands of Jews from Lodz were about to be sent to the Lublin region in sealed freight cars.[64]

In Warsaw, the largest Polish city, the RSHA had already dissolved the existing Jewish council and appointed a new one under the leadership of Adam Czerniakow. This *Judenrat* completed the required census of the Jewish population just days after Himmler's visit; there were 359,827 Jews then in Warsaw. About a week later the creation of the Warsaw ghetto began.[65] Ghettoization was a policy that Heydrich had once opposed for German Jews, but it was now certainly a way to isolate and pauperize Polish Jews—stages in the overall strategy.

Lublin, in eastern Poland, near the Russian lines, and with a normal population of just over one hundred thousand, was the reception point for deportations of Jews from western Poland. It had become a vast concentration camp, with congestion, stench, poverty, disease, and chaos unparalleled on earth. A Jewish journalist who had just arrived described it vividly:

Men die like flies in the thoroughfares, their bodies strewn on the roadway like old cinders. . . . At night everything is pitch black. . . . Chairs, wardrobes, even beds have long since been chopped up for firewood. Window-panes have been shattered, and there is no glass to mend them. The winds whistle through the desolate houses. Foodstuffs are unobtainable. The whole city is girt with barbed-wire fences, and the Nazis allow no traffic to pass through it. The water has turned foul and cannot be drunk. Cholera and typhus were already rampant [upon his arrival]. . . .[66]

On October 30 Himmler issued a new ordinance that charted out the resettlement operations for the next four months: removal of all Jews from Polish territories annexed by Germany (Danzig–West Prussia, the Wartheland, East Upper Silesia), removal of all Poles who had moved to the area in recent decades (the so-called Kongress-Polen), removal of a still-to-be-determined number of particularly hostile Poles from the provinces of Posen, South Prussia, East Prussia, and East Upper Silesia.[67]

Just eight days later, Higher SS and Police Leader (Wartheland) Wilhelm Koppe and Krüger signed an agreement regarding deportations from the Wartheland to the Government General. The ensuing winter deportations of many thousands, with only the clothes on their backs, and to places without accommodations, caused untold misery and countless more deaths.[68]

While the executions and resettlement operations in Poland continued, Himmler also had to prepare for the next stage of the war. Even before Britain and France rejected Hitler's peace feeler in early October, the Führer set about preparing the German military for an attack in the West, issuing a series of directives in October and November for "Case Yellow," an invasion of France through Belgium, the Netherlands, and Luxembourg. Hitler, typically, wanted to attack almost immediately after the end of the Polish campaign, whereas the German military leadership pressed for more time to prepare. Unlike the campaign of mid-1940, however, Hitler's main target in late 1939 seems to have been Britain.[69] The invasion in the West was designed not to conquer all of France, but to secure the channel ports and thereby provide a base for an air-and-sea war against Britain. Bolstered by optimistic estimates of what damage Göring's Luftwaffe could inflict, Hitler expected, according to one highly illuminating intelligence report, that the campaign against Britain might be over in two months.[70]

Bad weather hampered preparations and forced postponement of the attack into 1940, and then the Allied capture of a German courier carrying the instructions for the offensive nullified the element of surprise. Case Yellow was deferred, and a new strategy was eventually adopted.

In the midst of the fall military planning came an unexpected explosion. On November 6 Himmler headed to Munich in preparation for the annual celebration of the unsuccessful Nazi uprising of November 8–9, 1923. But, as in 1938, the ceremonies in the Bürgerbräukeller, one of the city's main beer halls, did not go according to plan. On that fateful evening of November 8, Hitler unexpectedly cut short his evening address and rushed off to catch a train back to Berlin. Himmler went with him. About twenty minutes after they had left, a bomb planted in one of the pillars exploded, killing seven Nazi officials on the platform in the beer hall.[71]

When they received the news, Hitler and Himmler immediately concluded that the British Secret Service was behind the incident. Years earlier Himmler had become attracted by the mystique of the British Secret Service, and he retained this respect throughout his life.[72] Hitler may really have believed that the British were involved, or he may simply have wanted additional grounds (i.e., propaganda) for his impending military preparations for an attack against Great Britain. He would not have had much difficulty convincing Himmler to take some specific action against the British.

It happened that one of Heydrich's most promising subordinates, Walter Schellenberg, was then in the midst of an operation in which he posed as a member of an anti-Nazi conspiracy within Germany, hoping to mislead and draw information from two British agents in the Netherlands. Himmler telephoned Schellenberg in the middle of the night and ordered him to drop his plans; he was to arrest the British agents and bring them back to Germany instead. When Schellenberg hesitated, Himmler made it plain that this was Hitler's order and must be obeyed. The kidnapping on neutral territory of the two Britons at Venlo went better than Schellenberg had a right to expect, but the operation turned out to be quite pointless, since the British had no connection whatsoever with the assassination attempt, which had been carried out by a disgruntled cabinetmaker whose brother had spent time in a concentration camp. RSHA interrogators wasted a great deal of time trying to get the potential assassin, Georg Elser, and the two British agents to confess to a broader conspiracy. Himmler was unhappy with the lack of results, telling Schellenberg that Hitler simply would not believe in a lone assassin, and that he wanted a great propaganda trial directed against the British.[73]

On November 18, apparently thinking of Hitler's plan to attack Britain, Himmler made an effort to obtain amphibious transport vehicles for his SS military force. The next day Heydrich, perhaps incognito, made a trip to the Belgian port of Ostend to look at the facilities there.[74] Then, five days later, Hitler called a meeting of the commanders-in-chief of the armed services in order, he said, to give them some insight into his thoughts about the coming events.[75] It was time to place more of his cards on the table, and perhaps also to get rid of those who objected to the way that he was playing his hand.[76]

Hitler explained that his fundamental goal was to restore a proper relationship between the size of the German population and its territory. The solution could come only with the sword. War now was no longer a pure military operation, but a racial struggle. For the moment, Germany had the option to fight a war on one front. Russia, he said, was not dangerous for the time being (a year or two), its military having been weakened (by the purges). Besides, there was the treaty, which the Russians would respect as long as it served their interest. Germany could challenge Russia only if it was free in the West. And Germany had to attack soon, for time was basically on the side of Germany's enemies, and the death of either Stalin (!) or Mussolini could seriously damage

Germany's foreign-policy situation. Hitler alluded to the bomb in the Bürgerbräukeller as an example of how easily death could remove a key player from the scene. The fate of Germany depended upon him, and he had reached the unalterable decision to attack France and England at the earliest opportunity. He dismissed the significance of violating Belgian and Dutch neutrality and stated bluntly that he wanted to annihilate the enemy.[77] Himmler was not present for this speech, but there would have been nothing new to him in it. He too was contemplating a racial struggle and the annihilation of the enemy.

CHAPTER 4

▼▼▼▼▼▼▼▼▼▼▼▼▼▼▼▼▼

RACIAL PLANNING
AND EUTHANASIA

NAZI RACISTS saw the future as a zero-sum game: whatever the German race gained had to come at the expense of another race or other races. The supremacy of German "blood" guaranteed Germany's victory in the struggle for racial domination, and it justified whatever treatment the victors found it necessary to impose on the defeated races. So there were two related tasks in newly conquered Poland: to locate those of German blood and harness them to the German cause, and to subjugate or destroy Germany's enemies.

In early December 1939 the head of the Nazi Party's Office of Racial Politics, Walter Gross, sent Himmler a long analysis of the possibilities and prospects for a "new order" in Poland. Gross thought he could expect Himmler's approval and support, because the analysis followed the basic lines of Hitler's various statements and Himmler's own guidelines for resettlement in the Government General. The authors, two specialists named Erhard Wetzel and Gerhard Hecht, had cast much of their analysis in racial terms, differentiating racial types within the Polish population and selecting those most suitable for Germanization. They also placed into separate categories not only Jews and baptized Jews, but also those of Polish Jewish "blood" and Poles under Jewish influence.[1]

The authors predicted the likely population density of the Government General once the nonassimilable Poles, the Jews, and the gypsies were brought in, and they recommended a slightly more generous occupation policy toward the Jews than toward the Poles, partly because the Jews were more productive economically, partly because such a German policy would inevitably alienate these two races from each other: divide and rule. They did not want the Jewish population to increase, but they were not particular about how to hold it down or reduce it;

they also would allow continued Jewish emigration from the Government General. At the same time, Gross referred to the annihilation of those incapable of Germanization. ✗

"Germanization" and even "annihilation" were malleable terms. Germanization was a kind of assimilation into the new German order; some people could fit in and play useful roles, others could not. But to any true racist the capacity to become Germanized was not solely an acquired characteristic. The key to selection lay in hereditary characteristics—that ✗ is, in the blood. Annihilation might mean destruction of a group as a self-conscious community, the breakup of a people, or, conceivably, physical elimination.

In their references to the potential population density of the Government General, the analysts more or less ruled out the most radical approach for the Government General. Their report took no notice of the tens of thousands of executions of Poles and Jews that had already occurred. They took account of Nazi ideology, but also of some practical considerations, and they did not carry racial hatred to its ultimate extreme. Himmler did not think much of moderation in this situation, and his SS had overshadowed the Nazi Party on racial policy.[2]

He paid little attention to the report. He was not particularly impressed with Gross, who had a relatively weak position within the Nazi Party and was not much in favor with Martin Bormann, the rising star of the Party Chancellery. Months later, when Gross inquired what had happened to the report, Himmler delayed again and then said that the racial policies would be realized after the war—a stock phrase he used to parry inconvenient requests and inquiries. In the meantime, when Ulrich Greifelt asked about possible RFV cooperation with Gross's Office of Racial Politics, Himmler ordered strict segregation.[3]

Judging from the available evidence, Himmler had already sketched ✗ out his own course for "annihilation" in the East. Not that he had a plan for the complete destruction of the Jewish race in Europe. In late 1939 Himmler was focusing solely on the problem of Polish and German Jews, and even there he was not yet seeking a total and uniform solution of the Jewish question. But he was weighing the possibilities for disposing of large numbers of Poles and Jews. Taking a more radical definition of annihilation, he then had to figure out how one could possibly accomplish it. His ideas seem to have been worked out not only with Heydrich but also quite possibly with Oswald Pohl, head of the SS economic enterprises and the SS construction operation. Later Pohl's various functions would be integrated into a single office called the Economic-Administrative Main Office (Wirtschafts-Verwaltungshauptamt or WVHA), but his function was the same from the beginning: to make the SS profitable enough so that it was financially independent of both the party and the state. Then Himmler could accomplish his plans without interference.[4]

Born in 1892 in the western-German city of Duisburg, the former naval officer Pohl was one of Himmler's most important subordinates, on a par with Heydrich (both were SS-Gruppenführer). In some ways, Himmler could rely more on Pohl than on Heydrich, who was too intelligent, powerful, and independent for Himmler's liking. Pohl had the Janus-form necessary for smooth cooperation with the Reich Führer SS. Toward his subordinates and other party and state authorities, Pohl was aggressive, assertive, and demanding. He knew how to wield power on his own, and he normally did not refer to the instructions he received from Himmler. He also discussed sensitive policies only with the smallest possible circle in the WVHA, the division chiefs.[5] Toward Himmler, Pohl was totally subservient. He went to see his superior only when he was summoned, and he regarded his every wish as an order. He never permitted others to voice a word of criticism of Himmler.[6] Apart from having charm, which Himmler lacked, Pohl was to Himmler very much what Himmler—until very late in the war—was to Hitler.

There is one incident from a later period that helps to illuminate the Himmler-Pohl relationship. In March 1942 Himmler suggested that the divorced Pohl visit a widow (with three children) whom he regarded highly. The suggestion fell on fertile ground—either because Himmler had made it, or because the couple hit it off. On December 12, 1942, Pohl married the wealthy Frau von Brüning, whose family had ties to I. G. Farben, in a ceremony held at Himmler's field headquarters.[7] It was a good match for Himmler: another SS man married off, and another SS link to I. G. Farben.

On the afternoon of December 5, 1939, Himmler met Pohl to discuss plans. Himmler wanted to go over the situation at the Buchenwald concentration camp, where a large number of Polish and Jewish prisoners had recently been killed. He listed brickworks as an item for discussion, apparently because he knew that there was going to be a huge demand for construction in the East, and this looked to be a promising arena for SS involvement. He wanted to discuss a concentration camp for women, either the one existing camp at Ravensbrück or, more likely, the establishment of a new facility.

Item 7 on Himmler's agenda was "crematorium-delousing units," a combination that at first sight seems puzzling.[8] There was a need for crematoria. Thousands of prisoners were already being killed or were dying under conditions of extreme privation in existing concentration camps within Germany, and disposal of the bodies was a messy problem, especially in winter, when the ground was frozen. Some of the camps already had crematoria. And lice represented a constant problem in concentration camps. But one fact is difficult to overlook. The gas chambers constructed in the extermination camps in 1941–43 were officially called "delousing units"; their actual function was not referred to.[9] The discreet Himmler would not create written evidence of mass murder— even in his private documents he went along with linguistic devices designed to camouflage reality. In his agenda list for Pohl he linked a crematorium and these "delousing units" with a hyphen and included them under the same item number—a sign that they were part of the same operation.[10] But one did not need a crematorium to dispose of dead lice.

The idea of the mass extermination of enemies in a concentration camp had a certain logic. There were so many people to eliminate that some sort of streamlined and quiet procedure was necessary. Why not make use of the most modern technology? Himmler's own handwriting thus provides the earliest evidence of a plan for a kind of death factory, with poison gas as the killing agent and crematoria to dispose of the bodies.

There are other signs of Himmler's interest in new technologies of mass murder. A week before his meeting with Pohl he had traveled about eighty miles east from Berlin to the town of Meseritz on the Obra River, within Prussian Pomerania, where there was an insane asylum called Obrawalde. He met with the Gauleiter and provincial governor, Franz Schwede-Coburg,[11] one of Hitler's earliest supporters, who had recently offered Himmler the use of all the mental asylums in his region as barracks for the Waffen-SS.[12]

Of course, Himmler could not use the buildings until they were emptied of patients. According to eyewitness testimony, in the spring of 1940 SS men transferred all the Jewish patients from Meseritz-Obrawalde, about five hundred, onto eight to ten large buses, which drove off to an unknown destination. The patients were never seen alive again. The rest of the inmates were removed similarly later.[13]

Even earlier were the changes at the Tiegenhof asylum, located outside the town of Gnesen in the Wartheland. During November 1939 the asylum dismissed its employees and hired a new staff, which drew up an alphabetical list of the patients. On the morning of December 7 the staff injected some of the patients with a strong sedative that dulled their senses and even put some in a trance. A van drove up. SS officers climbed out and began to load the patients into the vehicle. The first "evacuated" that day were Jewish women, and they were followed by most of the others in the following days and weeks. The van was not a means of transport but a final destination. Based on what happened with the same kind of vehicle later, it appears that all these patients were killed by bottled carbon-monoxide gas piped back into the closed freight area. As far as can be determined, the Jewish patients at Tiegenhof were among Nazi Germany's earliest victims of poison-gas technology.[14]

An hour and a half after his meeting with Pohl on December 5, Himmler had a brief session with the Führer, in which he discussed, among other things, the possibility of treating forty to sixty thousand Polish prisoners of war as political prisoners, thereby making them "eligible" to serve as concentration-camp laborers.[15] Martin Bormann told a subordinate at this time that Himmler was discussing all measures against the Jews directly with Hitler.[16]

On December 12 Himmler made still another trip to Lodz and Posen. One purpose was to inspect the preparations and the housing for the ethnic Germans transferred from Russian territory and from the Baltic States. But his visit also coincided with the worst phase of expulsions of Jews from Lodz. Herded onto unheated cattle cars, the deported Jews spent the next two or three days without food, water, or sanitary facilities.[17] Some twenty miles outside the city of Posen, the gas vans were still loading patients from the Tiegenhof asylum.

Himmler had shown a definite interest in the technique of killing by poison gas, which Hitler had advocated, in the mid-1920s, as a partial solution for Germany's Jewish problem. Given Himmler's loyalty to the Führer, it is hardly surprising that he borrowed an idea from *Mein Kampf*. And it was no accident that the Jewish patients at Obrawalde and Tiegenhof were the first victims in both asylums.

On the other hand, there is insufficient evidence for us to conclude that Himmler saw poison-gas technology as the only solution to the Jewish question. The number of Jews in the annexed territories and in the Government General was so large that only massive killing factories, not gas vans, could begin to cope. Himmler's idea of gas chambers and crematoria in one or more concentration camps might have been the beginnings of an answer, but he did not move to carry out the idea right away. And the killings of mental patients at Obrawalde and Tiegenhof must also be seen in the context of another program of mass murder— the so-called euthanasia program—authorized by Hitler himself.

EUTHANASIA was for Hitler a program to rid the German people of anyone considered mentally or physically deficient—any perceived weakness in the collective gene pool. In that sense it was the logical extension of the mélange of late-nineteenth-century racist and Social Darwinist ideas that Hitler had picked up as a youth. In his 1929 speech at the Nuremberg Party Congress, he had stated that, if one million children were born in Germany in a given year, and if the weakest seven or eight hundred thousand were eliminated, the German people would be strengthened.[18] In mid-1933 the Nazi regime issued a law providing for the involuntary sterilization of genetically suspect individuals.[19] In 1935 Hitler told his personal circle that he supported euthanasia but the political opposition was too great: perhaps it would be easier to implement such measures in wartime.[20] The SS newspaper, *Das Schwarze Korps*, called for euthanasia in 1937, and SD official Albert Hartl, a former priest, investigated the issue and the likely political reaction of Catholic authorities in 1938.[21] The approach of war provided a reason to prefer killing to sterilization: Germany could not afford to maintain "useless eaters" and hospital or asylum patients: this thinking prevailed in the Reich Interior Ministry.[22]

Hitler at first entrusted National Health Director Leonardo Conti with direction of this program in July 1939. But Philipp Bouhler, head of the Führer Chancellery, had already taken charge (with Hitler's approval) of a program to provide a "merciful death" to incurably ill or feeble-minded children. Bouhler complained about Conti's mission to handle adult euthanasia, and Hitler then transferred the mandate for "defective" adults to his personal physician, Karl Brandt, and to Bouhler. Also heavily involved in the programs for both children and adults was Dr. Herbert Linden, ministerial counselor within the Interior Ministry. Hitler directed his Führer Chancellery to avoid any appearance of a connection with the euthanasia operations. This command soon led to the establishment of a charitable foundation to serve as a front organization, and to the adoption of cover names by several participating officials from the Führer Chancellery: Viktor Brack, Hans Hefelmann, and Werner Blankenburg.[23] The program itself—or the portion of it directed at adults—was given the code name T4, after the address (Tiergartenstrasse 4) of the euthanasia-program headquarters.

In October 1939, when some of the doctors wanted more formal authority before they would carry out killings of patients judged "incurable," Hitler wrote out a brief authorization on his personal stationery for Bouhler and Karl Brandt, allowing them to widen the powers of selected doctors, who would at their discretion grant "incurable" patients a merciful death. But he refused all suggestions that he formally issue a euthanasia law.[24] Apparently he did not feel that the public was yet prepared to accept the killings of fellow Germans, whatever their mental or physical defects. There he proved to be correct; when rumors of killings of patients circulated later, there were public protests. Because of the need for absolute secrecy, the doctors could not dispose of large numbers of unwanted patients in hospitals and asylums themselves, and the methods and locations for disposal had to be selected carefully. Eventually there would be six major gassing centers in Germany (including Austria) to carry out the Führer's will and to dispose of the patients selected by doctors as incurable.[25]

Himmler and the SS leadership certainly knew what was taking place. Himmler may have been present when Hitler signed the euthanasia authorization, and the Waffen-SS Sanitation Office supplied the Führer Chancellery with medications.[26] More important, the few officials from the Führer Chancellery were novices in techniques of mass murder and had only a skeleton staff. They needed plenty of assistance to remove, transport, and dispose of large numbers of patients, and the assistance came, by and large, from Himmler's SS and police empire. Police experts in the RSHA Criminal Technical Institute (KTI) invented the gas van used at the Tiegenhof asylum in December 1939 and elsewhere subsequently.[27]

Himmler had no reservations about eliminating genetically "defective" Germans, but he did later show concern about the political risks of associating the SS with killings that the German public would overwhelmingly condemn if it learned of them.[28] So there were practical reasons for Himmler to involve the SS in the euthanasia program, and political reasons to keep the SS at a distance. But Himmler was not in charge of euthanasia, and he had more racial enemies to dispose of than he could handle; he must have wanted to solve his own problems. Still, the euthanasia operations could and did serve as a testing ground for the methods of mass murder used later in the Final Solution.

There was a logical as well as a technological link between Nazi euthanasia and genocide. The Nazi concept of a healthy and pure German *Volk* excluded a number of groups. Within Germany itself, the misfits were the mentally disturbed and physically deformed, the criminals and those considered socially deviant, and, of course, Jews and gypsies. Outside of Germany or in the annexed territories were Poles, Czechs, and other Slavs, whose racial status was regarded as inferior. Their treatment depended in part on Nazi plans for their territories and in part on how usefully they could serve the Nazi war machine. Actions to clear the Third Reich of all of these groups—either by expulsion, sterilization, imprisonment in concentration camps, or mass murder—were part of the same effort to purify and extend the German race.[29]

Of all the deviant groups, of all the targets of Nazi programs, however, Jews were considered the most dangerous. Not only were they seen as parasites, but, through racial intermingling, they had allegedly corrupted German blood. They were regarded as automatically hostile to the German cause and race; indeed, they were supposed to be part of an international conspiracy to rule the world. They were not so much a race as a permanent enemy of other races—in the words of one scholar, a "secularized Satan."[30]

Wherever and whenever there was opposition to Nazi objectives, at home or abroad, Hitler and Himmler believed that Jews were probably behind it. The biggest problem in extracting this malignant force was precisely Nazi concern about Jewish influence abroad. Heydrich had laid out the problem as early as September 1939: Himmler was presenting ideas on the Jewish question directly to the Führer, who had to make the decisions, because they had substantial repercussions on German foreign policy.[31] Only a decisive turn in the war could completely liberate Nazi Germany from this constraint. In the meantime, there was good reason to maintain secrecy about plans and activities designed to purify the Reich. The gas vans and gas chambers were attractive not only because they might become highly efficient; they also made it possible to carry out murder unobtrusively.

IN MID-DECEMBER 1939 Himmler took off for Rome by way of Innsbruck. There was important business to discuss with Mussolini, who had lately been annoyed with Germany, partly because of the Hitler-Stalin Pact.[32] On December 20 the two men met alone. Mussolini's German, though not good, was a lot better than the few words of Italian Himmler spoke, so the conversation would have been *auf deutsch*.

Italy was Germany's only trustworthy ally, and Himmler wanted to find out how Mussolini would react to the German expansion and "purification" in the East. Mussolini apparently complimented Himmler on how Germany had through its triumphs gained added respect and recognition.[33] Then it seems that Mussolini urged a future one-front war against Russia. He pointed out that Hitler had written in *Mein Kampf* that population density was a crucial factor in the health of a people, and that Germany had to expand to the east. Himmler added that this also meant solving the Polish question, the Slavic question, and the Jewish question. Himmler's fragmentary notes provide no details of his statements on the Jewish question, but in a letter that Mussolini wrote to Hitler eleven days later, the Duce referred to "your plan of concentrating them all in a large ghetto in Lublin."[34] Himmler may not have given Mussolini complete information, but there is no reason why he should have given him inaccurate information.

Mussolini spoke of writing the Führer a letter, promising that Italy would be on Germany's side in the war. On December 31 he warned

Hitler against further rapprochement with Stalin and urged Germany to turn to the East, with its Slavic and Asiatic masses under the sway of the Jews. Germany and Italy together, Mussolini wrote, would demolish Bolshevism; then they could turn to the West. But he held off from an immediate military commitment.[35]

Whether or not they were sincere, Mussolini's comments reinforced Himmler's own views about Germany's mission. Italian Foreign Minister Count Galeazzo Ciano wrote in his diary that the meeting had lasted about two hours, and that Himmler had emerged from the room looking very satisfied. Mussolini told Ciano only that Himmler had been anti-Russian and a bit depressed. Mussolini said that he reassured Himmler that he (Mussolini) would never permit a German defeat. Ciano then added: "That is already a great deal, but I'm afraid it already may have gone much further."[36]

In the first few days of January 1940 one of Heydrich's *Einsatzkommandos* operating in the area of Königsberg decided to move some 170 Poles who were considered to be members of the intelligentsia out of the detention camp at nearby Hohenbruch. Brigadeführer Otto Rasch required the Poles to sign statements that they agreed to be transferred to the Government General. The statements were a ruse. After the prisoners signed, they were taken away—to a forest, where the commandos executed them. Heydrich had ordered the killings as "retaliation" for the wartime massacre of ethnic Germans by Poles in Bromberg.[37] Such operations could not be kept secret for very long, and so Heydrich needed to find a suitable site and method for further liquidations. He hit upon Soldau, once a medieval German stronghold, now a town just over the German side of the East Prussian–Polish border.

Soldau was converted into a concentration camp where perceived enemies of the state and elements hostile to society were killed in secret.[38] This January 1940 incident and the subsequent use of Soldau as a killing ground represent one of the earliest examples of Nazi officials' use of the resettlement program simply as a cover for mass murder. Heydrich directly approved these killings, and probably gave the instructions to carry them out unobtrusively.[39]

Around the same time, Himmler saw good reason to set up new concentration camps in the East. In January 1940 he sent Oswald Pohl and Wilhelm Keppler to check out possible sites in the East for new camps —former prisons, mining areas, etc.[40] When SS Inspector of Concentration Camps Richard Glücks dispatched a commission in early January to inspect another site recommended by Oberführer Arpad Wigand, a police official in Breslau, that move came in the context of Himmler's own initiatives. Wigand proposed the former military barracks near the town of Auschwitz. The swampy area around Auschwitz had the advantage of being well situated, Wigand noted: isolated from the outside world, easily expandable, and accessible by rail.[41]

The enemies creating the most immediate concern for Himmler and Heydrich—and the first prisoners at Auschwitz—were Poles who had already caused trouble for Germany or who seemed likely to do so in the near future. Himmler told former Economics Minister Kurt Schmitt that he had a mission from the Führer to prevent Poland from ever rising again—which meant, according to Schmitt, a policy of extermination.[42]

As Himmler and his subordinates plotted out methods to deal with Germany's enemies, they also had to "rescue" ethnic Germans under Soviet control. The "good blood" was to move west, the "bad blood" east, and balancing the migrations was no easy matter.[43] Ethnic Germans from areas within the Russian sphere of influence were brought into the annexed regions of Poland. The first SS operation was simply to register these new subjects of the Third Reich and, if they seemed racially suitable, to provide them with citizenship. Late in 1939 Himmler had instructed Heydrich to put together a special team of experts from various agencies who would handle the examination and naturalization of the resettlers. As the number of ethnic Germans swelled after a formal agreement between Germany and the Soviet Union, the Immigration Central Office remained in Posen, but teams of experts traveled around to the reception camps, which the Volksdeutsche Mittelstelle maintained. SS Race and Settlement officials racially screened the newcomers and sifted out the undesirables in a process disguised as a medical examination.

Himmler had to work out arrangements with the Gauleiter and government officials to receive the new settlers in their territories. Himmler's RFV could sooner or later provide the ethnic Germans with confiscated farmland and housing, but they lacked furniture or household goods. There was a great deal of household property available in the cities, but it fell under the control of the Main Trusteeship Office, which was Hermann Göring's tool. So Himmler's officials had to negotiate arrangements for the sale of Jewish and Polish property to the ethnic Germans, with a special new government corporation, the German Resettlement Trusteeship Society, providing credit to the prospective new farmers.[44] (The notion of recycling Jewish property to deserving Germans found fertile soil, and the practice would branch out in later years.) All of these resettlement activities for ethnic Germans, which began in late 1939, contributed to Himmler's spending a good deal of time in January 1940 sorting out bureaucratic problems and overlapping jurisdiction in meetings with his RFV deputy Ulrich Greifelt, with SS Race and Settlement Office head Günther Pancke, with one of Göring's economic (and agricultural) experts, Hermann Backe, with Göring's staff and other officials involved with the new immigrants.[45]

In late January Himmler took a train trip on "Heinrich" to Przemyśl with an entourage large enough to require a second railcar: his chief of staff, Karl Wolff; his office manager, Rudolf Brandt; his bodyguard and adjutant; his favorite poet, Hanns Johst; his Tibet expert, Ernst Schaefer; and several others.[46] During the trip Himmler's young adjutant Jochen Peiper told Schaefer that Hitler had entrusted Himmler with the extermination of the Polish intelligentsia, and that Himmler had even taken part in one execution. Afterward, Peiper claimed, Himmler had not spoken for several days. Peiper also talked of the incident in which Ludolf von Alvensleben had executed his own relatives; they would all look at the potatoes from underneath, Peiper commented gaily. Alvensleben had told his relatives just before the execution that if he did not shoot them he would have to face them in the next war.[47]

Their main business in Przemyśl was to welcome the last arriving party of more than a hundred thousand so-called Volhynian Germans, ethnics who had lived in a section of eastern Poland now in Soviet hands. Mostly farmers, they were resettling in German-controlled territory, because Hitler and Himmler wanted them there, not in Russian hands, and Stalin certainly was not opposed to getting rid of Germans. Resettlement teams from the Volksdeutsche Mittelstelle had arranged transport by train and wagon convoys in the midst of a bitterly cold winter; there were some deaths during the trips. Rudolf Brandt observed that these settlers were superb raw material and had very good horses.[48]

From Przemyśl, Himmler's train went back to Cracow, where the men met up with Higher SS and Police Leader Friedrich-Wilhelm Krüger, the Lublin SS and Police Leader Odilo Globocnik, and Governor Hans Frank. Himmler and Frank talked mostly about the hard times before 1933, exchanging stories about how they had beaten up communists. Globocnik boasted of how he had just liquidated the inmates of a Polish insane asylum, which was almost certainly a reference to an event about two weeks earlier. On January 12, 1940, some Gestapo and SS men had entered an asylum at Hordyszcze (Chełm-Lubielski) around 4:00 p.m. They ordered the employees to leave at once, and then they herded the patients out into the yard, where about three hundred were shot. The next day the employees returned and buried the bodies in a mass grave.[49]

Himmler was concerned that Frank was resisting his plan to deport millions of Poles and Jews to the Government General—and that stories of Frank's opposition had begun to leak out. (In mid-January Himmler seems to have asked State Secretary Lammers to inform him of leaks about the deportations of Jews and about Frank's opposition. A couple of months later Lammers passed along an example—a description and denunciation of "the death march of Lublin."[50]) But Frank supposedly explained that he did not oppose the resettlement policy in principle, only the disorganized manner in which it was being carried out. The various local officials and RSHA bureaucrats had dumped far more people than expected in the Government General, and local authorities were unprepared to cope with them. Himmler seems to have accepted the criticism, but he explained that the RSHA had now established a special section (IV D 4) to coordinate all deportations. Frank let Himmler get the impression that the fundamental problem was resolved and only the details remained to be worked out.[51]

Back in Berlin, after a morning session with Himmler,[52] Heydrich convened a meeting of the higher SS and police leaders of the annexed territories and the Government General, Deputy Governor Seyss-Inquart, and a number of other officials. Heydrich revealed Himmler's latest orders: produce a unified policy to implement the resettlement tasks ordered by the Führer. He then called for the removal of another forty thousand Jews and Poles from the Wartheland in preparation for more Baltic Germans, and for the deportation of some 120,000 Poles in the several Eastern *Gaue* to make room for the Volhynian Germans.

There were, of course, questions about what should be done with the Poles and Jews. Heydrich announced that Himmler had decided to make use of eight hundred thousand to one million Poles (in addition to Polish POWs) as laborers in the Reich. The remainder of the Poles, excepting ethnic Germans and racial minorities perceived as partly Germanic (Kashubians, Masurians, etc.), would go to the Government General. All Jews from the annexed territories and thirty thousand gypsies from the Reich would follow the Poles to the East. Heydrich also noted that the construction of a defensive wall on Germany's border with the Soviet Union and other projects in the East would probably provide an occasion to force hundreds of thousands of (male) Jews into compulsory-labor camps.[53] Actually, Heydrich understated Himmler's intention. In his February 2 conversation with General von Brauchitsch, Himmler spoke in favor of an antitank ditch on the Russian border that would provide work for 2.5 million Jews.[54] That number represented virtually all adult male Polish, Czech, and German Jews.

In the January 30 meeting, Heydrich at least hinted at the future. The families of the Jewish laborers, Heydrich said, would be dumped in with the other Jewish families already in the Government General, whereby the problem at hand might be solved.[55] If Heydrich was more explicit than that at the meeting, whoever was taking the minutes knew enough not to write his comments down. However, one of the high officials in the WVHA, in his postwar testimony, dated the beginning of the policy of annihilating Jews to early 1940, basing his judgment on information he had obtained from SS officers serving in Poland.[56]

HANS FRANK was president of the Academy of German Law. According to his secretary, his lifetime ambition was to become minister of justice. But his familiarity with legal principles had little impact on his actions, for Frank was also a believer in Nazi ideology and a man of great ambition. Only in comparison with a Himmler does Frank seem moderate. In the eyes of General Johannes Blaskowitz, the governor was a clever and talented man, but quite untrustworthy.[57] By February 1940 Himmler must have come to somewhat the same conclusion.

Frank had reason not to carry out Himmler's resettlement schemes. He apparently wanted to develop a stable domain. Raising the population density by adding up to eight million Poles, Jews, and gypsies from German territories, and depressing the standard of living to a bare minimum, was not likely to create stability or make life comfortable for Frank. He preferred to create a showplace of culture. A lover of fine music, Frank was particularly devoted to Chopin, and established a Chopin Museum in Cracow. He also organized and supported a first-rate philharmonic orchestra.[58] Although a strong German nationalist and a vicious anti-Semite, Frank clearly appreciated Polish culture and history more than Himmler did.

Frank began to develop a case for a different course. A long analysis prepared either by Frank or for him in January 1940 maintained that the annihilation of a people with the size and strength of tradition of the Poles was impossible and unprecedented in recent centuries; even a substantial reduction could be accomplished only under the most favorable circumstances. The mere fact that the author raised this argument showed that genocide was considered quite conceivable.

Willing to eliminate the "influence" of the leading elements in Poland, the author was prepared to have the Government General receive Poles and Jews from the annexed territories and to play them off against one another. But this stage would only be a preliminary step. Some three million Jews might then be shipped off to Madagascar, the surplus Poles deported farther to the east. But the remainder should be allowed a decent, if hard, existence, with the possibility of assimilation into German culture. Implicit in the report was the notion that Germany should create orderly conditions and stimulate economic development; that would leave the Poles less susceptible to Bolshevism.[59]

Only a couple of days before he met up with Himmler's visiting party in late January, Frank sent off a confidential memo to Göring's Office of the Four-Year Plan in which he argued that Polish economic resources ought to be used to add to German military strength. He envisioned moving at least one million Poles to Germany (here Frank, Himmler, and Göring were in agreement), where they were sorely needed as agricultural and factory workers. But he also wanted to stabilize the Polish economy and direct it toward military production.[60] Himmler's sweeping resettlement policy was hardly consistent with Frank's emphasis on immediate, practical economic and military objectives, not to mention his cultural aspirations. If economic considerations were the highest priority, Himmler's far-reaching plans for expulsions, immigration, and new settlements would be set back.

Frank's appeal to Göring was a skillful move. Head of the National Defense Council and still the dominant figure in the Nazi war economy, Göring had a natural interest in maximizing production. Perhaps the greediest of all the Nazi leaders, he had amassed his own industrial empire, the state-owned Hermann Göring Works. He was Himmler's most powerful competitor in the battle for confiscated property and resources in the East.

Göring invited Himmler, Frank, and the Eastern Gauleiter to a conference at his estate at Karinhall on February 12. In his introductory remarks, Göring made it clear that the foremost goal of German measures in the East was to strengthen the war potential of the Reich. The rest of the meeting did not go much better for Himmler. Göring opposed evacuation measures that would rob the Eastern areas of laborers necessary to maintain the economy there and of workers who could be brought into the Reich. He granted that the Government General should take in Jews from Germany and the annexed territories, but only in an orderly way, with prior notification of the governor. Frank pointed out that he had to take account of foreign-policy considerations. He noted sharply that previous resettlement policy had made it impossible to restore orderly administration. Even Himmler's scaled-down resettlement plans should be dependent upon prior resolution of food problems and the war-related considerations outlined by Göring, Frank said.

Himmler tried to minimize what his RFV agency had done. Not more than 300,000 out of 8 million Poles had been evacuated so far, he said, while 240,000 Germans had come into the newly Germanic territory. More Polish peasants in Posen, West Prussia, and southeastern Prussia would have to make way for Volhynian Germans in the course of the current year. But, with reference to the needs of the war, Himmler said that he had postponed the immigration of the Lithuanian Germans, as well as Germans from Bukovina and Bessarabia. He pledged to reach agreement with Frank on future evacuations.[61]

Frank boasted in his diary that Berlin had now abandoned the massive resettlement schemes, retaining only the idea of a Jewish reservation east of the Vistula. Even the deportation of the Jews from Germany, Frank wrote, would not occur within a year or during the course of the war.[62] Himmler's viewpoint was quite different. He was willing to defer those deportations of Poles designed to create space for the Volhynian Germans, but he had said nothing about the deportations still in progress in the Wartheland. He had canceled nothing. And he now carried on as if there were no serious problem.

At the meeting of January 30 Heydrich had spoken of first deporting forty thousand Jews and Poles from the Wartheland to create space for the Baltic Germans, and Himmler continued to aim at that target. On February 20 he decided to select the "Congress" Poles (Polish families who had migrated from central Poland in recent decades) first, along with members of organizations hostile to Germany, up to a total of forty thousand. Poles with close relatives in the German armed forces were to be exempted. In the future, Himmler decided, selections would be made on the basis of racial considerations as well as political ones.[63] The only real change from earlier resettlement plans was Himmler's concentration on the removal of Poles at this stage.

Himmler explained some of his motives and problems in his secret speech to the party Gauleiter and Reichsleiter on February 29. The Führer had given Himmler a mission, he declared, which was to ensure that at least the annexed territory become Germanic in the near future, which meant dissolving Polish nationality. The Polish problem, the Slavic problem generally, would come back to haunt Germany again and again unless it was fully resolved.

Himmler offered his own "historical" analysis of the problem. A once-Germanic ruling class in the East had gradually intermarried with the Slavs, creating a substantial element of mixed blood. In times of German political weakness, the Poles took advantage of the situation to assimilate the ethnic Germans and those of mixed blood. Even racially pure Germans came to regard themselves as Poles, which was a dangerous combination. Himmler argued that the admixture of Nordic blood had transformed the Poles, the Czechs, the Slovaks, the Gorals (a mountain people in the area of Teschen[64]), and the Hungarians from tribes into nationalities, and that the Nordic element among the Slavs made them dangerous to Germany. If there were no German blood among them, there would be no real nationalism or leadership skills. Germany now had to recapture that lost blood, Himmler maintained, or eliminate it.

These basic principles, Himmler said, had impelled him to act, and he would continue to do so. He would stubbornly hold to the goal, but adjust his means of pursuing it. He then told the audience that his remarks were for their own ears only. At the beginning of the war it was necessary to intervene in a very harsh way, especially in West Prussia, to strip the enemy of its leaders (insurgents, political organizations, intelligentsia). Many had suggested alternatives to him and warned him that German troops themselves would suffer damage from serving as executioners, but there was no other way to resolve the problem. He added that those who presumed to give him advice had never actually seen what took place, implying that he had been there. To witness such scenes was hideous and frightful, he confirmed, but Himmler rejected the charge that the executions were un-German; it was un-German to allow oneself to be deceived and defeated.

Once the war ended, Himmler said, there would be a racial sifting of the Polish population. Those suitable could remain in the German provinces in the East or go to the rest of Germany. The pure Mongol elements, the Mongol mixed bloods, and the Huns would go to the Government General. For every German brought into the East, two or three Poles and/or Jews had to be removed, he calculated.

Himmler presented limited information about his policies toward Jews in the East. He indicated that, in contrast to the Poles, Jews could be deported *en masse* to the Government General, assuming there was sufficient food supply and reception capacity there. He announced that the normal emigration of Jews (which he exaggeratedly estimated at some six to seven thousand per month) to places such as Palestine, South America, and North America would continue. He warned the Gauleiter not to develop false hopes; it would take some time before most of their *Gaue* would be free of Jews. The Jews were to be deported from the Eastern provinces of Germany, Austria, and Bohemia-Moravia first, about 1.1 million of them.[65] The rest of the Reich would come later.

It was not really necessary to "educate" the party officials on the Jewish question, as he had done with the Slavs; the belief that Jews were a pernicious influence and the desire to remove them from German territories were widespread. The tone of Himmler's speech indicated (in at least one passage) that he was even less concerned about the loss of Jewish lives than about the deaths of Poles. Himmler was not prepared to discuss anything beyond emigration and resettlement of Jews before such an audience. But we should keep in mind what he had said about his policies toward the Poles: he intended to be stubbornly inflexible in his goal, adaptable in his implementation of it.

Frank agreed with Himmler on a few points but disagreed with much. At a meeting in Warsaw on March 2 with district officials, SS officers, representatives of the Four-Year Plan, and high officers of the armed forces, Frank proclaimed that the Government General was an independent entity, the legal government of Poland, and not a province of Germany. He alone was responsible to the Führer and to the Reich, and he could permit no special interests within his realm and no policies established by Reich agencies. Since the Führer wanted to remove the Government General from the war zone, Frank said, his basic policy was to establish calm. The authorities had to neutralize potentially dangerous organizations such as the intelligentsia, the church, and the "militant" element. But the Jewish question, Frank added, represented no immediate danger, and the Government General had no need of the Reich's racial laws.[66] Frank took a practical approach—get rid of those causing or likely to cause immediate problems.

Around mid-March Frank complained to Göring about the continuing deportations into Poland, and as a result Göring sent out a secret telegram forbidding further deportations without his approval and without proof that Frank had already agreed to them. Also around this time, Frank announced publicly that the Government General was the homeland of the Polish people, and that Polish rights and property would not be violated.[67] Even if Frank issued this propaganda merely to reassure the Poles or mislead foreign observers, Himmler could not have been pleased.

Himmler tried a move behind Frank's back. He issued an unpublished order to bar the emigration of Jews from the Government General, not only to Germany, but to all other countries.[68] On the surface, the move made sense only in reducing the competition for German Jews seeking to obtain havens in other European countries or visas to the Western Hemisphere countries. But German Jews were in a better position to get to Italy or Portugal anyway, and in the case of American visas, Poles did not come under the same quota as Germans. The annual quota for Germans seeking U.S. immigrant visas was more than twenty-seven thousand; the corresponding quota for Poles was tiny. The ban contradicted Germany's expressed policy of allowing Jews to emigrate in order to be rid of them, and the apparent logic behind it was faulty. But if there was a secret political-ideological reason not to allow Polish Jews to emigrate, Himmler's order made perfect sense. The political-ideological motive was revealed seven months later.[69]

On April 27 Himmler flew into Płock, a port city on a branch of the Vistula River, about sixty miles northwest of Warsaw. Officially, he had come on an inspection tour, not of Poland, but through nearby south-eastern Prussia—so read the itinerary prepared by Higher SS and Police Leader Wilhelm Rediess. And Rediess, East Prussian Gauleiter Erich Koch, and District Governor Paul Dargel were among those who accompanied Himmler's convoy. If he followed the itinerary, Himmler must have inspected the Fifteenth SS Death's Head Standard in Płock and observed the training given to the self-defense force and ethnic Germans from Lithuania there as well. Then he had a chance to indulge his military and historical interests in the area.[70]

The Army High Command would soon be preoccupied with the Western front. In that sense, it was a logical moment to accelerate resettlement activities in the East. Himmler probably wanted a firsthand look at the territory and consultations with local subordinates such as Rediess, Security Police Inspector Dr. Otto Rasch, and Oberführer Roch, all of whom were part of his entourage. They had all taken a direct role in the shootings of Poles at Soldau. In fact, Rasch subsequently wrote that he considered it his duty to attend all phases of the operations at the Soldau camp, including the shootings that he himself had ordered.[71]

Gruppenführer Rediess asked Himmler's permission to borrow the highly efficient unit under Sturmbannführer Herbert Lange that had carried out gassings from mental asylums in the Wartheland. Rediess's subordinates then gathered more than 1,500 mental patients from East Prussian facilities and another 250 to 300 from Zichenau at the Soldau camp. The "movers" from the vans, now decorated with the name of a coffee firm, loaded one group aboard, headed off, disposed of the bodies, and returned hours later for the next victims. Between May 21 and June 6 the euthanasia patients gathered at Soldau were all "evacuated" in this way.[72]

Lange not only carried out activities quietly; he also left no documentary record for prying bureaucrats and historians until a dispute broke out. Wilhelm Koppe was having trouble meeting all his expenses in the Wartheland area, so he tried to make a profit off the gassing experiments. When Rediess asked him for the use of Lange's squad, he stipulated that Rediess pay a bonus to the squad—ten marks for every person killed—and Rediess supposedly agreed. In fact, Rediess's subordinate Rasch paid Lange an advance of two thousand marks before the operation at Soldau began.[73] Then, however, the squad and Koppe waited in vain for the rest of the money. By October Koppe was forced to write a detailed letter to Rediess's successor retracing the history of the affair and asking for payment. Rediess, who had since become higher SS and police leader in Norway, responded by mail, denying that he had ever taken Koppe's request for money seriously.[74]

From these letters and telegrams we learn the details of the Soldau "evacuations," as they are called in the documents, and of Himmler's direct involvement. According to Rediess, Himmler held the gassing operation to be particularly important, and after the men completed their "difficult task," Himmler ordered them to take a vacation, which they chose to spend in Holland.[75]

Himmler conducted a similar inspection tour of the Wartheland and the Lublin region the next week. He again visited Lodz, Lublin, and Chełm and conferred with the senior SS-police officials: Koppe, Krüger, and Globocnik.[76] Globocnik, the SS and police leader for the Lublin area, was junior to Koppe and Krüger, but he was the most aggressive and forceful of the three, which did not escape Himmler's notice.

Globocnik was another of the many Austrians in the upper ranks of the SS. The son of an officer, born in 1904 in the city of Trieste on the Adriatic Sea, he was too young to have fought in World War I. He had attended military school and vocational school, and eventually became an architect. He joined the Austrian Nazi Party very early, in 1922, and was brought to trial for high treason five times before the Nazis took over Austria in March 1938. All of this made Globocnik a perfect candidate for promotion, and he was named Gauleiter of Vienna. But his sharp elbows and his willingness to cut corners got him into trouble in 1939, when he was accused of misappropriating party money (reimbursing himself for alleged undocumented expenses). Nazi Party Treasurer Franz Xaver Schwarz insisted on punishing Globocnik, and he was removed from office, pending resolution of the case against him. In spite of his own personal scrupulousness in matters of finance, Himmler had no qualms about using a man like Globocnik in the SS. In fact, Globocnik's vulnerability—the party's case dragged on into 1941—made it more likely that he would go out of his way to earn Himmler's favor.[77]

As SS and police leader for the Lublin district, Globocnik was in a critical post for the Jewish resettlement program. In the battles over jurisdiction and policy between the SS and Frank, Globocnik chose not to try to serve two masters. As a result of his independence and arbitrary brutality, Frank and his provincial governor, Dr. Ernst Zörner, made an unsuccessful effort to force Globocnik out. Friedrich-Wilhelm Krüger, well aware of Globocnik's activities and his difficulties with the civil administration, urged Himmler not to give in and remove Globocnik. In June 1940 Krüger suggested that Himmler award him a decoration instead. Himmler deferred the decoration, but assured Krüger that he had no intention of transferring Globocnik.[78]

Globocnik had established an impressive record of using violence. In one incident in the spring of 1940, he had his men chain together hundreds of convicts and Jews and drive them to the Bug River, near Lublin, where they were to be drowned. But the river was still frozen, and the men were able to flee to the opposite bank, where Russia's zone of occupation began. The Russian soldiers drove them back. Globocnik's men opened fire to prevent them from returning. Finally, the Russians blasted holes in the ice, and the men were drowned according to the original plan.[79] This was one way to dispose of unwanted people, and it was quite consistent with SS goals and methods.

As the SS official in charge of Lublin, site of the planned Jewish "reservation," Globocnik was in a perfect position to implement evolving plans to resolve the Jewish question. The Nazi death threats against German and European Jews ever since the fall of 1938, and the prewar SS plan for phases of persecution leading to the mass murder of remaining German Jews, made it clear that Himmler and Heydrich considered the Jews the most dangerous and irreconcilable of the Third Reich's enemies. Heydrich had already written that the "final goal" in Poland with regard to the Jews would take time to carry out, but that one could get there by stages.[80] If the Polish intelligentsia was now being killed off, could large numbers of Jews be far behind? In this sense, Himmler's idea of crematoria and gas chambers in concentration camps, Heydrich's approval of camouflaged killing at Soldau, Himmler's conception of using male Jews for hard labor on the eastern border, and his ordering of new concentration camps in the East represented steps toward what became the Final Solution.

▼▼▼▼▼▼▼▼▼▼▼▼▼▼▼▼▼▼

CHAPTER 5

RACIAL EDUCATION
AND THE MILITARY

GENERAL JOHANNES BLASKOWITZ, commander-in-chief of the
army's Eastern sector since the end of October 1939, was Himmler's
military *bête noire*. With his headquarters situated not far from Lodz,
Blaskowitz had received plenty of information about *Einsatzgruppen* killings and atrocities. During November and December Blaskowitz had
twice complained and reported in detail to von Brauchitsch and to the
Army High Command about the army's difficulties with Himmler's
forces. Blaskowitz did not mince words in his protests. His soldiers, he
wrote, did not want to be associated with the atrocities of the police
squads, and they refused to cooperate in any way with squads whose
methods had created chaos rather than order. Blaskowitz court-
martialed one of his soldiers, who had helped an *Einsatzgruppe* carry out
a raid against Jews.[1] He called the *Einsatzgruppen* an unbearable burden
for the army, because they created a problem of discipline within the
army and a danger to security within Poland. And he called upon his
superiors for a change in occupation policy. The commander-in-chief
did announce that he expected model conduct from his soldiers and, if
necessary, energetic intervention with the use of force to preserve the
reputation of the army, but this gesture was hardly a solution adequate
to the problem.[2]

Hearing of Blaskowitz's views, Hitler denounced the army leadership
for its foolish notion that one could use "Salvation Army" methods in
Poland. He claimed that he had long distrusted Blaskowitz, who, he said,
ought to be removed.[3] Meanwhile, Hitler had approved additional arms
and artillery for the SS troops in the Government General and throughout the Eastern sector, which had to be obtained from the military.
Himmler had ordered Friedrich-Wilhelm Krüger to get the arms from

Blaskowitz, but Blaskowitz had refused to supply the weapons, and all Krüger could do was complain to Himmler. If Himmler had gone back to the Führer to report that he and his men had been unable to extract the arms they needed, it would have been a sign of weakness. So Himmler chastised Krüger: "I don't need an Obergruppenführer to send me a notice of failure and to conduct unsuccessful negotiations. Anyone else who can write memos could do that job equally well. . . ."[4]

Blaskowitz's denunciations began to affect the behavior of some officials in the High Command of the Army, the High Command of the Armed Services, and the army commanders in the West.[5] Blaskowitz prepared another scathing report about SS activities in the East and presented it to Brauchitsch in mid-January. At first Brauchitsch refused to risk another confrontation with Hitler, and Blaskowitz came away convinced that the commander-in-chief was "spineless." But other generals as well put pressure on Brauchitsch to do something about a problem that was ruining morale and creating a loss of confidence in the military authorities. So he invited Himmler to an afternoon tea a week later. Heydrich had already obtained a copy of Blaskowitz's latest report on the atrocities, so Himmler knew what was on Brauchitsch's mind.[6]

Himmler was conciliatory, expressing his pleasure at the invitation. Brauchitsch asked whether there was any value in prosecuting those who were involved in the reported incidents. The two men apparently agreed that they would take no action, but they would make a concerted effort to prevent any further cases of this kind. When that understanding failed to satisfy the military critics, Brauchitsch sent an officer to conduct a special investigation of conditions in Poland. Then he raised the issue again, at a second tea, on February 2.

At first Himmler seemed to be the very embodiment of moderation and rationality. He pointed out that the SS and the police had a difficult task in the East, but admitted that they had made some mistakes. He claimed he had intervened to discipline some who had been involved, and that some of the guilty had even been shot. He said he intended to carry out his task with as little bloodshed as possible. On the other hand, Himmler maintained, the army had been guilty of misdeeds—not only unauthorized killings (for which soldiers allegedly received bonuses), but also social contacts with Polish large landowners. In attacking German officers who socialized with Polish aristocrats, Himmler was repeating part of Hitler's October 17, 1939, diatribe to General Keitel.[7] He was probing, not too gently, a very sensitive wound.

Again Himmler asked Brauchitsch to notify him if he learned of further incidents. Brauchitsch, however, told his staff to pass along only the most serious cases. Such lukewarm steps were hardly likely to satisfy

Blaskowitz, Abwehr Lieutenant Colonel Groscurth, or General Ulex, all of whom continued to press for significant action. Ulex demanded the dissolution of the SS and police units in Poland. Blaskowitz observed that the slaughter of thousands of Jews and Poles was not only not pacifying the country but also stirring up widespread hatred against Germany. He wanted the guilty brought to justice.[8]

This ferment among some high-ranking officers exemplified a more general problem. Almost all the senior military officers had been unhappy with the Weimar Republic, and in spite of some misgivings about Hitler as a leader at first, they were pleased when Nazi Germany pursued a more aggressive foreign policy and expanded the army. Serious opposition among the senior officers to Hitler's increasingly radical foreign-policy goals in 1938–39 led to talk of a coup, but after the shakeup of the army leadership in early 1938 and the Munich Pact, the top men went along with the Führer, and the rest of the army naturally followed.[9] The quick military victory over Poland strengthened Hitler's hold over the army.

But Himmler was not Hitler. The Waffen-SS was increasingly a serious rival to the army, and the racial policies of the SS went far beyond the chauvinism and social anti-Semitism customary among many aristocratic officers. Even among army officers who supported Hitler loyally as the head of state and were willing to follow him into war against the West, some had a marked dislike for Himmler and the SS. Himmler was not stupid. He knew that he had some friends among the army elite, but that a number of officers were outright enemies and others reserved, and he regarded the military with suspicion. If the SS was to grow and to accomplish its radical goals, something would have to be done about the army.

One of Himmler's friends among the Gauleiter (Terboven) suggested that the army might want to invite Himmler to speak before commanders in the West to smooth the waters. Brauchitsch's first inclination was just to let tempers die down. When it became clear that simply ignoring the military critics might jeopardize his own capacity to command, he changed his mind. On February 20 General Werner von Tippelskirch invited Himmler to give a lecture to commanders in the West—not to justify himself, Tippelskirch explained, but to educate them.

This time Himmler was angry and defensive. He preferred to talk before men he could trust—commanders such as Fedor von Bock, Walter von Reichenau, and Günther von Kluge—but Tippelskirch noted that it was precisely the skeptical ones who needed to be educated. Himmler then launched an attack on some of his enemies in the military: General Wilhelm von Leeb was hopeless; he would never meet with

General Georg von Küchler, who had called the SS a disgrace; Generals Blaskowitz and Ulex were out of the question.[10] After some time passed and he cooled down, Himmler reconsidered and agreed to a mid-March presentation.[11]

If Himmler was going to speak to the army commanders, there was another matter that he could not entirely avoid, one almost as sensitive as the executions in the East. On October 28, 1939, he had set off a controversy when he issued an extraordinary "order" for the entire SS and police to father as many children as possible so as to compensate for the loss of the best German blood in the war. This order explicitly stated that in these circumstances men and women might overstep the boundaries of law and common practice and produce children outside of marriage. Himmler pledged to provide generous support for mothers and children without differentiating between married and unmarried women; his SS men would not have to worry about the financial consequences of fathering children.[12]

A few months later, at a secret meeting of the Reichsleiter and Gauleiter, Himmler explained that he had long been concerned whether there would be a sufficient number of successors to the current generation of Nazis. When it became clear that the war would continue even after the victory over Poland, he felt compelled to do something, because the next phase in the West would surely bring more casualties than had occurred in the East, and precisely the bravest, most self-sacrificing men would suffer the highest losses. Himmler then told a poignant story about the father of an SS soldier who had died in the Polish campaign. The father, who had lost his only child, supposedly went around asking the son's comrades whether his boy had had a girlfriend—in the hope that he might uncover the existence of an illegitimate child. Himmler praised the father for overlooking social conventions and for recognizing the oldest truth—the need for the continuation of the family and the preservation of the blood. After he had learned of this case, Himmler said, he had drafted his order, presented it to the Führer, and got it approved.[13]

In this same speech, Himmler discussed the demographic reasons for his order at some length. There were up to half a million women between the ages of thirty-five to forty-five who had not borne children, either because their husbands had fallen in World War I or because they had been unable to find husbands subsequently. Another huge demographic burden was the existence of so many homosexuals. Himmler stated that in 1933 there were more than 1.5 million members of homosexual organizations in Germany. As a result of government suppression, these organizations had been unable to recruit members, so now, Himmler maintained, the number was down to about five hundred thousand—still a serious problem. Himmler did not discuss how the imprisonment of homosexuals in concentration camps had contributed to the decline. Moreover, all his figures were gross exaggerations.

The need to increase the population could not be resolved simply by stressing the importance of marriage and condemning unmarried mothers and illegitimate children, Himmler said. Illegitimate children of good blood were valuable members of the racial community, and only the marriage that produced many children represented the nucleus of the *Volk*.[14] Fundamental re-education in this area would require a clash with Christian influences that could occur only after the war, Himmler implied.

The re-evaluation of marriages according to their capacity to produce children was not a matter of abstract ideology for Himmler. His own wife, Marga, was now forty-seven. She lived in Gmünd, on the Tegernsee in Bavaria, with their adopted son and their natural daughter, Gudrun, while her husband spent most of his time in Berlin and in travels across Europe. Meanwhile, Himmler had become friendly with an attractive, unassuming staff secretary twelve years younger than he. In 1941 she left her job and semiformally became his mistress. During the next few years she bore him two children.[15] Himmler practiced what he preached about illegitimate children.

If the Nazis had won the war, there is no telling how radical Nazi population policy would have become. Himmler had told the select group aboard his train in late January 1940: "It is important for us to consider that one man can have ten children a year from ten women, whereas one woman can have only one child a year from ten men."[16] Hitler later spoke positively about polygamy under circumstances in which there was a shortage of men.[17] As usual, there was a very close correspondence between Himmler's and Hitler's private views.

Even the published views, however, were enough to cause quite a controversy. When Himmler's order had become known within the army, officers and troops alike had reacted angrily. Some had expressed concern about the encouragement of immoral behavior; others had regarded the order as an unleashing of young men at home to pursue the wives, daughters, or sisters of soldiers at the front. When the Army High Command had sent Lieutenant Colonel Groscurth to investigate reaction elsewhere, he had learned that the Air Force High Command had originally believed the order to be so outlandish that it had to be a forgery, and that Göring himself had supposedly disapproved of it. In this case, Brauchitsch had written a strong letter of protest to General Keitel. Then the SS newspaper, *Das Schwarze Korps*, had added a new irritant when it proclaimed that a girl who refused to perform her highest duty in this way was equivalent to a man who refused to perform military service. Lieutenant General Groppe then had angrily told his troops that such an order in a Christian state was an abomination. But when Brauchitsch had sent the strongly pro-Nazi General Reinecke to Himmler to lobby for a modification of the order in January 1940, Himmler had told Reinecke that the order had gone out with the approval of the Führer. Himmler had indicated, however, that he might issue a commentary on the order, and that he might perhaps withdraw the statement published in *Das Schwarze Korps.*[18]

Himmler had heard from his own sources that the military were greatly agitated over the October order,[19] so he prepared a response in a draft dictated on January 14,[20] even before his first tea with Brauchitsch, ten days later. Typically, Himmler said nothing to Brauchitsch about his own move, and as late as February 2, when Brauchitsch gave Himmler the text of his forthcoming statement to the troops about the controversial order, the Reich Führer SS left Brauchitsch in the dark. In his own pronouncement to the troops, Brauchitsch defended marriage as the foundation of the family, but also accepted the vital need for more children.[21]

Himmler's statement was not really apologetic. SS men were subject to the same standard of comradeship and respectability as anyone else; no one should move in on the wives of soldiers in the field, Himmler declared. Besides, he noted, the overwhelming majority of SS men were on the front, and German women were themselves the best guardians of their own honor. He denounced those who spread false interpretations of his order.[22]

Himmler won in another area as well. Groppe, who had publicly criticized Himmler's order, was relieved of his command, although he was not subjected to disciplinary proceedings as Himmler had wanted.[23] Still, Himmler was able to boast to the Reichsleiter and Gauleiter on February 29 that he had handled the whole matter directly with Brauchitsch and avoided going to the Führer, which, he declared, would only have sharpened the argument.[24] He was probably right; he certainly had better command of his temper than did Hitler.

By March Himmler was ready to address the commanders of the individual armies in the West. Himmler preferred, Karl Wolff reported to the army command, to give a presentation in the evening, if possible, in conjunction with a dinner. Not only were such arrangements easier to work into Himmler's schedule, but, Wolff stated, a speech in the evening would have a greater effect on the audience and would provide a comradely setting, more favorable for handling these difficult problems. Himmler also wanted to speak to the commanders somewhere in the West, rather than in Berlin, to expand the audience down to the level of division commanders, and to include some of the SS commanders of similar rank. The subjects were to be the order of October 28 and the resettlement policies in the East. Three days later Himmler inspected the SS Death's Head Division, the concentration-camp guards converted to soldiers, in its new quarters, near Kassel. He ordered Commander Theodor Eicke to crack down on all cases of misbehavior—brawling with civilians or soldiers had been a frequent problem in the past. It was time to make a better impression on the military.[25]

As was his custom,[26] Himmler had prepared only an outline of his speech. He was hardly a rousing speaker, but he was smart enough not to give himself an additional handicap by reading a speech. This was not an academic exercise, and precision was less important than producing the right effect upon the audience. Himmler began by discussing his order regarding the production of more children, but apparently quite briefly. With all the criticism he had received, he would have avoided statements that highlighted the contradictions between the Nazi standpoint on illegitimate children and Christian morality. He would certainly not have wanted to discuss the demographic problems caused by homosexuality. (False accusations of homosexuality against the army commander-in-chief in 1938, General von Fritsch, had forced Fritsch to resign and allowed Hitler to dispose of an important opponent in the military, but the episode had angered some of the senior army officers.) He would most likely have said something about the casualties in both world wars and the need for more children if Germany was to remain strong.

In contrast, his notes indicate that Himmler went into the racial problems in Poland in some detail. The thirty-four million inhabitants of Poland, he said, included Poles, Ukrainians, White Russians, Jews, Kashubians, Gorals, and others, with racial types ranging from the Nordic to the Mongol; the upper class was Germanic, Himmler claimed. The admixture of German blood had helped Poles develop national consciousness, which made them dangerous to Germany. Adolf Hitler had made Germany strong enough to solve this age-old historical problem by annexation, purges, and Germanization. Since fusion of the Germans and Slavs was impossible, Germany had to use other methods. He then ruled out the Bolshevist method, which he claimed would be like a knight's lowering his sword before his opponent. He finally proposed the execution of the leading figures of the opposition—a harsh but necessary solution.[27]

What did Himmler mean by "the Bolshevist method"?[28] Stalin's purges—his disposal of alleged political and social opposition forces and classes—were certainly well known to the Nazi leadership. On the surface, it seems plausible that Himmler was equating Bolshevist methods with outright liquidation of the Slavic population—and that he was rejecting genocide. As we shall see, two months later Himmler wrote something along these lines. But why would liquidating the racial enemy be equivalent to a knight's lowering his sword? We also know from other sources that Himmler certainly did not regard the liquidation of an enemy population as uniquely Bolshevist.[29]

More likely, Himmler borrowed his concept of Bolshevist methods from Hitler, who had an eccentric and ideologically distorted view. According to Walter Schellenberg, despite numerous intelligence reports to the contrary, Hitler insisted that Stalin had systematically pursued a secret policy of racial mingling within the Soviet Union, with the goal of allowing the "Mongol" element to predominate. During 1941 Hitler laid both the policy of racial mingling and that of mass extermination at the door of the Bolsheviks. In 1942 he claimed that the Ukrainian support forces fighting with the Germans contained men of the Mongol type—a clear result of the Bolshevik policy of racial mixing.[30]

So Himmler was arguing that, if the Nazis manipulated the "races" in Poland in this way, they might well prevail more easily for a while, but the perpetuation of the Mongol racial type in Poland would threaten Germany in Himmler's eyes. And the partly Germanic groups would continue to spread their blood to the Slavs, giving them the talent for leadership and warfare. That was equivalent to a knight's lowering his sword before the enemy.

Himmler proceeded to tell the commanders in no uncertain terms that the executions of the leading figures of the opposition in the East were authorized at the highest level. His notes state: "[I was] myself there: no wild affair of the junior officers any more than it was mine alone." Later in his notes he wrote: "———— know[s] very precisely what takes place." General Ulex recalled that Himmler had said: "I do nothing that the Führer doesn't know." Ulex was astounded that Himmler had traced the executions back to Hitler's orders. Himmler had apparently done so reluctantly, but there was little alternative. Nothing else seemed likely to dampen the criticism.[31]

Himmler then spoke of his plans for the Germanization of the Eastern provinces and the transfer of non-Germans to the Government General, in somewhat the same language as he had used with the Reichsleiter and Gauleiter. The time for accomplishing the Germanization of the East, the creation of a new German empire, would come after the "other" problem, in the West, was resolved, he promised. The military commanders at least shared Himmler's hope for the success of the Western offensive. Himmler concluded with an appeal to his "colleagues" to cooperate, under the leadership of Adolf Hitler, in the establishment of a greater German and greater Nordic empire.[32]

In his March 27 speech to the air-force officers at Essen, Himmler covered the same ground as he had with the army. He spoke of the "hard fist" necessary in the East. He mentioned the plans to bring in ethnic Germans and to remove Jews—also to bring about Jewish emigration from Germany. Once again, he concluded with a call for the military to cooperate in the establishment of a greater German Reich after resolving the Western problem.[33] Then Himmler added another lecture to the series. This time, on April 5, the audience was composed of Gauleiter Terboven and twenty-eight prominent industrialists.[34] Although we do not know the identity of the businessmen, it is likely that they were selected according to their significance to the economy, rather than for their close connection with Himmler or the SS. (At least, this seems a reasonable inference, given the nature of the speech.)

This time Himmler noted that his concentration camps had taken on important economic functions. He again stressed the importance of racial principles, racial purity, and careful selection of men for the SS; quality of the blood was their highest value. Next he explained that the Führer had given him the task of resolving the Eastern situation, which was not so much a political problem as a racial problem. He retraced the history of the Slavic peoples and the previous efforts to deal with them, and he summarized the *temporary* solution under way: ruthless intervention, inflow of some ethnic Germans, "evacuation" of the others. But everything, he said, was limited for the time being by economic difficulties.

After the war, Himmler continued, there would be three possibilities. The first would follow the Bolshevik model. The second possibility was the method used by Genghis Khan; although his notes do not spell out the obvious, this option clearly was the extermination of entire enemy populations. The third possibility Himmler called the "German solution"—sifting out the racially valuable from the racially useless and sending the latter to the Government General.[35] More clearly than before, Himmler made it plain that his term "Bolshevik method" was not outright mass murder of the entire enemy population: wholesale liquidation he attributed to Genghis Khan instead. Yet Himmler declared that he preferred the more humane option of liquidating only the enemy leadership and expelling the racially useless to the Government General.

We would be justified in regarding Himmler's statements with at least some skepticism. Himmler was not accustomed to laying out his plans and intentions to any group—let alone to industrialists who might not have a real commitment to the Nazi movement or to senior military commanders, some of whom were clearly opposed to Nazi ideology. Even with high-ranking SS men, Himmler usually held private conferences with individuals when giving out sensitive or controversial instructions.[36] What Himmler did in his three successive speeches (four, if we count the speech to the Reichsleiter and Gauleiter) was really to justify what had already been done, not to delineate his future plans in all areas. Even so, his remarks about the three options represented a revealing glimpse at the range of possibilities that existed in early 1940. And at least one Krupp official drew the conclusion from speeches that Himmler and Alfred Rosenberg gave in 1940 that the Nazi-Soviet treaty would not last long, that Germany intended to break it.[37]

To the industrialists Himmler also spelled out some of the cultural and archeological activities of the SS, which he himself promoted and which he thought might appeal to his well-educated audience. At the close, he returned to a theme stressed in his previous lectures—the need for cooperation between the armed forces and the Nazi movement. The work of the Wehrmacht would be impossible without the party, he stated, and the work of the party inconceivable without the Wehrmacht. The current friction, he stressed, had to be overcome. Himmler regarded these businessmen as potential allies in the future, and he must have been aware that some of them had close business and personal connections with the military elite.

These lectures indicate the importance that Himmler attached to resolving outstanding difficulties with the military. There were pressing reasons to act. Himmler and his Waffen-SS commanders were trying to acquire heavy artillery, other weapons, and transport vehicles from the military bureaucracy in time for use in the spring offensive. They also wanted the SS units to be prominent in the initial assault, but military authorities controlled the assignments.[38] That alone provided sufficient reason for conciliatory steps.

Wittingly or not, the armed forces were aggravating his difficulties with Governor Frank by demanding vast amounts of land in the Government General for training and maneuvers. What is more, the military's acquisition of land was to be for an indefinite period; it was to be considered permanent. If the military got its way, 20,000 to 30,000 Polish small farmers would be displaced very soon, and the total would eventually rise to 150,000 to 170,000. Sending the displaced farmers to Germany as laborers was under discussion, but they would hardly be eager to give their all for the Third Reich under the circumstances. In a meeting on April 4 with military representatives and Albrecht Schmelt, an SS-and-police official from the Breslau area, one of Frank's appointees explicitly stated that, after the governor had declared the Government General to be the Polish homeland, they could not simply expropriate these farmers and dump them on the street. Moreover, many of these Poles had opposed the former Polish government and were friendly to the new German rulers. He suggested compensating the displaced farmers with good farmland in the Chełm region. (Himmler's RFV was in the process of removing ethnic Germans from Chełm to the annexed portions of Poland, farther to the west.) But Greifelt, Himmler's RFV deputy, knew that Himmler wanted to preserve the large farms in Chełm for future German possession—quite possibly for the SS itself. The military's demands and Frank's response jeopardized Himmler's existing resettlement policy in the Government General—and raised the issue of who was in control, as Greifelt warned his boss. Himmler responded firmly that the Führer had entrusted him with resettlement policy and that he would carry it out.[39]

When Gottlob Berger, chief of the Replacement Office of the Waffen-SS and a close Himmler associate, visited Poland later in April, he saw further disquieting developments. Blaskowitz seemed to be preparing to draft ethnic Germans in the Government General into a new regiment, which would be competition for the Waffen-SS. The civil authorities were considering the use of a Goralian police force—without even consulting Himmler. When Blaskowitz himself showed up in Cracow, he was not at all happy to see Berger, and he seemed to dominate Frank, Berger reported to Himmler.[40]

All of these complications represented distractions for Himmler, some of them serious obstacles. If an implicit alliance formed between Frank and the military, or if Blaskowitz was able to gain control over the Government General, Himmler would face a long and difficult campaign to carry out his will and his plans in the East.

There was one good way to deal with Blaskowitz. Himmler already knew Hitler's views about Blaskowitz; perhaps all he had to do was put the matter to the Führer in the right way at the right time. In May 1940 Hitler dismissed Blaskowitz as commander-in-chief in the East and prevented General Ulex from becoming his successor.[41] By July, with the added impact of military victory in the West, the climate had improved so much that Brauchitsch instructed army authorities: "The soldier who comes to the East from the West must not criticize the way the political authorities conduct the ethnic struggle (Jewish problem) in the East. These tasks were given to the *political* authorities by the Führer and are no concern of the *military* authorities."[42]

CHAPTER 6

▼▼▼▼▼▼▼▼▼▼▼▼▼▼▼▼▼

TO MADAGASCAR
AND BACK

HIMMLER'S WAFFEN-SS did not play a part in the rapid conquest of Denmark and Norway in the spring of 1940. The German military took Copenhagen in twelve hours, but the battle for Norway, prolonged by Norwegian resistance and limited British and French intervention, dragged on for some weeks. On April 30 a British cruiser evacuated King Haakon, the Norwegian government, and the country's gold reserves. Yet, even without a direct military role, Himmler was able to extend his bureaucratic tentacles to the new sphere. About two weeks after the invasion of Norway, Hitler named Wilhelm Rediess to the post of higher SS and police leader for Norway and ordered a small *Einsatzgruppe* there to help the police pursue his policy.[1] It was but a prelude to further SS gains in the West.

On the afternoon of May 9 Hitler slipped out of Berlin from a small suburban junction, his train supposedly headed for Norway but actually moving to an improvised military headquarters on the Western front, near Münstereifel, which Hitler had named Refuge on the Rocks (Felsennest). The military had prepared two other sites for the Führer, one in the Palatinate and one in the Black Forest, but Hitler liked Felsennest best because of the rocky landscape, the climate, and the primitive and wholly warlike installations. After receiving satisfactory weather forecasts, he ordered the attack against Belgium, the Netherlands, and France to begin at 5:35 a.m. on May 10. The Armed Forces High Command sent out the code word for the general attack in the West: "Danzig."[2]

A day later Himmler's special train, "Heinrich," departed from Berlin's Anhalter Bahnhof. The train headed for Altenkirchen in the Westerwald, about thirty miles east of Bonn. That first evening Himmler, Ribbentrop, and Lammers were all in good spirits, as favorable news filtered in from the front. Himmler was exultant that Queen Wilhelmina of the Netherlands had refused to surrender; now the Führer would not have to show any consideration for her, and Holland could be *returned* to Germany.[3] Himmler considered the Netherlands as having properly belonged to Germany since the Middle Ages. Even though Waffen-SS troops had no role in General Guderian's decisive tank thrust through the Ardennes Forest in southern Belgium and Luxembourg and the penetration of France's vaunted Maginot Line, they did play a prominent role in the conquest of the Netherlands.[4]

There was another triumph too, if a less complete one. The High Command of the Armed Services was expecting to set up a military administration for the Netherlands, but on May 17 or 18 Hitler gave the military leaders a rude shock by naming Arthur Seyss-Inquart as executive for the country.[5] Seyss-Inquart's appointment meant that Himmler and the SS would not have to struggle with military authorities over implementing racial and ideological policies in the Netherlands. Seyss-Inquart's first order was to arrest German refugees who had come to the Netherlands since 1933; after ten days in a concentration camp, they would be sent to Poland.[6] The move foreshadowed the fate of Dutch Jewry two years later.

Hitler did, however, allow the creation of military-administration regimes in Belgium and France, perhaps because these occupied territories were supposed to serve as the base for the expected invasion of Great Britain. The Armed Forces High Command had already indicated its own "racial policy" in February 1940 guidelines for the future occupation administration in Belgium and the Netherlands. Since these areas were not to be annexed, Jews were not to be singled out from the rest of the population; there were to be no measures against Jews (or Freemasons) *per se*. Himmler had no intention of simply allowing the military's inhibitions to prevail. One sign of future events was a May 23 telephone conversation between foreign-intelligence expert Walter Schellenberg and Himmler's office manager, Rudolf Brandt. In response to Brandt's previous call, Schellenberg provided information about the racial composition of the population in the Netherlands and in Belgium.[7]

Himmler could not resist another inspection of conquered territory. With Karl Wolff and four other SS officers, he rode around the Netherlands and Belgium incognito, observing the sights and the people, who, Himmler noted, would clearly be a (racial) benefit to Germany.[8] Immediately afterward he went on to Hitler's headquarters at Felsennest. Sometime before May 22 Himmler gave Hitler a position paper he had written on the treatment of foreign peoples in the East.[9] He thus caught the Führer at a favorable moment—when he was beginning to savor an overwhelming military victory. On the 20th German units captured the French cities of Amiens and Abbeville, and advance forces reached the channel coast at Noyelles, threatening to cut off the British and French forces to the north and east.

Himmler lobbied Hitler for some additional equipment for the Waffen-SS, and he recommended a new book by a well-known German writer, Edwin Erich Dwinger, on Polish atrocities against ethnic Germans in Poland at the outset of World War II. He wanted to know whether the Gestapo should bring Captains Best and Stevens, the British agents seized at Venlo in November 1939, to trial. Hitler said yes, at the appropriate moment, which *he* would determine. Himmler also wanted to know the Führer's reaction to the position paper on the treatment of foreign peoples in the East, but Hitler had not yet read the memo.[10] On May 25, with the German armored thrust temporarily halted, Himmler apparently gave Hitler another copy of the six-page memo. Hitler seems to have read it on the spot and announced that he was very much in agreement. He wanted the memo to remain confidential, with a limited number of copies distributed to key individuals.[11]

Probably written after Himmler's trip into Poland in early May and after further consultation in Berlin with Friedrich-Wilhelm Krüger,[12] Himmler's position paper was harsher than the 1939 analysis from the Nazi Party's Office of Racial Politics. Wetzel, Hecht, and Gross of the party office had tried to balance economic and racial considerations in their recommended occupation policy, and they had sought to permit Poles to form nonpolitical organizations and to engage in some cultural activities—even to possess a sort of citizenship (*Staatsangehörigkeit*), though of course no political rights.[13] Himmler's basic notion was to carry out a racial selection in the East to salvage and assimilate the racially valuable inhabitants and to inhibit the growth of national consciousness among Poles and various minorities in the Government General. Their sense of ethnic identity would have to disappear. Virtual elimination of education would help ensure German domination in the East. Non-German children would have no need for any but the simplest primary education—they could be taught to count to five hundred (at the most), to write their names, and, above all, to obey Germans as a divine command. Children of good racial stock might apply for further education, but German authorities would approve only if the parents allowed those children to be sent permanently to Germany. "As inhuman and tragic as each individual case might be," Himmler wrote at the end of this section, "this was nonetheless the mildest and best method if one rejected the Bolshevist method of the physical destruction of a people on grounds of conscience as un-German and impossible."[14] The mere mention of the destruction of an entire people as a possibility showed that Himmler was operating in a different universe from Wetzel and Hecht. He derived his conception not only from extreme racist doctrines but also from his sense of what Hitler was likely to consider and accept.

Himmler's use of the term "Bolshevist method" to describe extermination suggests that he was trying to discourage Hitler from pursuing this course with the Poles. Previously he had alluded to mass murder with references to Genghis Khan's methods.[15] But that phrase would not work very well here, since Hitler had a favorable opinion of the Mongol chieftain.

Left in Poland after the execution of these policies over the next ten years, according to Himmler, would be a racially inferior population, including the elements deported from Germany, who would serve as a reservoir of labor. These people could be used as migrant laborers, stone breakers, and construction workers for streets or buildings.

Taken as a whole, Himmler's memorandum had a dual audience: Hitler and various Nazi authorities with semi-independent status. The whole point of the memorandum was not only to establish the basic line of policy, but to get some of Himmler's rivals to recognize it—and to recognize his jurisdiction. That would not end all Himmler's problems with the Gauleiter, Frank, and Darré, but it would surely reduce them. Hitler gave him what he wanted—the right to give or send the guidelines to Frank, Darré, and Gauleiter Erich Koch, Albert Forster, Arthur Greiser, and Josef Wagner, with Hitler's endorsement.[16]

Surprisingly, Jews are almost absent from Himmler's memo. In one section he wrote that the concept of a Kashubian people would entirely disappear within four to five years; the other nationalities would take longer. In the midst of these musings, Himmler expressed his hope that the concept of Jews would be extinguished through "the possibility of a great emigration of all Jews to Africa or elsewhere into a colony." Wetzel and Hecht had discussed at considerable length the economic productivity of the Eastern Jews and recommended granting them a favored position with respect to the Poles; Himmler grasped for a way to make them disappear from European territory and consciousness.[17]

His reference to Jewish emigration to Africa represented something of a departure. Previous plans for dealing with German and Polish Jews had depended upon prior deportation of Jews to a reservation in the far corner of the Government General, where adult males were to be put in labor camps and the remainder of the Jews decimated. But Nazi opponents as diverse as Göring, Frank, and the military authorities had resisted the deportations to Lublin.

It was not that Frank opposed all killing. In a speech to police officials in the Government General on May 30, he observed that atrocity propaganda, perhaps stirred up by the Americans, the French, the Jews, or the Pope, had caused problems within Germany.

> ... it was terrible in these [past] months to have to listen to the voices from the Propaganda Ministry, from the Foreign Ministry, from the Interior Ministry, yes, even from the Wehrmacht, that this was a regime of murder, that we had to stop these atrocities, and so forth. Of course it was clear that we also had to state that we would not do it any longer. And it was just as clear that, while the world spotlight was on this area, we could not accomplish anything substantial of the sort. But now, with the 10th of May, the world has become fully indifferent to this atrocity propaganda. Now we must use the moment that is available to us. When every minute and second thousands out there in the West of the best German blood have to be sacrificed, then we as National Socialists have to think of our duty [to ensure] that the Polish nation does not rise at the cost of this German sacrifice.

Frank had clear instructions from Hitler not to burden German authorities with the liquidation of the potential Polish leadership: "We don't need to drag these elements off first into concentration camps in the Reich. . . . We will do it in the form that is simplest."[18] Unlike Himmler, however, Frank believed that the Polish Jews presented no immediate danger to the Reich.[19]

Himmler believed that taking on the Jews involved far greater numbers and greater risks than coping with the Polish ruling class. Heydrich had stated the basic constraint in September 1939: Himmler presented policy decisions on the Jews directly to Hitler, because they had particular repercussions on foreign policy.[20] Hitler was still hoping to reach a settlement with Britain and to avoid war with the United States.[21] Even the deportations of Jews to the Lublin region had brought unfortunate publicity to Germany, tarnishing its image. Frank and Göring had resisted Himmler's deportation policy and Himmler's authority, which only made it more likely that conflicts and leaks would continue, barring explicit written orders from Hitler giving Himmler full control over the Jewish question—an unlikely possibility. On the day when Himmler first presented his memorandum on the Eastern peoples to Hitler, Frank insisted on canceling the ban on Jewish emigration from Poland.[22]

Himmler's progress on the Jewish question in Poland was blocked. The German and Polish Jews were not yet all concentrated in the right region, the camps with necessary facilities were not yet established, and the technology of killing was perhaps not sufficiently developed. After Sonderkommando Lange took a vacation in mid-1940, the mobile gas vans with carbon monoxide seem not to have been used for some months; they may have been considered inadequate.[23]

Africa was already under discussion in May 1940, because the Führer was speaking of demanding the return of German colonies there as part of a settlement with the British. Himmler would have known this well before Hitler said as much to General Jodl on May 20.[24] So Himmler took advantage of the prevailing political wind.

In one respect, Himmler's reference to Jewish emigration to Africa represented an apparent radicalization of his strategy. His previous short-term goals had concerned German and Polish Jews; his memo now proposed moving all Jews from Europe to Africa. His acceptance meant that work toward a continent-wide program could begin. That work could prove useful whether or not the Jews actually ended up in Africa.

Despite his comment about Bolshevist methods' being un-German, Himmler was probably not repudiating the idea of exterminating the Jews.*[25] Would the obedient Himmler have risked taking a clear stand against a view that the Führer had once expressed openly to the Reichstag? On the other hand, Himmler had not yet committed himself to the complete extermination of European Jewry. Himmler remained consistent in regarding the Jews as a special category of unassimilable people—one that had to be physically removed to Africa to avoid contaminating and endangering the German Reich.

Scholars have debated over the years whether the Nazi regime ever took seriously the idea of mass shipment of Jews to Africa (what became the Madagascar plan). If Hitler had already decided upon the policy of complete extermination, why use resources to send Jews all the way to Africa? Some have thus suspected that the Madagascar plan was simply a ruse while planning for the Final Solution in Europe proceeded. Or was Madagascar supposed to be the site of the Final Solution, of the gas chambers? At the opposite extreme, other writers have taken the Madagascar scheme at face value—something that the Nazi leadership wanted and fully intended to carry out. Millions of Jews would have tried to live, under Nazi supervision, in an African reservation. Only

---

*Partly for organizational reasons. The sentence about the Jews comes well before the statement about rejecting Bolshevist methods; the latter follows the section on educating non-Germans. In any case, Himmler would not have discussed in written form, intended for distribution to some rivals, an actual policy of exterminating Jews.

when transportation to Africa proved impossible did the leadership turn to other options.[26]

Since we lack definitive evidence of Hitler's real intentions, the controversy will likely continue, but both extremes seem to distort reality. Himmler's primary purpose in mentioning the emigration of Jews to Africa was probably instrumental. He required a policy that would for the moment satisfy Hitler, Göring, and Frank, give the appearance to the outside world that Germany was not behaving "irresponsibly," and draw Jewish policy under the tighter control of the SS. The plan for mass Jewish emigration to Africa was the best bet.

In November 1938, in a conversation with Göring, Hitler had endorsed the idea of a Jewish reservation in Madagascar.[27] Himmler could not be sure that Hitler still favored the idea, but there was one way to find out. His uncertainty might well explain why his memo referred to Jewish emigration to Africa so briefly and tentatively. It was not a full-blown plan but a trial balloon.

Göring was also a major player in economic and settlement matters in the East. So Himmler tactfully went to Göring's train on May 27 and gave him a copy of the memo approved by the Führer.[28] Frank would be happy with any plan that did not dump masses of Jews into the Government General, and even happier with a plan that would ship Polish Jews elsewhere. Frank supported a Jewish reservation in Madagascar,[29] an idea that the rabid anti-Semite Julius Streicher had also occasionally championed in his paper *Der Stürmer*.[30] Before 1939 Polish authorities had discussed with the French and the British the possibility of shipping large numbers of Jews to Madagascar, so Nazi propagandists could maintain that the Third Reich was merely carrying out an idea developed by other Europeans.[31] As outlandish and impractical as the whole scheme seems, what became the Madagascar plan satisfied Himmler's immediate political needs.

Whether millions of Jews could be moved to Africa depended upon other future events: an end to the war in the West, and availability of shipping and financing. There are some hints, as we shall see, that Himmler took the idea seriously. In the end he would not make the decision —Hitler would. If Hitler was interested, so was Himmler.

That did not mean, however, that Himmler was thinking of a peaceful and thriving Jewish state in Africa. He had no intention of letting Jews escape from Nazi control. The problems posed by climate, disease, and a limited economic base in Madagascar had already been publicly aired. If a Jewish reservation in Africa had materialized, it would have possessed even less hospitable conditions than in Lublin. Since Himmler had not yet invested major resources in the construction of Jewish camps in the East, he could be open to another possible method to decimate European Jewry.

Almost immediately after his success with the Führer on May 25, Himmler had to deal with an ugly incident involving his beloved Death's Head Division. Remnants of British units near the French town of Le Paradis were surrounded in a farmhouse on May 27 by the division's Fourteenth Company, which had already suffered heavy casualties. After British marksmen killed and wounded several more SS men, they ran out of ammunition and raised a white flag. They then marched out without weapons, with their hands raised. Obersturmführer Fritz Knöchlein placed the one hundred prisoners against a barn wall and had them executed, as two heavy machine guns created a crossfire. Afterward SS soldiers walked among the bodies with fixed bayonets, stabbing or shooting anyone still moving. (Two British privates, however, managed to play dead, and later surrendered to a regular-army unit. They survived the war and were able to tell their story.) This atrocity was the direct result of Commander Eicke's training methods, which stressed hatred of the enemy.[32]

Himmler and Wolff visited Le Paradis shortly after the massacre.[33] We do not know what was said, but there is some indication of the tenor from the letter that Eicke wrote to Wolff shortly afterward. Eicke explained apologetically that his men had been unable to bury dead SS soldiers because they had suffered another attack almost immediately.[34] It does not appear that Himmler was particularly concerned about the enemy's dead. The Death's Head Division was temporarily grouped under the Sixteenth Panzer Corps, commanded by General Erich Hoepner. Although Hoepner wanted to have a full investigation of the incident, neither Eicke nor Knöchlein was punished, and if there were any written references to the incident, they were destroyed.[35]

While Himmler continued to travel around the front and the conquered areas, the Foreign Office got to work on planning the future shape of Africa. Ribbentrop asked two close associates for suggestions.[36] On June 3 Franz Rademacher of the Jewish desk within the new Germany Department of the Foreign Office requested the foreign minister to choose among three options on the Jewish question: all Jews out of Europe; removal of Western European Jews from Europe to Madagascar (listed in parentheses with a question mark), while the Eastern Jews were held hostage at Lublin to neutralize the American Jews; and establishment of a Jewish national home in Palestine. Rademacher, a former assistant judge, discouraged the last option by citing the danger "of a second Rome."[37] He assumed that Ribbentrop had the power to make a choice.

On June 14 Paris fell to German forces. Two days later Himmler and Rudolf Brandt lunched at the Ritz and visited the wonders of Versailles. They were inspecting more SS troops when they received word, on June 17, that the new French government under Marshal Pétain had requested an armistice. Himmler immediately decided to return to the Führer's side, no doubt to help him celebrate his great triumph. Hitler was overjoyed when he received the news at his new headquarters ("Wolf's Gorge") at Bruly le Peche in southern Belgium.[38]

Shortly after Himmler arrived, Hitler, accompanied by Ribbentrop, took off for Munich to meet Mussolini and Ciano. There, in discussing the shape of the peace settlement, Hitler approved the concept of using Madagascar for the Jews. Two days later he told Admiral Raeder the same thing. What Ribbentrop specifically proposed to Ciano on the 18th, however, was a Jewish settlement in Madagascar under *French* supervision.[39] Ribbentrop's remark may have been disinformation, but it is entirely possible that he was sincere, since he had proposed something of the sort a few months earlier.[40] By one account, Hitler also spoke to Mussolini of establishing a Jewish *state* in Madagascar.[41] But he had no intention of creating a Jewish state.

Hitler reserved the key role in Jewish policy for Himmler and the SS. On June 24 Heydrich wrote a short but pointed letter to the foreign minister, reminding Ribbentrop that in January 1939 Göring had entrusted Heydrich with authority over Jewish emigration. Since there were now some 3.5 million Jews under German control, emigration could no longer provide a solution: "a territorial final solution is therefore necessary." Heydrich asked to participate in all forthcoming discussions dealing with the "final solution" of the Jewish question.[42] He inserted himself squarely into the process: the Foreign Office was not to be the controlling agency.

One interpretation of this letter is that Heydrich and Himmler were simply defending their jurisdiction against bureaucratic and political competitors. On the previous day Philipp Bouhler, head of the Führer Chancellery, had asked Hitler for an unspecified colonial assignment, and Hitler had turned him down.[43] (A couple of months later, in spite of instructions to work closely with Himmler's office, Franz Rademacher proposed that the Führer Chancellery handle the transportation of the Jews to Madagascar.) So Bouhler may have tried to grab a piece of the Madagascar project for himself and the Führer Chancellery.[44] But the SS prevailed instead. Having won that battle, Heydrich tried to forestall another, with the Foreign Office.

Heydrich's language suggests that there was more than bureaucratic competition involved. One official in the Reich Chancellery testified after the war that Hitler himself used to use the term "final solution" at different times to refer to different measures against the Jews, but that he reserved the right to choose the "final solution" himself: "The word is a collective concept of different measures that Hitler contemplated or held out the prospect of."[45] Rademacher later wrote: "the Führer had entrusted Gruppenführer Heydrich with the implementation of the solution of the Jewish question."[46] Heydrich certainly would not have imposed himself on Ribbentrop if he did not think he had the Führer's support.[47]

Mid-level bureaucrats continued to consult and compete over the "rights" to Madagascar.[48] In Eichmann's office there were at least fifteen to twenty meetings with twenty to twenty-five people present, working out details of a Madagascar plan.[49] Their superiors held back, awaiting events and decisions that would determine the feasibility of shipping Jews there.

London failed to respond to Hitler's peace feelers, and the British fleet stood in the way of German colonial expansion. On July 2, the OKW informed military authorities that Hitler had decided to prepare for a landing in England under certain conditions. But Hitler was still not enthusiastic about such a risky venture into the lair of the British lion. A week and a half later the Führer told General Halder that England's hopes rested on the United States and the U.S.S.R.[50] If he could knock out the Soviet Union, the British might either collapse or concede what Germany wanted. The possibility of achieving his longtime dream of a war for living space for the Aryan race in the East appeared nearer than ever before. If the war continued, either in the West or in the East, Madagascar would not come into question for the duration, whatever the French attitude about turning the island over to Germany. The Madagascar plan would have to be postponed, modified, or abandoned.

On July 3 Heinrich Müller reported to Rudolf Brandt that Himmler had decided: "the other half should remain."[51] This typically veiled reference to an otherwise unrecorded conversation seems to involve the RSHA's plans for the Jews. One of the options that Rademacher had originally proposed on June 3 was to ship the Western European Jews to Madagascar and to hold the Eastern Jews "hostage" in the East.[52] Rademacher had since recommended deportation of all European Jews, but there were good reasons why Himmler might have preferred what was on the surface the less radical course. To leave the *Ostjuden* in place was all the more reasonable in light of the prospect of an early and decisive war with the Soviet Union. With massive warfare, after all, came fine cover for killing operations.

Himmler preserved his options by allowing the plans for a large emigration to Madagascar to go forward, and by retaining large numbers of Jews in the East for disposition there. Adolf Eichmann later explained the logic of destroying only the Eastern Jews. The biological foundation of Jewry was in the East; the Western Jews did not have the same fecundity, and they would never recover from the loss of their brethren in the East.[53] So it was more important for the SS to strike at the Jews in the East.

As Himmler must have anticipated from the beginning, news of the emerging Madagascar plan brought about a temporary improvement of his relations with Hans Frank. In late June Frank was still complaining pointedly, in a letter to Reich Chancellery Secretary Lammers, that continuation of the resettlement operations was unbearable. The Government General was already overpopulated, he noted, and the Wehrmacht was demanding more and more land for training grounds. Further evacuation of Poles and Jews from the Reich to Poland, Frank wrote, was "completely out of the question."[54]

Then Himmler met with Krüger in Berlin, and Krüger told Frank on July 10 that the Reich Jews would not be sent to Poland, because they were destined for Madagascar. At the same time, Krüger explained, expulsions of Jews from the Government General scheduled for August (Frank was trying to clear Cracow of Jews[55]) were also canceled for the same reason.[56] In other words, the Madagascar plan allowed Himmler and Frank to agree on freezing the status quo: no more Jews in, but no Jews expelled right away either. Frank told his subordinates that this was a "colossal relief," and he immediately called a halt to the construction of ghettos within his domain.[57] There was no need for ghettos when, "within the foreseeable future," the Government General would be free of Jews. Frank also announced another triumph: on July 8 the Führer had accepted his proposal to make the Government General formally a part of the German Reich. There was to be no difference between the Lublin district and the rest of the country; Germany had taken permanent possession, and there would be no more talk of a rump Polish state.[58]

Frank managed to hold his apparent gains in a July 31 meeting in Cracow with Greiser and Koppe.[59] They pointed out the overcrowded conditions in the Wartheland, especially in the Lodz ghetto, and asked Frank to accept the 250,000 or so Jews from Lodz on an interim basis —until they could be shipped overseas. Frank refused. Himmler had notified him officially, Frank said, that, according to a Führer order, the Government General did not have to accept any more Jews.[60] He softened the blow to the Wartheland officials, anxious to be rid of their Jewish problem, by describing conditions in the Government General in such dark colors that they seemed worse than what Greiser and Koppe faced. But that was partly to defend himself against new pressures, for now that Jews were no longer a pressing issue for the Government General, the others wanted him to take in gypsies and Poles displaced from Germany and the annexed territories.

That broader agenda too was in accordance with Himmler's most recent plan. He had written up guidelines for the Germanization of the Eastern provinces and presented them to Hitler aboard the train on June 30; Hitler had said that they were correct on every point.[61] Himmler had recommended settlement by German and Nordic peasant farmers; history showed that otherwise the areas would never be secure. Foreign labor could be used temporarily for construction, but expulsions of the non-Germans would proceed step by step. Roughly one-eighth of the non-German population—Poles and other minorities—selected according to racial criteria—could settle in villages and cities where needed, whereas the remaining seven-eighths would have to go to the Government General. Hitler's approval meant that sooner or later Himmler would push this program to the limit, and the limit here meant seven million additional Poles for the Government General. So the pressure on Frank to take in more Poles was only beginning.

At the same meeting the Gauleiter and SS officials raised the issue of what was now to happen with the Jews. Greiser, who had spoken to Himmler the previous week,[62] said that Himmler had told him of the intention to deport the Jews to specified territories overseas. Krüger mentioned plans under consideration for the deportation of all Jews from the Government General abroad. Neither specifically mentioned Madagascar. Bruno Streckenbach, as commander of the Security Police and SD for the Government General, a subordinate to Heydrich and Himmler, stressed that precise information was lacking. His office had the task of determining how many Jews there were within Germany and the occupied territories, he said:

According to the plan up to now, the Jews are supposed to be shipped to Madagascar. When and how the shipping takes place is a question of the peace settlement. Whether they actually are supposed to come to Madagascar is also not yet finally determined.

Streckenbach's last comment, in particular, raised doubt as to whether any Jews would actually go to Madagascar. And he was in a position to be exceedingly well informed; he had met with Himmler and Dr. Gerhard Klopfer from the Party Chancellery only six days earlier.[63] He would have heard the latest about Himmler's and Hitler's viewpoint.

Madagascar was at best only one contingency plan. What was settled was that the Jews were to be removed in one way or another. And previous plans had already raised the idea of mass murder.

Hitler's own statements added further uncertainties. On August 3 he met with the new German ambassador to Paris, Otto Abetz, to discuss issues related to France. Hitler confirmed that he wanted to resolve the Jewish problem for all Europe, and that he wanted to force the conquered countries (and persuade Germany's allies) to send their Jewish citizens away. According to Abetz's postwar testimony, however, Hitler referred not to Madagascar as the destination, but to the United States. With a population density less than that of Europe, the United States was in a position to take in several million Jews.[64] The limited contemporary evidence of this conversation supports the notion that Hitler merely endorsed the idea of removing all Jews from Europe, not the concept of sending them specifically to Madagascar.[65]

Given Germany's recent inability to dispatch even thousands of Jews to the United States,[66] Hitler's mention of America was an absurdity—or a conscious evasion of realistic possibilities. He would have known that the United States was unwilling to absorb anything like the millions of Jews that Nazi Germany wanted to dispose of. What seemed to interest Hitler most was preparing people to accept the idea of removing all Jews from Europe, not determining a precise destination.

Perhaps one reason for Hitler's evasiveness was his new military objective. He had informed Brauchitsch and Halder that he intended to order the invasion and destruction of the Soviet Union in early 1941. Actually, Hitler's original inclination was to attack the U.S.S.R. in the fall of 1940, but practical objections raised by Jodl and Keitel apparently persuaded the Führer to change his mind. Russia could wait until the spring. The military authorities gave out a few basic instructions for preparations, but written orders were forbidden in July. Hitler's first instructions for "Operation Barbarossa," named after the red-bearded Holy Roman Emperor Frederick I who had led the First Crusade, did not come out until December.[67]

As early as July 11 Himmler had given a strong hint that he knew of the forthcoming campaign against the Soviets when he assured his SS recruitment chief, Gottlob Berger, that the Death's Head Division and the Police Division would not be demobilized (in spite of pressure from the army): "everything else verbally another time," Himmler added. He would not and could not put more in writing, even to Berger. Another sign that Himmler was already well informed about the Führer's intentions came on July 30. He asked Krüger to report to him every week on the progress of the antitank barrier being constructed along the border with the U.S.S.R. with the use of forced Jewish labor.[68]

Heydrich and Himmler had first mentioned this antitank ditch in early 1940 as a project that would employ a huge number of Polish Jews capable of labor. Heydrich had then alluded to separating the Jewish men capable of hard labor from their families, who would be thrown in with the Jews in the Government General, whereby the Jewish problem, he had said vaguely, might be resolved.[69] But military objections and Frank's opposition to resettlement had prevented the concentration of the bulk of Jewish laborers along the Eastern frontier.

Then, in May 1940, an energetic but disreputable accountant named Oscar Dirlewanger enlisted the help of the Führer Chancellery to gain entry into the Waffen-SS. Years earlier Dirlewanger had been convicted of having sex with a girl under the age of fourteen; he was sentenced to two years in prison. The Führer Chancellery had become convinced that judicial authorities had "erred," and Dirlewanger, a decorated World War I veteran who was partially disabled, was allowed to volunteer to fight in the Spanish Civil War. After his return to Germany, he was cleared. One of his supporters was Gottlob Berger, who brought Dirlewanger to Himmler's attention and who may have dreamed up a scheme to put Dirlewanger in charge of a battalion of poachers.[70] Himmler liked the idea and linked it up with the antitank barrier.

In mid-1940 Himmler suggested to Hitler that poachers serving time in prison, who were barred from military service, might be well employed in the East. A vegetarian, Hitler was a vehement opponent of hunting —he did not like the slaughter of helpless animals. But the Führer reacted with enthusiasm to Himmler's proposal to make better use of the men in the East.[71] Poachers had experience killing animals; they could instead help manage another species considered subhuman—the Jews. According to Berger, Hitler issued a written order to weld the prisoners into a commando unit to serve on Germany's eastern border.[72] On June 15, 1940, Himmler formally named Dirlewanger as Obersturmführer in the Waffen-SS and authorized him to collect poachers from the prisons.[73]

In a postwar interrogation, Berger claimed that Dirlewanger's unit suppressed banditry in the forests around Lublin.[74] Actually, Dirlewanger's battalion was first placed in charge of supervising several thousand Jewish laborers constructing a portion of the antitank line that Himmler had earlier suggested, filling a defensive gap between the Bug and San rivers.[75] No less a man than Odilo Globocnik praised Dirlewanger's leadership in glowing terms: "during the work on the Bug [River] ditch construction and in leadership of the camp for Jews at Dzikow, Dirlewanger managed his unit in outstanding fashion." Globocnik called Dirlewanger's activities "special employment" under his command.[76] Just what that praise meant for the Jewish laborers was hard to imagine.

According to an SS judicial investigator, Dirlewanger afterward, in the Lublin region, allegedly "caught Jews, imprisoned them and either had them shot or else released only if they could pay a certain amount of money; . . . he caused an entire section of Lublin to be surrounded, systematically looted and subsequently had the plunder sold by Jews; . . . shocking atrocities such as 'scientific experiments,' tortures etc. were performed on Jews." Dirlewanger also succumbed to his old weakness, having sex with some of the Jewish women.[77] If Himmler had had his way, the bulk of Polish Jews capable of labor would have been captives of men like Dirlewanger and Globocnik, who struck Himmler as the right sort for a tough job—supervising and punishing the Jews capable of hard labor.

A military campaign against the Soviet Union would have serious repercussions upon the Jewish question in the East. The Lublin reservation would no longer be "out of the way"; it would now be near the front lines, and the Nazis would perceive Jews as an immediate threat to their security. If the SS had earlier wanted to dispose of as many Jews as possible, the new phase of the war would provide all the more reason and opportunity to do so.

A war against the Soviet Union also called the whole Madagascar project into question, but planning for a massive deportation to the island continued. Perhaps there was still a chance of deporting the Western European Jews to Madagascar, where those who survived the climate and the hostile conditions would be hostages against the British and Americans. Or perhaps Himmler was not ready to reveal his hand even to the Jewish specialists in the RSHA. It is hard to draw firm conclusions about his intentions, given the lack of written evidence. Nonetheless, there is a kind of logic in the sequence of events in the West.

THE PRINCIPAL authors of the RSHA version of the Madagascar plan, probably Eichmann and Theo Dannecker, completed their specific proposal in August.[78] Madagascar was particularly suited to the creation of a Jewish reservation, they wrote, because of its "insular" character. Of course, Germany would have to exclude from the beginning "any possibility of Jewish self-rule" and to prevent any attempts at influence by the United States. The authors also calculated that with 120 ships carrying an average of fifteen hundred Jews each, the process of transporting four million Jews (from Germany, the Government General, the Protectorate of Bohemia-Moravia, Belgium, Holland, Luxembourg, Denmark, Norway, Slovakia, and France, but not from Spain, Portugal, Hungary, Rumania, Bulgaria, Greece, Italy, or Yugoslavia) would take about four years. All of this was to be financed through the confiscation of Jewish wealth, especially in the areas outside Germany. The director of the whole project would be Heydrich; there was little sign that anyone outside the SS would have a role.[79] Eichmann may have been gullible enough to believe the RSHA plan feasible, but the more experienced Heydrich probably was not.[80] There were too many diplomatic and military obstacles, and the whole project seemed to be of little purpose. Still, higher authorities did not openly reject the proposal.

Eichmann did not try to keep the project secret. In fact, he talked about it widely even before the plan went to the Foreign Office. In a series of conversations with the heads of the Berlin Jewish community during July, Eichmann explained that the fate of Europe's Jews was to go to Madagascar; the plans were all ready, he said.[81] But Eichmann in mid-1940 was not the insider that he later became. He certainly had no power to make any decisions, and it is most unlikely that he knew then what was going to take place.[82] He had to wait.

To be sure, the RSHA did not halt activities against Jews while awaiting a policy decision. In August, when other German authorities in occupied France began to lay the groundwork for separating the Jews from the rest of the population, Heydrich gave his approval but warned that the active participation of the Security Police experts in France was essential. He specifically noted that the German police authorities in France had already built the closest ties with their French counterparts, which would be useful in implementing measures directed against Jews within the occupied zone.[83]

The first noticeable steps, however, came in territory destined for annexation by Germany. Alsace and Lorraine, two provinces whose destiny had been determined by wars for centuries, became the first Western proving ground for Nazi measures to clear out Jews and other despised groups.

On July 1 Hitler conferred with Robert Wagner, Gauleiter of Baden, and Josef Bürckel, Gauleiter of the Saar-Palatinate, the two nearest German regions, regarding future policy in the areas. The Führer appointed Wagner as Reich representative in Alsace and Bürckel as chief of the civil administration in Lorraine. Not only did both provinces quickly receive a German administration; Germany also restored the customs borders that had existed from 1870 to 1918, when the provinces were German.[84]

There was little doubt that Hitler intended to annex Alsace and Lorraine. It was, however, clearly inadvisable to announce the annexation openly to the French. At the time, Hitler was anxious not to alienate the new Vichy government, out of concern that the French might throw their support and their fleet to the British, if the latter chose to fight on.[85] (On July 3, fearing that the French would surrender their fleet to the Germans, the British attacked and destroyed a major portion of the French fleet at Mers el-Kébir, Algeria.) Alsace and Lorraine were destined to be part of Germany, but they would have to wait for the formalities. On the other hand, there was little reason to delay a purge of groups and individuals regarded as hostile to Germany.

Later that month some three thousand Alsatian Jews were expelled into the unoccupied zone of France.[86] This expulsion suggested the possibility of parallel Nazi policies in the East and the West; like the Government General, Vichy France could be used as a dumping ground for undesirables purged from German territory. Having lost the war, the French were less able to prevent the deportations than Governor Frank was in the East. In the continuing armistice negotiations between General von Stülpnagel and the French General Huntziger at Wiesbaden, the French agreed to accept all Jews from Alsace and Lorraine with French citizenship.[87]

In spite of this apparent parallelism, Himmler did not practice massive dumping of Jews in the West. To send Jews over the demarcation line in France was to cede control over them to Vichy. Even though the Vichy regime was itself mistreating and incarcerating Jews, both out of domestic anti-Semitism and in order to court Germany (rather than as the result of German pressure),[88] there were no guarantees on how long this hostility would continue or how far it would go.

In early September Himmler made another inspection tour in the West, visiting Alsace, Lorraine, and Luxembourg. Although he gave some speeches to Waffen-SS audiences, he conducted more important business in private. After a briefing from the higher SS and police leader for Württemberg and Baden, Kurt Kaul, who had now taken on similar functions for Alsace, Himmler decided not to deport to France Alsatians of good racial stock who did not cause political difficulties. Such expulsions would simply give the French the benefit of German blood and leadership ability. Some Alsatians in this category had been included in the first round of deportations, which had begun in July, but Himmler's new policy was supposed to change that. There are indications that Himmler wanted the same policy for Lorraine.[89]

During the trip Himmler stopped at quarries at Senons and Natzweiler. Natzweiler was in the middle of the Vosges Mountains in Alsace, near a ski resort called Struthof. It was particularly isolated, windy, and normally cold, even in September—a good site, in other words, for a concentration camp, which the Nazis began to build a few months later. It could have become another place, like those camps in Silesia and at Mauthausen, where Jews could be worked to death. As it later turned out, however, Natzweiler was used primarily for other victims. The twenty-five thousand prisoners who later died at Struthof included captured members of the French resistance, Russian POWs, and eighty-seven Jews whose skulls and skeletons were needed for an anatomy collection by Professor August Hirt at the Reich University in Strasbourg.[90]

On September 25, 1940, the Führer held a second conference with Wagner and Bürckel, which Martin Bormann attended. After the two men gave a presentation about the situation in their new domains, Hitler said it was too soon to be thinking about introducing German laws into the provinces; first, the Gauleiter had to establish conditions similar to those in Germany itself. Hitler then pointed out that in the East the Gauleiter had the necessary "freedom of movement" to carry out the tasks that he assigned to them "through whatever means"—this was to be the situation in the West as well. Their basic task, he continued, was to carry out the Germanization of the regions within ten years, and he would not interrogate them about what methods they used to accomplish it.[91]

Bormann was deliberately circumspect in his summary of Hitler's instructions. To create conditions similar to those in Germany, as Wagner later specified, meant that the Führer had approved the "cleansing" of all aliens, patients, and unreliable elements. In other words, Hitler wanted to dispose of at least the Jews, gypsies, blacks, and patients who would in Germany fall victim to the euthanasia operations.[92] In his eyes, all of these groups represented either sources of contamination or defects in the German genetic pool.

Bürckel's interpretation of his mandate was even more extreme; he intended to expel the entire French-speaking population of Lorraine to clear the way for ethnic German settlers. When (Lorraine) Higher SS and Police Leader Berkelmann questioned him closely, Bürckel conceded that this policy was not precisely ordered by Hitler; it was his own decision, which he had communicated to the Führer. Bürckel was so impatient that he was unwilling to wait beyond the spring of 1941; all the Lorrainers were to have left by March 1 or April 1. He preferred to send the Lorrainers east in order to salvage the good blood, but if he had to dump them in France instead to meet his deadline, he would do so.[93]

SS and RSHA officials recognized that Alsace and Lorraine, under the circumstances, would each have different policies, and that these differences would cause complications.[94] With the Gauleiter citing their direct mandate from the Führer, however, the SS chiefs were not in a strong position. They could negotiate and try to postpone deadlines, but they could not reverse the policies outright.[95] Himmler and his subordinates had to adapt to what the two Gauleiter had initiated—all the more because they had no clear, preferable alternative. This constraint applied in much the same way to the deportation of the Jews. During the latter half of 1940 Himmler still had no place to put large numbers of Jews.

So it was that, between July and December 1940, 105,000 Alsatians— mainly Jews, gypsies, other aliens, criminals, "asocials," the insane, Frenchmen, and Francophiles—were deported into the unoccupied zone of France.[96] Wagner and Bürckel managed to carry their expulsion policy one step further—to extend it to their own domains within Germany proper.

The subject of expelling Jews from Baden and the Saar-Palatinate seems to have come up at Hitler's September 25 conference with Wagner and Bürckel, who probably wanted to clear out Jews from their *Gaue* there even more than from Alsace-Lorraine. One well-informed report specifically indicated that Wagner and Bürckel had proposed the deportations from southwestern Germany.[97] Less than a week later, the RSHA was carrying out investigations in Baden, and one subsequent RSHA memo declared that Hitler himself had ordered the deportation of the Jews from Alsace and Lorraine.[98]

On October 22, with notice ranging from fifteen minutes to two hours, 6,504 German Jews from Baden and the Saar-Palatinate carrying nothing more than a suitcase apiece were rounded up, placed on sealed trains, and sent to Lyon to the surprised French authorities there. The RSHA guidelines were that all Jews capable of transportation were to be included, and that mixed-bloods were exempt. One of those judged capable of transportation was at least ninety-seven years old. Not everyone made it; eight Jews in Mannheim and three in Karlsruhe committed suicide. The police sealed the vacated dwellings.[99]

Eichmann, who was not really in a position to know, later testified that Himmler had approved this deportation "impulsively," ignoring the complications.[100] The evidence suggests that Hitler gave his approval and that Himmler then acquiesced. But Eichmann's statement does convey the sense that Himmler was more attentive to the situation in the East than in the West, and that the deportations to the unoccupied zone of France did not really fit into Himmler's plans. Even in late October,

Himmler was not ready to ship German Jews to the East. Wagner and Bürckel had an immediate solution to their problems; Himmler did not.

The deportations westward could still be squared with the concept of shipment of Jews to Madagascar. One German report that reached the Foreign Office claimed that other German Jews, to a total of 270,000, were supposed to follow the route west, but that Vichy had protested and further deportations were suspended. The French government, which had decided to imprison those Jews already received in camps near the Pyrenees, would send them on to Madagascar when the sea route opened up, it was stated. A better intelligence report reached American diplomats in Switzerland. Some of the Jews would be sent to Madagascar, but others would be moved to the East.[101] That turned out to be about half right.

By this time the earlier hopes for Madagascar had faded. The Battle of Britain had failed to break the British will to resist, and the royal fleet stood in the way of any German quest for an African empire. The Madagascar plan continued to serve a purpose. It accustomed officials to the idea that the Jews were to be shipped off somewhere, and that the RSHA and the SS were in charge. Beginning in August 1940 Eichmann sent representatives to various states to prepare the way for subsequent deportations.[102] The SD opened branch offices in Nancy (Lorraine) and Besançon (Franche-Comte) for the purpose of seizing all Jews, Freemasons, and provocateurs as well as carrying out research on the racial makeup of the population.[103] The Madagascar plan was highly effective in enhancing the authority and reach of the RSHA—and of Heydrich. But Heydrich never signed off on the overall plan; Eichmann was still waiting for a decision from above in December.[104] SS activities in Silesia and the Government General had progressed by then, so Himmler did not tarry much longer.

On August 8, 1940, Himmler lunched at the Reich Chancellery and heard the Führer's latest pronouncements.[105] Two days later he held an unusually large conference in his office in the former Prince Albert Hotel, now the headquarters of the RSHA. Himmler rarely met with more than a few people at a time, but on this morning eleven key subordinates were there simultaneously.[106] If anyone kept notes, they do not survive, but it is not too much to assume that Himmler wanted to alert his subordinates to the forthcoming war against the Soviet Union and to elaborate on how this conflict would affect the SS empire in the East. Racial sifting of the Eastern population had been on Himmler's mind in June, and the presence of Otto Hofmann from the SS Race and Settlement Office is a good clue that that was one of the topics. If Himmler had decided to keep at least half of Europe's Jews in the East, as his

July discussion with Heinrich Müller seemed to indicate,[107] this may well have been the moment for Himmler and the others to consider how best to make use of these Jews.

Several times Hitler had spoken of annihilating Germany's enemies and of tackling sensitive problems in the event of war and under the cover of war. The Jews, the ultimate racial and ideological foe of Hitler and the Nazi movement, had not yet been the main target, because of perceived foreign-policy constraints. But the impending war against the Soviet Union was also, in Hitler's and Himmler's eyes, a war against a stronghold of the world Jewish conspiracy. One could not secure German rule over the vast expanse of Russia without dealing ruthlessly with the Jewish-Bolshevik menace. This was Hitler's long-established view,[108] which Himmler must have heard in private many times. If Himmler and the SS were not ready to help the Führer accomplish his goals, some competitor would step forward.

Some steps already taken moved the Nazis closer to the goal of making the East *judenfrei*. Both the imposition of labor under brutal and primitive conditions and the ghettoization policy in Poland, which was about to resume, were bound to lead to a high rate of attrition; meanwhile, profits from economic activities could be used within the SS empire. Himmler implicitly recognized the importance of economic considerations in the SS empire in a September 9 speech to SS officers in Metz:

> If the entire Corps [i.e., the SS] really is an order . . . [then everyone recognizes that] one part is not conceivable without the other. . . .
> We are not conceivable without the economic enterprises. Part of this must remain unknown to most of you, because it is never to be spoken of. I want to tell you a little piece more: the construction of housing, which is the precondition for a sound and social foundation for the entire SS as for the entire leadership corps, is not conceivable if I do not get the money from someplace or other. No one gives me the money as a present—it must be earned, and it is earned by putting the scum of humanity, the inmates, the habitual criminals, to work.[109]

To Himmler, Jews capable of labor certainly qualified as the scum of humanity.

The first step had to be to concentrate Jewish labor under tightly controlled conditions. Since Frank had temporarily prevented the concentration of all German and Polish Jews in the Lublin district, a more diverse geographical plan was necessary. Just how far the discussion went at that August 10 meeting or afterward can only be estimated by subsequent hints, statements, and actions. Two days later Pohl spoke with Rudolf Brandt about getting tools for the antitank ditch in the East, so the use of Jewish labor there was still part of the picture.[110]

Further plans for forced-labor projects came out in September when Erich von dem Bach-Zelewski, higher SS and police leader for Silesia, met with Himmler in Berlin. Himmler and Bach-Zelewski both still wanted to deport the Silesian Jews to the Government General, but Frank's opposition had made this impossible, Bach wrote in a letter to Karl Wolff. Consequently, he continued, Himmler had decided to round up the Jews and also the unemployed Poles in the area, to place them in closed camps in Silesia, and to use them for stone breaking and road construction. Bach-Zelewski also noted that this new task would take years, which was longer than was envisioned for the planned war against the Soviet Union.[111] So those Silesian Jews were not destined for Madagascar and not for the Government General either.

Silesia, where Deputy Gauleiter Fritz Bracht was highly cooperative, provided plenty of opportunities for forced-labor projects and land for new concentration camps. In fact, at least one new concentration camp in Silesia, Gross-Rosen, was established in August 1940. In the company of Bach-Zelewski, Himmler inspected the stone-breaking operations there on October 28.[112] But the establishment of labor camps and concentration camps was not limited to Silesia. Himmler soon approved a new branch of Mauthausen to be called Gusen.[113] Not far from Vienna, Mauthausen was at that time the deadliest of all the concentration camps. Other steps, such as the digging of canals, work on river-control mechanisms, and the building of roads and railways, took place in Silesia, the Wartheland, and the Government General. The Nazis used primitive labor camps for these Jews, and forced-labor columns for heads of families whose other members remained behind in ghettos.[114] Together they represented a more systematic effort to harness Jewish labor for the profit of the SS.

Given the severe shortage of labor and the SS's need for funds, this labor policy was nothing if not practical. Yet it was clear from the beginning that profit was not the only, or even the dominant, motive behind the use of forced Jewish labor. In many places the conditions were designed to work Jews to death: minimal food and clothing, exhausting labor all day long every day.[115] That was not how one maintained a productive labor force for any length of time.

There were other clues in the summer and fall of 1940 that the regime of forced labor was merely a step along the road to a *judenfrei* East. In a letter to Interior Minister Frick on August 21, in response to the ministry's proposal to introduce the Nuremberg Racial Laws in the newly annexed Eastern territories, Ulrich Greifelt discouraged use of the laws in the East at this time. Uniform guidelines for deciding who belonged to the German *Volk*, Greifelt wrote, were still being worked out. He revealed that a Führer directive had set the maximum number of assimilable Poles in the annexed territories at one million—this was, of course, Himmler's formula, which Hitler had approved. Then Greifelt explained that he saw no reason to introduce laws to protect the non-assimilable Poles from breeding with Jews, since "a final cleansing of the Jewish question and the mixed-blood question was foreseen for after the war."[116]

On September 11 Reinhard Heydrich wrote a memo for the files that is even more revealing, though it contains no mention of the Jewish question. Analyzing proposals for the Germanization of the mixed-blooded (German-Slavic) elements in Bohemia-Moravia, Heydrich pointed out that the first necessary step was a racial census of the population. Then one could decide what percentage of German blood was necessary to qualify a person for Germanization, and then one could look at subjective qualities (such as behavior). Those of good stock who were unfriendly to Germany might be sent into Germany proper; if they refused to go, at least their children might be taken away and sent, Heydrich wrote. Those not suitable for Germanization presented a problem. If they were all pushed into a reservation in Bohemia, how could one make Bohemia entirely German? One could only set the *imaginary goal* of "evacuating these remaining Czechs to a *currently imaginary Government*" [my italics].[117]

Heydrich's basic consideration in the fall of 1940 was not how to make the best use of non-German labor. Hitler and Himmler had decided, on grounds of racial ideology and because of the need to provide living space for Germans, that only a limited number of foreigners would be acceptable within German territory in spite of the shortage of labor. Foreign laborers who were brought in were to be segregated carefully. The most fundamental problem was where to put those who did not fit in or who represented a threat—or how to get rid of them.

The Jews were considered completely unassimilable and dangerous. There had once been a place to which Jews could be deported temporarily—the reservation in the Government General—but first Governor Frank refused to take more in, and then the impending war with the Soviet Union precluded leaving Jews there to die off or gradually be killed. As the Nazi leaders saw it, a Lublin reservation would have been a breeding ground of opposition to Nazi rule over an Eastern empire. The same logic would apply to the existence of Jewish ghettos in the major Polish cities. What remained was an imaginary goal of evacuating Jews to an identified but unfeasible destination—Madagascar. With Madagascar serving as a cover, Himmler and the SS leadership had to work out the actual plans for disposing of large numbers of Jews in the East.

The establishment of closed ghettos in other major Polish cities was not a sign of any decision at the top to maintain Jewish lives. Whereas ghetto administrators deliberated over the problems of keeping Jews alive and producing on minimal rations, Heydrich was thinking along different lines. One of the officials on Frank's staff told anti-Nazi German diplomat Ulrich von Hassell in October 1940 that there was an open campaign to exterminate Polish Jews and the Polish intelligentsia systematically. Sometime after the closing of the Warsaw ghetto behind high walls in October–November 1940, Heydrich told the chief SS physician, Ernst Grawitz, that he should start an epidemic there and exterminate the Jews in that way. Grawitz claimed to have resisted the idea.[118]

In December 1940 a Pole living in Warsaw wrote a long analysis of conditions and Nazi policies in Poland, which he managed to get to the United States Embassy in Berlin. The unnamed Pole pointed out that about 40 percent of the Jews in Poland had already been forced into closed ghettos, which were designed to isolate them and make them absolute paupers. Once they were eliminated from Polish society and proved to be superfluous, the Nazis would be able to exterminate them after Germany won the war. Extermination would then be a purely technical matter. It was as good a description as any of the strategies that the American diplomat Geist had forecast before the war: concentration, isolation, pauperization, disposal of as many as possible by force.[119]

One man who had already developed a more advanced method of disposing of substantial numbers of people was Viktor Brack, the section chief in the Führer Chancellery who was running the "euthanasia" operations. The son of a doctor, Brack was an engineer who had long been close to the head of the Führer Chancellery, Philipp Bouhler. The six killing centers within Germany equipped with gas chambers and crematoria that Brack had built up constituted a system that was eliminating thousands of people each month.

The prevailing practice in the "euthanasia" program was to have doctors select those patients in hospitals and asylums who were incapable of performing useful service to society. People so designated were gathered up and shipped off to the killing centers. The question arose whether Jewish patients were to be treated any differently. In April 1940 Dr. Herbert Linden asked local officials to report to him the number of Jewish patients in their asylums. During the summer these Jewish patients were moved from their original institutions into certain designated asylums. Beginning in July there were a number of selections of Jewish patients who were quickly sent off to the gas chambers, regardless of their capacity for work.[120]

On August 30 the Interior Ministry issued a circular calling for all Jewish patients to be concentrated in a single institution within each state or province.[121] On September 13 Brack met with Himmler in Berlin to discuss common business, which may have included the liquidation of these Jews in the gassing facilities.[122] Coincidentally or not, in November 1940 Brack received a promotion to Oberführer in the SS and an honorary appointment to Himmler's staff.[123]

The next time Brack was scheduled to see Himmler was on December 13, two days after a scheduled meeting of the Reichsleiter and Gauleiter, but Himmler canceled the appointment.[124] Still, from a letter that Himmler wrote to Brack shortly afterward, we know some of what was on Himmler's mind. More and more information about the "euthanasia" killings was leaking out to the public, and the criticism was affecting the reputation of the SS. In the vicinity of the mental institution Grafeneck, in Württemberg, Himmler wrote:

> The population recognizes the gray automobile of the SS and think they know what is going on at the constantly smoking crematory. What happens there is a secret and yet is no longer one. Thus, the worst feeling has arisen there, and in my opinion there remains only one thing to do, to discontinue the use of the institution in this place and, in any case, disseminate information in a clever and sensible manner by showing motion pictures on the subject of inherited and mental diseases in just that locality. May I ask for a report on how the difficult problem was solved.[125]

In fact, Grafeneck was quickly shut down.[126]

If Himmler was not entirely happy with Brack's euthanasia operation, Brack was not quite at ease with the direction of Jewish policy. Knowing that Jews from the asylums were being killed as Jews, regardless of their capacity to work, Brack must have sensed the forthcoming direction of Jewish policy. After the war a skilled American interrogator, Fred Rodell, pried an account out of Brack under circumstances that maximized the likelihood of honest, if not complete, testimony.[127]

> With knowledge of the plans of the leadership of state to destroy the Jews fully, I and my coworkers, however, adopted a contrary viewpoint. In spite of all the damage that the Jews might have done

to Germany, I was of the opinion that this sort of radical solution was unworthy of the German people and of humanity generally. On account of this I first developed an idea that, to my knowledge, was thrown into the debate by my coworker Dr. Hefelmann—that is, to create for the Jews their own state. The island of Madagascar was foreseen for such a purpose. . . . This suggestion was worked out in writing and presented to Reichsleiter Bouhler. . . . I do not know whether the Reichsleiter then took this suggestion to the Führer or passed it on to the Reich Führer SS [but it was not accepted].

Brack could not recall exactly when he had written up this proposal, but dated it no later than the end of 1940. Otherwise, he said, Madagascar could not have even been considered.[128] His next suggestion, mass sterilization of the Jews, can be found in the surviving records; since it first appears in March 1941, the Madagascar proposal had to be earlier. A 1945 inventory of Himmler's papers lists some statistical material on Jewish emigration, the death rate among Jews, numbers of Jews left in the Reich, and "suggestions to solve the Jewish question." This material was dated November 11, 1940.[129]

Rodell pressed Brack on the significance of his testimony:

Q: You know, your statement implies that the destruction of the Jews was already decided in 1940.

A: May I say on that that I in no case heard anything officially.

Q: What does it mean to hear nothing officially? It was an open secret in high party circles.

A: Yes, that is the right designation.[130]

Brack was not the only one to recognize the general course in the East that loomed ahead. Himmler's former mentor and current antagonist Walther Darré had once been the head of the SS Race and Settlement Office. He still had plenty of contacts in the SS. In November 1940 Darré wrote an article on the Jewish question for his own journal, *Odal*, in which he revealed that the Nazis would not cease efforts to resolve the Jewish question even if the Jews reached Madagascar:

Is the goal achieved when Europe is cleared of Jews, when the last Jew emigrates to his new home overseas? We must answer no to this question, just as much for Europe as for Germany. One will never understand the full seriousness of this question if one simply follows the outward sequence of events.[131]

Darré clearly implied that there was a general goal already in existence that went well beyond emigration.

The first indispensable step still involved massive deportations to the East. To send Jews to Poland meant to overcome Hans Frank's resistance to all further deportations, which was not an easy matter. Himmler needed help from above to break the deadlock. This was accomplished in stages. On October 2 Hitler held a conference with Frank and several high party officials in his own residence in Berlin. Frank reported that the Jews in Warsaw and other cities were now shut up in ghettos, and that Cracow would soon be free of Jews; his policies had been successful. But others demanded that the Government General now take in their Jews. Hitler managed to avoid saying anything (or at least Martin Bormann did not record anything) about the Jewish question, but he did specify that he didn't care how high the population density in Poland went; it could go higher. The Poles were born to be unskilled workers, and Poland was to be a reservoir of cheap labor for Germany—one vast labor camp. The lowest German worker and farmer must be at least 10 percent better off than any Polish counterpart. The Polish elite, he said, were to be killed. If that was not enough pressure, Hitler later told Frank of his urgent wish that the Government General accept more Poles.[132]

Actually, even before Hitler's second meeting with Frank, there had been a significant change in policy toward Jews in the Government General. In late October the RSHA issued a new decree, banning the emigration of Jews from Poland,[133] a step that Frank had previously opposed. Frank wanted to be rid of some of his Jews, not forced to keep them.

The RSHA's explanation of the ban revealed that the Eastern Jews were particularly dangerous. Their emigration signified a "lasting spiritual regeneration of world Jewry," as a consequence of their orthodox religious attitude and the large numbers of rabbis and Talmudic scholars. These Jews could strengthen the Jewish organizations in the United States and enable them to wage their struggle against Germany even better. Hence the United States would probably give preference to these Jews from the Government General in immigration-visa applications, and for this reason Germany should deny them the possibility of leaving.[134] Following the same logic about the potential regeneration of world Jewry, the RSHA and the SS would have to get rid of the Eastern Jews permanently. But this conclusion would not have gone into a published decree.

On October 26 Himmler and Frank had lunch at Frank's castle in

Cracow. That evening they went together to the state theater, which put on a production of Gotthold Ephraim Lessing's *Minna von Barnhelm*.[135] Frank's choice of play was peculiar, given the cultural views of his guest. An eighteenth-century man of the Enlightenment, Lessing was famous for many achievements, but prominent among them was his play *Nathan the Wise*, an attack on the prevailing hostility toward Jews. Nathan, the hero, was an enlightened, wise, and humane Jew. If Frank could appreciate good culture whatever its political content, Himmler could not; his politics informed his aesthetic judgments. Lessing, though racially impeccable, was on Himmler's blacklist.

One way or another, Frank got the message that the new ban on Jewish emigration had sufficient backing in Berlin. On November 23 his office accepted the RSHA's viewpoint and notified district chiefs throughout the Government General to reject all Jewish applications to emigrate except those from Jews of foreign citizenship. Frank's office, it was stated, would decide in this last category.[136] Frank thereby preserved a shred of jurisdiction over the Jewish question.

Later, in Berlin, Frank had another opportunity to gauge the approved line of policy. On December 10 Himmler was the featured speaker at the meeting of Reichsleiter and Gauleiter in Berlin. Among other things, Himmler talked of the need to make the Eastern provinces German and of the limit of one million racially acceptable non-Germans. He explained also that there were to be primarily farm settlements in the East, but that cities and industry were acceptable, provided that population density did not exceed recommended levels. He stressed the need for merciless German domination of the foreign elements, and the use of foreign labor during the period of development. He spoke again of the struggle against the Polish intelligentsia. Finally, he referred to the Government General as the reservation for seasonal and one-time workers, and he said Jewish emigration would create more space for Poles in the Government General.[137] He apparently did not discuss the recent ban on Jewish emigration from the Government General, which might have seemed a divergence from the general line that Poland was to be cleared of Jews.

After the two-day meeting ended, Hitler had another opportunity to talk to Frank. This time he specified that the Government General had to take in Poles and Jews soon; after the war, he warned, there would be too many international difficulties.[138] Frank could no longer misunderstand or delay; Himmler had won.

Hitler intervened to prevent Frank from causing trouble about further deportations of Jews to Poland, and the RSHA had the authority to plan for the removal of all Jews from Europe. Himmler was working out plans to dispose of Jewish laborers profitably in the East. Globocnik had already begun the killing of Jews in his region, and the establishment of closed ghettos in major Polish cities represented a tightening of the noose on Jewish communities outside Lublin. By the end of 1940 Himmler had established the major elements of a general policy to resolve the Jewish question in Europe. The timing, methods, and numbers were far from settled, but the general goal was becoming clear even to some individuals outside the charmed circle of the SS leadership.

Judging from Frank's version of what Hitler told him on December 11, Hitler had at least hinted at what was to come. The Führer had told him of an old Japanese saying, which was still valid: "After victory, bind the helm faster." Then, in sympathizing with those who had to put up with the lice and Jews in the Government General, Frank commented: "In a year I could get rid of neither all the lice nor all the Jews (laughter). But in the course of time . . . , if you help me, that will be accomplished."[139] One did not get rid of lice by transporting them to Madagascar.

CHAPTER 7

▼▼▼▼▼▼▼▼▼▼▼▼▼▼▼▼▼▼

TOWARD THE
FINAL SOLUTION

HITLER'S determination to invade the Soviet Union came in the face of his previous concern about the danger of a two-front war. But an independent Russia, he later told Martin Bormann, bolstered British hopes of outlasting Germany, and time, he was convinced, was working in favor of the enemies. With the Americans becoming increasingly active in the diplomatic and economic sphere against Germany, he had to wipe out the Russian menace soon to avoid a war of endurance that Germany could not win. Russia's very existence, Hitler also observed, was a threat to Germany.[1] The conquest of *Lebensraum* in the East had been the focal point of Hitler's foreign policy since the 1920s; now his long- and short-term objectives, and his ideology, were all tightly fused together.[2]

Hitler's War Directive No. 21, entitled Case Barbarossa, reflected this combination. The German armed forces were instructed not only to crush Soviet Russia prior to the conclusion of the war against Great Britain in a rapid campaign; they were told of the final objective, a barrier against "Asiatic Russia" along the imaginary line from the Volga River to Archangel. If successful, Barbarossa would thus place most of European Russia in German hands.

There was no military reason to draw a line from the Volga to Archangel. Russian troops beyond that point would still have been a threat.[3] The line was not so much a destination for German troops as a goal for future German settlers. Hitler had to be thinking of a permanent racial boundary between Germans and Slavs: as much *Lebensraum* as the Aryan race needed and could control. In September 1941 he would tell his evening coterie that it was foolish to regard the the Ural Mountains as the automatic boundary between Europe and Asia; one could just as easily take one of the Russian rivers: "the boundary will be where the

Nordic-German population branches off from the Slavic." Germany's task was to make that boundary where it wished.[4]

Hitler and his military planners had crossed swords a number of times, once, for example, over whether the northern spearhead of the three-pronged thrust should head for Moscow or secure the Baltic States and Leningrad. Modifications of Barbarossa delayed Hitler's signing until December 18, 1940.[5] That same day Hitler gave a speech to a new class of officer cadets, and Himmler delivered one to the commanders of the Waffen-SS, in which he stressed the importance of unity and racial ideology within all branches of the SS.[6]

That evening Himmler went over to the Reich Chancellery.[7] There are no surviving records of what was discussed, but it is reasonable to suppose that Hitler spoke about the significance of what he had now ordered. Himmler would have been particularly interested in defining and securing the SS's role in the coming campaign against the Soviets. With Hitler's support, he had for some time been expanding and re-organizing the Waffen-SS.[8] The role of the police units in the U.S.S.R. was still to be determined.

During the invasion of Poland the *Einsatzgruppen* had liquidated thousands of prominent Poles and Jews under the cover of war. Likewise, the spring-1940 offensive in the West had allowed SS authorities to resume the executions of leading Poles. Now there was to be a gigantic new military campaign against a Jewish-dominated Asiatic foe—or so Hitler and Himmler believed. Whatever comments about the Jews Hitler made on this occasion, Himmler felt free to proceed with far-reaching plans over the next few months.

Toward the end of December Himmler received a letter from the Reich Commissioner of Holland, Arthur Seyss-Inquart, extending greetings and best wishes for the New Year. Himmler returned New Year's greetings and lauded Seyss-Inquart's task of restoring nine million Nordic-Dutch to the German people:

> We are both absolutely clear about the fact that this task of creating a Nordic community of some 110 million is the foundation for a truly great Nordic Reich. I would be very pleased if I could welcome you as my guest at Wewelsburg for a couple of quiet days this year. The quiet and the contemplation of the castle will give us the leisure and the opportunity to be able to discuss many important and ultimate matters.[9]

Himmler had extensively renovated this castle, once a mountain fortress used by the Saxons against the invading Huns, rebuilt into triangular shape in the seventeenth century. Concentration-camp laborers had extracted and transported new stone from a nearby quarry. Decorated with medieval or ancient swords, knives, suitable paintings, sculpture, and archeological discoveries from across Europe, Wewelsburg provided the right historical setting for Himmler and his elite in which to meditate and to work out the ideology of the SS. But the castle was officially camouflaged as an SS school.[10]

Erich von dem Bach-Zelewski later testified that at the beginning of 1941 Himmler had held a meeting of twelve SS-Gruppenführer, including Bach-Zelewski, at Wewelsburg.[11] Himmler claimed that the purpose of the Russian campaign was to reduce the indigenous population by some thirty million.[12] Whether or not all those millions were to be murdered, a population reduction on that scale would certainly create plenty of room for German settlers.

Alfred Rosenberg may have learned something about the scope of killings and designs for mass starvation in the U.S.S.R. a few months later. After he met with Hitler on April 2, he noted in his diary: "What I do not write down today, I will nonetheless never forget." Just before the attack on the U.S.S.R., Rosenberg told his subordinates of the hard necessity that lay ahead—a very sizable evacuation of Russians. The economic specialists for the East were more blunt during their preparations for the war: tens of millions of Russians (in the North alone) would die or be sent to Siberia.[13]

Heydrich had the reputation of being able to carry out any job immediately, and now he was put to the test. In January 1941 the administrative officials in the RSHA were instructed to prepare for a large police action in broad areas.[14] Heydrich's police units might not have a free hand in the Soviet Union, given their difficulties with the military in Poland. But Himmler's efforts during early 1940 to "educate" the officer corps were not entirely without results, and the Army High Command had become more pliant. In addition, the Bolsheviks were a traditional foe of the conservative German military elite. There were greater prospects now for cooperation between the SS and the army. Because of the scale of the planned killings in the Soviet Union, the huge area involved, and the need for the police units to move freely and quickly, such cooperation was essential if the *Einsatzgruppen* were to be successful.

Himmler and Heydrich would not have gone to the army before they were ready—and confident of Hitler's backing. Until now historians have found no trace of operational plans or of negotiations with the army until March 1941. Actually, Heydrich contacted the army hierarchy earlier, but managed to keep most of the deliberations secret and unrecorded.

A peculiar civilian unit known as Sonderkommando Künsberg, a Foreign Office commando unit commanded by an SS officer named Künsberg, accidentally uncovered some of these secret proceedings and left a record for posterity. During the Western offensive in the spring of 1940 Künsberg had seized foreign government records and precious metals in the Low Countries and France. Apart from the commander and his staff, Sonderkommando Künsberg had a scholarly section, an administrative section, and a transport section—just over one hundred men and a dog. Later Künsberg's unit underwent five weeks of additional training, going on long marches while carrying heavy loads, and by December Künsberg, with an expanded unit, was eager for more action. Eventually he got it, but not quite as he had thought or intended.[15]

In January 1941 Künsberg bombarded Himmler's office with phone calls requesting the admission of his unit into the Waffen-SS. The busy Himmler at first left the decision to Wolff, who seems to have turned Künsberg down, but Künsberg persisted in trying to reach Himmler directly.[16] Himmler confirmed that the kind of work done by Sonderkommando Künsberg did not really fit into the Waffen-SS. If Künsberg was so enthusiastic, however, Himmler knew where he could be used. Heydrich was already scraping up men to fill the *Einsatzgruppen*, Security Police units by another name. In early-February discussions with Künsberg and a liaison from the Foreign Office, Heydrich revealed that he had already begun negotiations with the commander-in-chief of the army regarding the use of the Security Police alongside the combat troops. Heydrich noted in passing that the negotiations with Brauchitsch had gone well, and that a formal agreement was expected soon. These police units would be SS units but would carry out "special tasks" in conjunction with the military and further police tasks, he said, including the capture and arrest of "persons of political interest" after the conquest of enemy territory. This was a most tactful way of describing what would eventually take place. Quite in contrast to Heydrich's methods, the Foreign Office man wrote all of this down and then put through a written request for equipment and other forms of support from the Security Police.[17] Whether because of the pressure of other business (war planning) or the sensitivity of the issues, however, completion of the agreement was delayed.

Other signs of forthcoming mass murder began to mount. On February 26 Göring told economic specialist General Georg Thomas of the High Command of the Armed Forces that with the occupation of the U.S.S.R. would come a rapid liquidation of the Bolshevik leaders. On March 3 General Alfred Jodl of the Operations Staff of OKW passed along to subordinates the Führer's guidelines for the planned military administration in the conquered areas of the Soviet Union. According to Hitler's instructions, the forthcoming war was more than a "mere armed conflict"; it was a collision between two ideologies. Accordingly, the Bolshevist-Jewish intelligentsia had to be eliminated. The military was to control as little territory as possible, its supreme authority restricted to the immediate areas of military operations. Civilian commissioners would rule over the rest, accompanied by police authorities. Whether the nonmilitary police (here Hitler referred specifically to organs of the Reich Führer SS) would also be needed in the operational areas was a matter that the military would have to clear with Himmler, but he added: "the necessity to neutralize Bolshevik leaders and commissars immediately is an argument in favor [of it]." With that, Hitler made the outcome of the military's talks with Himmler a foregone conclusion. He specifically excluded the use of military courts-martial for such operations; courts-martial would deal only with legal matters within the military. Two days later Quartermaster General Eduard Wagner told Army General Staff Chief Franz Halder that the army was not supposed to be "burdened" with administration in Russia. And on March 13 the redrafted OKW guidelines, now conforming to Hitler's wishes, provided for Himmler to carry out special tasks in the operational areas that were assigned by the Führer. He was to act independently and on his own responsibility in carrying out his mission, and he was to avoid disturbing military operations. He was supposed to arrange the details with the army directly.[18]

At least twice more that month Hitler emphasized the need to liquidate the bearers of Bolshevism, and on the second occasion, a speech to some 250 senior officers from the three armed services, he made it plain that the military too would have to play a role in this campaign. The German troops would have to hand over captured communist functionaries and political commissars to the *Einsatzkommandos*, or, if that was impossible, shoot the captives themselves; these people were not to be regarded as prisoners of war. Hitler's March 30 speech provided part of the impetus for one of the most infamous military orders of the war, which came to be known as the Commissar Order—the execution of alleged Soviet commissars without trial.[19] In all likelihood, there was more behind this order than a simple desire to liquidate the Communist political officials assigned to the Russian army. Nazi propaganda dating back to 1935 closely identified commissars and party functionaries with Jews, and many German officers had come to accept this equation. The Commissar Order was a means to make use of the German military's anti-Bolshevist sentiment, which years of indoctrination had enhanced. The order would involve the army in the planned liquidations of commissars and move it toward acceptance of the general killings of Jews. The Armed Forces High Command guidelines for the troops in Russia, in fact, called for merciless intervention against Jews, Bolshevist agitators, guerrillas, and saboteurs; Jews qualified simply because of their race.[20]

To be sure, not all officers would go along easily with measures to liquidate civilians without trial. According to the wartime testimony of a Major Bechler at Hitler's headquarters, Brauchitsch knew that the army commanders would object to the Commissar Order, so he sent Lieutenant General Eugen Müller around to explain the necessity of the order. There still were objections, particularly from Field Marshals von Bock and von Kluge, but Hitler insisted on compliance.[21]

During March Gestapo chief Heinrich Müller and General Wagner were working on a draft agreement to regulate the relationship of the army and the police units.[22] Himmler gave Heydrich specific instructions regarding this draft,[23] but the first version, completed on March 26, did not give the *Einsatzgruppen* a free hand. It conceded to the commando units the right to carry out Security Police tasks, but allowed the army commander-in-chief to exclude them from areas where they might disturb operations. Moreover, the draft mentioned only *Einsatzgruppen* activities in the areas of the rear army groups, away from the front lines. Heydrich noticed the omission and wanted a provision for arrangements on the front lines.[24]

When it became clear that personal animosity between Müller and Wagner was complicating the problems, Heydrich turned negotiations over to his foreign-intelligence expert, Walter Schellenberg, who was able to secure an agreement that mitigated the restrictions. In the new version, the *Einsatzgruppen* received their instructions from the chief of the Security Police and SD, but were subordinate to the commander of the rear army group with regard to marching orders, quarters, and rations. The army commander-in-chief had to approve measures that could affect operations. Since Brauchitsch had cooperated already on a range of other matters,[25] the agreement left the *Einsatzgruppen* reasonably free. And there was a new provision for smaller *Sonderkommandos* to operate directly with the regular troops in the fighting areas.[26]

The general idea of the extermination of millions in the East, born no later than January 1941, produced specific written arrangements between the RSHA and the army in late April. The orders, of course, could not be implemented until the attack on the Soviet Union, originally scheduled for mid-May and delayed until June. There was thus a hiatus of at least six months between the initial planning and the execution.

Heydrich's SD provided the biggest percentage of the leadership of the mobile police units, but Himmler reserved the final right of decision over the selection of commanders. The size of each of the four units (subdivided into *Einsatzkommandos* and *Sonderkommandos*) ranged between six hundred and a thousand.[27] An overall strength of just over three thousand was very small for the task at hand.

Even before the commanders were chosen, the RSHA provided some direction to a select group of its higher officials. Two different individuals later recalled that in March or April 1941 there was a secret RSHA meeting to discuss the role of the mobile police units in the coming campaign. Heydrich and/or Müller (the accounts vary) spoke about Hitler's decision to invade the Soviet Union, a war that Müller said would last eight weeks or so, and about the forthcoming role of the *Einsatzgruppen*. According to the more detailed account given by a former priest turned Nazi named Albert Hartl, Müller asked his desk chiefs who were responsible for the various enemy groups to submit written recommendations on the measures to be taken, and Adolf Eichmann offered a proposal to exterminate all the Jews in Russia. Eichmann subsequently boasted about his proposal to Hartl, who did not at first take him seriously.[28] Hartl's testimony about Eichmann is all the likelier in that Eichmann (contrary to his postwar statements) was by this time aware of a similar extermination policy for at least the German Jews, which had come down from above.

HEYDRICH needed a replacement for the Madagascar plan, designed to remove all Jews from the continent, in accordance with Hitler's statements of 1940. In early February 1941 letters to the Foreign Office expert on Jewish policy, Martin Luther (whom Heydrich was not likely to entrust with any secrets[29]), Heydrich reaffirmed the RSHA's intention to carry out a total evacuation of Jews from the continent; the destination could be chosen later, he said, probably disingenuously.[30] But it appears that he was working toward a total evacuation by geographical stages.

In January Heydrich had already approved a "near-term plan" to resettle, during 1941, 831,000 people from the Eastern provinces of Germany (and the Viennese Jews) into the Government General. Simultaneously, the military's demands for territory for training and maneuvers required the expulsion of another two hundred thousand. Frank and his subordinates continued to stress the difficulties involved, even if they no longer contested the fundamental decision. There was talk of getting outside assistance from the Reich to feed and quarter the newcomers.

This first plan included some Jews, but it was not fundamentally aimed at resolving the Jewish question: it was designed to clear space for ethnic Germans to settle in the Eastern provinces. The whole process—expulsion of Jews and Poles, immigration of ethnic Germans from Eastern Europe, seizure or creation of farmsteads for SS men or army veterans—was called "re-Germanization." It required further negotiations with Frank and his subordinates.[31]

Second, Heydrich also worked out a secret plan for the deportation of what seems to have been most Jews from the Old Reich (Germany's pre-1938 boundaries) to the Government General.[32] Two existing and independent (if imperfect) documents refer to this scheme. At a mid-March 1941 meeting in the Propaganda Ministry, Eichmann revealed that about two months earlier Heydrich had presented a plan to the Führer for the "final evacuation" of the (German) Jews to Poland, and that only the limited absorptive capacity of the Government General was temporarily holding up implementation.[33] In other words, Hitler had already approved it. In 1942 two German officials, one in the Foreign Office and one in the War Ministry, claimed to have seen a signed Hitler order, dated January 1941, to make Germany *judenfrei* by the end of 1942.[34]

If Hitler did in fact sign such an order, it would not have been unprecedented. He had used his own stationery and signature to provide general authorization for the Führer Chancellery to proceed with the euthanasia program in the fall of 1939. He had also used similarly vague language then. To those who knew nothing of the details, it did not sound quite so horrendous to consider granting a merciful death to the incurably ill. But the actual program was to kill those considered genetically defective or merely a burden upon the food supply. Similarly, to make Germany free of Jews was a goal that did not sound so criminal. There were various ways to rid Germany of its Jews, but the SS had long since possessed a plan to kill as many as possible.

Himmler had taken the same approach for Poland: forcing adult male Jews to work under conditions where many would die, ghettoization as preparation for the elimination of as many of the rest as possible. The RSHA had also worked out a plan for the deportation of Jews from most of the countries of Europe, and had sent Jewish advisers to some of them. Though Hitler had by now rejected Madagascar as a destination, those Jews could soon be directed to Poland, where they would receive the same treatment as the Polish Jews.

A more "moderate" option was a proposal to sterilize millions of Jews. Euthanasia manager Viktor Brack had thoroughly investigated the possibility of sterilizing people through the use of powerful X-rays. After consulting an expert physician, Brack described a procedure in which an official, sitting behind a counter, would go through the motions of requiring individuals to fill out some forms for two or three minutes. While the subjects were engaged, the official would activate an X-ray machine without his subjects' knowing it. Brack estimated that at a reasonable cost some twenty installations of this kind could each sterilize 150–200 persons per day in this way—a total of three to four thousand per day. The only disadvantage was that side effects would soon show up, and the men and women would eventually learn what had happened. In his late-March 1941 memo to Himmler, Brack did not discuss who the intended subjects were, but after the war he admitted that this proposal was another effort to resolve the Jewish question short of mass murder.[35] At the rate Brack projected, the sterilization procedure could have dealt with the entire German Jewish population in no time, and even the remaining masses of Polish Jews could have been processed in a couple of years.

In actuality, research on "concealed sterilization" had a longer history and was considered for even broader use. According to reports by a Swiss doctor named Theo Lang who worked at the Munich Psychiatric Institute until 1941, the idea arose initially because of growing resistance to application of Germany's law for compulsory sterilization of genetically defective persons.[36] A number of doctors and health officials in 1937 then decided to pursue the possibility of a concealed sterilization procedure designed to weed out impurities in Germany's racial base. After the conquest of Poland, Dr. Bruno K. Schultz of the SS Race Office, Dr. Herbert Linden in the Reich Ministry of the Interior, and Dr. Carl Heinz Rodenberg, also in the Interior Ministry, took up this possibility for use in Poland. Lang told a British Secret Service agent in December 1941 that he knew definitely that Himmler's staff had been considering "for a long time" the sterilization of all adult Poles.[37] Himmler's later expression of interest in the process was not for a solution to the Jewish question;[38] Hitler had already refused to consider it for that purpose, according to Brack.[39]

Events and documents from early 1941 suggest that Hitler had already made a fundamental decision to exterminate the Jews. Brack's postwar testimony indicates that others were aware of this course in early 1941, and that Hitler and Himmler had rejected their alternative proposals. Under the circumstances, whether the witnesses saw Hitler's signature on a document is not really critical. A document stating that the Führer wished to make at least the Reich and Bohemia-Moravia *judenfrei* would, in combination with his public and private statements, convey the same message: the fundamental decision was made, even if it was not yet irrevocable. The longstanding disposition to kill Jews, combined with plans for a continent-wide solution, and the rejection of major alternatives, made the goal clear. Based on past experience, Hitler would have wanted to use the war against the Soviet Union as a cover for killings in the East. And he expected the war to put all the continent's Jews within reach.

Hitler's January 1941 order or wish to free Germany of Jews by the end of 1942 represented a general authorization for Himmler and Heydrich to prepare themselves for the appropriate moment—not an order to begin deportations immediately. Operational and scheduling decisions would have to follow later. But why did Hitler allow almost two years to clear German territory of Jews?

Once again, we need to see what traces of a top-secret matter filtered down to the SS. It happens that just around this time an SD official wrote a lecture on the Jewish question, which he or someone else submitted to Himmler. Sturmbannführer Paul Zapp began with the usual Nazi accusations against Jews—that they sought world domination, that they had used Bolshevism to come to power in Russia, that they controlled banks and corporations, that they were opposed to all non-Jews, and simultaneously that they worked hand in hand with Freemasons and the churches. These charges were almost clichés in the Third Reich. Less common was Zapp's argument that the Nazis could successfully resolve the Jewish question only on a worldwide basis:

> One can first conceive of the absolute cleansing of the Jewish question when one succeeds in striking decisively at world Jewry. The political and diplomatic leadership of Adolf Hitler has [already] built the foundation for the European solution of the Jewish question. From this vantage point the solution to the world Jewish question will be tackled.[40]

If world Jewry was the eventual target, then world domination was the obvious answer, and that was not likely for some time—at least a year beyond the conquest of the Soviet Union. Zapp could not have been too far off the mark, for he was subsequently selected to command Einsatzkommando 11a, which set about killing Jews and others in the Ukraine.

In January 1941 Hitler was probably still concerned about the possible foreign-policy repercussions of the mass murder of Jews. Himmler and Heydrich had to wait for a settling of accounts, one way or another, with the British and Americans before the killings of German Jews (and perhaps other Western European Jews) began. Keeping the United States out of the conflict had once represented reason for restraint in foreign policy and secrecy on Jewish policy, but American intercession in behalf of Britain seemed increasingly obvious by early 1941. In January President Roosevelt had introduced the Lend-Lease Bill, which allowed the United States to provide destroyers and other equipment to the British, with the president free to decide upon British repayment in kind, property, or other benefits. The bill passed both houses by solid majorities in early March. Hitler now had to expect that American military intervention was just a matter of time. There was no longer any reason for him to consider the feelings of what he regarded as the Jewish clique around FDR. The likelihood of American intervention was now grounds for conquering Russia and destroying the Jews first.

A day after Sturmbannführer Zapp's speech reached Himmler's office, Hitler gave his lieutenants further encouragement to accelerate their efforts to clear the continent of Jews. In a speech at the Berlin Sportpalast on January 30, 1941, the eighth anniversary of the Nazi seizure of power, Hitler referred to his prophecy two years earlier to the German Reichstag: if Jewry brought about another general war in Europe, the result would be the end of the Jewish role in Europe.[41] He added that the Jews might have laughed at his prophecy, and that they might still be laughing, but that the coming months and years would show that here too he had seen things correctly. He gave every indication that he had made up his mind about his future course.

In this same speech Hitler also referred to the rise of race consciousness among one nationality after another; he said that he looked forward to the day when even Germany's current enemies would recognize the greater internal enemy. They too would join the front against international Jewish exploitation and parasitism against nations.[42] This speech contained plenty of evidence that the resolution of the Jewish question on a continent-wide basis was still dear to him.*

Whenever Hitler gave a violent speech against the Jews, Eichmann later testified, something would come down from Himmler. If he did not take the initiative, Bormann would complain that not enough was being done, and Himmler would fly into a rage.[43] This time Bormann did not have to complain.

On March 17 Governor Hans Frank came to Berlin to meet with Hitler in his private rooms in the Reich Chancellery. It was a very private

---

*Hitler's army adjutant, Gerhard Engel, who reconstructed his experiences after the war, wrote that on February 2, 1941, Hitler told a small group of intimates that he had been thinking of sending a couple of million Jews to Madagascar but the war had prevented this; he was now thinking of something else, which "was not exactly friendlier." Hildegard von Kotze, ed., *Heeresadjutant bei Hitler 1938–1943: Aufzeichnungen des Major Engels* (Stuttgart, 1974), 94–95. There has been discussion among historians regarding Engel's reliability as a source, but other sources, cited earlier, now support this version of Hitler's reported comments.

conversation—"under four eyes," as the Germans describe it. Frank undoubtedly raised some of the difficulties that he was having with Heydrich's latest "near-term plan" to deport Jews from the Eastern provinces to the Government General. Hitler agreed to limit settlers according to the Government General's capacity to take them. At the same time, and there is considerable irony here, Hitler stated that, as a reward for its achievements, the Government General would become the first territory to be made free of Jews. This ill-defined reward guaranteed that Frank would hang after the war. Only three days later, in the meeting at the Propaganda Ministry, Eichmann referred to Heydrich as being in charge of the "final evacuation of the Jews" to the Government General.[44]

There was only one way to have a "final evacuation" of the Jews to Poland and simultaneously to make Poland free of Jews—namely, to do away with all the Jews originally in Poland and those who had been sent to Poland. SS and RSHA officials had already used "evacuation" as a euphemism for the operations of the "euthanasia" program, but "final evacuation" was really definitive terminology: Hitler had approved the mass murder of the Jews in Poland. The locations and methods were apparently still open; they would have been up to Himmler to figure out.

If the goal and basic policies were now clear, the specific plans were not. The gas vans previously used in Poland had disposed of relatively small numbers; technological development was by no means completed. The *Einsatzgruppen* were not big enough to take care of the task in the Soviet Union alone. Himmler and Heydrich had yet to work out the ways and means. The exact moment when Heydrich's plan to rid Germany of its Jews and the plan to have the *Einsatzgruppen* execute Jews and other enemies in the Soviet Union were fused with a systematic effort to destroy European Jews in the Government General may never be known, but the first operational decisions came in July.

Himmler did hint at new plans and at his choice of personnel in April. After Friedrich-Wilhelm Krüger wrote to Himmler about Globocnik's proposals for Jewish labor in concentration camps, Himmler responded that he wanted to discuss the matter with Krüger in person during his next visit to the Government General. He specifically raised the possibility of a new task for Globocnik.[45]

The RSHA had already started to reach beyond the boundaries of the Government General and the Reich to capture control of foreign Jews. Hauptsturmführer Dieter Wisliceny in Eichmann's Jewish section was sent to Slovakia in September 1940, to serve as Himmler's special deputy and adviser to the Slovak government. When the Foreign Office tried

German blood for the Reich was part of the task of developing the Greater German Empire.

A spokesman for the Burgenland Germans thanked Himmler on behalf of all ethnic Germans, and then Himmler spoke about the miserable condition of Germany when the ancestors of the Burgenlanders had emigrated some 140 years earlier. Now, Himmler declared, the Eastern provinces—East and West Prussia, Upper and Lower Silesia—were German provinces and would be settled by Germans. He would allow no compromises and concessions. The racial struggle had to be conducted harshly if peace was to be established: "The Führer has raised us all not to seek temporary solutions but solutions for centuries." Himmler still cited the Government General as the place for Poles and Jews, his only reference in the speech to Jews. He then naturalized fifty of the Burgenland German families and distributed citizenship applications to the other ethnic Germans present, while the organist played a version of "Deutschland über Alles."[54]

Later that month Himmler had the occasion to visit Dachau. He noticed that a Jewish prisoner was in the infirmary, which violated an order dating back before the war that Jewish prisoners should receive medical attention only if they were indispensable. Himmler now issued an order that all Jews who reported sick should be killed.[55] By the spring of 1941 he had few inhibitions about putting Jews to death.

On May 20, 1941, Walter Schellenberg notified police officials in France and Belgium (as well as the Foreign Office and General von Stülpnagel in France) that any emigration of Jews from those countries would restrict the ability of German Jews to make use of the few options left for Jews to emigrate. Because of this problem, and "in view of the surely approaching Final Solution of the Jewish question," the police were to prevent Jewish emigration from France and Belgium.[56] This was about as much as the RSHA could state in a document to be distributed externally without openly repudiating the emigration policy. To change the course openly would have required an explanation to officials who were not privy to the secret of the Final Solution, such as Alfred Rosenberg.

After an early-May trip to newly conquered Greece,[57] Himmler returned to Berlin only to find new problems there, the result of Hitler's recent appointment of Rosenberg as his deputy for central work on the Eastern living space. Because of his prickly personality and poor past performance in various offices, Rosenberg was neither widely liked nor respected within the Nazi elite,[58] but he was a Baltic German who had a good deal of knowledge about the East, and he had been a formative influence upon Hitler in the early 1920s. At any rate, Hitler gave him a chance to work on Eastern problems and, after the invasion of the U.S.S.R. began, named him minister for the occupied Eastern territories. Hitler assured Himmler that he would not be subordinate to Rosenberg in carrying out his tasks in the East.[59] But, either out of inattention or calculation, the Führer did not make that fact clear enough to Rosenberg, or Rosenberg refused to accept his subordination. Rosenberg started to make demands upon Himmler, asking for reports on his preparations regarding the East and suggesting that his appointments in the East had to be cleared with him, Rosenberg.

Himmler complained in strong terms to Bormann: Rosenberg had made demands that even the Wehrmacht had not dared to make; "working with or even under Rosenberg is the most difficult thing there is in the Nazi Party." Bormann tried to arrange for superior powers for Himmler in the East on all matters related to security.[60] He wrote to Reich Chancellery Secretary Lammers about the supreme importance of the tasks of the police there: "especially in the first weeks and months, in the carrying out of their really difficult task, the police must under all circumstances be kept free of all obstacles that could arise out of disputes over jurisdiction."[61] Bormann's intervention did not fully resolve the question of authority and jurisdiction for the East, but it was already clear that Himmler and Bormann had better information than Rosenberg about the Führer's views regarding necessary "executive measures."[62]

Rosenberg, a longtime anti-Semite, had been one of the more enthusiastic supporters of the Madagascar plan. In October 1940 he had written an article entitled "Jews to Madagascar" and sent it to the Führer via Martin Bormann. Bormann had notified Rosenberg that Hitler had decided not to allow publication for the time being—perhaps it could appear in a few months. Rosenberg then heard nothing more on the matter. In March 1941 he was scheduled to give a speech at the opening of the new Institute for the Research of the Jewish Question at Frankfurt am Main. Lacking a clear sense of where Jewish policy then stood, Rosenberg again contacted Bormann to find out whether in his speech he could discuss resettlement on Madagascar.[63] Bormann's answer, if any, does not survive, but Rosenberg managed to perceive the situation accurately somehow. His speech omitted any mention of Madagascar. Rosenberg said that the Jewish question would be solved only when the last Jew left Greater Germany.[64] That was considerably more modest than Himmler's goal.

The Hess affair probably strengthened Himmler's cooperation with Bormann around this time. The specter of disloyalty drove the two true believers together. On May 10 the Führer's Deputy Rudolf Hess, acting on his own initiative, flew a plane to England in a desperate effort to convince the British to make peace with Germany before Barbarossa began. Hitler was furious, but not so distraught that he neglected to have Himmler and Ribbentrop question the Foreign Office specialist on Britain, Dr. Fritz Hesse, as to whether Hess had any chance of succeeding. Himmler gave the official a courteous briefing on Hess's flight. But he showed a flash of anger when Hesse implied that Hess might tell the British too much about the Führer's intentions. Himmler was clearly worried about a leak of the Nazi plans for Russia.[65]

Bormann and Himmler gave out the story that mystics, astrologers, and nature healers had manipulated a disturbed Hess. One result was that Bormann brought a Führer order to Heydrich to crack down on subversives of this kind, and Heydrich hastened to comply.[66] Bormann did not assume Hess's old title, but as head of the Party Chancellery he became more powerful than Hess had ever been.

At the end of May Himmler toured Mauthausen with Oswald Pohl.[67] Perhaps the deadliest of all the existing concentration camps, Mauthausen offered Himmler an opportunity to see the results of a retaliatory measure he had ordered against Dutch Jews. In February 1941 Dutch storm troopers (WA) of the NSB (Dutch Nazi Party) had taken to raiding the Jewish quarter of Amsterdam for excitement and plunder. The Amsterdam Jews had formed self-defense organizations, and had driven back the attackers a number of times. In one case a WA man was seriously wounded; he died some days later. The higher SS and police leader for the Netherlands, Hanns Rauter, had claimed that a Jew had ripped open the trooper's artery and sucked his blood. As a consequence, German and Dutch authorities sealed off the Jewish quarter on February 12. But there were still Jews living in other parts of the city. On February 19 a German police patrol attempted to enter an ice-cream parlor in southern Amsterdam owned by two German Jewish refugees, and the policemen were sprayed with ammonia. A police firing squad executed one of the owners, and Rauter recommended to Himmler more far-reaching action against the Jewish quarter. On February 22 and 23 German police squads seized more than four hundred Jews "of Asiatic type" between the ages of twenty-five and thirty-five off the streets of the quarter. After the victims were beaten and tossed around, they were sent off; most arrived at Mauthausen in May.[68] According to Seyss-Inquart, Himmler had personally ordered this measure as retribution.[69] The Mauthausen guards treated the Dutch prisoners in such a way that many chose to commit suicide. None in the group survived. After Himmler's visit to Mauthausen, the same thing happened with a second group of Dutch Jews seized in Amsterdam in June.[70]

In early June Himmler began an inspection in the Wartheland, the domain of Higher SS and Police Leader Koppe, and he toured the Lodz ghetto. He stopped at the office of the ghetto administration and visited one of the tailoring factories.[71] The ghetto administration was then under the control of Hans Biebow, a former coffee importer from Bremen, who had joined the Nazi Party only in 1937. Some months earlier he had used public funds to purchase food for starving Jews in the ghetto. Biebow had championed the idea of creating a viable ghetto economy in Lodz, causing a deputy (who wanted the Jews to die out as rapidly as possible) to leave in protest. By the summer of 1941 there were some forty thousand Jews at work in the ghetto, moving it toward its eventual status as the most industrialized ghetto in Europe.[72]

Although Gauleiter Greiser had already pretty well secured control of most of the wealth produced by Jewish labor in Lodz, Himmler did not openly disapprove of putting Jews to work in the ghetto. The day after his visit, an optimistic Biebow met with *Gau* food authorities in Posen and persuaded them to increase rations for the ghetto. But the improvements never materialized. Biebow's policies contradicted an unannounced general course that local and regional authorities became aware of only gradually. Jewish policy in the Wartheland actually moved in the opposite direction, with more Jews and gypsies brought in despite the lack of food. By the end of 1941 there was a new and quicker way to dispose of them than overwork and starvation.[73]

THE PREPARATIONS for the campaign against the Soviet Union went slower than anticipated, and the original mid-May invasion date had to be postponed until June 22. By early June Hitler was already anticipating the victory and considering the next step. His Directive No. 32, dated June 11, 1941, began with flat statements: "After the destruction of the Soviet Armed Forces, Germany and Italy will be military masters of the European Continent, with the temporary exception of the Iberian peninsula. No serious threat to Europe by land will then remain." Although the rest of the document contains some mention of exploiting the newly conquered lands in the East, the main thrust was to focus on future steps against British influence in the Mediterranean and in Asia, through German pressure or attacks in such far-flung places as Gibraltar, Turkey, Iran, and Iraq. Only someone with the "confidence of a sleepwalker" could have given his armed-services chiefs instructions to work on such plans for the period *after* Barbarossa.[74] Barbarossa simply happened to be the largest military campaign in history.

The evidence that the Nazi leaders expected the Soviet Union to crumble quickly is not limited to Directive 32. Himmler and Heydrich were already preparing some of their military and police units for a war that had little or nothing to do with securing immediate military objectives but, rather, with a long-term objective of establishing racial hegemony and providing sufficient living space for Germans in the future. On May 26 Himmler assigned a group of Waffen-SS units to what he called the Kommandostab Reichsführer SS, which became in effect his own private army. The Waffen-SS troops assigned to the campaign against Russian soldiers were under military authority, but Himmler was free to use his private command force as he saw fit. This little-known force, composed of men from the Order Police and the Waffen-SS, soon grew to some twenty-five thousand men, who were to engage in actions behind the lines against partisans and Jews but also against communist officials, gypsies, allegedly dangerous Asiatics, and the mentally ill (considered deviant and a burden rather than an enemy). For most, their political and racial qualities automatically made them threats to German security in Himmler's eyes, whatever their behavior. Himmler specifically stated that he did not want these troops used simply to occupy positions; they were required for what he euphemistically called "other tasks."[75]

June 17 was a special day for Himmler—the fifth anniversary of his appointment as chief of the German police. Some of his subordinates provided him with the perfect occasion to reminisce about the past by organizing a ceremony and presenting him with a special gift—a published volume of essays written for his fortieth birthday the previous October by some of his SS associates and even one by Falk Zipperer, Himmler's boyhood friend, now a professor of law. The two boys had played war games endless times more than a quarter of a century earlier; now Himmler was getting ready for the real battle in the East, and this time he had a real army to play with. The volume also contained a glimpse at the anticipated future. Werner Best, the SS legal and administrative expert, contributed an article comparing the various methods of administering and ruling over large empires throughout history.[76]

Heydrich was busy on that day arranging for his own gift to Himmler. He summoned the newly appointed commanders of the four *Einsatzgruppen*, the twelve *Einsatzkommandos*, the *Sonderkommandos*, and some others (a total of perhaps thirty or forty men) to the conference room of RSHA headquarters in the Prinz Albrechtstrasse.[77] The men in the police units, officers and the ranks, had been training and exercising for some weeks at a Border Police school at Pretzsch, on the Elbe River, northeast of Leipzig.[78] Then Heydrich summoned the leadership back to Berlin to give them special instructions orally. The information was not suitable for all the troops, only for the elite. No one is known to have taken minutes or recorded the event shortly afterward; we must depend largely on postwar recollections to establish what Heydrich said.

After the war the officials who were already known to have participated in the mass executions in the East had reason to recall Heydrich's orders quite specifically, because the orders at least placed them under some degree of compulsion, whereas those who could plausibly deny involvement in mass executions had reason to remember only Heydrich's generalities. In short, no one's motives were pure, and perhaps memories were different in any case. So there remains some disagreement among historians about which witnesses to believe.[79]

One of the witnesses, an SD man named Walter Blume, later testified that Heydrich had told the group that Eastern Jewry provided the "reservoir of intellectuals for Bolshevism," and that the Führer and the leadership of state held the view that it must be destroyed.[80] Months later, after hundreds of thousands had already been executed, Heydrich told a newly appointed commander exactly that: the information about the Führer's view and order was not to go beyond the commanders of the *Einsatzgruppen* and heads of the *Einsatzkommandos* and *Sonderkommandos*.[81] This account is persuasive not only because it is consistent with other, independent accounts of earlier proposals to destroy the Jews in the East, but also because of the language. Jews appear frequently as the "intellectual reservoir of Bolshevism" in Hitler's diatribes, a phrase that had also been used in an RSHA decree of October 1940 banning the emigration of Polish Jews.[82] This was exactly the kind of remark that Heydrich was likely to make.

There also was testimony, again marred by some discrepancies and contradictions, that the police-unit leaders had received instructions at Pretzsch a couple of days later from Heinrich Müller and/or Bruno Streckenbach.[83] An RSHA official who knew both colleagues well testified after the war that both Müller and Streckenbach went to Pretzsch between June 15 and 20.[84] One commander of an *Einsatzkommando*, under prolonged interrogation, for some time could not "remember" anything given at Pretzsch except vague instructions to provide for security in the East and to eliminate resistance ruthlessly. After conceding that Streckenbach had spoken to the leadership separately at Pretzsch at a social gathering a few days after Heydrich's meeting in Berlin, he finally admitted that Streckenbach had revealed Hitler's general order: "The Führer has ordered the liquidation of all Jews, gypsies, and [communist] political functionaries in the entire area of the Soviet Union in order to secure the territory." Another witness remembered the Müller-Streckenbach speeches referring to the destruction of all the people who were enemies of the National Socialist world-view.[85] After reviewing the troops shortly thereafter, Heydrich called upon the men to carry out their duties faithfully and to be "harsh but not brutal."[86] Himmler had used the exact same phrase when speaking to SS men serving on the Eastern border in late 1939.[87]

The day after Heydrich met with the leadership of the police units in the Prinz Albrechtstrasse, Himmler summoned one of his favorite writers there too.[88] Edwin Erich Dwinger, forty-three years old, was no hard-line Nazi. As late as 1936 he was not only not a Nazi Party member, but was even suspected of participation in Otto Strasser's Black Front resistance movement. But Dwinger, a decorated veteran of World War I who had been held prisoner by the Russians during the civil war after the Bolshevik Revolution, had other outstanding qualifications for the SS. He had written several books about his wartime experiences, lauding the performance of heroic German soldiers, exactly the kind of historical works Himmler loved. He was an expert on Russia as a result of his wartime and postwar experiences. Moreover, he was a farmer as well as a writer. (In 1941 Himmler would write that he and Dwinger looked at agricultural problems in exactly the same way.) So Dwinger was recruited into the SS in 1937.[89]

Dwinger's reputation grew when he published excerpts from the diary he had kept while fighting in the campaign against the French in 1940.[90] Another book, *Death in Poland*, revealed the "shocking" story of Polish atrocities against ethnic Germans in Bromberg and elsewhere in Poland. The organized killings of Polish civilians by the SS and police far outnumbered Polish murders of Germans, but the former was not an appropriate topic for a nationalistic German writer, and Dwinger did not hesitate to magnify the number of German victims: "General murder reached a high point that history had not seen since the time of Genghis Khan."[91] It was an analogy that must have pleased the Reich Führer SS. Himmler liked Dwinger's book so much that he gave a copy to Hitler.[92]

By June 1941 Himmler was convinced that Dwinger was the right man to describe the impending events in the East. He told Dwinger he was a "chronicler of our times" and said that he would like Dwinger to serve as his personal-staff expert on the East—to observe the liquidation from a special vantage point. Himmler said he knew from reading Dwinger's books that Dwinger was tough, and such a quality would be needed, because "we will not be able to avoid liquidating perhaps three million party functionaries." When Dwinger supposedly objected to killing on such a scale, Himmler replied that the policy was beyond discussion; any other plans violated the will of the Führer and were virtually treasonous.

Himmler wanted Dwinger to come with him to his headquarters in the East. Perhaps wary of too close an association with the Reich Führer

SS, Dwinger pointed out that General Heinz Guderian had already assigned him a special mission. Could Himmler wait for him until after the conclusion of the fighting? Himmler could hardly object to a soldier's being loyal to his division, so he agreed: Dwinger would switch over to Himmler's command in Moscow in six weeks. "In six weeks?" Dwinger asked in disbelief. Himmler replied that the Führer himself had declared that Moscow would fall by August 4, and that the Soviet state would collapse like a house of cards.[93]

The day before the invasion of the Soviet Union began, Himmler gave a presentation to the Führer regarding the possible use of poison gas in the campaign. Poison gas warfare was outlawed by the Geneva Convention, but that did not stop Himmler. If the Waffen-SS or the regular army was going to use poison gas, the troops needed equipment and training, and that required the establishment of training grounds at an appropriate location. Himmler apparently suggested a training site in the Wartheland, but Hitler decided not to proceed for the time being.[94] The discussion had no further consequences, but it demonstrates two important facts. Himmler knew that poison gas was potentially available; the subject was on his mind. But only Hitler could make this kind of decision.

As it happens, one of the gases the army had expressed interest in as early as the fall of 1939 was a form of prussic acid or hydrogen cyanide. The army had wanted the Degesch corporation, a pesticide manufacturing firm in which I. G. Farben held an interest, to stabilize prussic acid and make it possible to use it for chemical warfare.[95] It would not be long before Himmler's men would use the same compound against another enemy.

CHAPTER 8

▼▼▼▼▼▼▼▼▼▼▼▼▼▼▼▼▼▼

CLEANSING THE
NEW EMPIRE

IT LOOKED like a mismatch, though not in terms of quantity. The German army threw more than three million soldiers into Operation Barbarossa. Norway sent some 67,000 men to fight with German troops on the Finnish northern border. Finland itself, fighting technically independently, mobilized half a million men, and the Rumanians supplied 150,000. Against them was an even larger Russian force, but with many untrained and uncoordinated elements. Stalin's purges of the officer corps in the 1930s had severely weakened the Russian army, which had performed during the 1939–40 "Winter War" against Finland like an orchestra whose players could not keep time.[1] With the exception of the air war over Britain, Germany had won every campaign in astonishingly short order. Sober Western analysts calculated not whether the Soviet Union could hold out, but how long. Initially, most thought no more than a few months.[2]

Moreover, the Germans had the element of surprise. Although preparations for an undertaking of this kind could hardly be kept entirely secret, the Russian defenders were caught largely unprepared and confused on June 22, 1941. Within hours, German troops controlled every bridge across the border rivers from the Baltic Sea to the Carpathian Mountains.[3] German tanks began racing east, and the Luftwaffe wrecked many Russian planes on the ground. The destruction of the stronghold of Bolshevism had apparently begun.

Since Hitler and Himmler were firmly convinced that the Slavs were an inferior race, the first reports may have confirmed their feeling that they could wrap up the campaign quickly. At any rate, by the afternoon of June 23 Himmler felt free to play tennis with members of his staff.[4]

But he had already set others to work. That same evening the commander of Einsatzgruppe A, Dr. Franz Walter Stahlecker, arrived at
police headquarters in the East Prussian city of Tilsit, close to the border
of Lithuania. Referring to special powers given to him, Stahlecker ordered the Tilsit police to clear out a twenty-five-kilometer band of Lithuanian territory to the east of the German border. Jews as well as
Lithuanians suspected of being communists were to be subjected to "special treatment," which meant that they were to be liquidated. When a
policeman claimed that there were not enough men to do this job, Stahlecker replied that the SD office in Tilsit and, if necessary, the protective
police in Memel, could help out. The first mass executions were carried
out on June 24 or 25 in the Lithuanian city of Garsden, where 201
people, mostly Jews, were killed.[5] It was a sign of things to come.

For every enemy of the race removed, there was more room for Germans. On June 24 Himmler met in his office in the Prinz Albrechtstrasse
with Professor Konrad Meyer-Hetling from the University of Berlin.
Himmler had selected the professor to head his planning division, later
upgraded into a planning office, within the Reich Commissariat for the
Strengthening of the German People.[6] For the moment, Himmler asked
Meyer-Hetling to supply him with a sketch of settlement opportunities
in some of the Eastern areas. Meyer-Hetling's first draft of what was
soon to be called the "general plan for the East" no longer survives, but
subsequent references make it seem that he envisioned German settlement not only of Polish territory, but of the Baltic States, Byelorussia,
and parts of the Ukraine. Such settlement could not take place without
vast displacement of the existing inhabitants one way or another, but
Himmler had already spoken of doing just that.

By the time Meyer-Hetling's rough draft arrived at Himmler's new
headquarters in East Prussia in mid-July, however, it was too limited to
be of use. The rapid advance of the German forces toward Moscow and
Leningrad and into the Ukraine already had Himmler thinking on a
grander scale. Never loath to look ahead, Himmler marked Meyer-
Hetling's cover letter "obsolete."[7]

On June 25 Himmler headed out on his special train toward the
Führer's new headquarters in the East, just outside Rastenburg, East
Prussia. Two days earlier the Führer had taken his own train to the
headquarters he had named "Wolf's Lair," where newly constructed
concrete bunkers, roads, and train tracks joined the wooden huts shel-
tered by thick trees.[8] Himmler soon made his base at Angerburg (We-
gobork), at the edge of a large lake and about twenty miles northeast of
Rastenburg. He and his adjutants Peiper and Grothmann lived and
worked aboard "Heinrich," which rested about an hour away from the

Führer's more permanent facilities. Later, after it became clear that the war would not end quickly, Himmler established a more extensive base, complete with barracks and reinforced concrete bunkers, southeast of Angerburg, near Grossgarten. He called it "High Forest."⁹

From Angerburg, relatively close to the initial front, Himmler monitored two different but related campaigns. There were by now some 160,000 Waffen-SS troops under his authority. Most of them were delegated to fight with the regular army (under army command) against the Russians, and, despite a few exceptions, these troops proved formidable in combat, which undoubtedly strengthened Himmler's faith in the importance of will and ideology for a soldier.¹⁰ But a second campaign, involving the police units and Himmler's private army (Kommandostab Reichsführer SS), was designed to wipe out the enemies of Nazism behind the lines—that is, in the Eastern areas already conquered by the troops.

No careful commander sends his troops into battle without some calculation of the strategy most likely to achieve his goal, and Himmler was meticulous to a fault. He was so careful, in fact, that there is no surviving blueprint for the murder campaign in the U.S.S.R. Certain documents nonetheless hint at advance instructions that he or Heydrich must have issued. Perhaps the clearest example came in Stahlecker's October 1941 report about the activities of Einsatzgruppe A: "the goal of the cleansing operation of the Security Police, *in accordance with the fundamental orders*, was the most comprehensive elimination of the Jews possible [my italics]." Sturmbannführer Rudolf Lange, commander of Einsatzkommando 2 in Latvia, also wrote that his goal from the beginning was "a radical solution of the Jewish problem through the execution of all Jews."¹¹ These comments and the flow of events conform to a general pattern. The very first SS plan for German Jews had culminated in the killing of as many Jews as possible, and Stahlecker's remark suggests the same kind of initial instruction for the U.S.S.R. What was possible in one area might well be different from what could be done in another, which would help to explain some of the regional variations in killing targets and percentages.

Geography and demography made it impossible to wipe out the huge population of enemy groups—five million Jews alone—in one fell swoop with such limited manpower. If only part of the job could be accomplished right away, it was necessary to do so in a manner that could serve as preparation for the rest. That might mean that the police units had to encircle, trap, or otherwise gain control of those enemies it could not immediately kill.¹² Within the context of what we know about their plans since 1939, it is logical that Himmler and Heydrich gave *Einsatzgruppen* commanders instructions to eliminate the most dangerous enemies first, if they could not deal with everyone. So it is not really surprising that in some areas police units murdered Jewish men, women, and children from the very beginning, while in others they limited their killing to Jewish men, or, even more narrowly, to Jewish intellectuals and potential leaders.[13]

The four *Einsatzgruppen* began to send daily radio reports (and written reports by courier) on their movements and activities back to RSHA headquarters, where they were compiled and issued to selected RSHA offices and, of course, to Himmler in East Prussia.[14] Heydrich and Müller also issued further instructions to these killing units as time went on. On some occasions the commanders telephoned in reports to Himmler's office directly.[15] Himmler maintained another line of authority over the *Einsatzgruppen* by making each commander subordinate also to the higher SS and police leader in the region where the *Einsatzgruppe* and its subdivisions were operating. The three higher SS and police leaders for the Soviet Union (Ostland, Central Russia, and Southern Russia) were themselves subordinate directly to Himmler; in fact, they were known as "little Himmlers." These same men were also in charge of the regional operations of the various units of the Kommandostab Reichsführer SS sent out from East Prussia or Poland to conduct killings behind the lines.[16]

On June 30 Himmler and Heydrich set out from Himmler's field headquarters in East Prussia for a tour of the conquered Polish cities of Augustowo (Augustów) and Grodno in the former Russian zone of Poland.[17] Augustowo was just over the East Prussian border, and Grodno only a little farther to the east. Grodno, a city of some fifty thousand, had a Jewish population of more than twenty-one thousand before the war, most of whom were probably still there. Yet Himmler and Heydrich found no police killing units in the city whatsoever. The next day Heydrich sent out an order to the *Einsatzgruppen*, reminding them of the need to keep pace with the military developments and to take the initiative. So, on July 3, police and SD units moving out from the East Prussian city of Tilsit killed 306 men and ten women in Augustowo. In Grodno a number of prominent Jewish intellectuals were shot, and then the police unit forced Jews between the ages of fourteen and sixty to report for compulsory labor.[18]

Otto Bräutigam of the Ministry for the Occupied Eastern Territories testified after the war that, although he did not know the specific order, he had the impression that the SD (*Einsatzgruppen*) had been directed to carry out the liquidations of Jews as quickly as possible behind the troops, to make it seem as though these killings were part of the war itself.[19] Haste was necessary, since the war was only expected to last a matter of months. The shorter the war, the more the SS would have to rely upon other, more easily concealable, but as yet untested methods of mass murder after the expected conquest. The results of the first week or so of fighting could only have fortified the idea that it was best to hurry. Even the supposedly sober professional Chief of the General Staff, Franz Halder, wrote in his diary on July 3: "It is very likely not saying too much when I observe that the campaign against the Soviet Union has been won in less than fourteen days."[20]

The police units often needed the cooperation of the army commanders in the field. This time Hitler himself had instructed the army generals that the war was a collision between two ideologies, and that it was necessary to eliminate the Bolshevist-Jewish intelligentsia.[21] There was enough anticommunist sentiment within the military to make some Nazi goals in the East seem justifiable to more than a few high-ranking officers and to the military hierarchies.[22] Still, it remained an open question how all the generals would react to the killing of women and children. And some of those who had protested against the killings of civilians in the past were still very much on the scene. General Küchler, commander of the Eighteenth Army, for example, was headed for the Baltic States, where there were many Jews, which meant that Einsatzgruppe A, under the command of Stahlecker, might have to be particularly careful.

Fortunately for Stahlecker, the Baltic States of Estonia, Latvia, and Lithuania were initially well disposed toward their German occupiers, which made his tasks easier. The Soviet Union had forcibly occupied the formerly independent republics only in 1940, as a consequence of the Nazi-Soviet Pact, arresting or abducting many notables. A good number of Baltics considered the devil they knew as the greater enemy. There were also some native residents who agreed with the Nazis that Jews and communists were closely linked. Within hours of their arrival in late June, the *Einsatzkommandos* established auxiliary police forces in the cities, composed of dependable local volunteers, which were used partly to identify communists and partly to combat partisans.

Though he boasted of his successful cooperation with the military in dealing with partisans, Stahlecker later described some of the difficulties he faced with the actions against Jews. His police force was

> determined to solve the Jewish question by any means and with complete resolve. It was desirable, however, that the Jewish question not be raised immediately, as the unusually tough measures would also have created shock in German circles. It had to appear to the outside that the indigenous population itself reacted naturally

against the decades of oppression by the Jews and against the terror created by the Communists in recent history, and that the indigenous population carried out these first measures of its own accord. . . . It was the duty of the Security Police [*Einsatzkommandos*] to initiate these self-purging actions and to guide them into the proper channels, so that the goal set for cleaning the area is reached as quickly as possible.[23]

Himmler himself probably dictated this strategy even before Heydrich telegraphed it to the *Einsatzgruppen* on July 2; the first step was to incite pogroms surreptitiously.[24]

In the Lithuanian capital of Kowno (Kaunas), Stahlecker succeeded in contacting the leader of one of the local militias on June 25. As a result of the advice the Germans gave him, this Klimatis arranged the first pogrom that night, during which more than fifteen hundred Jews were killed and several synagogues and some sixty Jewish homes were destroyed. In the next few nights further actions, apparently under the command of a Lithuanian First Lieutenant Norkus, killed twenty-three hundred Jews, all, as Stahlecker later boasted, "without any visible indication to the outside world of a German order or of any German suggestion."[25]

Since the communists were said to have destroyed the local Latvian establishment, it was not so easy to get a Latvian pogrom started, Stahlecker later explained.[26] Still, after Einsatzkommando 1a and part of Einsatzkommando 2 entered the Latvian capital, they organized a four-hundred-man auxiliary police force under Latvian First Lieutenant Weiss. On July 3 the auxiliary police plundered Jewish homes. And two other Latvian groups carried out pogroms, killing some four hundred Jews and destroying all synagogues.[27]

Stahlecker's men took photographs and even films of the actions in Kowno and Riga, to enable them to prove that Lithuanians and Latvians conducted executions "spontaneously."[28] In Estonia there were only a couple of thousand Jews left: most had fled with the Russian troops across the border. There the *Einsatzkommandos* and the Estonian forces they recruited dealt initially with murdering and arresting communists.[29]

After the pogroms ended and order was restored, the second stage of murder operations began. The local militias were dissolved, and the German police units selected Latvian and Lithuanian volunteers from among those who had fought the Russians, to serve as executioners. In Kowno two companies of auxiliary police were placed directly under Karl Jäger's Einsatzkommando 3, one to guard a concentration camp for Jews and to carry out executions.[30] In Wilna Lithuanian police units subordinated to the *Einsatzkommando* drew up lists of the local Jews, particularly identifying intellectuals, activists, and the wealthy. Then they searched Jewish houses, seized property, and executed ninety-three of the Jews during three days in early July, with the Lithuanians participating in the shootings. The *Einsatzkommando* then barred members of the German army from entering the Jewish quarter of the city. By the second week in July executions of Jews and saboteurs had reached five hundred per day.[31]

In the Ukraine, the police units had some success inciting pogroms in the early days of the invasion, but also encountered some reservations on the part of Ukrainians.[32] In Byelorussia and the Central Russian sector, pogroms were less frequent and less effective. Where the *Einsatzkommandos* were forced to act first, their shootings were frequently described as reprisals against Jewish partisans or Jewish looters. These reprisals reflected the general policy that Jews were automatically considered to be hostile; whenever a German was shot, whenever there was looting, the assumption was that Jews were responsible. At the same time, casting such murders as reprisals concealed the general policy, planned in advance, of eliminating all Jews, to the greatest degree possible. To tie executions to specific Jewish crimes was a way of making them easier to carry out for the men who did the killing and for army officers who might have had difficulties of conscience with an open policy of genocide.[33] Himmler, higher SS and police leaders, and the *Einsatzgruppen* commanders employed this device on a number of occasions.

In the Polish city of Białystok, Jews allegedly looted shops after Russian troops withdrew and before the Germans arrived. On July 1 Order Police Battalion 322 swept through the Jewish and Polish quarters and seized a mass of property assumed to be stolen from the Germans. Later that day Himmler and Order Police Chief Kurt Daluege showed up unannounced, asked for a briefing on the battalion's experiences, and inspected the booty. That evening, Higher SS and Police Leader von dem Bach-Zelewski gave a dinner in Himmler's honor. According to Bach-Zelewski, Himmler personally ordered him to execute two thousand Jews as punishment for the looting.[34] An original document provides a better picture of Himmler's apparent order, as well as what actually occurred. Bach-Zelewski soon ordered a police regiment commander to execute inconspicuously all male Jews between the ages of seventeen and forty-five. Members of a police battalion and an *Einsatzkommando* shot these Jewish "plunderers." The police regiment commander advised the battalion commanders and company chiefs to lessen any psychological effects upon their men (the executioners) by holding social gatherings for them in the evening and by teaching the men about the political necessity of these measures—instructions apparently received orally from Himmler.[35]

Another example of masking the general order to kill Jews came on July 1 in the Polish city of Lemberg, where what was soon to be called Einsatzgruppe C had just arrived. This main city in eastern Galicia was of mixed Polish, Ukrainian, Jewish, and ethnic-German population. Commander Dr. Otto Rasch informed his men that Jews in Lemberg and some other inhabitants had killed a number of people in the city before the Russian troops had retreated. Although this "crime" did not affect the German forces, that mattered little. The Ukrainians had already created a local militia under a military commandant, which the Germans decided to use. Together with the militia, Einsatzkommandos 4a and 6 and a police unit brought in from Cracow rounded up some three thousand suspects, mostly Jews, in the municipal stadium. The next day Rasch informed the men that he had received an order from Hitler that all those guilty or even suspected of involvement were to be executed. Rasch personally supervised the executions on July 2 and 3. Actually, another five thousand Jews in the city died around the same time as a result of Ukrainian pogroms and police killings on the streets.[36]

In August Jews were supposed to have fired on a German military unit in the Southern Russian city of Jassy, or, in another variation, had threatened the ethnic-German residents of nearby Ananjew. Although Rumanian fascists had already purged Jassy of almost twenty-five hundred Jews, Himmler ordered the execution of several hundred Jews in Ananjew.[37] Even in September, well after word of the general policy to kill Jews had leaked out, Himmler issued an alleged reprisal order that one soldier recalled as follows:

Soldiers of the Army and of the Waffen-SS! On 1st September, 6 SS-officers were found in the Weniza forest in the following condition: They had been stripped of their clothing and hanged with their legs up. Their entrails had been taken out. Such an act demands revenge, and since it were Jews who did it, we will utterly extirpate them. Even the brood in the cradle must be crushed like a swollen toad. We are living in an iron time and have to sweep with iron brooms. Everybody has there fore to do his duty without asking his conscience first.

Himmler[38]

Whether the Russian atrocity was real, magnified, or entirely invented is less important than the fact that it was used as justification and cover

for a policy already determined. German reprisals against Jews co[...]
fact take place in many areas where there were still Jews alive, but kil[...]
of Jews proceeded in virtually all areas—with or without anti-Germ[...]
activity.

Cooperative generals such as Heinrich von Stülpnagel and Karl von
Roques adopted a variant of the SS line in the Soviet Union during the
summer of 1941. When there were acts of sabotage or guerrilla warfare
that could not be traced, they assumed that Jews were responsible and
took retaliatory measures, which were carried out by regular-army
forces. By October Field Marshal Walter von Reichenau argued that
events had proved again and again that Jews had instigated partisan
warfare, and General Erich von Manstein explained that Jews served as
liaisons between the Red Army and the partisans in the rear.[39] These
arguments justified army "retaliation" against many tens of thousands
of Jews, who were held collectively responsible and punishable. In this
fashion, the regular army played a significant role in the killing of Jews
in the East.

Pogroms, regular executions of small numbers, and "reprisal actions"
could eliminate Jews entirely from smaller communities, but not in the
larger cities or the areas of heaviest Jewish population. There a more
gradual approach was needed, but even so the violence during the first
few weeks promoted the overall objectives. Nazi officials persuaded or
forced Jewish leaders or arbitrarily chosen representatives to cooperate
in the process of relocating entire Jewish communities into closed
ghettos—allegedly for their own protection.

In Kowno, where Stahlecker had persuaded Lithuanian elements to
conduct pogroms in late June, Lithuanian "partisans" under German
direction seized thousands of Jews and imprisoned them in one of the
chain of fortresses outside the city built by the Russian tsars. This "Seventh Fortress" lay atop a large hill and was surrounded by a moat; it
had a vast underground area with concrete cellars invisible from the
outside. During the first week of July, about eight thousand Jews were
beaten, tortured, and then killed in and around this fort.

On July 7 Jäger summoned five of the most prominent Jews of the
city to his office, which was adorned by expensive carpets taken from
Jewish homes. Jäger blamed the Lithuanians for the violence and said
he could not allow it to continue. Since the Lithuanians no longer wanted
to live with the Jews, he said, the Jews had to move into a ghetto in the
suburb of Viliampole, where they would have plenty of room. The re-
location was carried out between July 15 and August 15; given the prevailing antipathy of Lithuanian authorities, Jewish leaders felt that they
had no alternative but to cooperate.[40]

This example illustrates the general pattern for the cities with large concentrations of Jews. After early pogroms and executions, the establishment of ghettos and concentration camps placed the remaining Jews in captivity. The Nazis could dispose of them at their convenience, after their labor was no longer needed, or when it could be done inconspicuously. Even though the largest killing actions usually occurred months or even a year later, the whole process was calculated in advance. When an *Einsatzkommando* liquidated fifteen thousand Jews in Rowno, in the Ukraine, in November 1941, it was described as a long-planned killing action.[41]

All in all, both with the killings they carried out directly and with their preparations for the future, the *Einsatzkommandos, Sonderkommandos,* and Order Police and Waffen-SS battalions devoted to the murder campaign were able to accomplish a significant part of their goals within the first several weeks of the Russian war. And the war against the Soviet Union was proceeding so well that Himmler was actually able to divert troops to the murder campaign.[42]

German forces were not the only ones to carry out pogroms and mass executions of Jews. Einsatzgruppen C and D were operating in the South, in areas where the Hungarians and Rumanians were also fighting the Russians and occupying territory. Neither country was initially informed of Himmler's special mission in the East. While the Hungarian forces generally did not take part in actions against Jews and even prevented some killings, the Rumanians carried out numerous atrocities against Jews in Bukovina and elsewhere. Rumanian killings culminated in the massacre of nearly sixty thousand Jews in Odessa in October 1941 as a reprisal for partisan attacks.[43]

Heydrich, however, was not satisfied with Rumanian behavior in the East. In early August he withdrew the Jewish adviser assigned to the German Embassy in Bucharest as a sign of displeasure, and then specifically accused the Rumanian troops in the newly occupied territories of repeatedly displaying a "strong friendliness to the Jews."[44] Einsatzgruppe D had reported cases of Rumanians' making use of Jewish labor in the East and had concluded that the solution of the Jewish question was in the wrong hands with the Rumanians. The head of the force, Otto Ohlendorf, added that, "until the Final Solution of the Jewish question for the entire continent" began, Germany was better off working with the Ukrainians. As late as mid-October, the Rumanian ambassador to Germany angrily protested the inaccuracy of this calumny that "high SS circles" had raised: in Rumania, he said in defense of his country, there was "an old and elemental hate of the Jews."[45]

None of these Nazi complaints blots out the significance of Rumanian mass murders in the Soviet Union. They do, however, illustrate just how radical Nazi Germany's course was. Traditional anti-Semitism and even vicious pogroms were not sufficient. Only thorough, planned measures and complete subservience satisfied Himmler and Heydrich.

ON JULY 13 Himmler went to the German port city of Stettin to address some replacement Waffen-SS troops about to leave for the Finnish front. In a speech to the officers, Himmler stressed that the will to take the offensive was the key to victory. Hitler himself, Himmler said, had stated that a setback did not matter as long as the troops could rise and attack again. Himmler was reporting the facts: the will to victory was Hitler's constant refrain during the war. In 1943, when German officers explained that their troops could not drive the Allies out of Sicily because they could not cross to the island, Hitler replied that will, not ferries, was decisive.[46]

Himmler's second speech in Stettin, to the ranks, raised broader ideological issues. He offered the troops a vision of racial conflict throughout history, in which the Jews played a critical part.

This is an ideological battle and a struggle of races. Here in this struggle stands National Socialism: an ideology based on the value of our Germanic, Nordic blood. Here stands a world as we have conceived it: beautiful, decent, socially equal, that perhaps, in a few instances, is still burdened by shortcomings, but as a whole, a happy, beautiful world full of culture; this is what our Germany is like. On the other side stands a population of 180 million, a mixture of races, whose very names are unpronounceable, and whose physique is such that one can shoot them down without pity and compassion. These animals, that torture and ill-treat every prisoner from our side . . . these people have been welded by the Jews into one religion, one ideology, that is called Bolshevism, with the task: now we have Russia, half of Asia, a part of Europe, now we will overwhelm Germany and the whole world.

When you, my men, fight over there in the East, you are carrying on the same struggle, against the same subhumanity, the same inferior races that at one time appeared under the name of Huns, another time—1,000 years ago at the time of King Henry and Otto I—under the name of Magyars, another time under the name of Tartars, and still another time under the name of Genghis Khan and the Mongols. Today they appear as Russians under the political banner of Bolshevism.[47]

In Himmler's eyes, as in Hitler's, the threat to Germany from the East went back for centuries, even if the Jews had increased it since 1917. The implication of Himmler's historical vision was that the methods of Genghis Khan had to be turned against the successors of Genghis Khan—not only against the Jewish and Bolshevik leaders, but against the subhuman races themselves.

The next day Himmler's office discussed with Gottlob Berger the publication of a picture book illustrating the subhuman races behind the Bolshevik cause. The original idea came from Hitler, who wanted to publish a piece of propaganda with limited text that would serve to "immunize" the German people against communism. The Führer gave this job to the Propaganda Ministry, but then rejected the first two drafts from Goebbels's agency. At that point Himmler took over the job and gave it to his protégé Berger, who in turn assigned it to a subordinate. Berger's man had his own difficulties; Himmler rejected his first four drafts. Finally, Himmler invited the author to spend two weeks at Hegewald, a settlement near his field headquarters, and during that time they worked out a book that Hitler, who gave it to his own propaganda expert, finally approved. Himmler took considerable pride in the book, entitled *The Subhuman* (*Der Untermensch*), filled with pictures of threatening, un-European visages supposedly of the enemies to the east.[48]

Other Nazi propaganda organs took up similar themes. A short book issued in 1942, part of a series edited by Georg Leibbrandt, a high official in the Ministry for the Occupied Eastern Territories, declared that more research on the racial composition of Turkestan was needed. The Tadzikhs and Uzbeks seemed to be of Iranian (and hence Aryan) stock, whereas the Turkmen had Mongolian characteristics, such as a long head.[49]

Some of these racial and pseudo-historical pronouncements seem so ridiculous that one is tempted to discount them as mere propaganda. But the same kind of assertions crop up in private or restricted communications. The Party Chancellery, for example, later analyzed the racial composition of the Soviet Union as a whole as follows. The Soviets supposedly had relatively few Europeans and equally few pure Mongolian types. The scarcity of Europeans resulted from the fact that the Bolsheviks had considered them dangerous and exterminated them. But the scarcity of pure Mongolians was deceptive, because the more common, indeterminate racial types came anthropologically from very ancient European and Asiatic races which had little in common with the contemporary European races. Even someone with the right skin, hair, and eye color was not likely to be Nordic or eastern Baltic, and therefore remained dangerous. The prototypical Russian features as depicted in

Nazi caricatures were more likely to be found, along with Far Eastern and Jewish racial elements, among the Russian officers. One could find the same characteristics, the Party Chancellery concluded, in German prisons and concentration camps. This analysis was part of a collection marked "secret" and designed only for internal party use.[50]

This fear of Asiatics was part of Himmler's view of the world and of history, and it was also Hitler's. During a July 21, 1941, meeting with Marshal Kvaternik, Croatian defense minister and commander-in-chief of the Croatian armed forces, Hitler compared the Russian troops to those of Genghis Khan, and said that the powerful Mongolian race was pressing against Europe. Although it was difficult to get a clear picture of the racial composition of contemporary Russia, photos of Russian POWs indicated that 70–80 percent of the Russian people were of Mongolian stock, though there were still some Slavic types and a few other racial groups, Hitler added. Kvaternik recalled that during World War I the Russian army was primarily composed of Russian peasants. Hitler responded that Bolshevism had exterminated them.[51]

In mid-July the *Völkischer Beobachter* had explained that, after the tsarist regime had created the preconditions for far-reaching decomposition of its people, the Bolsheviks had carried out the job. Only the colored peoples of the Eastern realms retained their old features: there supposedly were no more Russians in the true sense. It is easy to determine the origin of this line of anthropological analysis. As early as 1940 Himmler had followed Hitler in arguing that the Bolsheviks had carried out a conscious policy of racial mixing.[52]

In a radio broadcast on August 24, Winston Churchill observed that the German police-troop executions in Russia surpassed anything since the Mongol invasions of Europe in the sixteenth century: "there has never [since] been methodical, merciless butchery on such a scale, or approaching such a scale."[53] Hitler and Himmler might have appreciated the comparison.

The SS campaign against the inferior races of Asia, moreover, was not limited to propaganda. There were efforts in 1941 to decimate peoples considered successors of the Huns or Mongols or these believed to be linked with the Jewish conspiracy. Some of these policies had nothing to do with securing territory or even liquidating communist officials, as we can see from the strange and tragic experience of the exiled Turkmen.

There were hundreds of thousands of Turkmen living in exile in the Baltic States, the Russian zone of Poland, and in the Ukraine. Originally they had been involved in the attempt, during the Russian Civil War and the 1920s, to establish a republic of Turkestan. After the Soviet

Union crushed their fledgling republic and liquidated the national leaders who had disguised themselves as communists, many Turkmen went west, some settling in Germany.[54] But in 1939, as the approach of war with Poland became obvious, their former President Tschokai ordered them to leave Germany, and they ended up with others who had settled to the east. They fell into the grasp of Nazi Germany after Operation Barbarossa began.

At the outbreak of the war against Russia two police officials arrested Prince Veli Kajum Khan, who had remained as Turkman observer in Berlin. Prince Kajum Khan had studied economics and agriculture at German universities and was well connected with the German intellectual elite. That did not help him with the police. Sent to jail in Berlin-Steglitz, he was asked to provide lists of Turkman Freemasons and Jews; he was accused of being a Freemason himself, and he was subjected to various forms of torture when he denied membership and knowledge of Freemasonic and Jewish activity. Kajum Khan was told later that Heinrich Müller, head of the Gestapo, had ordered his arrest. He was held for four or six weeks, then released after a professor intervened in his behalf.

During this time Kajum Khan received information that the Germans had rounded up Turkmen and put them into a camp. Although he could not confirm the reports, the German radio, press, and posters were filled with propaganda about the inferior races of Asia, with pictures of Nordic men and Asiatics used to prove the case. In late July or August 1941 some scholars offered him the opportunity to visit a camp, since he was needed as an interpreter. In the first camp he found at least twenty thousand of his countrymen imprisoned under horrible conditions, many wasting away, literally living in holes in the ground. The prisoners told him that each day SS men came and made a selection. Those judged to have long noses or "Mongolian" slit eyes were sent to the left, removed from the camp, and murdered in a forest outside the Polish town of Suwałki. Another method of selecting those to be killed was to check for circumcision.

The situation was little different at a second such camp that Kajum Khan visited. Although he was risking his own life, he wrote a letter of protest and sent it to the Ministry for the Occupied Eastern Territories and took other steps to get the information out. It turned out that the ministry was unaware of these camps, for it sent a commission to investigate, which confirmed the story. Count Friedrich Werner von der Schulenburg, former German ambassador to the Soviet Union and heavily involved in the anti-Nazi resistance, later told Kajum Khan that Müller had issued a secret order for the liquidation of all inferior races in

Turkestan, and that Schulenburg himself had seen a copy of the order.[55] The German army never penetrated to the eastern side of the Caspian Sea into Turkestan itself, but the Turkmen living outside their homeland were well within reach.

Other sources supply supporting evidence. The *Einsatzgruppen* reports to Berlin contain a number of references to the liquidation of Asiatics. In Mogilev the SD and police combed the POW camp of Russians identified as Jews and Mongols. After the conquest of Kiev in September 1941, German physicians arrived to work at a "pathological institute"— in essence, a center for killing and medical experiments comparable to the euthanasia institutes in Germany. According to one of the doctors who took part in the killings, normally by administering lethal doses of morphine, the first large-scale action was directed against Turkmen and "other low-grade Caucasian races." Other victims included Jews, gypsies, politically unreliable people, and the mentally or hereditarily ill—a total of eighty to one hundred thousand. The SD delivered the victims to the institute. A unit of Mongols removed the bodies and disposed of them in a nearby crematorium.[56]

In all likelihood, this order to liquidate Turkmen and low-grade Caucasians came out of the bundle of proposals submitted to Müller at the secret RSHA meeting several months before Barbarossa.[57] In other words, it probably occurred at the same time and in the same way as the order to kill Jews in the East. The whole campaign in the U.S.S.R was clearly planned well in advance. There was no military necessity for this murder policy; the only logic behind it was racial and ideological.

This is not to say that the SS (or Nazi) attitude toward Asiatics was identical to that toward Jews. Jews remained the most important target, the arch-enemy throughout the war. There was, however, an arbitrariness to some other racial judgments, which allowed for significant changes over time. As the war dragged on and German manpower ran short, even the Waffen-SS found it possible to redefine its racial categories so that inferior races—including the Turkmen—could supply Himmler with additional troops.[58]

HIMMLER did not attend a small but important meeting at Rastenburg on July 16. By this time the German forces were bearing in on Leningrad in the north and Kiev in the south. In the center, not only Minsk but Smolensk, a mere two hundred miles from Moscow, had been captured. Russian losses were huge. The meeting at Rastenburg was a business meeting, but it was also a kind of victory celebration. Hitler turned his attention from the seemingly minor military problems that remained to the task of carving up and administering the vast conquered areas of the Soviet Union.

The Führer first presented the general guidelines to his attentive audience: Göring, Bormann, Lammers, Keitel, and Rosenberg.[59] He declared that Germany should not divulge its aims to the world; declarations were unnecessary and would only make its path more difficult. As with Norway, Denmark, Holland, and Belgium, Germany would say nothing about its intentions—only maintain that it was forced to occupy, organize, and secure the territory. Of course, Germany would nonetheless take all measures necessary for a final settlement, such as shooting and deportation. And those present had to understand fully that Germany would never leave the conquered regions. To the inhabitants, however, Hitler declared, the Germans should proclaim that they were bringing freedom.

Since the Russians had issued an order to conduct partisan warfare behind German lines, Hitler continued, Germany could turn such operations to its advantage by exterminating anyone who represented opposition. Germany would prevent any significant military power west of the Ural Mountains—even, Hitler said, if it had to carry on the war for one hundred years. Only the German should bear arms, not the Slav, Czech, Cossack, or Ukrainian. The whole Baltic territory would be incorporated into the Reich.

Rosenberg wanted to distinguish among the nationalities in the East; he regarded Ukrainian national consciousness and education, for example, as useful to Germany, because it could be exploited against the Russians. But Himmler had already undermined Rosenberg's pro-Ukrainian tendency, arguing behind the scenes that the Nazis should decimate the Ukrainian intelligentsia, leaving the Ukrainian masses an obedient herd.[60] Göring emphasized that the first priority was to guarantee Germany's breadbasket in the East and to secure the economy generally. The group talked about boundary changes and appointments to administrative positions in the East, and there were the usual squabbles over jurisdiction and patronage. Rosenberg wanted to be sure that Ribbentrop, who had put in a claim for Foreign Office involvement, would not tie his (Rosenberg's) hands in the East. Hitler decided that Rosenberg's ministry merely had to send a liaison to the Foreign Office. Ribbentrop would be the least of Rosenberg's problems.

When the six men finally got around to considering Himmler's functions in the East, Bormann's minutes state, a long discussion developed. Yet the record here, unlike elsewhere, does not contain details—a sign that it traversed sensitive ground. Bormann delicately stated that there was concern expressed at the meeting about Himmler's functions in the East conflicting with Göring's responsibilities. However, Hitler and Göring "repeatedly" pointed out that Himmler needed the same sphere of jurisdiction that he had in the Reich, that he would not have different powers in the East, but that his powers were absolutely necessary. What was behind this disagreement?

One could not very well have a long discussion about Himmler's jurisdiction in the East without touching on his functions, which is to say the functions of the SS and police there. Ever since its founding, the SS empire had had a mission to deal with Germany's internal enemies, and now the impending annexation of Eastern territory meant that the future German Reich would have millions more subjects, whose racial and political qualities made them suspect. Hitler's directives at the meeting about security in the East were blunt: "shoot anyone who even has a cross look." Most or all of those present would already have known that Hitler was determined to eliminate German Jews, and that Madagascar and sterilization were no longer options. The implication of the minutes, then, is that the same thing would happen to the Eastern Jews as was planned for the German Jews—and that Himmler needed the same kinds of powers to carry this off. Another conclusion can be drawn from experience: if the group got into a specific discussion of the Jewish question, Hitler would not have been a mere spectator.

Rosenberg (and possibly Lammers) likely made reference to Göring's economic concerns and responsibilities, because mass killings and resettlement operations would disrupt the economy and infringe on Rosenberg's domain.[61] But Hitler and Göring "repeatedly" supported Himmler's authority in the East. Whatever Göring's economic goals in the East, he was willing to accept mass killings of perceived enemies. Rosenberg had no recourse but to submit.

The result was to give Himmler a mandate over all security-related matters, which Hitler formalized the next day with a decree signed by himself, Keitel, and Lammers. This decree specified that, even after the introduction of a civil administration in the East, Himmler would have the right to issue directives regarding security to civilian authorities. Himmler's higher SS and police leaders were only nominally subordinated to Rosenberg's commissioners; in terms of their functions, they were subordinated to Himmler.[62] At the end of the five-hour meeting, Hitler reassured the group that in practice disagreements would quickly disappear. This was easy for him to say; no one ever challenged his authority.

Though no one pronounced the verdict, Rosenberg was the weak man at the conference, his choices for appointments questioned or criticized, some appointments made over his head, his authority left vague. His pro-Ukrainian approach was openly repudiated within weeks of the conference. Later Rosenberg tried in vain to argue that Hitler's decree of July 17 was supposed to protect his authority against Himmler's encroachments—which by August involved economic matters in the East as well as police matters. Himmler launched a trial balloon, arguing that his powers as Reich Commissioner for the Strengthening of the German People extended into the newly conquered areas. Because he was unsure of success, however, Himmler had Greifelt take responsibility for this step, rather than risk his own standing.[63]

Göring came off relatively well on July 16, though it remained unclear how Himmler's assigned tasks in the East would square with Göring's economic concerns. The other winner was the absent Himmler, and Bormann quickly sent him a copy of the minutes.[64]

Other Nazi officials also sensed that Himmler and Bormann had teamed up to carry out Hitler's wishes, even against the resistance of Rosenberg, Frank, and some of the Gauleiter. A few weeks earlier Gottlob Berger had heard Nazi Party Treasurer Franz Schwarz openly criticize Frank and Gauleiter Erich Koch, and show signs of uneasiness about Rosenberg's appointment as minister for the East. Schwarz had described Himmler's brainchild, the higher SS and police leaders' posts, as one of Himmler's greatest achievements. Schwarz had also declared that he, Bormann, and Himmler had to stick together firmly, now more than ever. These three, Schwarz said, would be the rock against which the waves of opposition would break. Berger cleverly replied that Himmler was always striving to form such a coalition in the interests of the movement.[65] Since Schwarz controlled a sizable purse, it was wise to keep him on Himmler's side.

On July 20 Himmler went to Lublin for a meeting with Globocnik, whose drive, ambition, and ruthlessness made him a candidate for a star role in Himmler's emerging scenario. Globocnik had some weaknesses —longstanding charges of corruption against him were probably well founded. Nor did Himmler like the fact that Globocnik was a bachelor who had not yet produced offspring to assure the future of the race. (Only days before Himmler's July trip to Lublin, Globocnik became engaged—without, however, submitting the medical and genealogical data on his fiancée needed for SS approval.)[66] But Himmler needed Globocnik for a harsh task.

Three days before Himmler headed for Lublin, he appointed Globocnik his deputy for the creation of SS and police strongholds in the newly conquered Eastern territories. This was a move toward Himmler's idea of settling peasant-warriors in the East; he intended to have the SS and police put down roots and live with their families in these bases, and he was prepared to have the SS build residences for them.[67] Globocnik was also eagerly promoting German settlement in Lublin and nearby Zamosc,[68] and Himmler visited these two cities on July 20.

Zamosc, in the southeastern portion of the Lublin district, was a noteworthy tourist attraction with a history that must have appealed to Himmler. Founded in 1580 by Johann Zamoyski, who had studied in Padua, the town was modeled after Padua by German and Italian architects. Its marketplace in the center of town sprang directly from the late Italian Renaissance. A few years later Zamosc joined other German and Eastern European cities in the Hanseatic League, a trading organization of independent city-states. In the early seventeenth century it added strong fortifications, which it needed to hold off numerous attacks of Tatars, Russians, and Swedes. It formed an outpost of German culture and civilization in the East, or so Nazi officials liked to think.[69]

Himmler liked what he saw and gave Globocnik at least general approval to go ahead with renovation, expansion, and a permanent SS settlement in Lublin, under the name "Program Heinrich." To supply labor and turn out necessary goods, Himmler ordered Globocnik to build a new concentration camp (which became Maidanek) for twenty-five to fifty thousand inmates in the Lublin area. The existing smaller camp was to be devoted to auto repair and carpentry, and a third facility would be established to make clothes and carry on other trades. Himmler specifically mentioned that large tailor shops could use female Jewish labor. By November 1941 these projects were already consuming vast amounts of construction materials, which had to be shipped in by rail.[70]

This specific plan was apparently only the first step of a larger project—the postwar resettlement in the East. Once before, Himmler had spoken of lifting a magnet over the annexed Eastern territories and the Government General to lift up those made of racial "steel." Now he needed an even larger magnet for a vast new empire. In July Himmler ordered the Ethnic German Liaison Office to register ethnic Germans throughout the Soviet Union and to lay the cornerstone for German leadership there. He also was prepared to take—that is, to seize—Germanic children of pure blood immediately.[71] By early August officials in the SS Race and Settlement Office were already discussing how they could go through the Russian population and select the racially valuable, without showing much concern for the others. The idea, wrote Otto Hofmann, head of the office, was premature, since only a small part of the Soviet population could be imprisoned in camps. Hofmann promised to clarify some of the basic issues in his discussions with Himmler.[72] In mid-August Martin Bormann wrote that Hitler would defer until after the war a decision about just how much Eastern territory would be rapidly and completely Germanized, but that Himmler had already calculated that at least the Wartheland, East Prussia, and the Government General would be affected. The real German colonial empire, Bormann wrote, lay not in Africa but in the East.[73]

Himmler authorized Globocnik to carry out a geological and geographical survey of the Eastern territories as far as the Ural Mountains, to plan police strongholds scattered throughout that vast area, to construct model farms with up-to-date living quarters and equipment, to recondition existing farms, and, in a nice anthropological touch, to study ancient national costumes to be worn by German immigrants. Globocnik was allowed to recruit a staff of architects, interior decorators, contractors, drainage experts, surveyors, and historians. In August 1941 he also formed a corporation to sell household goods to the incoming Germans. To pull all this off, Himmler needed a large source of funds independent of the Reich Finance Ministry.[74]

Something else important and imminent was under consideration on July 20. Rudolf Brandt wrote that he had waited up on the night of July 20–21 until 1:00 a.m. for an important phone call from Himmler from Lublin—not a normal occurrence in his schedule.[75] A second clue came several months later when one of Globocnik's subordinates wrote to the head of the SS Race and Settlement Office explaining that Globocnik regarded the "cleansing" of Jews and Poles from the entire Government General as necessary to secure the area, and that he had developed far-reaching plans to attain this objective. Globocnik's subordinate specifically noted that Himmler was in agreement with Globocnik's idea, though Frank and his associates posed an obstacle. Globocnik's intention, his subordinate later wrote, was to create economic and biological pressure on the Polish population, as a way of cleansing the Government General of Poles.[76] There was nothing about the plans for cleansing Poland of Jews—a hint that these ideas went beyond what one could or should put on paper. The letter was also an indication that by October those plans were already set.

There is another way to speculate about Himmler's and Globocnik's discussions and agreements. The next day Hitler gave Croatian Marshal Kvaternik a review of the Russian campaign and a glimpse at his plans for the future. After only four weeks, Hitler boasted, Germany controlled Soviet territory that was larger than Germany before the annexation of Austria. He was not worried about the historical precedents; it was not he but Stalin who would suffer the fate of Napoleon. The Russian armies were virtually destroyed, and within six weeks, he predicted, they would hardly be capable of putting up serious resistance anywhere. Success allowed Hitler to ruminate about other goals.

There were situations in which one had to strike quickly to avoid a much greater bloodbath later on, he noted. Some people could not be incorporated within a state: even education, instruction, and imprisonment could not reform criminal and asocial elements who lived only to exploit others. There was only one way to deal with them: to destroy them. If they were not so dangerous to the community, one could shut them up in a concentration camp and make sure that they never again got out. Later Hitler described the Jews as a center of pestilence for humanity. Telling Kvaternik that the Jews would be removed from Europe, Hitler explained that any state retaining Jews would provide a new seat of infection and decomposition, whereas a Europe free of Jews could be unified. Although he apparently mentioned Madagascar or Siberia as a new site for resettlement of the Jews,[77] these references merely veiled the thrust of his argument: since the Jews were inherently criminal and parasitical, they had to be destroyed or shut up in concentration camps from which they would not emerge. Considering that Kvaternik was a foreigner, Hitler was surprisingly candid; only a little of what he said was designed to deceive.

More evidence of what Himmler told Globocnik the previous day may still emerge from Polish archives or trial records, but there is already enough to suggest that they discussed what Eichmann had earlier called the "final evacuation" of the Jews to Poland—to a system of concentration and extermination camps. Deportations of Jews from the Polish ghettos and from the Reich to the Lublin region would create a need for more manpower and more efficient techniques of killing, both of which required advance preparation. If Himmler had not discussed detailed plans earlier with Globocnik, he had to do so now, for time was getting short.

In a speech to his officials on July 22, Hans Frank spoke of issuing orders imminently to clear out the Warsaw ghetto. Hitler had again recently promised Frank to transfer the Jews from the Government General first. In the future, Frank said, the Jews would enter the Government General only for transit. Frank could not have believed that Jews would head for Madagascar via Poland, and it made little sense to think that Western European Jews were to be resettled in the Soviet Union when the SS and police were already massacring Jews there.[78]

Even before Himmler's discussion with Globocnik, the Reich Führer SS had taken the first steps to create an extermination camp at Auschwitz.

▼▼▼▼▼▼▼▼▼▼▼▼▼▼▼▼▼▼

CHAPTER 9

HEYDRICH'S PLAN

THERE IS some postwar testimony about Himmler's unwritten operational plans during the summer of 1941, and we must try to calculate, based on what is known of his movements and contacts, when he unveiled his intentions to others. His plans emerged then, because he had to tell a number of subordinates what actions to take; it was time to convert plans into action. We may also look at Himmler indirectly—through the reactions and activities of others. This process is a little like deducing the existence and the position of an invisible star—a black hole—by its pull on other stars, comets, or planets, whose movement would otherwise be inexplicable.

The most important postwar account came from Himmler's longtime acquaintance, Auschwitz Commandant Rudolf Höss. In spite of his relatively modest SS rank, Höss had outstanding credentials: World War I service in Turkey and Palestine, a conviction for participation in a political murder during the Weimar Republic, a jail sentence, membership in the Munich section of the Nazi Party since 1922, and years of experience under Theodor Eicke at the Dachau concentration camp.[1]

Beyond that, Himmler had been acquainted with Höss since 1921 or 1922. They had met in General Ludendorff's apartment in Munich, when both men were involved in the Bavarian Free Corps, and from 1930 on they had known each other quite well. They were both enthusiasts of farming; they had much to talk about. Höss was entirely reliable and discreet. One of his SS evaluation reports later noted that he did not push himself into the foreground; he let his achievements speak for themselves.[2]

Shortly after he was apprehended and recognized by the British in

1946, Höss began to clarify his role in the Final Solution. He stated that in June 1941 Himmler had summoned him to Berlin for a secret, private meeting. Not even Himmler's adjutant was present, so Höss's account is our only direct source.[3] Unfortunately, Höss then proceeded to describe how Himmler told him about the operation of the extermination camps of Belzec and Treblinka, which were not even under construction in June. During this interrogation he had his dates confused, and he probably injected some things that Himmler did not tell him until 1942.[4] Later, after he had had time to reconstruct his activities better, Höss abandoned the claim that extermination camps already existed at the time of this meeting—he spoke more vaguely of extermination places in the East,[5] which could well apply to sites where the *Einsatzgruppen* carried out executions. And Höss now dated the meeting as sometime during the summer of 1941, but he could not remember exactly when.[6]

Himmler was not in Berlin very often during the summer of 1941, especially after the invasion of the U.S.S.R.[7] It seems most likely that he actually met with Höss sometime during July 13–15. He spoke roughly as follows:[8]

The Führer has ordered that the Jewish question be solved once and for all and that we, the SS, are to implement that order.

The existing extermination centers in the East are not in a position to carry out the large actions which are anticipated. I have therefore earmarked Auschwitz for this purpose, both because of its good position as regards communications and because the area can easily be isolated and camouflaged. At first I thought of calling in a senior SS officer for this job, but I changed my mind. . . . I have now decided to entrust this task to you. It is difficult and onerous and calls for complete devotion notwithstanding the difficulties that may arise. You will learn further details from *Sturmbannführer* Eichmann of the Reich Security Main Office who will call on you in the immediate future. . . .

You will treat this order as absolutely secret, even from your superiors. After your talk with Eichmann you will immediately [alternatively, "within four weeks"[9]] forward to me the plans of the projected installations.

The Jews are the sworn enemies of the German people and must be eradicated. Every Jew that we can lay our hands on is to be destroyed now during the war without exception. If we cannot now obliterate the biological basis of Jewry, the Jews will one day destroy the German people.

Höss wrote later that at the time he regarded Himmler's reasoning as correct. In any case, he had received a sacred Führer order, and it was his duty to carry it out. The only thing unusual was that Himmler had summoned Höss and given an explanation—he could have merely sent an order.[10]

There are undoubtedly gaps in what Himmler told Höss, and more of them in Höss's recollections five years later. It would not be suprising if Himmler neglected to mention that he was deputizing Globocnik with similar tasks on the eastern border of the Government General; this information was not something Höss needed to know yet. But there is some wartime evidence of this Himmler-Höss meeting. Höss told others that he had received his orders to prepare for the Final Solution directly from Himmler, so his version of a summer-1941 meeting is not a convenient postwar invention.[11] And in spite of some defects, Höss's account approximates the known facts and the sequence of events better than any comparable one.[12]

Höss's conference with Himmler would fit into a sequence with Himmler's July 20 meeting in Lublin with Globocnik. It would even explain why Himmler's office manager, Brandt, waited up until 1:00 a.m. on the morning of July 21 for a phone call from Lublin, where Himmler must have been determining Globocnik's role in the coming Final Solution. And, finally, this Himmler-Höss meeting certainly casts additional light on Hitler's July 21, 1941, comments to Marshal Kvaternik: one either destroyed criminal and parasitical elements, or one threw them into concentration camps from which they would never emerge.[13]

Höss's testimony and the sequence of events both indicate that the fundamental decision to kill the Jews of Europe came before any determination of the exact method of killing. After all, Heydrich was not fastidious about how he got rid of Jews; what mattered was to get the job done quickly.[14] Like Höss's task at Auschwitz, Globocnik's job must have been to determine how best to dispose efficiently of the huge number of Jews to be brought there. And Himmler would have wanted to check out other likely sites.

On July 29 Himmler flew from Lötzen in East Prussia to Kowno, Lithuania. Higher SS and Police Leader Hans-Adolf Prützmann had carefully laid out a three-day itinerary for Himmler. But there was an extra meeting right at the start: Order Police Chief Daluege asked to see Himmler. He explained that there were urgent problems in the Ostland that he wanted to discuss, but that he had to be back in Berlin for an important meeting on July 30.[15] Daluege did not normally tell Himmler that he had critical prior commitments—they must have been very critical indeed. The meeting likely involved Heydrich and his subordinates; the Order Police and the Security Police both had a role to play in the deportations of Jews to the East. And the next day Heydrich took a big step forward with the Final Solution.

Daluege's problems in the Ostland involved the newly installed chief executive Hinrich Lohse, who had already caused Himmler's men some difficulty. Lohse was Rosenberg's man, but he was not well liked by Hitler or Göring.[16] He seemed to want to put Jews in ghettos, but not much more. On July 27 he had given oral instructions to his regional commissioners regarding the Jewish question. Einsatzgruppe A complained that some of the commissioners had gone to the *Einsatzkommandos* in their regions and tried to stop the executions of Jews and communists. Daluege appears to have briefed Himmler on the problem.[17]

In Riga, Himmler inspected a company of the Latvian defense units, which he had authorized only a few days earlier. He made it known that he intended to send the Lithuanians, Latvians, Estonians, Ukrainians, etc., away from their native lands to serve elsewhere.[18] This idea stemmed from the fact that the Nazis could manage "security" with small numbers of native policemen in these areas, whereas their officials in Byelorussia were shorthanded. It probably also reflected Himmler's concern about encouraging nationalist sentiment among peoples that Germany intended to subjugate. He did not want the support forces to start styling themselves as national armies.

By the time Himmler arrived in Riga, the police had registered all Jews in the city. Immediately after Himmler left, Nazi authorities introduced new regulations. First, police ordered all Jews to wear a yellow star of David on the left breast. Two days later a new order switched the star to the right breast; those who did not hear of the change and therefore did not comply were arrested. Jewish women were forced to perform labor as well, and by the end of August it was announced that the Jews would be forced into a ghetto to be created in a suburb of Riga mainly inhabited by Russians until then.[19]

Himmler flew on to Baranowicze, where Erich von dem Bach-Zelewski had established his headquarters.[20] A descendant of impoverished aristocrats, Bach-Zelewski was a longtime soldier. He had entered the army during World War I at age fifteen after the Russians invaded his Pomeranian homeland and burned down his family's house. He had also managed to remain in Germany's small postwar army, so he had plenty of military experience. In other respects, however, he was not well equipped for the tasks Himmler would now give him. His two sisters had both married Jews, and as a result Bach-Zelewski had become socially unacceptable to his fellow officers. He and his wife no longer received invitations, and he had resigned his military commission, taken his pension, and entered a border-defense force. The Nazi movement offered him a new career, but his family situation made him even more vulnerable. In March 1941 he tried to avoid responsibility for the coming bloodbath by asking to be given a commission to fight the Russian forces. Himmler made him higher SS and police leader for Central Russia instead. Later Bach-Zelewski implied that he had reached too lofty a position to give it all up.[21]

Before setting out on his tour, Himmler had ordered two SS cavalry regiments, under the command of Hermann Fegelein, Eva Braun's brother-in-law, to assemble in the Baranowicze area. Such cavalry regiments, Himmler believed, were particularly suited for use in the swampland, where motor vehicles were at a disadvantage. Bach-Zelewski was supposed to use them, Himmler ordered, to "cleanse" the Pripet River region, near the border of Byelorussia and the Ukraine. In the marsh areas, Himmler concluded, all villages had to be strongholds either for the Germans or for the enemy. Ukrainian villagers or other minorities hostile to the Russians or the Poles might provide friendly bases for German forces, but Poles and Russians were enemies, as were other racially inferior and criminal elements. All people suspected of supporting partisans were to be shot, Himmler continued; women and children should be shipped off, food and livestock seized, and the villages burned to the ground.[22]

Himmler had issued these general written instructions even before his arrival in Baranowicze, but he was willing to be more specific in person. The adjutant of the Second SS Cavalry Regiment radioed to the troops the next day Himmler's express (oral) orders: "All Jews must be shot. Drive Jewish females into the swamps."[23] Himmler was not trying to spare the women; he was apparently trying to spare his soldiers the upsetting experience of shooting the women. Later Bach-Zelewski would say, with vague reference to murder commands: "there was no need for pressure such as 'you must do this, or you will be shot.' There were entirely open, clear commands, . . . not any more secret than other secret commands. . . ." Perhaps to assuage any qualms of conscience, Himmler offered Bach-Zelewski one million marks for provisions at his headquarters.[24]

July 31 was a long and eventful day. Around the time Himmler was getting on a plane in Baranowicze to fly back to East Prussia, Heydrich was sitting down for a talk with Göring in Berlin. Heydrich had brought with him a draft "order" that he wanted Göring to sign.[25]

Complementing the task already assigned to you in the decree of January 24, 1939, to undertake, by emigration or evacuation, a solution of the Jewish question as advantageous as possible under the conditions at the time, I hereby charge you with making all necessary organizational, functional, and material preparations for a complete solution of the Jewish question in the German sphere of influence in Europe. In so far as the jurisdiction of other central agencies may be touched thereby, they are to be involved. I charge you furthermore with submitting to me in the near future an overall plan of the organizational, functional, and material measures to be taken in preparing for the implementation of the aspired final solution of the Jewish question.[26]

Heydrich went through the motions of deferring to Göring's authority over the Jewish question, but he and Himmler were really asking Göring to share responsibility for the Final Solution. One of the main purposes of the draft may have been to make it plain to others, who, like some at the meeting on July 16, had sought to use Göring to restrain Himmler, that Göring was on board. The Foreign Office expert on Jewish policy, Martin Luther, would write that Heydrich had stated in January 1942 that Göring had commissioned him at the Führer's instructions.[27]

Göring's behavior in August supports that conclusion. When Himmler put in a claim on several factories in conquered Latvia, hoping to add them to the growing array of SS economic enterprises, Göring decided to give in—though he warned that any more such requests would impair the unity of the war economy. The Reich Marshal did not willingly give away factories to others. But this time he knew that Himmler had received a powerful mandate, and he was aware of at least the general thrust of Jewish policy. Two weeks after his meeting with Heydrich, Göring declared that Jews in territories dominated by Germany had nothing more to seek; only in closely guarded concentration camps, and when necessary, could they be allowed to work; and he preferred hanging them to shooting them, since shooting was too honorable a death.[28]

Göring's commission of Heydrich formalized what earlier evidence had only suggested: with the words "complete solution of the Jewish question in the German sphere of influence in Europe," Himmler and Heydrich were planning arrangements for a continent-wide solution of the Jewish question, and they wanted Göring to sign off. And he did so without putting up difficulties, for he knew the Führer's views. The next day Heinrich Müller wired the commanders of the *Einsatzgruppen* that the RSHA was keeping the Führer constantly informed of their activities; they were asked to send visual material—photos, placards, fliers—as well as their regular reports.[29]

The Final Solution was and was not a resettlement plan. Western and Polish Jews would first be sent to various locations in the East, and they would be given the impression that they were to be employed there. But high SS officials knew what resettlement really meant. In early August, just after Himmler's visit, Prützmann mentioned to some subordinates in his office in Riga that Himmler had instructed him to resettle the "criminal elements." When someone asked where they were to be resettled to, Prützmann replied that the questioner had misconstrued the situation—they would be sent into the next world.[30]

Lohse was also taken to task around the same time in such a way that he got a good glimpse of the SS's intentions. Lohse's original draft decree on the Jewish question basically assumed that he and his subordinates had jurisdiction; it supposedly did not refer to cooperation with, let alone the competence of, the Security Police.[31] The main purpose of these guidelines was to provide for the registration, identification, isolation, and expropriation of the Jews in the Ostland.

Prützmann and Stahlecker both objected strongly. Stahlecker specifically warned Lohse not to use the model of the Government General —that was passé. The Jews would create unrest in the East, he argued, and there had to be a radical treatment of the Jewish question. The Security Police, he wrote, had received fundamental orders from higher authorities, which were not to be written down, only transmitted orally. These orders were connected, he wrote further, with the impending complete purge of all Jews from Europe.[32]

Lohse took the advice and modified his guidelines. At the outset he conceded that the Security Police were not affected by his provisional guidelines, which were to serve as minimum standards for the general commissioners and district commissioners subordinate to him. They would apply wherever and as long as further measures for the "final solution of the Jewish question" were not possible.[33]

Himmler's pursuit of execution sites and techniques continued in August. In Minsk he had a meeting with Criminal Police Chief Arthur Nebe, commander of Einsatzgruppe B.[34] Minsk, the capital of Byelorussia, had a Jewish population of more than fifty thousand, few of whom had managed to escape or hide at the outset of the war.[35] There had already been killings of Jews in Minsk, but on a limited scale— primarily the Jewish intelligentsia—as well as communist functionaries, "Asiatics," and criminals. Jewish doctors had been exempted, as had the mass of the Jewish populations.[36] In fact, the Nazis had brought in additional Jews from the nearby towns of Igumen, Slutsk, and Uzda, so that the total number in Minsk soon reached or exceeded eighty thousand. The first task was to register all these Jews, and then, on July 20,

Nazi authorities issued a directive establishing a closed ghetto, surrounded by barbed wire rather than brick walls and guarded by German
police and a Jewish order force. Transfer of the Jews into the ghetto
lasted until early August.[37]

Minsk, like Riga, was soon to become a dumping ground and killing
center for German Jews, and Himmler probably wanted to see whether
the facilities and the authorities were capable of handling the additional
people. Another factor may have been Himmler's concern about Nebe's
views. In spite of his long years of service under Himmler, Nebe was
not a racial fanatic and perhaps not quite adjusted to his new role as
Einsatzgruppe chief. (Later he was to become heavily involved in the plot
to assassinate Hitler, and he paid for it with his life.) Nebe had reported,
for example, that Byelorussia was so thickly populated with Jews that
only mass expulsion after the war could get rid of all of them.[38] Neither
the timing nor the goal was what Himmler had in mind.

Minsk had suffered badly from the recent fighting and from what
Nazi officials persisted in describing as arson. Entire blocks were destroyed, and the Germans who walked about the city crunched pieces
of glass with each step. The smell of smoke was everywhere. Remarkably,
one of the largest buildings in the city, the modernistic skyscraper called
the Lenin House, where the Byelorussian Parliament used to meet, was
basically undamaged. Himmler put aside political and aesthetic feelings
and spent the night there.[39]

The next day he told Nebe he wanted to see a demonstration of a
liquidation. So Nebe picked out at least one hundred alleged partisans
from the city's large jail; all but two were men. (By one account, Himmler
told Nebe to seduce the two women before shooting them—in order to
get information on what the partisans were planning.) There was a blond,
blue-eyed youth among the men. Before the shooting began, Himmler
asked him:

Are you a Jew?
Yes.
Are both of your parents Jews?
Yes.
Do you have any ancestors who were not Jews?
No.
Then I can't help you![40]

Members of Einsatzkommando 8 and Police Battalion 9 had to do the
dirty work. One group at a time, the victims were led toward a deep
ditch that had been prepared for them. They were forced to climb in

and to lie face down. The police unit then fired a salvo from above. After each round of killing, the bodies were covered with earth, and the next group, which had been kept waiting at some distance, was brought to the killing and burial site. After one round, Himmler complained that a victim was still alive. The chief of Einsatzkommando 8, Dr. Otto Bradfisch, placed a gun in the hands of a reserve police officer, Paul Dinter, and told him to finish the man off, which he did.[41]

As the executions proceeded, Himmler became more and more uncomfortable. Bach-Zelewski took advantage of his momentary weakness to press Himmler to spare not the victims but the policemen. Pointing out how shaken the executioners were, he complained that these men were now finished for the rest of their lives: they would either be neurotics or savages. (In fact, one member of the police battalion soon had a breakdown in Mogilev.) Himmler gave a short speech in which he explained to the men that Nazi Germany would soon extend to the Ural Mountains, and that it had hard tasks to carry out. He said he was responsible—they were simply carrying out a repulsive but necessary duty. They were to obey their orders unconditionally; in any case, those orders were based on harsh necessity. Combat was a law of nature, and human beings had to defend themselves against vermin, he concluded. Bradfisch later remembered Himmler's saying that the orders had come personally from Hitler, and that he and the Führer alone bore responsibility for them.[42]

Himmler then visited an insane asylum in Minsk, where he ordered Nebe to grant the inmates an end to their "suffering" as soon as possible. Still shaken by what he had just witnessed, however, he said he was now convinced that shooting was not the most humane method. Nebe supposedly suggested the use of dynamite. Bach-Zelewski and Karl Wolff both objected (at least according to Bach-Zelewski), but Himmler sided with Nebe. So Nebe received authorization to experiment with explosives.[43]

Around or shortly after the time Himmler left Minsk, Eichmann came to Auschwitz to discuss the details of the extermination program, as Himmler had wanted. Eichmann himself had learned of the order for the Final Solution from Heydrich, and probably only shortly before he went to Auschwitz. He told Höss that there was as yet no firm starting date for the operation, that plans were still in the preliminary stages, and that Himmler had not yet issued the necessary orders. But Eichmann did reveal tentative plans to deport Jews to Auschwitz from eastern Upper Silesia, the annexed areas of Poland, then simultaneously from Germany and Bohemia-Moravia, and then the Jews from the Western European nations.[44]

Höss and Eichmann also discussed methods of killing. Because of the large numbers of Jews involved, shooting was out of the question: it would have placed too heavy a burden on the executioners, Höss said. Eichmann told Höss about the gas vans used in the East for euthanasia killings. Their capacity, however, was too limited. The euthanasia killing centers in Germany dealt with larger numbers, but employing this model meant constructing many buildings, and it was questionable whether there was a sufficient supply of bottled carbon monoxide. So there was no easy answer. Eichmann said he would try to find a gas available in large quantities that would not require special installations. In the meantime, the two men picked a suitable site for a killing center—a secluded peasant farmstead in the northwest corner of nearby Birkenau. Höss then sent Himmler a detailed location plan, which was never formally acknowledged, but which, as Eichmann later told Höss, Himmler had approved. The plans have disappeared; they were never even entered into Himmler's correspondence log.[45]

HIMMLER had wanted a neater, cleaner, less upsetting way of killing large numbers of people, and poison gas was the obvious solution. Some of the technology was already tried and tested through the euthanasia program. Therein lay one problem. The mobile gas vans employed in East Prussia and the Government General during 1939–40, which made use of bottled carbon monoxide, had handled relatively small numbers of euthanasia patients,[46] not the millions projected now. The somewhat larger permanent euthanasia gassing facilities were in the Reich, closer to the victims, who were mostly "defective" Germans. The experienced gassing executioners were also busy with the euthanasia program—until August 24.

The leaks of information regarding the euthanasia program had finally become a serious political problem for the Nazi regime. On August 3 the Catholic Bishop of Münster, Count Clemens August von Galen, openly accused the government of carrying out mass murder of the mentally ill at the Marienthal Asylum, and he condemned the concept that any human being might be unworthy of life. Not only was the sermon mimeographed by the thousands and spread by hand; the British got hold of a copy, duplicated it, and dropped it from their planes. Although one Nazi official suggested hanging Bishop von Galen, Martin Bormann said that the Führer was worried that such punishment might impair the war effort. Indeed, Goebbels expressed concern that with any move against von Galen the Nazis would have to write off Münster's support for the war. Hitler took the only practical step he could: he stopped the euthanasia program—at least officially.[47]

On August 27 Heinrich Müller told his Gestapo subordinates that Himmler had made a fundamental decision regarding activities and expressions of opinion hostile to the state, which he said had increased in number since the attack on the U.S.S.R. Himmler had ordered the imprisonment in concentration camps of all clerics who "incited" the public, of Czechs and Poles hostile to Germany, as well as communists and similar rabble. They were to be offered long-term accommodations there, and they were not to be informed of the reason for their punishment.[48]

Because of Hitler's decision, the gassing specialists were now available for other duties, and no one recognized this fact quicker than Himmler, who had just left the scene of the unsatisfactory police execution at Minsk. Heydrich's plan for a continent-wide solution of the Jewish question was already approved, but, despite the killings in the East, the Nazis had not yet tackled the Jews in most countries. In other words, the Final Solution was still a plan; as Eichmann had told Höss, Himmler had not yet issued all the necessary operational orders.

Poison-gas technology offered the prospect of a better and quieter way to exterminate additional millions. The SS and police had helped out the Führer Chancellery on the euthanasia killings in Germany; now it was time to take over the men and equipment and use them in the East for the Final Solution.[49] The availability of these resources impelled Himmler to act upon Heydrich's plan.

But Himmler could not make such a decision himself. Hitler had originally authorized the euthanasia killings, and Hitler had nominally called the program to a halt. Himmler could at best suggest the transfer of the gassing specialists under the Führer Chancellery, which he did not control, to extermination camps in the East, where poison gas would be the primary weapon. Unless Hitler approved or had already approved the concept of killing millions of Jews, Himmler could not proceed. On August 26, however, Himmler's office manager telephoned one of Heydrich's aides to say that Himmler had agreed to Heydrich's plan.[50]

By another account, sometime during the summer of 1941 Himmler consulted one of his medical experts, Grawitz, who was not only chief SS physician but also president of the German branch of the Red Cross. Grawitz said Himmler had told him that Hitler had ordered the destruction of the Jews. Grawitz advised the use of gas chambers as the best way.[51]

Four independent pieces of evidence help to demonstrate the link forged in late August 1941 between Heydrich's plan and Himmler's new extermination camps. First, on August 28, in a letter to the Jewish specialists in the Foreign Office, Adolf Eichmann referred to the "coming Final Solution now in preparation."[52] Second, in the late summer of 1941 the gassing specialist Christian Wirth told another Nazi official that he had just been transferred from the euthanasia killing center in Brandenburg to a new facility in the Lublin area.[53] Third, postwar testimony by Viktor Brack, who ran the euthanasia program for the Führer Chancellery, clarifies the reasons for Wirth's transfer.

> In order to retain the personnel that had been relieved of these duties and in order to be able to start a new euthanasia program after the war, Bouhler [head of the Führer Chancellery] asked me—I think after a conference with Himmler—to send this personnel to Lublin and place it at the disposal of SS-*Brigadeführer* Globocnik.[54]

Actually, Brack wrote even during 1942 that "a long time ago" Bouhler had directed him to place a contingent of his men at Globocnik's disposal for implementation of Globocnik's special task, and that Himmler had directed him to proceed as rapidly as possible with the killings in order to disguise them.[55]

On September 2 an official from the SS Main Office proposed a list of men with special rank to be given an assignment with Globocnik in Lublin. These were obviously Brack's men from the Führer Chancellery. Himmler approved the list two days later.[56]

Himmler did not like to waste time or resources, and the euthanasia institutions in Germany were still available. So he ordered the transfer of Jewish inmates from the concentration camps to the euthanasia sites, under cover of the more general program of ridding the camps of mentally and physically deficient people. At this time Buchenwald Commandant Koch sent a transport of three or four hundred Jews to the euthanasia facility at Bernburg, where they were gassed.[57] They were not killed because they represented a security threat to Germany; they were already prisoners in existing camps. They certainly did not fit the standard profile of the euthanasia victims.

The big new project, however, was the construction of new killing facilities in the East. Himmler had to issue a specific order before any SS construction project could go forward. On the afternoon of September 10—the same day he approved the transfer of gassing specialists to Globocnik—he held a discussion with several subordinates from the SS Economic Office concerning "plans for construction." These same men—Oswald Pohl, Dr. Hans Kammler, and Sturmbannführer Heinrich Vogel—were heavily involved in the planning, construction, and administration of concentration camps. They appear to have drawn up plans for at least three new camps: Maidanek, Belzec, and Birkenau.[58]

Maidanek was a mixed-purpose camp, with a need for real workers. In the fall of 1941 Globocnik took over a sizable area on the outskirts of Lublin for the camp with workshops that Himmler had ordered in July. His first workers, who arrived that fall, were Russian POWs already in an exhausted condition. There was no housing or sanitary facilities for them, and they were given little food, so their number diminished as they carried out the task of building facilities at the camp. In December 1941 Maidanek received its first Jews, from the city of Lublin itself. They lasted no more than a few months; by the end of February all remaining Jews in the camp were shot. By March 1942 Maidanek was receiving Jews from elsewhere, with the fittest ones selected to work in an underwear factory and other plants, and the others sent directly to their death. By July 1942 Maidanek had a crematorium, about two months later a set of gas chambers.[59]

Belzec was the first pure extermination camp to begin operations in the region. There were only a few hundred worker Jews there (at a time), most used in the killing facilities or in the recovery of clothing and items of value from the dead. The first SS men showed up at Belzec in October 1941 to recruit construction workers to build the facilities. Himmler's office had reported Globocnik's progress to Oswald Pohl, head of what soon became the SS Economic-Administrative Main Office (WVHA), preparing Pohl for cooperation with Globocnik. Pohl's office had reported to Himmler that it could no longer obtain sufficient clothing or textiles for the Waffen-SS and the concentration camps. Himmler replied that he could make available a large mass of raw materials for clothing, and he gave Globocnik responsibility for delivering them.[60] Their owners were not likely to object. The gassing at Belzec began in March 1942 under the supervision of its first commandant, Christian Wirth. Ninety-one others from the Führer Chancellery who had worked with him on euthanasia gassings ended up at Belzec, Sobibor, or Treblinka—all of which were designed to gas Jews and were under Globocnik's supervision. The gassing experts lived separately from the other SS and police, and they were not carried on the list of Globocnik's regular troops.[61]

Before gas chambers were constructed, there was plenty that Globocnik could do with more traditional methods of killing. In October 1941 Captain Kleinschmidt, the company leader of a transport unit, came to the barracks in Lublin and ordered fifteen men to go with him. Each of the fifteen was given a truck and had to drive it to the concentration camp nearby. There they loaded about thirty on each of the fifteen trucks—a total of about 450 Jews—and carried them to an abandoned airport located approximately twenty-five miles from Lublin. The prisoners had to dig ditches six cubic meters in size. After finishing the ditches, ten of the victims took off their clothes and were given corrugated-paper shirts reaching halfway down the thighs. The bottoms of the ditches were lined with straw. The victims were ordered, ten at a time, to lie in the ditches, alternately head to foot. Then Globocnik's men threw hand grenades into the ditches, and heads, arms, and legs quickly filled the air. The troops shot anyone still moving after the explosion. Then they spread lime over the remains, and a new layer of straw was spread on top of the lime. Three or four layers of bodies, ten in each layer, were placed in such a grave. During the executions the other victims had to watch and await their turn. Women were kicked in the stomach and breasts, children smashed against rocks. According to an eyewitness to this particular episode, Globocnik's men killed approximately seventy-five thousand Jews in this general manner.[62] Apart from the sadistic killings by hand, it was about as far as one could go in streamlining the process of mass murder without more advanced technology.

Globocnik was not the only one experimenting with methods of execution. Arthur Nebe summoned the explosives-and-chemical experts from the RSHA's Criminal Technical Institute to Byelorussia. They locked a group of mental patients from Minsk in a bunker and blew it up, but the first explosion did not kill all the patients, so they had to try again. Afterward they had to retrieve the parts of bodies sprayed over the area, some hanging from trees. That experiment was not a spectacular success, but another one, using car-and-truck exhaust pumped through a hose into a sealed room in a mental asylum in Mogilev, extinguished five patients without difficulty. So the practice soon gained larger dimensions. After a German doctor visited the asylum in Mogilev, apparently to make a selection, as many as twelve hundred people were gassed.[63]

Another possibility was to use the transport trucks themselves, with their own exhaust serving as the source of carbon monoxide. In September 1941 the chemists, transport officials, and mechanics of the RSHA Criminal Technical Institute designed a tightly closed truck with the cab sealed off from the freight section. They then made arrangements with a body-work firm to convert Saurer truck chassis into vans with closed compartments that could hold about fifty people. The Criminal Technical Institute's chief mechanic made the alterations to divert the exhaust gas into the storage area.[64]

This new type of gas truck was tested on some Soviet POWs in Sachsenhausen. The results were so satisfactory that production was stepped up, and other vehicles—an Opel-Blitz truck and two Dodges—were also converted.[65] As it happened, the first deployment of the new gas trucks came in the Ukraine, [66] but there was also an urgent need for them in the Wartheland.

In July one of Eichmann's subordinates had raised the idea of finishing off the Jews in the Wartheland "in humane fashion," saying at that time that the idea seemed fantastic but was practical.[67] An extermination camp in the Wartheland could sweep Jews out of the Lodz ghetto. But Himmler had a problem with the mayor of Lodz and the district administrator, who were protesting plans to deport German Jews to Lodz. It would have been easier if Himmler could have said that Lodz's Jews would soon be liquidated, but he was not yet willing to tip his hand. "Naturally," Himmler wrote to District Administrator Uebelhoer, "it is not pleasant to get new Jews. But I should like to ask you in all cordiality to show for these things the same natural understanding which has been extended by your Gauleiter." When a polite suggestion did not do the trick, Himmler had to use firmness: "read your letter once again. You have adopted the wrong tone. You have obviously forgotten that you have addressed a superior." After the deportations to Lodz began in mid-October, and after Gauleiter Greiser interceded to smooth over the situation, Himmler magnanimously said he would bear no grudges.[68]

He did not delay much further. That fall Herbert Lange, commander of the unit that in 1940 had carried out gassings in vans using bottled carbon monoxide, rode around the Wartheland looking for a suitable site for a camp. He found an unoccupied castle along the Ner River, at a place called Chełmno, thirty-five miles northwest of Lodz, where a camp was established in late October or early November. Nearby was a forest where the gas trucks could operate discreetly. Gassings of Jews from the Wartheland were first carried out on December 8, 1941. Chełmno became, in effect, the first death camp in operation.[69]

But the gas trucks had powerful competition. Just around the time that Himmler was assigning poison-gas experts to Globocnik, Höss's subordinates were breaking new ground at Auschwitz. Auschwitz had been receiving trainloads of Soviet commissars and other POWs who were subject to liquidation. Höss's men had shot previous shipments of Russian prisoners, but on September 3 Höss's enterprising subordinate Hauptsturmführer Fritsch thought of an expedient new method based on the camp's own experience. The buildings, many of them former Polish army barracks, were full of insects, and the camp administration had previously brought in the Hamburg pesticide firm of Tesch and

Stabenow to get rid of them. Two experts had fumigated particular buildings with a patented insecticide, Zyklon B, a crystalline form of hydrogen cyanide that turned gaseous when exposed to the air.[70]

Tesch and Stabenow owned the rights to market Zyklon B east of the Elbe River. Zyklon B was manufactured by a Frankfurt firm called Degesch, an abbreviation for German Corporation for the Control of Vermin, in which I. G. Farben held an interest. Degesch had carried out experiments in order to find a gas that would kill all kinds of pests within a reasonably short period of time. Precisely that characteristic made it lethal to humans as well. So the exterminators at Auschwitz took extreme precautions to avoid accidents—no one was allowed near the buildings while they were being fumigated, nor could anyone come back for two days. The process made an impression on camp officials. Later they sent some of their own personnel to Hamburg for training, so that they could delouse buildings on their own.[71]

On September 3 Fritsch decided to experiment. First he crammed five or six hundred Russians and another 250 sick prisoners from the camp hospital into an underground detention cell. Then the windows were covered with earth. SS men wearing gas masks opened the Zyklon-B canisters to remove what looked like blue chalk pellets about the size of peas, creating a cloud of poison gas. After they left, the doors were sealed.[72] Höss wrote later that death was instantaneous. Perhaps that was what he was told. But he was not present to witness the event; he was away on a business trip. Other sources indicate that even the next day not everyone was dead, and the SS men had to release more insecticide. Eventually all the prisoners died. When Höss returned to Auschwitz, he heard about the successful experiment. On Eichmann's next visit to Auschwitz, Höss told him about the possibilities of Zyklon B, and, according to Höss, the two decided to use the pesticide and the peasant farmstead for extermination.[73]

Back in June the Auschwitz camp had asked whether the firm Heerdt-Lingler could supply special delousing chambers, designed specifically for the Degesch process, to the camp. Only ten cubic meters in size, these chambers were probably to be used for delousing clothing. Heerdt-Lingler was eager for the business but warned that there would be a delay of eight to ten weeks before delivery. Then the firm heard nothing for some time. In October a branch of Hans Kammler's SS construction office began work at Birkenau, the area near Auschwitz designated for a death camp.[74]

By November Heerdt-Lingler learned that Auschwitz had ordered five hundred kilograms of Zyklon B, which indicated that the camp was going to carry out delousing on a very large scale, all the more surprising in that Zyklon B could not be stored long—it deteriorated after three months. Zyklon could not safely be used for delousing without the special chambers. Yet Auschwitz had still not placed an order for Heerdt-Lingler's delousing chambers. Heerdt-Lingler asked a firm associated with Degesch why Auschwitz had ordered so much Zyklon: could the company still expect an order for the delousing chambers? The response was that the reason for Auschwitz's large order was unknown.[75]

After the war Erich von dem Bach-Zelewski explained that the extermination camps arose because Germans and Central Europeans were not suited to be mass executioners. Stalin, he said, always had people to employ for this purpose—for example, the Latvians. Although the Nazis found some individuals to serve as killers, there was no collective eagerness to do so. The extermination camp—Bach-Zelewski said Auschwitz, but used it as a generic term—was something that the Russians could not accomplish: it reflected the German gift for organization. Bureaucrats created it, he concluded.[76]

HITLER had miscalculated how long the war against the U.S.S.R. would take. By September 1941 it was clear that his original forecast of an eight-week campaign was wrong. But even the unexpected continuation of the war did not seriously delay implementation of the Final Solution. What Hitler had formerly been willing to defer to the end of the war, now he wanted immediately.

In June 1941 he had refused to approve a complicated measure from Frick regarding the legal status of German Jews, because, as Lammers told Justice Minister Gürtner confidentially, Hitler was of the opinion that after the war there would be no more Jews in Germany anyway.[77] Just after Himmler discussed "construction plans" with Pohl, Kammler, and Vogel on September 10 came a change in schedule. On September 18 he wrote to Gauleiter Greiser in the Warthegau about plans to send more Jews there. The Führer, Himmler explained, wanted to clear the Old Reich and Bohemia-Moravia of Jews as quickly as possible. They would be sent, in the first stage, to the annexed Polish territory; Himmler wanted the Lodz ghetto to absorb sixty thousand of them. But Greiser was not to worry—early in 1942 they would be sent "farther to the east."[78] By early 1942 Chełmno, Belzec, and perhaps even Auschwitz could be functioning as death camps for the Jews. These were the destinations "farther to the east" that Himmler would not spell out in a written document.

It is impossible to prove just how quickly Himmler apprised Hitler of the new possibilities for killing Jews. Hitler and Himmler both appear to have been in East Prussia between September 10 and 18.[79] If they met during that time, it would have been like Himmler to boast of the new technology. And it would have been like Hitler to conclude that he could now more quickly rid the Reich and the Protectorate of the people he considered vermin.

Hitler's decision to clear Germany of Jews before the end of the war and before the first death camps were ready to operate, however, created serious new problems for Himmler and Heydrich. It meant either providing temporary lodging in existing ghettos in the East, or using old-fashioned methods of shooting, or some combination of both. But the *Einsatzgruppen* and their helpers had far from finished their task of disposing of native Jews in the East: could they manage the German and Czech Jews too?

Hitler seemed to have few doubts. After a conference with Himmler and Heydrich on September 24, the Führer named Heydrich Reich Protector of Bohemia-Moravia, a move that gave him the opportunity to smash the Czech resistance by using the carrot and the stick, and also to push deportations of Czech Jews to Poland. On September 27 Himmler came through with a long-delayed promotion of Reinhard Heydrich to Obergruppenführer and general of the police.[80] But Heydrich did not live to see the final and highest form of recognition. After his assassination in mid-1942, the destruction of the Jews in the Government General of Poland—the killing action at Belzec, Sobibor, and Treblinka—formally became "Operation Reinhard."[81]

On September 25 Hitler spoke of extending Europe to the Ural Mountains and creating a human barrier against Asia.[82] By late September the military situation inspired the Führer with such delusions of grandeur. German forces had surrounded Leningrad, and Guderian and von Kleist had just destroyed the Russian southwestern army group near Kiev, capturing 665,000 prisoners as well as the city, a victory that was all the sweeter in that Hitler had plotted this campaign against the advice of his military experts. Now Hitler was planning a new offensive, designed to advance to Moscow and beyond. As with Leningrad, Hitler intended to starve the Russian capital into submission. On October 3 Hitler told the German people that the enemy in the East was broken and would never rise again, and a worried American military attaché in Moscow reported a week later that the end of Russian resistance was near. Respected military historians would later write that the Russian situation by October was actually worse than either the Germans or the Western Allies imagined.[83]

With Russia near collapse, and with his belief in the inferiority of the Slavs, Hitler would hardly have been pessimistic at this time. Once Russia was defeated, he believed, the final British hope of outlasting the Nazis would evaporate. Contrary to what some historians would later maintain,[84] Hitler was not frustrated by the military situation when the first extermination camps for Jews were being constructed. Himmler too was, by his own account, already looking ahead to the postwar period, though in late 1941 he reluctantly deferred some of the construction projects connected with the large settlement for SS men and their families in the Lublin area, because of the demands of the war.[85]

The Final Solution was an idea with some roots in the prewar period. Several key components—killing the Jews of Germany, Poland, and in the conquered Soviet territories—emerged as concrete plans by early 1941, at the time Hitler made the fundamental decision to destroy the Jews of Europe. But they were not implemented immediately, and the overall plan remained malleable into the summer of 1941. In short, the Final Solution came about gradually. Himmler's approval of a specific continent-wide program drawn up by subordinates, however, occurred in late August 1941, after he had settled upon the idea of gas chambers in extermination camps. By October 1941 several camps had moved beyond the planning stage.

The Final Solution was irrevocably set in motion when Himmler and the SS committed resources and manpower to planning and constructing extermination camps. All of this preceded any serious Nazi anxiety about military defeat, and it was largely uninfluenced by practical considerations about the food supply, shortage of laborers, or constraints on the transportation system, which were not too serious in any case. The Final Solution was the direct expression of Hitler's ideology and frequently expressed wish to destroy the Jewish race.

▼▼▼▼▼▼▼▼▼▼▼▼▼▼▼▼▼▼▼

CHAPTER 10

RIVALS INTO
COLLABORATORS

TWO OF the extermination-camp sites—Auschwitz and Chełmno—were technically within what was then considered the German Reich, though they were in relatively isolated areas of what had been western Poland. The others were on the far-eastern side of the Government General. To bring millions of Western and Central European Jews to any of these sites was a fairly complicated operation, and the logistics had to be carefully planned.

The Lodz ghetto in the Wartheland represented one convenient and immediate outlet for Jews deported from Germany. When the gas chambers at Chełmno were ready, it would not take long to relieve the overcrowded conditions in Lodz. Lodz and Chełmno, however, could handle only a fraction of the German Jews. If the *Einsatzgruppen* and similar units killed off enough Eastern Jews quickly, it would be possible to deport remaining German (and Austrian and Czech) Jews into the ghettos farther to the east, where they could soon be eliminated. In the conquered Soviet territories there was less danger that news of killing operations would leak out to the West, and squads of native auxiliaries were ably assisting the *Einsatzgruppen*, police regiments, and special brigades of the Waffen-SS in killing hundreds of thousands.

Still, Himmler had by no means resolved all the problems with the ongoing killings in the conquered Soviet territories. The whole process had to go smoothly and to remain secret. As German troops moved farther east, the military turned over basic jurisdiction to civilian authorities in the rear areas. It was no longer possible to use the fighting as a cover for mass executions, and it would not be so easy to pretend that the Latvians, Lithuanians, Byelorussians, and Ukrainians were carrying out mass murders on their own.[1] Himmler's men in the field also had to deal with rival German authorities: Hinrich Lohse's appointees in the new Reich Commissariat Ostland (the Baltic States and Byelorussia), Gauleiter Erich Koch's men in the Białystok region and also in the Ukraine, and Hans Frank's subordinates in Galicia and Lublin.

Alfred Rosenberg represented the most immediate and biggest problem. He was a vain man who persistently claimed expertise on policies in the Soviet Union and assiduously guarded what he regarded as his jurisdictional rights as minister for the Occupied Eastern Territories. He had a history of opposing Himmler, and he had appointed subordinates who had already made life difficult for Himmler's men and Heydrich's *Einsatzgruppen*. He and his appointees in the field stood in the way of SS domination of all security-related matters in the conquered Soviet territories and of SS claims to economic assets of the murdered Jews. So Himmler and Heydrich had to take a direct role in the course of events.

ON SEPTEMBER 18 Himmler flew from East Prussia to the port city of Libau in Latvia, beginning a three-day tour of the former Baltic States. The trip was pressing enough for him to disregard advance warnings that the weather was bad, and important enough for Heydrich to come along. The RSHA chief, a pilot, flew his own plane from Berlin. And Himmler added his settlement expert, Meyer-Hetling, to his usual entourage.[2] Heydrich's agency got rid of perceived enemies, Meyer-Hetling drew up plans for Germans to settle in the vacated territory: the two men symbolized the negative and the positive sides of the SS's resettlement.

It happened that there were still thousands of Jews in Libau, a development that could not have been to Himmler's liking. The situation there was a microcosm of what had taken place in a number of cities in the Ostland, with disagreements between the civilian authorities and the SS and police or the *Einsatzgruppen* delaying the process of clearing the Ostland of Jews. Himmler's stop in Libau seems to have had a direct impact on events there. Two days later a newly appointed local SS and police leader, Dr. Fritz Dietrich, arrived in the city. The idea of having a local SS and police leader to coordinate and supervise police activities in particular districts was Himmler's own,[3] and Libau was among the first locations to receive one.

On September 21 Jewish laborers were collected to clear the streets and the remnants of destroyed buildings. The next day sixty-one Jews in Libau were killed, the first of a series of executions carried out by Einsatzkommando 2 and Dietrich's subordinate Untersturmführer Kügler. These executions were limited to those older Jews, male and female, who were considered unsuitable for labor.[4]

After his subordinates reported police killings of Jews in Libau, Reich Commissioner Lohse prohibited further executions and took up the issue with Stahlecker. Stahlecker insisted that he had special orders from Himmler, which he could not discuss, and he specifically objected to Lohse's intervention to prevent executions in Libau. Lohse held his ground: "Yes, because you are subordinate to me, and I will not allow such things." Stahlecker then argued that he was subordinate to Higher SS and Police Leader Hans-Adolf Prützmann, not to Lohse: Lohse was free to complain about this if he liked. Lohse later claimed, probably with some exaggeration, that this was the first time he had heard that the police were not subordinate to him.[5]

In actuality, civil authorities collaborated freely in some actions against Jews. German officials in Latvia agreed in late September to the establishment of closed ghettos in the larger cities; all remaining Latvian Jews were to be kept there, and the rural areas were to be entirely cleared of Jews.[6] The objections to police operations in Libau and later in Riga (and in Schaulen, Lithuania) were based on the number of killings, the potential damage to the economy, the semipublic manner of execution, or just on the claim of superior jurisdiction over the police. If anyone objected to the principle, he did not say so publicly, and few Nazi officials objected to the principle of murdering Jews.

In most places, killing operations faced less resistance. From Kowno, Lithuania, for example, a mobile section of Einsatzkommando 3, under Hauptsturmführer Hamann, following orders given to him by Standartenführer Jäger, took his police unit and a battalion of former Lithuanian partisans out to execute Jews in one location after another. By the beginning of September they had already killed more than forty-seven thousand people—mostly Jews, some communists, criminals, mentally ill, and a few uncooperative officials.[7] According to one witness, the commandos used to go out in the morning and come back in the evening drunk, boasting of their executions. They also brought back with them clothing and valuables. The witness also saw Lithuanians hauling away the valuables on sleds and other vehicles. Hamann ran into serious opposition, as far as is known, only in the city of Schaulen, where both the district governor and the military tried with some success to protect thousands of Jewish laborers who were installed in a ghetto.[8]

Lohse and Rosenberg supposedly preferred ghettoization as a solution to the Jewish question. Rosenberg told some of his subordinates in Berlin that he could not see executing women and children. Ghettoization, on the other hand, had taken place even in the Middle Ages. The French

Revolution and the hated principles of liberty, equality, and fraternity had pushed ghettoization into obscurity, but he liked the idea.⁹

Not everyone in the Ministry for the Occupied Eastern Territories looked backward. The Jewish specialist there was Dr. Erhard Wetzel, the same Wetzel who was in the Nazi Party's Office of Racial Politics, the same man who had proposed a less extreme solution of the Jewish question in Poland in the fall of 1939. He had now learned better, and he wanted to make use of the most advanced technology. When Lohse apparently complained, in early October, that the mass executions in the Ostland were causing trouble, that Jewish laborers were still needed, and that some other method of resolving the Jewish question must be found,¹⁰ Wetzel suggested that Lohse use Brack's new gas trucks to dispose of those Jews unfit for work. He observed that Eichmann had agreed to this, although new trucks still had to be constructed. The goal was not only to speed up the executions but to make them more secret. Wetzel wrote:

> Incidents such as those that took place during the shootings in Vilna, according to a report I have on my desk, can hardly be sanctioned, keeping in mind that the executions were undertaken openly, and the new procedures assure that such incidents will no longer be possible. Jews fit for work, on the other hand, will be transported to work forces in the East.¹¹

Wetzel submitted this memo during October to Rosenberg for approval, but Rosenberg apparently deferred a decision.¹²

The reason for Wetzel's initiative was largely that he was better informed. Wetzel had a direct connection with the Party Chancellery—which is to say, with Martin Bormann—and he used to tell the others in the Ministry for the Occupied Eastern Territories what the chancellery wanted. Because of his situation, he was almost in a position to give orders on the Jewish question to others in the ministry.¹³ But Wetzel was only an ambitious and arrogant bureaucrat, not a real power or an innovator on the Jewish question. Whether he made suggestions or not, the same move to high-technology mass murder occurred anyway, as events in the Ukraine demonstrated. Once again, Himmler, not subordinates, set the course.

STALIN had unwisely ordered his armies to hold Kiev, the jewel of the Ukraine, which allowed the German panzer groups to encircle and decimate the Russian troops in the region. The fighting ended

September 24 with a glorious victory for an operation Hitler had ordered against the advice of the professional military planners. On the day Kiev surrendered, Hitler spoke at his headquarters of his intention to leave hardly anything standing in the city. One of those listening to his remarks wrote that the Führer generally intended to destroy Russia's large cities, to smash industry in the Ukraine, and to drive the Ukrainians back to the land.[14]

On September 30 Himmler set out on another tour—this time to the conquered regions of Southern Russia. In his party was an Untersturm-führer Dr. Albert Widmann, the head of the chemical section of the RSHA Criminal Technical Institute and one of the prime inventors of the new gas truck that recycled its own exhaust. A few weeks earlier Widmann had successfully gassed five mental patients in an asylum in the East with truck exhaust; then he and his colleagues in Berlin had gone to work on designing a closed truck.[15] In early September, Himmler had already decided to assign some gassing experts to the Ukraine, Russia's breadbasket, to carry on work there.[16] Since it was easier to modify existing trucks in the field to serve as mobile gas chambers than to produce the new trucks in Germany and to drive or ship them to the East,[17] Widmann accompanied Himmler to the Ukraine, where momentous events had just occurred.

The German military occupation of Kiev had not gone smoothly. Some officers were quartered in prominent undamaged buildings, several of which suddenly and mysteriously exploded. Next came a huge fire in the center of the city, destroying some of the most beautiful and representative buildings, and leaving about fifty thousand Russians homeless. German troops in Kiev uncovered two possible causes of the damage: time bombs left behind by Russian forces, and a spy-and-sabotage ring headed by a man with the code name Friedmann.[18] The situation was dangerous enough for even experienced soldiers to worry about security, and whenever there was a need to secure territory against enemy agents, the *Einsatzkommandos* had a quick solution.

The commander of Sonderkommando 4a, which had reached Kiev just behind the army, was Paul Blobel. Even among a crowd of mass murderers, Blobel distinguished himself through his crudity and blood-thirstiness. Early in the Russian campaign he had suffered from dysentery, which he attempted to treat with liquor. In spite of his cure, Blobel was able to carry out his duties, and his unit left a trail of blood along its route to Kiev. Perhaps his most barbaric action before Kiev was his execution of Jewish children from an orphanage in Bjala Zerkow in late August. Nor was Blobel the only guilty party there; the army became involved as well. After Colonel Groscurth tried to block the action in

Bjala Zerkow, General von Reichenau, commander of the German Sixth Army, allowed the completion of the executions.[19] If Reichenau had no objections to the killing of Jewish children, he would not blanch at broad actions to deal with the perceived Jewish threat to German security. So Blobel knew he had a free hand in Kiev.

After a meeting with Einsatzgruppe A Commander Rasch, Blobel recognized what had to be done. First he had explosives placed under the nearly nine-hundred-year-old Dormition Cathedral at the Perchersk Monastery and blew up a good part of that building. On September 28 he had the Ukrainian auxiliary police post notices on the walls of buildings ordering all Jews to appear at 8:oo a.m. at a designated location on Dekhtyarevskaya Street. He gave out word orally that the entire Jewish population was to be resettled. Actually there was to be a mass execution of a large number of Jews, as Blobel informed a few police drivers who had just arrived in Kiev and were waiting for their vehicles to be repaired. These Jews he described as asocial, without worth, and intolerable for Germany. In addition, there would be executions of patients in mental asylums and other "useless eaters." Because of the lack of manpower, Blobel said, the drivers would have to participate in the action too.[20]

More than thirty thousand Jews showed up on the morning of September 29 in spite of cold weather. A German minister stayed behind with the kitchen staff to make tea for the troops of the commando unit and the units of Police Regiment South, which had been called in to help. German forces blocked off the streets as the Jews were led in long lines in the direction of a ravine in the northwest part of Kiev, which was called Babi Yar. As they walked, the Jews chanted religious songs. One German policeman present thought that they knew what was in store for them.[21]

Blobel had his driver bring him to the top of the ravine, where he stood and watched as the Jews were marched in below, by this time clad only in underwear. They were forced to lie face down, and the executioners, also at the base of the ravine, equipped with Schmeisser automatic rifles, tried to shoot them in the back of the head, per instructions. Because of the mass of victims, some were shot several times over, others only wounded. Then the next batch came in and lay down on top of the first. According to one of the executioners, Blobel yelled frequently to his men below, complaining that the killings were not going fast enough. The killers worked in shifts, and they were kept supplied with ammunition and rum. At the end of the day lime chloride was spread on top of the layers of bodies.[22] After two days' work by Blobel's men and their helpers, Blobel proudly reported executing 33,771 Jews in an operation that had gone quite smoothly.[23]

On October 2—two days after the mass executions ended—Himmler flew to nearby Berdichev, where Friedrich Jeckeln picked him up. They led a convoy first to Zhitomir, formerly a city of about ninety thousand, which was badly damaged in the war. Two weeks earlier the entire Jewish population, about eighteen thousand, had been liquidated. From Zhitomir Himmler's party drove to Kiev, where Himmler spent the night. Himmler believed that Kiev was another ancient German city—he called it Kiroffo. The next day he took a tour of "Kiroffo."[24]

There were still some ongoing activities at Babi Yar. In an effort to clean up, Blobel had ordered his men to explode the sides of the ravine and cover up the bodies.[25] Perhaps he would have done this in any case to hide the evidence of the crime and to lessen the stench of the corpses, but he certainly could not leave such a mess for Himmler to see in case the Reich Führer SS wanted a tour of the now famous site. There were also additional executions, some of captured Soviet sailors and of other unknown victims. The killings at Babi Yar went on for at least a week after the big Jewish action and regularly thereafter.[26]

It is not known, however, whether Himmler included Babi Yar on his tour of Kiev. He was not fond of the old-fashioned method of killing, though he certainly appreciated the results. So did General von Reichenau. On October 10 he released a statement to the troops about their conduct in the Eastern territories. He called upon them to show "full understanding for the necessity of a severe but just revenge on subhuman Jewry."[27]

After Kiev, Himmler stopped in Krivoi Rog, Nikolayev, and Cherson. In Krivoi Rog the police units and the military had already shot a substantial number of Jews and communists in the surrounding county of Schirokoje.[28] In Nikolayev he met another prolific killer, Einsatzgruppe D chief Dr. Otto Ohlendorf. Ohlendorf's Einsatzkommando 12 had just killed about eight thousand Jews in Nikolayev, a city of more than a hundred thousand. Himmler tried to ease the burden on the executioners, telling them that they bore no responsibility for their deeds: he and the Führer were responsible; they were merely carrying out orders, as good soldiers must. According to Ohlendorf, Himmler also repeated the orders given out earlier: liquidation of all Jews and commissars. And Himmler made the task easier for Ohlendorf by giving him a promotion to Oberführer on the spot for having killed so many Jews—or so some of Ohlendorf's men claimed.[29]

In Cherson Einsatzkommando 11a had taken the Ukrainian police under its control, purged unreliable elements, and then made use of the Ukrainian force to block off areas during executions, to screen suspects, and to help out during antipartisan actions.[30] Outside Cherson lay an antitank ditch, which the SS and police forces then put to use. The five thousand Jews of the city had been loaded onto trucks and transported to the ditch, where the various German forces and Ukrainian auxiliaries shot them. In spite of receiving liquor and cigarettes first, several of the executioners lost their nerve during the killings and had to be relieved.[31]

A supposedly more humane method was at hand. Blobel later testified that he received the first gas truck in September or October, and one of his men, in a separate war-crimes proceeding, claimed that the first use of a gas truck occurred immediately after the action at Kiev—that is, in early October.[32] It would have made sense to have Widmann present to assess the results and make any adjustments in the equipment. By the time Blobel's unit moved from Kiev to Poltava, in November, two gas trucks were in use.[33]

The operator of the first truck, surprisingly, was Heydrich's own driver, Findeisen, a taciturn man who resisted inquiries as to why his boss had given him this not exactly pleasant job. As it turned out, the gas truck did not make things much easier for those who had to take part in this killing operation. As the truck drove its passengers to their final destination, the carbon monoxide gradually reached lethal concentration. Apart from the screams of the victims during their final five to ten minutes, there was the mess to clean up afterward—an unbelievable tangle of bodies covered with excrement. After these voyages Blobel used to look at the corpses, look away, and take another dose of schnapps.[34]

The addition of the gas trucks only reinforced the general picture. In the South, Jeckeln, Rasch, Ohlendorf, and subordinates like Blobel had made giant strides toward resolving the Jewish question. Himmler, who had recently been to the Ostland, could not have missed the difference in the Ukraine: Jeckeln had managed to get the military to cooperate, civil authority was not yet a problem, and the execution totals were far higher. So it may have been during this trip that Himmler decided to have Jeckeln replace Prützmann in the Ostland; in fact, the two men ended up switching positions in late October.[35] Himmler particularly wanted more rapid progress in the Ostland because of a new timetable laid down by the Führer.

While Himmler and Widmann were in the Ukraine, Heydrich informed the Führer of the scheduled deportations of German Jews to specific destinations in the Ostland.[36] Eight days later, at a conference in Prague with a group of subordinates, Heydrich passed along Hitler's reaction: the Führer wished the Jews to be removed from German space by the end of the year, if possible. All pending questions had to be resolved, and transportation difficulties should not be used as reason for delay.[37] Since none of the extermination camps was ready, the Führer's wish required rapid and massive shipments of German Jews to killing sites and ghettos in the East.

In fact, the urgency of the situation moved Heydrich to send both Heinrich Müller and Adolf Eichmann immediately to Kiev to confer with Himmler. Eichmann later claimed that he simply presented the final statistics on Jewish emigration, which may be partially true.[38] Himmler needed to know how many Jews were left and how quickly they could be transported to their death in the East. Of course, Eichmann was the transportation specialist, and it was logical for Himmler to consult him on the problem of shipping Jews to their death in Riga and Minsk.

Heydrich kept the Führer in touch with ongoing plans for the Jewish question through telegrams to Lammers and Bormann at the Führer's headquarters.[39] He also continued to coordinate his actions with Himmler. On October 18 the two men spoke by phone and agreed not to allow any Jews to leave German territory by going overseas.[40] With extermination camps under construction and on the drawing board, there was no good reason to allow even small numbers of Jews to escape.

Heydrich's moves increased the pressure on the Ostland, where some resistance to SS and police activities continued. Gauleiter Wilhelm Kube in Byelorussia complained that the SS and police were seizing gold, silver, and works of art from the region, and Rosenberg angrily told Lammers that Prützmann and Himmler were exceeding their authority generally. Himmler had not cleared his orders regarding political security in the Ostland with Rosenberg; instead, he had traveled about, "apparently in order to give oral instructions unknown to me. . . ." Rosenberg invited Lammers to join him in presenting these problems to the Führer.[41]

On October 24 Reich Commissioner Lohse had another frosty meeting with Sturmbannführer Rudolf Lange, who was on the staff of Einsatzgruppe A and commanded one section of Einsatzkommando 2. Lange had already taken steps to construct a large concentration camp for Jews near Riga, explaining to Lohse that he had acted according to Heydrich's orders, which required him to move quickly: the first transport of Jews from the Reich was due on November 10. General Commissioner Drechsler, who was also present, and Lohse objected to the SS's unilateral decisions.[42]

Meanwhile, Stahlecker had sent back word to his superiors in Berlin that Lohse had forbidden executions in Libau. As a result, the RSHA lodged a complaint with the Ministry for the Occupied Eastern Territories. On October 31, on behalf of the Ministry, Georg Leibbrandt asked

Lohse for a report on the matter, implying that Lohse had behaved improperly. Lohse's response, written by Government Counselor Trampedach in Riga, came on November 15, 1941:

> I have forbidden the wild executions of Jews in Libau because they were not justifiable in the manner in which they were carried out.
>
> I should like to be informed whether your inquiry of 31 October is to be regarded as a directive to liquidate all Jews in the East? Shall this take place without regard to age and sex and economic interests (of the Wehrmacht, for instance, in specialists in the armament industry) [this parenthetical note in different handwriting] Of course the cleansing of the East of Jews is a necessary task; its solution, however, must be harmonized with the necessities of war production.
>
> So far I have not been able to find such a directive either in the regulations regarding the Jewish question in the "Brown Portfolio" or in other decrees.[43]

Lohse was careful not to give the impression that he opposed the killings of Jews *per se*. But he thought it was acceptable to object to "wild" killings that became public knowledge. He also believed he was on relatively safe ground in trying to protect the interests of the economy. But his search for documents was bound to be in vain, since the orders were not given to the civilian authorities but to the SS and police. And discussion of liquidation was usually oral, not written.

On the evening of October 25 Himmler and Heydrich were among the guests at Hitler's headquarters. In the course of his remarks Hitler reminded them of his prewar prophecy that, unless war was avoided, the Jews would disappear from Europe. "This criminal race," Hitler continued, "has the two million dead of the [First] World War on their conscience, and now hundreds of thousands. Let no one say to me: we cannot send them into the mire. Who concern themselves about our men? It is good if preceding us is terror that we are exterminating the Jews. The attempt to found a Jewish state will fail."[44]

In early November the RSHA announced that the Ostland would soon receive fifty thousand German and Czech Jews. Half would go to Minsk, the other half to Riga. Apparently because the concentration camp at Salaspils, near Riga, was not yet ready, the first transports would arrive in Minsk beginning November 10. The Jews scheduled to reach Riga more than a week later might have to be diverted to Kowno if there was no space for them in Riga.[45]

Himmler made it quite clear to Jeckeln in November that all Jews in the Ostland would have to be killed. He also noted Prützmann's report that Lohse had opposed executions and liquidation of the Riga ghetto, and stated that the ghetto had to be liquidated whether or not Lohse approved: "Tell Lohse it is my order, which also reflects the Führer's wish." Shortly thereafter, Jeckeln arrived in Riga, gave the message to Lohse, and asked for his approval. According to Jeckeln, Lohse responded that he had nothing against the liquidation of the ghetto and that Jeckeln could interpret Lohse's agreement as an order. Lohse's more plausible version is that Jeckeln said that he had received the order and that he was responsible for everything, that Lohse was not to interfere.[46]

Rosenberg told Lohse he would try to raise the matter with the Führer. Lohse said he would forbid his subordinates to take part in executions of Jews, and that he would do what he could to prevent these measures, which damaged the economy.[47] Rosenberg then took up the theme of avoiding disturbances to the economy in his October 30 address to a large conference of government officials from various agencies concerned with the Eastern territories. Although he talked of settling fifteen to twenty million Germans in the East, and of recapturing land that the Jews and Russians had robbed from the ancestors of the Germans, Rosenberg made it clear that the economic demands of the war represented the highest immediate priority. And he estimated that the work in the East would take one hundred years.

Himmler did not bother to attend this conference, and he half-jokingly wrote Heydrich that as a reward for handling another matter Heydrich did not have to go either, since the meeting was concerned only with planning. Himmler could get away with sending his deputy Greifelt.[48] He did not disdain planning himself, but Rosenberg's long-range plans for the next century were another matter.

In spite of Rosenberg's emphasis on the war economy, Himmler's forces were already carrying out mass murders that removed valuable laborers. On October 27, for example, Reserve Police Battalion 11, with the assistance of at least two companies of a Lithuanian defense force, came to the Byelorussian city of Slutsk to carry out the liquidation of all Jews there. In spite of the protests of the district commissioner that most of the Jews were necessary for the local economy, and complaints about lack of advance notice, the commander unleashed his men upon the town, setting off wild butchery and looting that victimized Byelorussians as well as Jews. The district commissioner begged his superior, Gauleiter and General Commissioner Kube, to keep this battalion away from him in the future, and Kube too wrote an angry letter of protest, which was sent on to Heydrich in Berlin.[49]

Slutsk was not an isolated incident. On November 7 an SS-and-police unit, aided by Lithuanian and Byelorussian auxiliaries, raided the Minsk ghetto. They shot the elderly and ill and herded thousands of others into the main square. The Jews were forced to line up in rows of eight, and the men in front were given a banner that proclaimed: "Long live the 24th anniversary of the Great Socialist October Revolution." German cameramen filmed a march of the demonstrators, who were ordered to appear happy. When the filming stopped, the action began. The Jews were forced into the storehouses of the former NKVD division, thousands of people packed tightly together. After a couple of days those who still survived were told that they were to be resettled. Their guards led them to freshly dug graves outside the city, forced them to undress, and dispatched them with machine guns. Some twelve to thirteen thousand died. The ghetto now had room for the first shipment of German Jews, due to arrive any day. Six days later another seven thousand were executed.[50]

On November 15 came a kind of showdown. Rosenberg and Himmler had a four-hour meeting about a range of disagreements. Rosenberg presented a draft decree that subordinated the police to the civil administration. Himmler replied that he already had another draft, which he would take a position on; he had no intention of agreeing to Rosenberg's version. The two men then discussed Jewish policy. As usual, Himmler's written record of this section of the meeting was brief and only slightly informative. The two men agreed that Himmler's Jewish specialist would simultaneously become the specialist in the Political Section of the Reich Commissioner's Office. The same solution would be employed at lower levels.[51] This arrangement, which Himmler had used on a number of occasions, granted the Reich Commissioner for the Ostland some nominal personal authority over a specialist on Jewish policy, but in practice it meant that the higher SS and police leader would no longer face opposition from Lohse's staff, except insofar as Lohse could influence the Jewish specialist.

Did the two rivals discuss the substance of Nazi policies toward Jews in the East? Himmler's record of the meeting provides no evidence that they did, but this was precisely the kind of subject he avoided putting on paper. It certainly would have been hard to resolve the jurisdictional dispute without addressing the substance of policy itself. And there was another reason to be frank: the first German Jews had arrived in Minsk, and deportations to Riga were imminent. Even according to Himmler's own maxim of not telling someone more or earlier than he had to know, it was now time to enlighten Rosenberg. The tone of Himmler's memo made it clear that he left the meeting satisfied. Rosenberg had not put up a serious fight.

We may estimate what Himmler told Rosenberg about the Jewish question by looking at Rosenberg's statement shortly after this meeting. Only three days later he told German journalists at a confidential briefing that the Final Solution had begun; it was a "biological extermination of all Jews in Europe." No Jew could remain on the continent to the Ural Mountains; they would either be forced beyond the Urals or exterminated. The press was not to write about the extermination in detail, but the reporters could use stock phrases such as the "definite solution" or the "total solution of the Jewish question."[52]

On November 17 Himmler telephoned Heydrich and told him about the results of the meeting with Rosenberg, the situation in the Government General, and the "elimination of the Jews."[53] On November 29 Heydrich sent out invitations to the forthcoming government conference on the Jewish question, originally scheduled for December 9.[54] Complications such as the German declaration of war against the United States delayed the meeting, known as the Wannsee Conference, until January 20, 1942.

In the meantime, implementation of the Final Solution continued. On November 29 German police in Riga segregated men between the ages of eighteen and sixty who were capable of labor and settled them in a part of the Riga ghetto, which was sealed off. That evening Germans and Latvians raided the ghetto and assembled the Jews, killing or injuring many in the process. The next morning German policemen and Latvian auxiliary police drove a convoy of some fifteen thousand out of the ghetto with whips. A trainload of a thousand Jews from Berlin had just arrived in Riga, the first of the transports from Germany. Some had frozen to death in the unheated railway cars en route. The survivors joined the march of the Riga Jews to a nearby forest called Rumbuli. An eyewitness report passed back to some government officials in Berlin described the slaughter:

> The Jews . . . had to dig long trenches as mass graves, then undress themselves completely, sort out their clothes taken off in separate heaps, and then to lie down naked on the bottom of the mass grave. Then they were shot by SS men with pistols. The next group of those condemned to death had to lie down on top of those already executed, and were shot in the same manner. This procedure continued until the grave was filled. It was then covered with soil, and a steamroller was driven over it in order to flatten it out.

A week later at least another eight thousand were killed in the same way.[55]

As it happened, everything did not go according to plan on November 30, for the police who had organized the transport from Berlin had failed to take into account a policy that Himmler and Heydrich had adopted at the beginning of the month. The two men had discussed the idea of transporting elderly German Jews, and probably also decorated Jewish war veterans, to the special concentration camp Heydrich had established at Theresienstadt, in Bohemia-Moravia.[56] The elderly were no real danger to security, and they could not bear children. Decorated war veterans, also past their prime, had earned the privilege of living out the rest of their lives in a concentration camp. Although life in Theresienstadt was far from idyllic, the conditions were better than those in virtually any other camp in the East. Diversion of both groups to Theresienstadt would ease the strain on German executioners in Riga, Minsk, and Kowno.

In the first convoys from Berlin, however, were some elderly Jews and decorated veterans. The violation of policy was serious enough for Himmler, telephoning from the Führer's bunker at Rastenburg, to warn Heydrich on November 30: "Jewish transport from Berlin. No liquidation." The phone call was an attempt to halt the normal course of events—the official policy for all but the exempted Jews was liquidation. To save the few, it was necessary to defer the mass killings. As it happened, Himmler's intervention was too late; the executions had already taken place.[57]

Jeckeln reported to Himmler the success of his killing operations in the Ostland. No doubt he expected to be praised. But there had already been complaints from military and civil authorities in the Ostland; the killings were not secret enough. So Himmler said that shooting was too complicated an operation; it was better to use the gas trucks.[58] One particular reason for Himmler's dissatisfaction was that the complaints had actually reached Hitler. An eyewitness account of the shootings at Rumbuli was passed by a German military engineer through higher-level contacts until it finally reached Admiral Canaris. Canaris is reported to have given the Führer an account of the atrocities and the negative consequences, and Hitler is supposed to have replied: "You're getting soft, sir! I *have* to do it, because after me no one else will!"[59]

Himmler's dissatisfaction with the shootings of Jews, however, went beyond the particular circumstances in the Ostland and the criticism reaching the Führer. The fundamental problem, in Himmler's mind, was the effect of such killing on his men. So on December 12 he issued a general order, in slightly veiled language, to the higher SS and police leaders and their subordinates throughout the Eastern territories that was designed to mitigate psychological difficulties among the troops responsible for eliminating Germany's enemies. Commanders and officers were to take personal responsibility for ensuring that their men who carried out executions did not suffer damage to spirit or character. Himmler suggested social gatherings in the evening as a way of reinforcing camaraderie, but warned against abuse of alcohol on such occasions. A good meal, good beverages, and music would take the men to the beautiful realm of German spirit and inner life. There was, however, to be no discussion of their daily activities or of the statistics on killing. The orders and duties were absolutely necessary for the German *Volk*, but they were not to serve as subjects of conversation.[60]

On December 14 Rosenberg raised the Jewish question with Hitler in passing. He had planned to give a public speech in the Berlin Sportpalast, but Pearl Harbor had made certain sections of the speech obsolete, and Rosenberg asked for Hitler's guidance. Hitler told him not to mention that Germany would annex the Eastern territories. Rosenberg then said that he assumed it would be better not to refer in the speech to the extermination of the Jews. Hitler agreed, saying that the Jews had brought this war on Germany, and caused the destruction, and that they had only themselves to blame if they had to suffer the consequences.[61]

On December 18 Lohse finally received a formal answer to his November 15 inquiry whether there was a policy of executing all Jews without reference to the needs of the economy. The Ministry for the Occupied Eastern Territories replied that economic considerations were not to influence the handling of the Jewish question. This response was actually less specific than what Otto Bräutigam, deputy chief of the Political Division of the ministry, heard—namely, that the Führer had decided that the Final Solution of the Jewish question took priority over all else. Ministry officials suggested that Lohse negotiate arrangements for the Jews with the SS and police officials—precisely the ones who had caused the difficulties in the first place. At all cost, he should avoid raising the issue in such a way that it reached Hitler or Himmler.[62]

IN COUNTRIES where Germany had installed its own government of occupation, and where the men in power happened to be cooperative, Himmler and the SS could make relatively early preparations for deportations of Jews to the East. Arthur Seyss-Inquart testified at Nuremberg that Heydrich had visited him in the Netherlands in the spring of 1941 to explain that Jewish circles would put up the greatest resistance to Germany: Jews in the Netherlands would at least have to be treated like other enemy aliens—that is, they would have to be interned.[63] Once the Dutch Jews had been brought into camps controlled by the SS, sending them to the East would just be a matter of arranging the transportation. Likewise, some German preparations for deportations in the puppet state of Slovakia preceded Himmler's approval of the Final Solution.[64]

In spite of Himmler's preference for independent and clandestine action, however, the RSHA could hardly move against Jews in all the conquered or allied countries, or against Jewish nationals of countries within German territory, without getting clearance from those governments. If the Jewish question was Himmler's preserve, measures affecting Germany's foreign relations were the *raison d'être* of Foreign Minister Ribbentrop and his ministry. Sooner or later, Himmler and Heydrich had to bring the German Foreign Office into the negotiations. Himmler seems to have preferred it to be later.

The Foreign Office was not really capable of initiating the kind of racial policy to which Himmler was committed. It was too staid, too concerned about the rules of diplomacy, too addicted to precedent. Although he was without question loyal to Hitler, Ribbentrop was also widely regarded as incompetent in foreign affairs.[65] Some of his higher-echelon officials were old-line diplomats, often from aristocratic backgrounds, with no great love for the Nazi leaders. Others, even when they were party members, were nonetheless disagreeable. The new undersecretary of state, Martin Luther, sought his salvation in advancing his career as fast as possible. Himmler regarded him as "a common, unpleasant sort of fellow—slimy and uncouth."[66]

Besides the personal dislikes, there was a history of jurisdictional disputes between the SS and the Foreign Office. The SD had frequently played a clandestine role in German foreign relations independently of the Foreign Office, which Ribbentrop undoubtedly resented. The Foreign Office had its own Jewish section—D III—which sporadically and generally unsuccessfully tried to take a role in Jewish policy. Even if Heydrich had won the major battle by late 1940, there were still minor conflicts. In March 1941 the Foreign Office argued that Germany could take no action against alien Jews in Germany without its concurrence. The German Embassy in Croatia angrily raised complaints against the behavior of the SS head of the *Einsatzkommando* there—he disobeyed direct orders from the embassy and seemed to be conducting his own foreign policy. Another problem: the SS man serving as Jewish adviser to Rumania, formally attached to the German Embassy in Bucharest, was feuding with the German ambassador, an SA member whom the SS had almost assassinated in the Röhm Putsch of June 1934.[67] The number of irritants gradually mounted to the point where, by the summer of 1941, Himmler and Ribbentrop were barely on speaking terms.

So there was little immediate reason for Himmler to take Ribbentrop personally, or the Foreign Office generally, into his confidence. In spite of Ribbentrop's virulent anti-Semitism, the Foreign Office knew little or nothing of Himmler's plans for the *Einsatzgruppen* in the conquered Soviet territories, and even after the mass killings in the East began, it received no official notification for quite some time.[68] The overall plan, the Final Solution, was even more secret.

In early August, however, Himmler's adroit chief of staff, Karl Wolff, began the process of rapprochement. In a long lunch with Ribbentrop he was able to resolve a number of outstanding disputes, and the minister promised to invite Himmler to dinner soon. In fact, in late September Himmler was invited to go hunting with the foreign minister on his estate.[69] By this time the Foreign Office had learned a good deal about killings in the East, mostly from non-SS sources, and it had taken part in some negotiations involving the military, the Foreign Office, and the RSHA on the disposition of specific groups of Jews in Serbia. This was the context in which Luther was able to arrange a meeting with Heydrich in early October. Once again there was no written record of the conversation. But, under Luther's prodding, the Foreign Office decided to avoid complications posed by possible deportations of Jews to Rumania and to let Heydrich's men arrange to clear out the Jews in Serbia itself. Luther's willingness to cooperate in Serbia helped to forge a bond between the SS and the Foreign Office and set the groundwork for future events.[70]

Only a few days after his meeting with Heydrich, Luther responded knowledgeably to an inquiry from the Ministry for the Occupied Eastern Territories. The ministry had asked whether some Jews with foreign citizenship, such as the Slovaks, could be included in the police measures in the Reich Commissariat Ostland. In a written proposal for his superiors, State Secretary Ernst von Weizsäcker and Ribbentrop, Luther suggested that police measures should be expanded to all Jews. Even in the West, he continued, it would be a mistake to grant American Jews special exemptions from laws against Jews, when Germany was refusing to make exceptions for friendly states such as Spain or Hungary.[71] If Heydrich had not given Luther direct information about the Final Solution—for the moment Luther may still have thought of the long-defunct Madagascar plan as the Final Solution[72]—he had at least let Luther sense which way the wind was blowing. A Jew was to be considered a Jew, whatever the nationality and whatever the repercussions on German foreign relations.

By the end of October, however, both Luther and Franz Rademacher, head of the Jewish section of the Foreign Office, had more than enough information to recognize that deportations of Jews to the East within the framework of the Final Solution meant mass extermination. And at the same time, Heinrich Müller sent copies of the first five RSHA reports on the activities of the *Einsatzgruppen* to Ribbentrop.[73] Slowly the Foreign Office got the picture. Around this time Hitler discussed the Jewish question with Slovak President Tiso, Prime Minister Tuka, and Interior Minister Mach. Details of the conversation are unknown, but he seems to have expressed his own views, then used Ribbentrop to discuss specific application of policy with the Slovaks. It eventually became quite a regular pattern: Hitler would make a general approach, then Ribbentrop or Himmler would try to close a deal in his wake.[74]

On November 26 Ribbentrop held a reception for Bulgarian Foreign Minister Popoff, who mentioned that the Bulgarians were having difficulty extending their laws concerning Jews to foreign Jews living in Bulgaria. According to a memorandum Luther later wrote, Ribbentrop told Popoff that all Jews would have to leave Europe at the end of the war. The Führer had made this unalterable decision, which was the only way to master the Jewish problem. There had to be, Ribbentrop continued, a comprehensive solution introduced worldwide; individual measures would help little. Nor should anyone worry too much about protests of actions against Jews with foreign citizenship. The Germans were no longer accepting such protests from the United States.[75]

Coincidentally or not, on November 27 Hitler met in succession with high officials from Spain, Hungary, Italy, Croatia, Bulgaria, Finland, and Rumania. The only one of his late-November 1941 conferences that is well documented is probably the one where Hitler expressed his views on the Jewish question most openly, because he knew the feelings of his guest. On November 28 Hitler told the Grand Mufti of Jerusalem, Haj Amin el-Husseini, that Germany had declared an uncompromising war on the Jews, which of course meant that it was opposed to a Jewish homeland in Palestine. Germany was, Hitler continued, challenging the European powers to settle the Jewish question; when the time came, it would turn to the non-Europeans as well. Britain and Russia were both allegedly power bases of Jewry, and he would carry on the fight until the last traces of Jewish-communist hegemony were eliminated. The German army would in the future break through the Caucasus into the Middle East and help to liberate the Arab world, Hitler assured Husseini. Its only other objective in the region would be the annihilation of the Jews, he concluded.[76]

Finally, on November 29, Heydrich invited Luther to attend what became the Wannsee Conference. Responding to Luther's request, one of his subordinates listed Foreign Office goals that could be raised at this meeting. They included deportation of Croatian, Slovakian, and Rumanian Jews living in the Reich, deportation of Serbian Jews, deportation of Jews turned over to Germany by Hungary, and statements to the governments of Rumania, Slovakia, Croatia, Bulgaria, and Hungary of German willingness to deport to the East all the Jews living in these countries.[77] By December 1941 the Foreign Office had adapted quite well to the role that Himmler and Heydrich wanted it to play.

EVEN THOUGH Hitler had induced Hans Frank to accept in principle deportation of Jews to the Government General, there had still been difficulties over how many and how soon. Hitler had intimated to Frank that these Jews were not long for this world, but there could still be arguments over who had the right to dispose of them and their property. Himmler's recurrent battles with Frank left him with few illusions about establishing death camps inside the Government General—Frank and his men would undoubtedly create problems.

In February 1941, for example, Provincial Governor Zörner had barred the police from extracting the funds for Lublin labor camps from the Jewish council in the Lublin ghetto. In a mid-October letter, one of Globocnik's subordinates made it quite explicit: Globocnik would not be able to carry out his plans and ideas (including purging of Jews and Poles from the entire Government General) without the cooperation of Frank and the civil administration.[78]

In Polish Galicia, where there were more than half a million Jews, the civil administration had taken charge of registering Jews and organizing the Jewish councils; the police were at first relegated to suppressing the black market and running a few forced-labor camps. In the eyes of the SS and police authorities, the civil government, aided in some cases by the military, was impeding the solution of the Jewish question.[79] So it was necessary to weaken the civil administration in the Government General.

Heydrich had already begun to work on the situation. Typically, he tried a frontal assault. In mid-September he called Lammers to ask for a new Führer decree that would centralize police powers throughout all German-controlled territories. Heydrich wanted the decree to specify Himmler's right to give directives to the civil administration on all matters related to security. Hitler's decree of July 17, 1941,[80] had pretty well clarified Himmler's supreme authority on anything related to security in conquered Soviet territories, and Heydrich wanted a new, broader decree that would extend the precedent. Although he tactfully included some other territories—Bohemia-Moravia, the annexed provinces of Poland, Alsace-Lorraine—in his request, the main point was to make unmistakably clear Himmler's authority over the Government General. And Heydrich related the need for central control to the struggle against "the international class of criminals"—in other words, Jews. During the war, he wrote in a follow-up letter, this struggle was of decisive importance, and it had to be carried out without reference to geographical restrictions. Nor could he bother the Führer for a decision every time there was a question or a conflict with the civil administration, he wrote. Lammers considered the pros and cons, noted that Frank would oppose such a decree, and was on the point of taking the matter to Hitler for consideration. But on October 22 Himmler asked him to wait. Although Himmler did not spell out his exact motive, he was not working behind Heydrich's back; the next day he told Heydrich about his request for delay.[81] Apparently he had a good reason to postpone the initiative, which was connected with Frank's growing difficulties.

Anonymous letters had charged Dr. Karl Lasch, provincial governor for Lemberg and business director of the Academy of German Law, with various misdeeds. Frank was the academy's president, and Lasch was a close and valued subordinate. Lasch, a Nazi since 1931, asked the party courts to clear him. In November came the verdict—not the outcome Lasch had hoped for. The judges sustained several accusations, including the charges that Lasch had hired others to do his dissertation research, that he had misused the academy's funds and taken bribes. The court said that Lasch had showed weakness of character.[82] He was now politically crippled.

There were other charges of corruption against Lasch in his capacity as provincial governor. Knowing that Frank would likely protect his ally, Himmler supposedly told him that the judicial system in the Government General could handle the case. But Heydrich meanwhile exploited Lasch's weakness and took hold of some of the subordinate civil administrators. And he began to launch an attack on Frank's own role in the Lasch case.[83] The Lasch documents, together with the proposed Führer decree on the centralization of police power, resurfaced in the Reich Chancellery in December 1941.[84] That was probably not a coincidence; Himmler had decided that the time was right to press the issue.

Frank was nothing if not inventive. First he tried to avert a collapse by playing Himmler's subordinates off against one another. He secretly invited Himmler's RFV deputy Ulrich Greifelt to visit him and to discuss nationality policies. He probably intended to gain whatever goodwill he could that might help to preserve his power and that of the civil administration. But Globocnik learned privately that Greifelt had accepted the invitation; he quickly warned Krüger, who telegraphed Himmler.[85] Greifelt was not a powerful figure, and Himmler could not have wanted him to negotiate what Krüger said was on the agenda: Himmler's own fundamental demands. The visit did not take place.

Another thing that Frank could try was to give Himmler some of what he wanted. On November 29 the Government General was invited to send a representative to the Wannsee Conference. Frank did not yet know what was afoot; he had to get his deputy Josef Bühler to ask Heydrich what it was all about.[86] Bühler seems to have learned the gist of the matter. In a mid-December conference in Cracow, Frank then passed along the word to his subordinates. He claimed that he had begun negotiations in Berlin to push Jews farther to the east.

> Certainly a major migration is about to start. But what is to happen to the Jews? Do you think they will actually be resettled in Ostland villages? We were told in Berlin: Why all this trouble? We can't use them in the Ostland either; liquidate them yourselves! Gentlemen, I must ask you to arm yourself against all feelings of sympathy. We have to annihilate the Jews wherever we find them and wherever it is at all possible. . . . The Government General will have to become just as free of Jews as the Reich. Where and how this is going to happen is a task for the agencies which we will have to create and establish here, and I am going to tell you how they will work when the time comes.[87]

Frank was now close to Himmler's line, but still not completely informed. He did not know that construction of at least one death camp in the Government General (Belzec) had already begun. And he was under the illusion that he could maintain some control over the process, which could hardly have been Himmler's intention.

Rosenberg, Ribbentrop, and Frank—and the agencies they headed— were not the only ones who were brought into the picture well after Himmler's and Hitler's decisions. Other agencies were invited to Wannsee; other officials had to be informed. In early December Himmler or Heydrich had a conference with Wilhelm Stuckart, state secretary in the Interior Ministry.[88] We do not know the exact contents of their conversation, but several weeks later Stuckart was quite well informed. Another Interior official came to Stuckart on December 21 to pass along a story he had heard about the mass slaughter of deported German Jews at Riga. The official, Bernhard Lösener, had been involved in the formulation of the Nuremberg Laws in 1935, but now he wanted to resign.

Stuckart, the dominant figure in the ministry, replied: "Herr Lösener, do you not know that all this takes place on orders from the highest level?" An order from the highest level meant from Hitler himself.[89]

This backing was not the only reason Himmler was able to convert rivals into collaborators; his skillful campaign against Frank showed that he knew how to bide his time and exploit an opponent's weaknesses. But Hitler's support certainly made things easier.

CHAPTER 11

WANNSEE AND BEYOND

SINCE REINHARD HEYDRICH was president of the International Criminal Police Organization (Interpol), he had wanted Interpol headquarters in Berlin. So the RSHA acquired a large villa in a posh Berlin suburb overlooking the lake known as Grosser Wannsee. The house was supposed to be equally suited to work and to social gatherings, and it lent an air of refinement to the important gathering Heydrich had arranged there.[1] It was not actually Interpol business, but a German government matter.

The meeting at 56–58 Am Grossen Wannsee was originally set for December 9, but the Japanese attack on Pearl Harbor and the subsequent German declaration of war on the United States had caused a postponement. During the delay the German army experienced something of a crisis in the Soviet Union. A severe Russian winter and a fierce Russian counteroffensive, especially in the central sector, drove back the German forces and placed many in peril. Firmly convinced of Russian weakness, Hitler could only blame his generals. He dismissed Brauchitsch and took over operational command himself; other generals too resigned or were dismissed summarily.[2] But the worst was over by mid-February, and plans proceeded for a new German offensive in the spring.

The postponement of Heydrich's meeting until January 20, 1942, did not matter very much, because Heydrich did not call it to make fundamental new decisions on the Jewish question. Massive killings of Jews in the conquered territories in the Soviet Union and at Chełmno had continued in the interim, and new extermination camps were in preparation. The Wannsee Conference was designed to give an official stamp of approval to a prior policy. With the formal Reich Cabinet in dormancy,

229

the men gathered around the table at Wannsee represented a kind of *ad hoc* cabinet which collectively discussed Jewish policy for the first time during the war. But there was no collective decision-making where the SS was involved.

The SS representatives at the meeting (in spite of a few postwar denials) were old hands at the policy and the process of destruction: Heinrich Müller and Adolf Eichmann of the RSHA; Dr. Otto Hofmann of the SS Race and Settlement Office; Karl Eberhard Schöngarth, commander of the Security Police and SD for the Government General; Dr. Rudolf Lange, commander of the Security Police and SD for Latvia. Lange, the lowest-ranking man of the group, had the most experience in the field. His Einsatzkommando 2 had killed more than thirty-five thousand Jews and thousands of other victims during the six months of the German occupation of Latvia.[3] Heydrich, of course, chaired the meeting.

The other participants included men with SS rank, such as Dr. Gerhard Klopfer of the Party Chancellery and Dr. Wilhelm Stuckart, undersecretary in the Interior Ministry, but they and the non-SS men were there to represent their agencies: the Reich Ministry for the Occupied Eastern Territories, the Interior Ministry, the Office of the Four-Year Plan, the Ministry of Justice, the Office of the Governor General of Poland, the Foreign Office, the Party Chancellery and Reich Chancellery. The government officials were senior civil servants beneath the cabinet ministers, and eight of the fifteen men participating held doctorates.

Heydrich opened the meeting by referring to Göring's entrusting him with the preparations for the Final Solution of the Jewish question. According to Martin Luther, who was present at the meeting, Heydrich also said that Hitler had entrusted him with this job.[4] The purpose of the meeting, Heydrich explained, was to bring all the agencies together and coordinate their activities. He made it clear, however, that Himmler's office was in charge of the policy everywhere; there were no geographical limits on the Reich Führer's authority.

Heydrich reviewed the history of the battle against the Jews, which he divided into stages. First they had forced the Jews out of the various sectors of German life; then they had physically removed Jews from German territory. The Reich Central Office for Emigration had accelerated the emigration of Jews, even though every agency was aware of the disadvantages of emigration. Heydrich had said this much—and probably a good deal more—at the meeting of SS-Gruppenführer in January 1939.[5] At the time, no other way to remove Jews from German territory was possible, Heydrich now explained.

Heydrich claimed that, between the Nazi takeover in 1933 and the end of October 1941, emigration removed some 537,000 Jews. Then Himmler formally ended Jewish emigration, because it was too danger- ous during war and because there were other possibilities in the East, Heydrich said. Hitler had then authorized "evacuation" of Jews to the East, he explained, which itself was a temporary measure, though it provided practical experience of great importance during the coming Final Solution. "Evacuation" here was a euphemism for the deportations, ghettoization, and mass killing actions that had preceded the establish- ment of the extermination camps.

Heydrich listed the numbers of Jews believed to be in each European country, from a mere 200 in Albania to more than 5 million in the Soviet Union, a grand total of more than 11 million. He did not consider the political or military status of the country as a factor. England's 330,000 Jews and Ireland's 4,000 were listed next to Finland's 2,300 and Italy's 58,000. The figures, Heydrich claimed, were low estimates, since in many countries the statistics were based on religion, not on racial definitions of Jews.

All eleven million plus were to be included in the Final Solution of the Jewish question. Based on Heydrich's comprehensive approach, what Hitler had already told the Grand Mufti of Jerusalem two months earlier, and what Sturmbannführer Paul Zapp had submitted to Himmler at the beginning of 1941,[6] it seems clear that Himmler and Heydrich intended to seize Jews wherever German control or influence extended—even- tually throughout the world.

The Final Solution of the Jewish question that Heydrich set before this meeting was only a slightly modified design of what American dip- lomat Raymond Geist had reported before the war began; now it was expanded for all the Jews in Europe. In the course of the Final Solution, Heydrich explained, these Jews would be shipped to the East for what Heydrich called "labor utilization." Separated by sex, those Jews capable of labor would be used to build roads in such a way that a large part would die, or, as Heydrich more delicately put it, would fall away through natural reduction. Heydrich apparently did not explain what would hap- pen to those incapable of hard labor.

Those who survived labor utilization, Heydrich said, would be the toughest elements of Jewry. If they were freed, they would become the germ cell for Jewish regeneration. This was the lesson of history. So, Heydrich concluded, they would have to be dealt with "appropriately." Europe would be combed of Jews from West to East, although the Reich and Bohemia-Moravia would go first, to clear residences for Germans and for general social-political reasons. At first Jews would be evacuated to transit ghettos; later they would be transported "farther to the east." He then explained the use of Theresienstadt as a special camp for those over sixty-five and for decorated and disabled Jewish war veterans.

The Foreign Office, Heydrich said, would have to get together with the Security Police and SD to approach foreign governments. In some cases, however, such as Slovakia and Croatia, the key questions had already been resolved. Heydrich did not go into details. In Slovakia authorities had concentrated Jews beginning in 1940, and in the fall of 1941 full-scale ghettos were established. The Nazi adviser to the Slovak government, Dieter Wisliceny, testified after the war that the plan was to impoverish the Jews, and create a social and economic problem that would be solved by deportation.[7] Martin Luther did observe that there might be problems in some of the Nordic countries. In view of the small number of Jews involved, he recommended postponing the evacuations there for the time being.

According to the official record, a good deal of time was spent on the treatment of the part-Jews—the *Mischlinge*. The participants did not manage to resolve the thorny problem of what to do with the part-Jews, or the Jews married to Germans, though there was some support for sterilization. The less extreme racists had to weigh the unwanted Jewish blood against the value of German blood in these cases, and the deportation of Jews or part-Jews with Christian spouses posed political problems and risks to the secrecy of the extermination camps. On the other hand, there was pressure from above. Himmler regarded the combination of German and alien blood as particularly dangerous. Even where a part-Jew was exempted from the Final Solution, Himmler wanted to scrutinize his or her descendants for signs of racial inferiority—for three or four generations. It was the kind of check one made with plants or animals, the former agronomist later told Martin Bormann.[8] Hitler also repeatedly expressed concern that the mixed-breeds were being treated too generously. He wanted to regard a *Mischling* as a German only when the person had made a positive contribution, such as early activity in behalf of the Nazi Party during the 1920s, before he or she was conscious of being categorized as a *Mischling*.[9]

Since Heydrich wanted to keep the Wannsee meeting relatively short, these perplexing problems were deferred for subsequent meetings and correspondence about the "Final Solution of the Mischling Question."[10] The Wannsee Conference lasted only an hour to ninety minutes. There were no objections to the fundamental policy of exterminating the Jewish race throughout Europe. The meeting then broke up into small groups and private discussions about the work to be done. Heydrich, Müller, and Eichmann remained afterward, and Heydrich told them how pleased he was with the way the meeting had gone. He had anticipated resistance to a coordinated policy; he got virtually none. Even Hans Frank's State Secretary Josef Bühler and the legalistic Wilhelm Stuckart had been enthusiastic. Heydrich and Eichmann drank a round of cognac together.[11]

In his official summary, Eichmann polished up the comments, using the customary euphemisms and ambiguous terms suitable for an official document. Even so, Heydrich revised the summary three or four times before he let it be copied and distributed. One of the deletions was a discussion of the exact methods for killing Jews. On the other hand, Heydrich wanted some of the state secretaries' comments down in the record in order to bind them to the policy—to nail them down, as Eichmann later put it.[12]

The Wannsee Conference was necessary for logistical reasons as well. The seizure and deportation of millions of Jews to the East was no simple police measure. Rail lines and railcars would be needed across Europe. The killing process was still being refined, and more resources would be required. Concentration-camp labor would need employers nearby —either SS enterprises or private firms. Disposal of Jewish property and belongings would require financial arrangements and transfers of funds. However inflexible the government bureaucracy was, the SS could no longer operate its Jewish policy behind the back of the ministries. It now had to have government cooperation for a much-expanded program of genocide. So Himmler and Heydrich had to let select government officials in on the secret.

On January 25 Himmler and Heydrich discussed sending the deported Jews to camps, where those suitable for labor could be profitably used.[13] Himmler's original conception, which Heydrich apparently continued to support, had been to kill all Jews deported to the extermination camps immediately; Himmler's decision to exempt temporarily those capable of hard labor represented a concession to difficult circumstances. The unexpected military setbacks on the Russian front, the huge death rate among Russian POWs (half a million died from mistreatment and disease between November 1941 and January 1942), whom the Reich had foreseen as laborers, and the longstanding shortage of labor within Germany created urgent pressure for exploitation of all possible sources of labor. Oswald Pohl's SS Economic-Administrative Main Office had to respond to this situation, which led Himmler to approve use of some Jewish labor for war-related production. But this policy was clearly designed to be limited and temporary, not a fundamental change of a racial-ideological goal. The Final Solution proceeded in spite of the dire need for labor. Later in the year Hitler expressly rejected the idea of allowing German industrial firms to make use of fifty thousand Jews as slave laborers in the Reich. Those Jews who were selected for labor rather than immediate execution at such camps as Auschwitz and Maidanek (or in the work ghettos in the conquered Soviet territories) were treated like doomed subhumans, not valued workers.[14]

On January 26 Himmler notified Richard Glücks, inspector of the concentration camps, that the camps would now take on great economic tasks; he should expect to receive a hundred thousand male Jews and fifty thousand female Jews in the next four weeks to use as laborers. The Jews were needed, Himmler said, because no more Russian POWs were expected for the time being; these arriving Jews had previously emigrated from Germany. The last part was partially true. Himmler instructed German military authorities to turn over all Jews and communists in the occupied zone of France, and they included some German émigrés.[15]

Three days later Himmler or Heydrich sent Rosenberg a draft of their guidelines for the Jewish question. The document was suitable for distribution within the Ministry for the Occupied Eastern Territories; it said enough to those who knew, but not too much. The Jewish question, according to the draft, was going to be solved for all of Europe at the end of the war, if not before. All current measures in the occupied Eastern territories must help prepare for this goal: native pogroms against Jews, if they were not too disruptive of law and order; identification of Jews and separation of the Jewish population from the non-Jewish; elimination of Jewish influence over the Russian people; and introduction of compulsory hard labor.[16] The document did not specify the final stage of persecution, but it was the same basic phased strategy that Geist had described in 1939.

On January 30, 1942, after Hitler and Himmler had both returned from East Prussia to Berlin, Hitler reaffirmed to the German public his prewar prophecy that a world war would result in the destruction of Jewry. Three days later, in private, he told Himmler and other evening guests: "Today we must conduct the same struggle that Pasteur and Koch had to fight. The cause of countless ills is a bacillus: the Jew. . . . We will become healthy if we eliminate the Jew."[17] Two months later Hitler associated himself completely with Himmler's broad plans for Germanization of the East. According to what Gottlob Berger heard from a firsthand source, Hitler told a group of officers whom he decorated with the Iron Cross with oak-leaf cluster:

I know exactly how far I have to go, but it is so that the whole East becomes and remains German—primeval German [urdeutsch]. . . .

We don't need to express our ideas about that now, and I will not speak about it. That [task] I have given to my Himmler and he is already accomplishing it.[18]

Here was the politician calculatingly allowing subordinates to carry out his dirty work.

Before the Final Solution could proceed smoothly, Himmler wanted a showdown with Hans Frank. He had to be sure that Frank would obstruct neither the killing nor the recovery of Jewish effects. By March 1942 Himmler had lined up his evidence and his allies carefully. On the afternoon of March 5, in the salon car on Himmler's train, Lammers, Bormann, and Himmler confronted Frank with a series of charges raised against him. Lammers said at the outset that they wanted to handle these matters in a personal and comradely manner; they did not want to have to bring them to the Führer.

Frank defended himself with dramatic rhetoric against the charges of corruption, and maintained that he was subordinate only to the Führer. But Himmler described the morass of corruption in Poland revealed by a recent trial—the lack of distinction between private and state property, the purchase of objects from the ghettos by individuals. Still worse was the fact that Frank's own sister had had personal dealings with Jews, and that his wife had hired relatives for key positions. Bormann observed that the Führer had strong views on the subject: relatives should not hire relatives. Frank lamely said it was the first he had heard of the Führer's opinion. After these charges and more were discussed, and after Himmler stressed how they had done Frank a service by raising these matters with him and not with the Führer, Himmler got to the main point—the relationship of the SS-and-police hierarchy with the civil administration. Frank agreed to appoint Friedrich-Wilhelm Krüger as his state secretary for all police business and resettlement matters. The group also concluded that Lammers should arrange for a Führer decree giving Himmler the power to issue directives on security and resettlement to the Government General and to the new state secretary. Finally, there was unanimous agreement to legalize Globocnik's own private police force. Globocnik would also be allowed to become SS and police leader and regional governor together.[19] The meeting gave Himmler everything that he wanted—even if Frank tried subsequently to recapture some lost ground. The Führer decree was finally issued in May 1942.[20] By then the deportations to the death camps in the Government General had begun.

Heydrich did not see the full application of his far-reaching plan. He fell victim to Czech assassins' bullets shortly after deportations of Jews from Western Europe to Auschwitz and from the Government General to Belzec and Sobibor began. Just after Heydrich was shot and a few days before he died, Governor Frank issued a decree transferring control of all Jewish affairs in the Government General to the SS and police— to avoid misunderstandings, the decree stated.[21]

Himmler, however, lived to see and speed implementation of the plan—and the gas chambers that he had envisioned in the fall of 1939 and approved in the late summer of 1941. On July 17, 1942, he flew from East Prussia to the Silesian industrial city of Kattowitz, where he picked up Gauleiter Fritz Bracht, Higher SS and Police Leader Ernst-Heinrich Schmausser, and Auschwitz commandant Rudolf Höss and then drove to the now expanded Auschwitz camp. Over the main gate stretched a slogan in large letters: ARBEIT MACHT FREI. Labor makes one free.

According to Himmler's appointment book, he simply inspected the farming operations, the main concentration camp, and the women's camp. But Rudolf Höss tells us that Himmler inspected everything at Auschwitz—land reclamation, plant and stockbreeding centers, nurseries, laboratories, and nearby Birkenau, which had a Jewish sector, a Russian sector, and a gypsy sector. The women's camp was not yet located at Birkenau, but this area did have an airtight underground bunker surrounded by a wall. It was a primitive gas chamber, which had first been used to dispose of a transport of Jews some ten weeks earlier.[22]

Though it is not mentioned in his appointment book, Himmler watched the selection of able-bodied Jews from a transport that had just arrived at the camp from the Netherlands and the procession of the remainder to the gas chamber. Auschwitz made use of Zyklon B, which did the job quickly. Himmler watched the whole process, saying very little. Instead he unobtrusively observed the SS officers engaged in gassing the Jews.[23] Later Himmler commented that these were battles that the coming generation would not have to fight.[24]

That evening he attended a dinner at Gauleiter Bracht's residence, where he also spent the night, and he was in the best of spirits. He engaged in lively conversation with Frau Bracht and Frau Höss, drank a few glasses of red wine, and even smoked, which he rarely did. The next day, after further inspection of the camp, Himmler told Höss that he would have to live with the overcrowding and other difficulties at the camp. The orders Himmler had given the Security Police would not be changed under any circumstances. Eichmann's program would be intensified. Himmler authorized a major expansion of the camp at Birkenau: Höss was to proceed with the destruction of Jews unfit for labor and gypsies there. Then he announced that he was promoting Höss to

Obersturmbannführer. Finally, Himmler toured the nearby I. G. Farben plant for synthetic rubber that made use of concentration-camp labor.[25]

Himmler also wanted to see the gas chambers that made use of carbon monoxide. He went straight from Auschwitz to Lublin, where Globocnik held a tea for him.[26] It is not clear whether Himmler attended the swearing in that day of some of the German personnel involved in the gassing operations. Each man was supposed to swear that Hauptsturmführer Höfle, Globocnik's chief of staff, had thoroughly informed him:

1. that I may not under any circumstances pass on any form of information, verbally or in writing, on the progress, procedure or incidents in the evacuation of the Jews to any person outside the circle of the *Einsatz* [Operation] *Reinhard* staff;
2. that the process of the evacuation of Jews is a subject that comes under "Secret Reich Document," in accordance with censorship regulations. . . .[27]

So even the men doing the gassing had to make use of the euphemism "evacuation of the Jews." When two of the men talked a bit too much a month later, they were executed—at least, this is what Globocnik told some SS visitors.[28]

Himmler spent another two days in the Lublin area; plenty of construction and other preparations for Germanization were in progress. This time his appointment book offered a hint of his other interests, recording a visit to an unidentified camp for "effects" and a treasury.[29] By this time the Lublin region had two operating death camps, Belzec and Sobibor. With transports arriving frequently and the gas chambers doing their jobs, the personal effects of the dead Jews were piling up: clothes, shoes, suitcases, jewelry, gold fillings from teeth, even hair, and money.

A survivor of Sobibor later wrote that one day in late July 1942 she saw Himmler, six SS officers, and three civilians arrive there. They went immediately to camp three, which had the gas chambers. They may have bypassed the early stage of the process, which had the deputy commandant of the camp, wearing a white coat to give the impression that he was a physician, announce to Jews arriving at a barrack that they would be sent to work. First, however, he said, the Jews had to bathe and undergo disinfection. Inside the barrack were signs indicating that they should proceed to the cashier's room. The cashier often gave the Jews receipts for their money and valuables to convince them that they would get their things back later.[30]

After they undressed, an SS man and Ukrainian auxiliaries took the group to the actual gas chambers, disguised as showers. Sometimes they beat the Jews and set a vicious dog upon them to hurry them to the showers. Most victims did not know what was taking place until the doors were closed and locked and the gas began to filter in, so the process usually went quite smoothly. Carbon monoxide took about eighteen minutes to do the job. Himmler's group stayed an hour, watched, gave instructions to the commandant, and left abruptly. They did not partake of the delicacies that had been prepared for them.[31]

Carbon monoxide worked slower than Zyklon B, but it worked well enough for Himmler to proceed. While he was still at Lublin, he sent a written order to Krüger: the "resettlement" of the entire Jewish population of the Government General was to be completed by December 31, 1942. With the exception of a few collection camps for Jews in some major cities, no Jews were to remain in Poland. All Jewish laborers had to complete their jobs or be transferred to one of the collection camps. These measures were prerequisites for the Nazi "new order" in Europe, since any remaining Jews would stimulate resistance and provide a source of moral and physical pestilence.[32]

On July 22, two days after Himmler's departure from Lublin, deportations began from the Warsaw ghetto to the newest death camp in the Lublin region, Treblinka. The same day, Globocnik wrote to Karl Wolff:

> The Reich Führer SS . . . has given us so much new work that with it now all our most secret wishes are to be fulfilled. I am so very thankful to him for this, and he can be sure of one thing, that these things he wishes will be fulfilled in the shortest time.[33]

Globocnik certainly tried his best to accomplish his task. According to Rudolf Höss, he was always eager to receive more transports of Jews.[34]

On July 24 Himmler flew from Berlin to his new headquarters at Zhitomir in the Ukraine. Once again he had found a location near the Führer, who had set up his own field headquarters at Vinnitsa, about seventy miles away. With victory over the Russians again tangibly within reach, Himmler had allowed himself some extravagance. There were banquet rooms and elegant houses, as well as barracks and a huge underground bunker with thick concrete walls. In preparation for Himmler's move, Einsatzgruppe C chief Dr. Max Thomas had insisted that the last Jew had to disappear from the Ukraine. In mid-July Thomas had passed along an order to liquidate immediately remaining Jewish laborers in the Vinnitsa region. Even the Ukrainian workers in the area were not to be trusted; they were to be sent to the Reich as forced laborers.[35]

Himmler invited some of the local SS and police officials to dinner on July 25. He talked about the ethnic Germans so dear to his heart, and then he moved on to discuss the partisans. He hesitated, as if to reflect on possibilities. Then he said that he would master the partisans too; he was thinking of putting out the eyes of captured partisans to terrify and deter others. There was dead silence for a few seconds, and then Karl Wolff, always the diplomat, defused the situation by suggesting that perhaps it would be better to cut off their hands. Himmler, not yet committed, said that something or other would occur to him.[36]

The next day Himmler called a halt to efforts to work out a legal definition of "Jew" in the occupied Eastern territories. Any such regulation, he warned Gottlob Berger, would only tie his hands. The occupied Eastern territories were to become free of Jews. The Führer had entrusted him exclusively with this heavy burden, and he would not allow anyone to interfere.[37]

A month later Himmler returned to visit Globocnik at Lublin. Brandt's brief note on the meeting mentions that the Reich Führer SS and Globocnik discussed the struggle against partisans, a term meant to include the anti-Jewish measures, as well as the Polish resistance. But two days later Globocnik gave a more detailed if somewhat exaggerated account of the meeting to SS Officer Kurt Gerstein and one of Eichmann's subordinates, who were delivering him a supply of Zyklon B. Globocnik claimed that Hitler, who he said was also present, ordered that the killings of Jews be speeded up. Hitler wasn't there, but Himmler was, beyond a doubt, and he may well have passed on a Führer order to accelerate Operation Reinhard.[38]

Serious, pragmatic arguments against the mass killings could only delay the process in particular areas, not change the fundamental decision. In the occupied Russian city of Pinsk, for example, the labor force in some factories producing goods for the German military was more than 70 percent Jewish. When military economic authorities learned of the plan to eliminate all Jews from the region, they complained that these factories would be crippled. Civilian officials in the Ukraine refused to challenge the SS, but the complaint went up the military hierarchy to Berlin. Himmler then personally decided to leave some one thousand Jewish workers alone until the firms had completed their contracts for the military. He nonetheless ordered the liquidation of the Pinsk ghetto.[39]

Hitler's failure to anticipate the protracted nature of the war in the East had not damaged Himmler's faith in his Führer. In one of his lunchtime conversations in September 1942, Himmler announced that fate had compensated Germany for its lack of sufficient manpower with the person of the Führer. Only rarely in the life of a nation—once every two to five thousand years—could it overcome such a disadvantage.[40]

As the gassings of Western European and Polish Jews mounted in the fall of 1942, there were choices to be made about the next step—the next targets. On a recent trip to Finland, Himmler had cautiously sounded out the Finns, who were fighting alongside Germany against the Soviet Union, about their attitude toward their Jews. Prime Minister Rangell had explained that there were only a couple of thousand Jews, who were well integrated, including soldiers fighting in the Finnish army: "We have no Jewish question," he emphatically concluded. Himmler had not pressed the matter.[41] (Under different circumstances, Bulgaria and later Denmark were also able to fend off deportations of their Jews.) On the other hand, preliminary preparations had been made to arrange deportations from Rumania, Croatia, and the Italian-occupied zone of France. But these were matters of high policy, and Himmler alone could not decide them.

Even in his own notes for a completely private meeting with the Führer, Himmler used euphemisms: "how should the Jewish emigration be further pursued?" And he did not record Hitler's response, except for a check mark that indicated the Führer's approval of Himmler's suggested course.[42] The next day Himmler responded to a suggestion from Fritz Bracht, who was so impressed by what he had seen at Auschwitz that he now wanted to call the world war the "Jewish war," since it revolved, in the final analysis, "around the power of Judah." Himmler rejected the idea, "because we would thereby make [the name of] Jewry eternal."[43] With the array of extermination camps in operation, Himmler could foresee the complete disappearance of all Jews.

In October Himmler traveled to Rome to brief Mussolini on the military situation and on Germany's Jewish policy. Mussolini had not yet turned over any Italian Jews to Germany, and Himmler had to prepare the groundwork for later resolution of this problem, either by Hitler himself or by Ribbentrop.[44] Himmler told Mussolini of Hitler's hope that the two dictators could meet as soon as Germany's military situation allowed him time off. He presented an optimistic assessment of progress on the Russian front: Stalingrad was as good as conquered, he asserted. Mussolini bragged that he and the Fascist Party had the Italian people firmly in their hands, in spite of wartime difficulties and food shortages. The Pope would not create too many obstacles; he was at heart a good Italian. The king was old and anyway loyal, and the crown prince was a good fascist, the Duce explained.

Himmler revealed that Germany was removing Jews from all the areas it controlled, because they were the cause of sabotage, espionage, and resistance. In Russia it had been necessary to shoot a considerable number of Jews—men, women, and children—since even the women and children had worked for the partisans. Mussolini agreed that this was the only solution. Himmler then explained that the other Jews were sent to concentration camps and used for hard labor in the East, and that the mortality there was very high. After some other elaborations and fictions of this kind, Himmler brought the meeting to a satisfactory close.[45]

By December Himmler was ready to dispose of an estimated six hundred thousand French Jews and other enemies there. He brought the matter to Hitler, who decided (as Himmler recorded it) to "do away" with them. Hitler did ask Himmler to wait until he had spoken to French Premier Pierre Laval, but these Jews were later deported to Auschwitz. Slightly more unusual was Himmler's idea to set up a special camp for those Jews from France, Hungary, and Rumania who had influential relatives in the United States. Himmler described these Jews, whose number he estimated at ten thousand, as valuable hostages. They would work in the camp, but under conditions that would allow them to remain alive, Himmler wrote just after the meeting.[46]

At the same time Hitler reluctantly approved Himmler's proposal to release some Jews in exchange for ransom payments, but only if this brought in large amounts of foreign exchange.[47] Military and economic realities were beginning to intrude on the Führer's dream of complete extermination. Events did not bear out Himmler's October prediction of imminent victory at Stalingrad, and the German army got no farther. And, in spite of Globocnik's best efforts, the extermination camps failed to complete their assigned task by the end of 1942.

Himmler nonetheless had to find out just how much "progress" had been made. He already had a professional statistician on his staff to help analyze the size and changes of population. This man, Richard Korherr, was to a degree an outsider, independent of the RSHA and the extermination-camp commanders. He was better qualified in several respects to measure the course of the Final Solution. So, in January 1943, Himmler instructed Korherr to draw up a detailed report, and he informed the RSHA not to compile its own statistics.[48]

Korherr's job was complicated by the fact that, even in a report designed for Himmler, he was not supposed to spell out the facts in black and white. It was easier to state how many Jews were still alive than what had happened to the others. To be sure, Korherr could state that through various means the Jewish population in the Reich and the Government General had diminished by 3.1 million between 1933 and 1942. In spite of his generous use of the term "evacuation," however, which Himmler seconded, to mislead those who would read the document in later years, Himmler had to correct Korherr's wording in one place. Where Korherr had written of the "special treatment" of the Jews, Himmler insisted on either the "transportation of the Jews from the Eastern provinces to the Russian East" or the "sifting of the Jews through the camps." These were among the officially approved terms to camouflage the realities of the Final Solution.[49]

On at least one occasion Himmler violated his own rule. In October 1943 Himmler delivered a long speech at a meeting of the SS-Gruppenführer at Posen. As usual, he spoke from notes, but he had begun the practice of recording some of his talks on a red oxide tape wider than what is used today. Early in the speech Himmler stopped and played the tape back to see if the recorder was picking up his voice properly.[50] He unquestionably knew that he was being recorded, but he was speaking to a very select audience, and he didn't think there was any danger of the recording's falling into the wrong hands. Even in the fall of 1943 Himmler was convinced that Nazi Germany would eventually win the war—it was a law of nature, he said.[51]

His voice was of middle range—neither deep nor high-pitched. He spoke clearly, deliberately, and emphatically, but for the most part dispassionately, much like a schoolmaster reviewing a long and somewhat complicated lesson for his pupils. At one point he actually talked about giving out a grade if he had to judge a certain performance.[52]

Himmler reviewed the military situation and the political situation on each front, but, as always, his analysis was colored and rendered useless by his racial judgments. In spite of Russia's successes, Slavs were incapable of constructing anything themselves, he claimed. Every few centuries the blend of races in Asia produced a great leader—an Attila, a Genghis Khan, a Tamerlaine, a Lenin, or a Stalin—who could make something out of the Slavs. These leaders possessed traces of German blood, which gave them their ability, but good leadership was not enough. In the end German racial superiority would help Germany to overcome the more numerous but inferior Slavic masses.

About two hours into the three-hour-and-ten-minute speech, Himmler decided to raise a weighty matter about which the SS could never speak publicly—"the evacuation of the Jews, the extermination of the Jewish people." It was necessary to speak about this once, Himmler said. It was one thing to put the phrase "exclusion of the Jews" or "extermination of the Jews" in the Nazi program and quite another to carry it out. In principle, Germans supported persecution, Himmler noted with some sarcasm, but then each of them tried to save the one good

Jew that he knew. These people had no sense of what it was like to see one hundred or five hundred or one thousand bodies lying there. Himmler boasted that the SS had maintained this program and, apart from some exceptions brought about by human weakness, had remained respectable. It was "an unwritten and never to be written page of glory in our history." And as he spoke, the reel of tape continued to turn and to record.

If the Jews had not been dealt with, Himmler continued, Germany would then be in the situation of 1916 or 1917, where Jews had infected the German body politic. "We had the moral right, we had the duty with regard to our people, to kill this race that wanted to kill us." It was the future Himmler had sketched out in 1938, the day before Kristallnacht, with much the same audience and much the same justification; now the prediction was partially fulfilled. Then, his voice rising to an angry snarl, Himmler continued: "We do *not* have the right to enrich ourselves even just with a fur or a watch or a Mark or with a cigarette!" It was the most strident and most emotional moment in the whole speech. The architect of mass murder remained in his own eyes a moralist to the end.

EPILOGUE:

HIMMLER IN RETROSPECT

IN SPITE OF Nazi efforts to destroy most of the extermination camps and erase the evidence of the millions of murders, more than a few traces of the physical installations of the Final Solution remain. One may still see the ruins of a gas chamber and the second crematorium at Birkenau, as well as the ARBEIT MACHT FREI sign and many of the buildings in Auschwitz I. Recently there has been an angry dispute among some Jews and Catholics over whether the presence of a Carmelite convent at Auschwitz dishonors the memory of the Jews who were killed there. That is another sort of legacy of the Holocaust.

At Globocnik's Maidanek, even more of the killing apparatus escaped destruction. The building housing the gas chamber remains—the sign outside reads ENTRANCE TO THE BATHS, and one can still see the shower heads and pipes designed not to carry water but to mislead the victims. The ovens of the crematorium are largely preserved, and the smokestack still reaches bleakly to the sky.

Just over fifty years after the start of World War II and ninety years after Himmler's birth, evidence of the master architect of the Final Solution is harder to come by. British officers buried him secretly; only a few know where his physical remains are. Himmler's villa in Berlin was seized by American authorities at the end of the war; it was razed to create space for the construction of housing for the American armed forces in Berlin, now no longer necessary. The headquarters for Himmler's personal staff and for the Gestapo (later RSHA) on the Prinz Albrechtstrasse, and the SD headquarters around the corner on the Wilhelmstrasse, are gone, apart from some underground jail cells. Once they were the centers of all the planning against the assorted enemies of the Third Reich. What Allied bombers did not destroy during the war, West Berliners tore down or blew up during the 1950s.[1] Perhaps it was a matter of urban renewal; perhaps also they wanted to forget the more gruesome aspects of the German past. Ironically, what was the Prinz Albrechtstrasse is today just a path a stone's throw away from where the Berlin Wall used to stand— another sort of atrocity fading into memory.

A new and wiser attitude eventually developed in West Berlin. There is today a small museum in the vicinity of the former Prinz Albrecht-strasse with details not only about the design of the former Prinz Albrecht Hotel, but also about the occupants of 8 and 9 Prinz Albrechtstrasse during the Nazi era: with documents, photographs, and model buildings. The geography and topography of the agencies of terror are to this degree preserved in our memory. But even there not much still stands that allows one to grasp Himmler the man.

Through the mountain of documents that Himmler, his SS subordinates, and other Nazi officials left behind, it was and is nonetheless possible to get an excellent sense of Himmler the politician and ideologue. Himmler was an idealist of sorts. Throughout most of his life he romanticized and idealized the German race, the German soldier, and the German farmer; he developed fixations about those who he believed threatened his cherished causes—above all, about the Jews. He considered the gypsies a similar source of racial impurity and parasitism; he held Freemasons and Jesuits, as well as Marxists, to be politically hostile and dangerous; he undoubtedly shared Hitler's view that elimination of allegedly defective Germans would strengthen the future German race. None of the other victims of Nazi murder programs, however, shared all the dangerous characteristics of the Jew. He became a strong racial anti-Semite well before he met Hitler; afterward he became a complete fanatic. He did not allow normal human emotions or concern for the individual to hinder him from pursuing his goals to their logical extreme.

Himmler's life and activities illustrate the potential repercussions of the belief that all behavioral characteristics are hereditary—in the blood, as he would have put it. If heredity is crucial, then the most efficient way to mold the future of a people is to ensure proper human breeding, favoring those considered well endowed and eliminating those considered defective or dangerous. In spite of his mystical side and his outlandish beliefs, Himmler was a stickler for efficiency.

Himmler was also a vehement anti-Bolshevist, but, like Hitler, he regarded Bolshevism as a surface manifestation. A Marxist might use the term "mere superstructure" for such an ideological threat. For Himmler, Bolshevism was only a part of the Jewish conspiracy. And whatever Jews did—or did not do—was less important to Himmler than what they were by nature, by heredity. A statement by Chaim Weizmann that Jews everywhere would stand on the side of Germany's enemies only confirmed what Himmler and Hitler long since believed.[2] If Weizmann had not made this statement, SS policies would have been no different. This is quite obvious to anyone who studies either man during the 1930s. The original *raison d'être* of the SS was to deal with the enemies at home, and the SS had a prewar plan to exterminate Jews remaining in Germany.

The Eastern races posed another major obstacle to Hitler's and Himmler's racial and geopolitical goals. The menace in the East was quite real in Himmler's mind. Sooner or later, in the twentieth century or in future times, Asiatic races would again threaten Europe unless the Nazis destroyed them, pushed them far back and weakened them, or placed them under a firm yoke within the German empire. Hitler's wartime conversations are also filled with diatribes against the East. Both men were indeed concerned about "Asiatic deeds," but not for the reasons or in the sense that Ernst Nolte argued.[3] They saw Asiatic barbarism as beginning long before Bolshevism took root in the Soviet Union. It represented a separate problem from the world Jewish conspiracy, though it was related.

The Final Solution began with ideological obsessions that Hitler, Himmler, and numerous other leading Nazis shared. The evidence presented here indicates that Hitler's prewar verbal threats against Jews were accompanied by a general SS strategy envisaging escalating persecution leading to mass murder. It is therefore impossible to regard Hitler's diatribes as purely emotional outbursts without practical consequences. Himmler and the SS took the Führer quite seriously and started to make plans. Since they began before the outbreak of the war, they were not much influenced by wartime constraints such as food shortages or lack of places to "put" the Jews. The idea of killing Jews was on the SS agenda from at least late 1938 on.

Yet it is hard to argue that the Final Solution was completely predetermined. Himmler moved only gradually toward a comprehensive plan for all Jews. The first known SS plan dealt with the German Jews who were to remain in the country. As Poland was conquered, the strategy of phased persecution was extended to the Polish Jews, but not necessarily to all of them. Some contemporary documents contain the phrase "as many as possible," and what was possible at a given time depended on a variety of circumstances—especially on perceived political and foreign-policy constraints.

Attempts to ban the emigration of Polish Jews during 1940 suggest that Himmler considered these Eastern Jews even more dangerous than German Jews, and the evidence presented here suggests that Himmler regarded the Madagascar plan only as a possibility for Western Jews.

Emigrating Jews were believed to stimulate "infection" and anti-Semitic reactions in countries receiving them, so the SS could even accept some Jewish emigration.

The technology for mass murder on a gigantic scale was still being developed. Although Himmler contemplated gas chambers and crematoria by December 1939, he did not move quickly to carry out this project. The scope of killing also depended upon Germany's military and diplomatic situation. The SS "only" killed thousands of Jews in Poland during and after the fall-1939 conquest because of the perceived influence of international Jewry in the West. Once it became clear that there would be no compromise peace with the West, the Jews under German control lost their value as hostages. Military victories in the West gave Hitler and Himmler the confidence to set in motion the plans for a vast killing operation during the forthcoming campaign in the Soviet Union.

By March 1941 the Final Solution was just a matter of time—and timing. This date is months earlier than the juncture most specialists have selected, but the evidence is compelling. Hitler had rejected other, lesser plans (Madagascar, sterilization). He had already approved a liquidation plan for Jews in the Reich and Bohemia-Moravia (at the minimum). Heydrich had already started negotiations with the army regarding the *Einsatzgruppen* in the Soviet Union, and the RSHA had sent Jewish specialists to other European countries to prepare for deportations. Emigration of Polish Jews had been banned months earlier, and closed ghettos and work camps had created the preconditions for easy disposal of Jews in Poland. Eichmann spoke of the "final evacuation" of the Jews *to* Poland at a time when Hitler was promising to remove all Jews *from* Poland. A month later Himmler referred to a new task he had for Globocnik. Extermination in Poland was a purely technical problem. So the argument does not rest on Hitler's rhetoric alone. None of these sources spells out everything; none of them is a perfect contemporary blueprint. But they are all independent sources and, taken together, they form a coherent picture of far-reaching plans and fundamental decisions made during the preparations for the campaign against the U.S.S.R. As Hitler had told Hans Frank in December 1940: "After the victory, bind the helm faster."[4] Plans, of course, are still only plans until they are implemented, but it would have taken a political or military earthquake to have derailed the process.

Early victories over the Russians gave Hitler and Himmler the impression that they had little to fear, so in July 1941 they went beyond the killings in the Soviet territories and took steps to implement continent-wide deportations of Jews, although other decisions, including the one to construct gas chambers in extermination camps, came slightly later. The actions taken in the summer and fall of 1941 were operational, following up on earlier, more fundamental decisions.

There was a clear evolution of policy regarding how many Jews would be killed, when, and how. This progression was influenced to a degree by the military situation. Military success fed the Führer's lust for more and more Jewish blood.[5] Later military difficulties did not diminish it much.

So there was both planning for, and evolution toward, the Final Solution, but the improvisation that occurred had little to do with food shortages, failures of resettlement, or military frustration in the East. The sequence of planning and, in some cases, the partial implementation of those plans rule out explanations based on a "late" decision for the Final Solution. No wartime constraints forced the Nazi elite to abandon less extreme solutions to the Jewish "problem."

The fact that Hitler, Himmler, and Heydrich made the primary decisions on the Final Solution does not exculpate other German officials in other institutions. The shootings in the East required the cooperation and sometimes the direct participation of the German army; transport officials arranged the deportations to the extermination camps.[6] Large German corporations as well as the SS made use of camp labor under conditions akin to a slow death sentence. Doctors selected those to be gassed and carried out gruesome medical experiments on Jews and other victims. Lawyers and civil servants helped to strip Jews of their rights and their property. Much of the apparatus of government, in one way or another, was connected with the escalating persecution of Jews from 1933 on. Raul Hilberg has long since described the operation of the interlocking bureaucracies—the state, the party, the military, corporate industry, and, of course, the SS and police. Since then a number of other scholars have emphasized the significance of the participation in the persecution and murder of Jews and others by particular professional elites.[7]

There are, however, differences among the prime movers, the large circle of direct participants in the Final Solution, and the even bigger society that did not, by and large, object to the program even when it learned of, or heard rumors of, mass murders of Jews. The decision-makers placed the Final Solution on the agenda in the first place and, when necessary, forced it through; the participants helped to implement it; the society was not inoculated against Nazi anti-Semitism and therefore created a permissive climate. All levels bear some measure of responsibility, even if all individuals do not. To limit responsibility to the men at the top alone is to provide a convenient excuse for all the others involved. But to emphasize the role of bureaucrats and the men in the field resolving practical problems and to overlook the ideological fanaticism and substantial direction from the top is to ignore historical reality—and to risk drawing the wrong lessons from the past.

Historians are not the only ones who pass judgment on the participants in the Final Solution. Although suicide prevented Hitler and Himmler from being tried at the end of the war, many of Himmler's chief subordinates did not escape legal sanctions. Still, the number of men, and in some cases women, who committed what are commonly called war crimes but were usually crimes against innocent civilians, and who were left untouched in the postwar period, was very high. There are explanations for why the Western democracies and West Germany did not move more aggressively to try suspected Nazi criminals in the first decade after the Nuremberg trials, but these reasons are not good enough. In spite of more serious efforts since then, especially in West Germany, the result is that only a small percentage of the mass murderers and the bureaucrats who made arrangements for them paid for their crimes.

Even after almost fifty years, substantial numbers of these people survive. They live not only in Germany but in many Western democracies, whose loose immigration policies in the immediate postwar period allowed many thousands of self-professed anticommunist refugees to enter without careful examination of their wartime activities. The Himmlers, the Heydrichs, the Eichmanns are gone, though one of Eichmann's chief assistants still lives in Syria. A good many of their junior helpers remain with us. They include people who actually carried out the shootings and gassings, and among them are a good many non-Germans who joined voluntarily in the killings of Jews.

As I write these words, Britain is still deliberating over the need for a law to give it jurisdiction over current British residents or citizens accused of World War II crimes on the continent. Only in relatively recent years have the United States, Canada, and Australia had legal weapons and resources to use against suspected Nazi war criminals in their midst. The research accumulated for this book has also played a very small role in facilitating some of the Western legal investigations and proceedings. Himmler might have appreciated the synergy, though not the goal.

Himmler was a human being—above average intellectually, below average physically and emotionally—who became willing to sacrifice tens of millions of people for what he regarded as the future of the German people. He did not really consider his victims human, so was not at all concerned about their suffering or their fate. They were like the pests and vermin that any farmer had to dispose of if he was going to sustain himself and his family.

Himmler, in short, was not a simple, bloodthirsty, sadistic monster. His brutality was more learned than instinctive and emotional. If a sadist is one who delights in personally inflicting pain or death on others, or in witnessing others inflict them, then Himmler was not a sadist. He even understood that his executioners might have psychological difficulties carrying out their jobs, and he tried to make things easier for them. The magnitude of their task required systematic planning and the use of deception to mislead the victims; the need to spare the SS killers led to exploitation of the latest technology. As Bach-Zelewski said, the death camp was the creation of bureaucrats. Himmler was the ultimate bureaucrat.

Himmler was also a dedicated student of history. His interest in the past was longstanding, vivid, and sincere. Of course, he infused his own emotional need for heroes and villains into what he read, but he made use of historical works and events to create political myths that he and his organization then pursued. So he saw in the past only what he wanted to believe. The real historian can and should describe and analyze events to make it difficult for others, like Himmler, to wear blinders when they gaze upon the past and fashion their own myths. Historians cannot demythologize the past if they are willingly blind to inconvenient facts that do not fit into their grand theories. This caution is important to remember in times when some writers deny that there ever was a Final Solution, when others claim that Hitler was not involved.

NOTES

INTRODUCTION

1. Raul Hilberg, *The Destruction of the European Jews* (Chicago, 1961); 2nd expanded ed., 3 vols. (New York, 1985). An extremely valuable German work is Helmut Krausnick and Hans-Heinrich Wilhelm, *Die Truppe des Weltanschauungskrieges: Die Einsatzgruppen der Sicherheitspolizei und des SD 1938–1942* (Stuttgart, 1981).

2. Affidavit of Isaak Egon Ochshorn, 14 Sept. 1945, National Archives (hereafter NA), Record Group (hereafter RG) 238, NO-1934.

3. *The Goebbels Diary* (New York, 1982), 157, 30 Oct. 1939, cited by Christopher R. Browning, "Nazi Resettlement Policy and the Search for a Solution to the Jewish Question," *German Studies Review* 9 (1986): 505.

4. Although Himmler's contact is not identified in this document stemming from British intelligence, it is quite clearly Himmler's masseur Felix Kersten, a Finnish citizen born in Estonia. Kersten began to treat Himmler in 1939 and remained with him during much of the war. He alone fits the description in the document: a man who knew Himmler intimately, who had seen him and worked with him almost daily for over five years, yet not a Nazi. Kersten's various memoirs are not at all reliable about details, but his picture of Himmler here is supported by other sources. Scavenger Special Report No. 2, 24 May 1945, copy in NA RG 319, IRR Files, Heinrich Himmler XE 000632. For a similar if less dramatic reading of Himmler's personality (as inwardly divided), see interrogation of Erich von dem Bach-Zelewski, 19 June 1947, NA RG 238, M-1019/R 4/152–53.

5. This report reached Wise through the Geneva office of the Jewish Agency for Palestine, based on the testimony of two men who had recently come from Poland. Copy in NA RG 59, Central Decimal File 740.00116 E. W. 1939/756, and summary in Welles to Taylor, 23 Sept. 1942, Triple Priority, NA RG 84, American Legation Bern, Confidential Correspondence 1942, 840.1 Jews. A similar report came to Jacob Rosenheim of Agudas Israel, who also gave it to Wise. Stephen S. Wise Papers, box 82, American Jewish Historical Society, Waltham, Mass. The portions of the reports about the liquidation of Jews from the Warsaw ghetto were generally accurate. The copy of Wise's "Denkschrift" referred to in Himmler's letter (see n. 6) is no longer to be found in Himmler's records, but based on the date given (Sept. 1942) and the subject, Himmler must be referring to what Wise

gave Welles and what Welles cabled to Taylor. In his news conference of 24 Nov. 1942 Wise also referred to the report about manufacturing fats. New York *Herald Tribune*, 25 Nov. 1942.

6. Himmler to Müller, 30 Nov. 1942, NA RG 242, T-175/R 58/2521486.

7. Interrogation of Erika Lorenz, 17 Oct. 1945, and interrogation of Franz Conrad, 17 Oct. 1945, NA RG 319, IRR Files, XE 096686.

8. This account is drawn from the interrogations of Himmler's adjutant Werner Groth-mann (13 June 1945) and his office manager, Rudolf Brandt (13 June 1945), immediately after they were captured. Copies in NA RG 319, IRR, Heinrich Himmler XE000632. I also consulted Roger Manvell and Heinrich Fraenkel, *Himmler* (New York, 1965), who interrogated some of the British soldiers involved but also made errors in their account. In cases of conflict between the interrogations and the Manvell/Fraenkel book, I sided with the interrogations.

9. Manvell and Fraenkel, *Himmler*, 244–47; quote on 246–47.

10. Ibid., 247–48. On Himmler's cyanide capsule, see interrogation of Marga Himmler, 26 Sept. 1945, NA RG 238, M-1270/R 6/841. Additional details in "The Gravediggers Return to Lüneburg," *After the Battle* 17 (1977): 1–3, including quote on p. 3. I am grateful to Paul Katsigiannis for calling this publication to my attention.

11. *Second Army Troop News*, 27 May 1945, reprinted in "Gravediggers," *After the Battle* 17 (1977):1.

12. Bradley F. Smith, *Heinrich Himmler: A Nazi in the Making, 1900–1926* (Stanford, 1971), 14–15.

13. Ibid., 25, 28–29.

14. Ibid., 24, 27, 41–42.

15. Ibid., 28–29, 47, 68.

16. Werner T. Angress and Bradley F. Smith, "Diaries of Heinrich Himmler's Early Years," *Journal of Modern History* 31 (1959): 206. Smith, *Himmler*, 25–26.

17. This material is to be found partly in the Hoover Institution's Himmler Collection at Stanford University and partly in Himmler's SS file, Berlin Document Center. Of the former, I used the microfilm copy in the National Archives, NA RG 242, T-581, particularly R 38A, 39A, 40A, 42A, 45A.

18. Smith, *Himmler*, 170.

19. Peter Loewenberg, "The Unsuccessful Adolescence of Heinrich Himmler," *American Historical Review* 76 (1971): 616–18.

20. Ibid., 635–36.

21. Smith, *Himmler*, 38–39. Loewenberg, "Unsuccessful Adolescence," 626–27. Diary entry of 25 Sept. 1914, Himmler Diaries, Hoover Institution. Comments about Himmler and women by Ernst "Putzi" Hanfstaengel, given the code name Dr. Sedgwick in NA RG 226, entry 171, box 8, folder 49, "Heinrich Himmler," pp. 7–8.

22. See, for example, diary entry of 29 Sept. 1914, Himmler Diaries, Hoover Institution. More generally, Angress/Smith, "Diaries," 207. Smith, *Himmler*, 35–38.

23. Smith, *Himmler*, 48–58.

24. Diary entry of 22 Nov. 1921, Himmler Diaries, Hoover Institution.

25. Smith, *Himmler*, 67–77. On Himmler's passion for farming, Rudolf Höss Aufzeich-nungen, Institut für Zeitgeschichte, Munich, F 13/5, 279. On the influence of agriculture on him, Günther d'Alquen Unterredung, 13–14 March 1951, Institut für Zeitgeschichte, Munich, ZS 2, 95.

26. Diary entry of 2 Nov. 1921, Himmler Diaries, Hoover Institution. Smith, *Himmler*, 85–86. Loewenberg, "Unsuccessful Adolescence," 620–22.

27. Diary entry of 24 Nov. 1921, Himmler Diaries, Hoover Institution, quoted in Loewenberg, "Unsuccessful Adolescence," 627–28. Slight variations in my translation.

28. Heinz Höhne, *The Order of Death's Head: The Story of Hitler's SS*, trans. Richard Barry (New York, 1979), 55.

29. Diary entries of 15, 31, and 26 Dec. 1919, Himmler Diaries, Hoover Institution. Smith, *Himmler*, 83, 87–88.

30. Diary entries of 19 Nov. 1919, Himmler Diaries, Hoover Institution.

31. Interrogation of Otto Ohlendorf, 23 June 1947, NA RG 238, M-1019/R 51/164.

32. Diary entry of 23 Nov. 1919, Himmler Diaries, Hoover Institution. This interpretation is consistent with both Smith, *Himmler*, 93, 136, and Loewenberg, "Unsuccessful Adolescence," 623.

33. Konrad Heiden, *Der Fuehrer: Hitler's Rise to Power* (Boston, 1969, orig. 1944), 307.

34. Angress and Smith, "Diaries," 217, 220–21. Smith, *Himmler*, 73–74, 91–92, 142–46. Diary entries of 27 and 30 Sept., 1–6 Oct. 1914, Himmler Diaries, Hoover Institution. Himmler's speech at Bad Tölz, 18 Feb. 1937, summarized in Josef Ackermann, *Heinrich Himmler als Ideologe* (Göttingen, 1970), 92.

35. Ullmann Aktenvermerk, 5 Dec. 1938, NA RG 242, T-175/R 112/2636601.

36. Diary entry of 22 Nov. 1921, Himmler Diaries, Hoover Institution.

37. Hanfstaengel's description of Gebhard Himmler's class in the year 1898 in NA RG 226, entry 171, box 8, folder 49, "Heinrich Himmler," 1–3.

38. Smith, *Himmler*, 152–53.

39. Ibid., 42, 59–60.

40. Helbing-Bauer, *Die Tortur*, Himmler Collection, Gelesene Bücher 1926–1934, no. 269, Library of Congress, German Captured Documents Collection, box 418. Alfred Krebs, *Tendenzen und Gestalten der NSDAP: Erinnerungen an die Frühzeit . . .* , quoted in Ackermann, *Heinrich Himmler*, 29.

41. NA RG 226, entry 171, box 8, folder 49, p. 10.

42. Michael R. Marrus, *The Holocaust in History* (Hanover, N.H., 1987), 3.

43. For instance, Yehuda Bauer, *The Holocaust in Historical Perspective* (London, 1978); Yehuda Bauer, *A History of the Holocaust* (New York, 1982).

44. This argument is particularly associated with Michael Stürmer. See his "Geschichte im geschichtlosem Land," in *"Historikerstreit": Die Dokumentation der Kontroverse um die Einzigartigkeit der nationalsozialistischen Judenvernichtung* (Munich, 1987), 36–39.

45. Here esp. Ernst Nolte, "Die Sache auf dem Kopf gestellt," in *Historikerstreit*, 223–31; Ernst Nolte, *Der europäische Bürgerkrieg: Nationalsozialismus und Bolschewismus* (Frankfurt am Main, 1987). For a more thorough review of the literature and a more detailed analysis, see Charles S. Maier, *The Unmasterable Past: History, Holocaust, and German National Identity* (Cambridge, Mass., 1988), esp. 66–99, and Richard J. Evans, *In Hitler's Shadow: West German Historians and the Attempt to Escape from the Nazi Past* (New York, 1989).

46. Jürgen Habermas, "Eine Art Schadensabwicklung," and "Leserbrief an die Frankfurter Allgemeine Zeitung," in *Historikerstreit*, 62–76, 95–97. Quote from Eberhard Jäckel, 12 Sept. 1986 article, originally in *Die Zeit*, reprinted in *Historikerstreit*, 115–22; quoted in Maier, *Unmasterable Past*, 53.

47. Gerald Reitlinger, *The Final Solution: The Attempt to Exterminate the Jews of Europe* (London, 1953), 80–84.

48. Adolf Hitler, *Mein Kampf*, trans. Ralph Manheim (Boston, 1943), 679. Eberhard Jäckel, *Hitler's Weltanschauung: A Blueprint for Power*, trans. Herbert Arnold (Middletown, Conn., 1972), 60.

49. Jäckel, *Hitler's Weltanschauung*, 77–79. Eberhard Jäckel, *Hitler in History* (Hanover,

N.H., 1984), 44–65. Lucy S. Dawidowicz, *The War Against the Jews 1933–1945* (New York, 1976), 206–19. Andreas Hillgruber, "Die ideologisch-dogmatische Grundlage der nationalsozialistischen Politik der Ausrottung der Juden in den besetzten Gebieten der Sowjetunion und ihre Durchführung 1941–1944," *German Studies Review* 2 (1979), 263–86. Hermann Graml, "Zur Genesis der 'Endlösung,' " in *Der Judenpogrom 1938: Von der "Reichskristallnacht" zum Völkermord*, ed. Walter H. Pehle (Frankfurt am Main, 1988), 160–75.

50. Karl A. Schleunes, *The Twisted Road to Auschwitz: Nazi Policy Toward German Jews 1933–1939* (Urbana, Ill., 1970). On p. 261: "The factional struggle for control over Jewish policy was not resolved until late 1938, after the SS had clearly emerged with the most effective proposals for a solution. Then, and only then, did Hitler commission it to prepare a coordinated policy toward the Jews."

51. The most important functionalist book is still Uwe Dietrich Adam, *Judenpolitik im Dritten Reich* (Düsseldorf, 1972). See also his "An Overall Plan for Anti-Jewish Legislation in the Third Reich?," *Yad Vashem Studies* 11 (1976): 33–55; and "Nazi Actions Concerning the Jews Between the Beginning of World War II and the German Attack on the USSR," in François Furet, ed., *Unanswered Questions: Nazi Germany and the Genocide of the Jews* (New York, 1988). Martin Broszat's best-known and most detailed article on this subject is "Hitler und die Genesis der 'Endlösung': Aus Anlass der Thesen von David Irving," *Vierteljahrshefte für Zeitgeschichte* 25 (1977): 737–75. Hans Mommsen has contributed quite a number of relevant articles, of which the best known is "The Realization of the Unthinkable: 'The Final Solution of the Jewish Question' in the Third Reich," trans. and reprinted in Gerhard Hirschfeld, ed., *The Politics of Genocide: Jews and Soviet Prisoners of War in Nazi Germany* (London, 1986), 93–144.

Because of substantial differences in interpretation with other functionalists, Christopher Browning's work (see n. 56) belongs in a separate category.

Readers in search of further articles and synthesis of this literature may wish to consult: Konrad Kwiet, "Judenverfolgung und Judenvernichtung im Dritten Reich: Ein historiographischer Überblick," in Dan Diner, ed., *Ist der Nationalsozialismus Geschichte? Zu Historisierung und Historikerstreit* (Frankfurt am Main, 1988), 237–64: Otto Dov Kulka, "Major Trends and Tendencies of German Historiography on National Socialism and the 'Jewish Question' (1924–1984)," *Leo Baeck Institute Yearbook* 21 (1985): 215–42; and Ian Kershaw, *The Nazi Dictatorship: Problems and Perspectives of Interpretation* (London, 1985), 61–105.

52. Adam, *Judenpolitik*, 310–16; Broszat, "Hitler und die Genesis," 759.

53. Arno J. Mayer, *Why Did the Heavens Not Darken?: The "Final Solution" in History* (New York, 1988), esp. 279, 289, 299.

54. Broszat, "Hitler und die Genesis," 756–58.

55. Mommsen, "The Realization," esp. 110–14.

56. Christopher R. Browning, *Fateful Months: Essays on the Emergence of the Final Solution* (New York, 1985), esp. 8–38. Christopher R. Browning, "Zur Genesis der 'Endlösung': Eine Antwort an Martin Broszat," *Vierteljahrshefte für Zeitgeschichte* 29 (1981): esp. 98, 103–9. Christopher R. Browning, "Nazi Resettlement Policy and the Search for a Solution to the Jewish Question," *German Studies Review* 9 (1986): 516–19.

57. Charles W. Sydnor, Jr., commentary on my paper "Himmler and the Origins of the Final Solution," Woodrow Wilson International Center for Scholars, 5 Dec. 1987.

58. This is particularly true of Dawidowicz, *War Against the Jews*, and Jäckel, *Hitler's Weltanschauung*.

59. Mayer made this statement (in English) in the course of a panel discussion of his book at the cultural center Am Gasteig in Munich on 17 Oct. 1989, for which I was present.

60. Gerald Fleming, *Hitler and the Final Solution* (Berkeley, 1984: German original, 1982).

61. David Irving, *Hitler's War* (New York, 1977), esp. xiv, 392, 504.

62. Fleming, *Hitler and the Final Solution*, 18.

63. Walter Laqueur and Richard Breitman, *Breaking the Silence* (New York, 1986). This book is a biography of Eduard Schulte, the German industrialist who leaked the first report about the Final Solution to reach the West.

64. NA RG 238, Office of Chief of Counsel for War Crimes, Berlin Branch SS, entry 205, box 41, reference to folder A 124: according to this summary, Brandt wrote Berger that he had destroyed records. On Frau Lorenz, see p. 7 above.

65. Himmler's notes for these meetings are in NA RG 242, T-175/R 94.

66. The bulk of these interrogations are in NA RG 238, M-1270 and M-1019.

CHAPTER 1: HITLER, HIMMLER, AND THE SS

1. On Himmler, see Konrad Heiden, *Der Fuehrer: Hitler's Rise to Power* (Boston, 1969, orig. 1944), 307; Walter Dornberger, *V2* (London, 1959), 179, cited by Gerald Reitlinger, *The SS: Alibi of a Nation 1922–1945* (New York, 1957), 20; Walter Schellenberg, *Hitler's Secret Service* (New York, 1971), 67.

2. Bradley F. Smith, *Heinrich Himmler: A Nazi in the Making, 1900–1926* (Stanford, 1971), 147.

3. Robert Lewis Koehl, *The Black Corps: The Structure and Power Struggles of the Nazi SS* (Madison, Wisc., 1983), 28–32.

4. As quoted by Otto Wagener in *Hitler—Memoirs of a Confidant*, ed. Henry Ashby Turner, Jr., trans. Ruth Hein (New Haven, 1985), 19–21, quote on 21.

5. SS Führerbesprechung, 13–14 June 1931, NA RG 242, T-580/R 87/Ordner 425, cited and discussed by Koehl, *The Black Corps*, 47–48.

6. Darré quoted in Hermann Rauschning, *The Voice of Destruction* (New York, 1940), 31. The speech may not be a pure rendition of Darré's conversation, but it is generally consistent with Darré's thinking. See the too-generous treatment of Darré in Anna Bramwell, *Blood and Soil: Richard Walther Darré and Hitler's "Green Party"* (Abbotsbrook, 1985), esp. 67–74.

7. Josef Ackermann, *Heinrich Himmler als Ideologe* (Göttingen, 1970), 110–12.

8. Heinz Höhne, *The Order of Death's Head* (New York, 1969), 166.

9. Ackermann, *Heinrich Himmler*, 101–26. On Himmler's role in marriage applications, Günther d'Alquen Unterredung, 13–14 March 1951, Institut für Zeitgeschichte, ZS 2, 95.

10. Höhne, *The Order*, 171–73.

11. Michael H. Kater, *The Nazi Party: A Social Profile of Members and Leaders, 1919–1945* (Cambridge, Mass., 1983), 134, 196. Koehl, *The Black Corps*, 241–42.

12. Reitlinger, *The SS*, has interesting ideas but is riddled with errors. Höhne, *The Order*, is much better, but still not adequately researched. Koehl, *The Black Corps*, is generally good as far as it goes, but it is quite thin on the wartime period. More specialized works of good quality are Ackermann, *Heinrich Himmler*; Hans Buchheim et al., *Anatomie des SS-Staates* (Munich, 1967); Michael Kater, *Das Ahnenerbe der SS 1935–1945: Ein Beitrag zur Kulturpolitik des Dritten Reiches* (Stuttgart, 1974); Ruth Bettina Birn, *Die Höheren SS-und Polizeiführer: Himmlers Vertreter im Reich und in den besetzten Gebieten* (Düsseldorf, 1986);

Enno Georg, *Die wirtschaftlichen Unternehmungen der SS* (Stuttgart, 1963). George C. Browder, *Foundations of the Nazi Police State: The Formation of the SIPO and SD* (Lexington, Ky., 1990), appeared too late to be used in this study. The Waffen-SS is a subject by itself. There is a good overview by George H. Stein, *The Waffen-SS: Hitler's Elite Guard at War* (Ithaca, 1966); and a fine monograph by Charles W. Sydnor, Jr., *Soldiers of Destruction: The SS Death's Head Division 1933–1945* (Princeton, 1977; revised edition, 1990).

13. According to Otto Ohlendorf, testimony of 3 Jan. 1946, in International Military Tribunal, *Trial of the Major War Criminals* (hereafter IMT) (Nuremberg, 1947), IV, 336.

14. Schröder to Himmler, 4 Dec. 1933, regarding an anniversary celebration of the occasion, NA RG 238, T-175/R 103/2625145.

15. Hermann Rauschning, *Men of Chaos* (New York, 1942), 24. Shlomo Aronson, *Heydrich und die Anfänge des SD und der Gestapo* (Berlin, 1967), 137–39. On Rauschning's limitations, see, among others, Theodor Schieder, *Hermann Rauschning's "Gespräche mit Hitler als Geschichtsquelle"* (Opladen, 1972).

16. Hans Buchheim, "Die SS—Das Herrschaftsinstrument," in Hans Buchheim et al., *Anatomie des SS-Staates* (Munich, 1967), I, 50–59. Höhne, *The Order*, 218–20.

17. Rauschning, *Men of Chaos*, 27–28. Once again, whether or not he reproduced conversations accurately, Rauschning had a generally accurate sense of Himmler's methods. See also Aronson, *Heydrich*, 137–39.

18. Reinhard Vogelsang, *Der Freundekreis Himmler* (Göttingen, 1972), esp. 52–78.

19. Keppler to Himmler, 13 Dec. 1939, NA RG 238, T-301/R 100/1006–7, NI-12301. See also interrogation of Wilhelm Keppler, 20 Aug. 1947, NA RG 238, T-1139/R 33/172–74, NG-3041; interrogations of Keppler, Sept.–Oct. 1945, NA RG 226, XL22953; NA RG 238, NI-15613.

20. Keppler to Himmler, 13 Dec. 1939, NA RG 238, T-301/R 100/1008, NI-12301; interrogation of Wolff, 16 Dec. 1946, NA RG 238, M1019/R 80/968.

21. "In Chemical Maker's Town, Germans Silently Disbelieve," *New York Times*, 17 Jan. 1989.

22. See, for example, how Himmler got extra workers for his concentration camps, over the opposition of the Ministry of Justice, through Hitler's intervention. Kamm to Lammers, 26 July 1939, NA RG 238, T-1139/R 5/35, NG-340. Also Sydnor, *Soldiers of Destruction*, 32–35.

23. Sydnor, *Soldiers of Destruction*, 30–31.

24. Ibid., 32–35.

25. For one of many examples of Himmler's agendas for Hitler, Besprechung beim Führer am 8 Nov. 1936, NA RG 242, T-175/R 94/272. Other agendas for other dates on this same roll. Hitler's *"willfähriges Werkzeug"* in interrogation of Werner Best, 30 Nov. 1946, NA RG 238, M-1019/R 6/1063; Fritz Günther von Tschirschky, *Erinnerungen eines Hochverräters* (Stuttgart, 1972), 139.

26. Interrogation of Rudolf Brandt, 23 Nov. 1946, NA RG 238, M-1019/R 9/654. Rudolf Höss Aufzeichnungen, Institut für Zeitgeschichte F 13/5, 280.

27. Schellenberg, *Hitler's Secret Service*, 102–3. Interrogation of Luitpold Schallermeier, NA RG 238, M-1019/R 62/1016.

28. Interrogation of Wilhelm Heinrich Scheidt, 12 July 1945, NA RG 238, M-1270/R 27/262.

29. Schellenberg, *Hitler's Secret Service*, 102.

30. Von Alvensleben to "Püppi" [Gudrun Himmler], 4 April 1939, NA RG 242, T-175/R 112/2636842.

31. Erzählungen und Aussprüche des Reichsführer-SS beim Mittagessen, 9 Jan. 1939, NA RG 242, T-175/R 88/2611408.

32. Michael Prawdin [Charol], *Tshchingis-Chan, der Sturm aus Asien* (Stuttgart, 1934). Michael Prawdin, *Das Erbe Tshchingis-Chan* (Stuttgart, 1935). Biographical information from Mrs. R. C. Prawdin, letter of 8 Nov. 1987. I am grateful to Walter Laqueur for putting me in touch with Mrs. Prawdin.

33. Ackermann, *Heinrich Himmler*, 55. Gelesene Bücher, 1926–1934, #332, German Captured Document Collection, box 418, Library of Congress.

34. Interrogation of Gottlob Berger, 30 Oct. 1947, NA RG 238, M-1019/R 6/666. Michael Prawdin, *Tshchingis-Chan und seine Erbe* (Stuttgart, 1938). Berger also mentioned the use of an earlier book on Genghis Khan, but he did not name the author.

35. Interrogation of Erich von dem Bach-Zelewski, 19 June 1947, NA RG 238, M-1019/R 4/140. Interrogation of Dr. Karl Gebhardt [Himmler's boyhood friend], 23 July 1947, NA RG 238 M-1019/R 20/710. There are other signs of the significant impact of this book on Himmler. According to Otto Heider, an official in the SS Race and Settlement Office, Himmler drew conclusions from this book about the need to keep the German race pure, the possibility of increasing the Germanic population limitlessly, and the need for European unity. Heider was one of those who got the book from Himmler as a present. Heider to Himmler, 3 June 1943, NA RG 242, T-175/R 29/2536755. The book also appears at the top of a long, undated list of books to be acquired for Himmler. See NA RG 242, T-175/R112/2636686. In 1944 guidelines written (apparently by Himmler) for the officers of the Waffen-SS Galician Division, composed of Ukrainian soldiers, the destruction of Kiev and the Ukrainian state by Genghis Khan and the Mongols was stressed. The lesson was that only Germany could protect the Ukrainians against Asia. See Central State Archives of the October Revolution of the Ukrainian S.S.R., Kiev, collection 4620, entry 3, file 378, 13.

36. Michael Prawdin [Charol], *The Mongol Empire: Its Rise and Legacy*, trans. Eden and Cedar Paul (London, 1967), 48, 195. The most recent scholarship concludes also that the Mongol conquests were a disaster on an unparalleled scale. Transoxiana and eastern Persia are said to have suffered something approaching genocide. See David Morgan, *The Mongols* (New York, 1987), 74.

37. Prawdin, *Genghis Khan*, 260–69.

38. Ackermann, *Heinrich Himmler*, 195–212. *Hitler's Secret Conversations, 1941–1944* (New York, 1976), 34, 25 Sept. 1941.

39. Prawdin, *Genghis Khan*, 53, 94, 60, 142, 205, 80, 87, 234 (quote), 131.

40. Heider to Himmler, 3 June 1943, NA RG 242, T-175/R 29/2536755.

41. Der Reichsführer SS, SS-Hauptamt-Schulungsamt, *Grenzkampf Ost: Der Kampf um die deutsche Ostgrenze*, n.p., n.d. Nur für Führer.

42. Prawdin, *Genghis Khan*, 507–18, 522, 529. Ackermann, *Heinrich Himmler*, 53–63, 88–92. On Hitler, see particularly *Hitler's Secret Conversations*, 6–7, 11–12 July 1941. For the favorable allusions to Genghis Khan, see Adolf Hitler, *Monologe im Führerhauptquartier 1941–1944: Die Aufzeichnungen Heinrich Heims*, ed. Werner Jochmann (Hamburg, 1980), 136, 367, 370; Henry Picker, *Hitlers Tischgespräche im Führerhauptquartier 1941–1942* (Stuttgart, 1963), 468, 497. For Himmler, Ackermann, *Heinrich Himmler*, 37, 206, and n. 35 above.

43. On Atlantis, see interrogation of Ernst Schaefer, 16 July 1945, NA RG 238, M-1270/R 27/186; Michael H. Kater, *Das Ahnenerbe der SS* (Stuttgart, 1974), 51.

44. Speech at Hegewald, 16 Sept. 1942, NA RG 242, T-175/R 90/2612890–95, men-

tioned by Michael Burleigh, *Germany Turns Eastward: A Study of Ostforschung in the Third Reich* (Cambridge, 1988), 8.

45. See Heider's comments in n. 35 above.

46. Interrogation of Karl Gebhardt, 23 July 1947, NA RG 238, M-1019/R 20/710. Gebhardt believed that Hitler hadn't actually read the book. But the fact that Hitler borrowed ideas from at least two sections, and the fact that Himmler was known to have given Hitler books to read, suggest otherwise.

47. This quote comes from the so-called Lochner version of the speech. Six days before World War II began, the well-known Berlin correspondent for the Associated Press, Louis P. Lochner, received some explosive intelligence. On 22 Aug., three days earlier, Adolf Hitler had given a speech at his mountain retreat at Berchtesgaden to the commanders-in-chief of the armed services. A high-ranking officer present at Berchtesgaden had taken notes, turned them over to the anti-Nazi resistance, which in turn had sought out Lochner and given him a summary. Lochner showed it to an American diplomat, who was too terrified of it to hold on to it, so Lochner turned over the document to the British councillor of embassy in Berlin, Ogilvie-Forbes, who sent it posthaste to London. After 1945 other records of Hitler's remarks on 22 Aug. turned up, which diverged somewhat from Lochner's document; they were less vivid and in some ways less extreme. The other, more official versions are in IMT 36, 338–44, 798-PS, and 523–24, 1014-PS. See Winfried Baumgart, "Zur Ansprache Hitlers vor den Führern der Wehrmacht am 22. August 1939: Eine quellenkritische Untersuchung," *Vierteljahrshefte für Zeitgeschichte* 16 (1968): 120–29; Klaus-Jürgen Müller, *Das Heer und Hitler: Armee und nationalsozialistisches Regime 1933–1940* (Stuttgart, 1969), 409–13. These two German scholars have argued persuasively that the man who took the original notes was Admiral Wilhelm Canaris, chief of the Abwehr, German Military Intelligence, and the man who edited them, perhaps bringing in additional information that he had from other sources, and arranged for them to reach the West through retired General Ludwig Beck, former Socialist Youth leader Hermann Maass, and Lochner, was Canaris's fiercely anti-Nazi deputy, Hans Oster.

For Lochner's version, Louis P. Lochner, *What About Germany* (New York, 1942), 1–5; *Documents on British Foreign Policy*, VII, no. 314, 257–60. The Lochner report appears in Office of U.S. Chief of Counsel for Prosecution of Axis Criminals, *Nazi Conspiracy and Aggression* (hereafter *NCA*) (Washington, D.C., 1946), VII, 752–54, L-003.

48. On Gebhardt's relationship with Himmler, see, for example, interrogation of Dr. Werner Kirchert, 3 Sept. 1946, NA RG 238, M-1019/R 35/298–99. Interrogation of Karl Gebhardt, 23 July 1947, NA RG 238, M-1019/R 20/709–710. The stenographer did not even recognize the term *Blutkitt*, and hence only a blank appears in the minutes here. But for proof that this was the term used by the interrogator, see the interrogation of Erich von dem Bach-Zelewski, 19 June 1947, NA RG 238, M-1019/R 4/140; interrogation of Otto Ohlendorf, 23 June 1947, NA RG 238, M-1019/R 51/165. The translation of Prawdin's passage into English (Prawdin, *Genghis Khan*, 143) unfortunately does not adequately convey the necessity of bloodshed. See Prawdin, *Tschingis-Chan und seine Erbe*, 136: "*In gemeinsamen Schlachten und Siegen war durch Blut ein Volk zusammengeschweisst worden. . . .*"

49. Prawdin, *Genghis Khan*, 57.

50. Interrogation of Karl Wolff, 26 Feb. 1947, NA RG 238, M-1019/R 80/955.

51. Intelligence Report, 12 Nov. 1943, from British Naval Attaché, Istanbul, NA RG 165, G-2 regional file: Germany 1933–1944, box 1193, Germany 3700.

52. See, for example, pp. 181–82, 241 below.

CHAPTER 2: PLANS FOR GERMAN JEWS

1. On the general Polish-German dispute over Polish Jews in Germany, see Eliahu Ben Elissar, *La Diplomatie du IIIe Reich et les juifs (1933–1939)* (Paris, 1981), 301–21; Emanuel Melzer, "Relations between Poland and Germany and Their Impact on the Jewish Problem in Poland (1935–1938)," *Yad Vashem Studies* 12 (1977): 193–229; Sybil Milton, "The Expulsion of Polish Jews from Germany October 1938 to July 1939: A Documentation," *Leo Baeck Institute Yearbook* 29 (1984): 169–99. For Himmler's express letters ordering the deportation, Trude Maurer, "Abschiebung und Attentat: Die Ausweisung der polnischen Juden und der Vorwand für die 'Kristallnacht,' " in *Der Judenpogrom 1938: Von der "Reichskristallnacht" zum Völkermord*, ed. Walter H. Pehle (Frankfurt am Main, 1988), 61.

2. Helmut Heiber, "Der Fall Grünspan," *Vierteljahrshefte für Zeitgeschichte* 5 (1957): 134–44.

3. Wolfgang Benz, "Der Rückfall in die Barberei: Bericht über den Pogrom," in *Judenpogrom 1938*, 15–16.

4. Well before the shooting of vom Rath, the SD considered the assassination of Wilhelm Gustloff (the Nazi official in Switzerland) part of a broader Jewish conspiracy. See Richtlinien und Forderungen an die Oberabschnitte, 21 April 1937, NA RG 242, T-175/R 588/408, which demonstrates the SD's role in the case.

5. Quoted in William L. Combs, *The Voice of the SS: A History of the SS Journal "Das Schwarze Korps"* (New York, 1986), 79.

6. Himmler himself recounted this story in his 30 Jan. 1943 speech to the higher officials of the Reich Security Main Office. See the text in NA, RG 319, IRR files 1903, Ernst Kaltenbrunner, XE 000440.

7. Shlomo Aronson, *Heydrich und die Anfänge des SD und der Gestapo* (Berlin, 1967), 53–56.

8. Himmler's speech, 30 Jan. 1943, NA RG 319, IRR 1903, Kaltenbrunner, XE 000440.

9. Ibid.

10. For Himmler's attacks on Jews, Freemasons, and Jesuits at this time, see Bradley F. Smith and Agnes F. Peterson, *Heinrich Himmler: Geheimreden 1933–1945 und andere Ansprachen* (Frankfurt, 1974), 57–58.

11. For Heydrich's views, Reinhard Heydrich, *Wandlungen unseres Kampfes* (Munich, 1935), 10–14. For the SD, Richtlinien und Forderungen, 21 April 1937, Abteilungsbesprechung II 112, 9 June 1937, NA RG 238, Office of Chief of Counsel for War Crimes, Berlin Branch, box 27, SS 5878. Götz Aly and Karl Heinz Roth, *Die restlose Erfassung: Volkszählen, Identifiziern, Aussondern im Nationalsozialismus* (West Berlin, 1984), 72–74.

12. Gerhard L. Weinberg, *The Foreign Policy of Hitler's Germany: Starting World War II, 1937–1939* (Chicago, 1980), II, 35–36.

13. Ibid., II, 378–464, esp. 452, 463.

14. Ibid., II, 467–68. Geist to Messersmith, 4 Jan. 1939, George S. Messersmith Papers, folder 1122, University of Delaware.

15. For a good, brief account of the positive SS attitude toward Jewish emigration from 1935 on, see Francis R. Nicosia, *The Third Reich and the Palestine Question* (Austin, 1985), 54–64, 151–56. Nicosia's view of the relationship between Heydrich and Göring, however, is different from the version presented here.

16. Report by Oberscharführer Hagen and Eichmann, 13 Sept. 1936, 4 Nov. 1937, NA RG 242, T-175/R 411/2936189–94 and 1936013–68, reprinted in John Mendelsohn, ed., *The Holocaust*, vol. 5: *Jewish Emigration from 1933 to the Evian Conference of 1938* (New York, 1982), docs. 4, 6. Circular of the Foreign Ministry, 25 Jan. 1939, *Documents on German*

Foreign Policy, ser. D, vol. 5, 931. Heydrich, *Wandlungen*, 10–14. That the Nazis used forced emigration to accomplish their goals is also the conclusion of historians Herbert Strauss, "Jewish Emigration from Germany: Nazi Policies and Jewish Responses (I)," *Leo Baeck Institute Yearbook* 25 (1980): 347; and Shlomo Aronson, "Die dreifache Falle: Hitlers Judenpolitik, die Allierten und die Juden," *Vierteljahrshefte für Zeitgeschichte* 32 (1984): 31, 45, 47.

17. Minutes of Refugee Committee, 9 Feb. 1939, Refugee Service 1939, American Friends Service Committee Archive, Philadelphia.

18. Wiley to Messersmith, 8 June 1938, Messersmith Papers, folder 1051, University of Delaware.

19. On his participation in the putsch, see Werner Angress and Bradley F. Smith, "Heinrich Himmler's Diaries," *Journal of Modern History* 31 (1959): 211, 221, 223.

20. See Karl Wolff's memo of 14 July 1938, which refers to the forthcoming Gruppenführer meeting scheduled for 9 Nov., Himmler SS file, Berlin Document Center. *Völkischer Beobachter*, 8 Nov. 1938, quoted in Benz, "Rückfall," 14–15.

21. Smith and Peterson, *Himmler*, 25–47. Also, NA RG 242, T-175/R 90, summarized portions on 261259–62, 2612582.

22. Wilhelm Treue, "Rede Hitlers vor der deutschen Presse (10 November 1938)," *Vierteljahrshefte für Zeitgeschichte* 6 (1958): 175–91, cited and summarized in Weinberg, *Foreign Policy*, II, 515–16.

23. Benz, "Rückfall," 18–19.

24. Ibid., 19–20. Uwe Dietrich Adam, "Wie spontan war der Pogrom," in *Judenpogrom 1938*, 77. See instructions about synagogues and businesses in NA RG 238, 1721-PS.

25. Adam, "Wie spontan," 77–78. Additional details of my account come from the pretrial interrogation of Wolff's personal assistant, Luitpold Schallermeier, 23 June 1947, NA RG 238, M-1019/R 62/1023–24, which, though not perfectly consistent or accurate, adds some useful details. Karl Wolff has Hitler in the famous Residenz in Munich, Heinrich Müller reporting the events to Himmler, then Himmler and Müller going in to see Hitler, which has the undoubted advantage (for Wolff) of removing Wolff from the scene with Hitler. Niederschrift der Unterredung Dr. Freiherr v. Siegler mit Karl Wolff, 12 Dec. 1952, Institut für Zeitgeschichte, ZS 317/1, 9–10. The first Gestapo telegram to local police offices is reprinted in IMT 25, 377–78, 374-PS.

26. Adam, "Wie spontan," 78. Quote from Schallermeier, 23 June 1947, NA RG 238, M-1019/R 62/1023–24. Second telegram issued from Munich 1:20 a.m., reprinted in International Military Tribunal, *Trial of the Major War Criminals* (Nuremberg, 1947), 25, 378, 374-PS.

27. Benz, "Rückfall," 31–32, 40. Full-length studies of Kristallnacht include Hermann Graml, *Der 9. November 1938, "Reichskristallnacht"* (Bonn, 1958); Rita Thalmann and Emmanuel Feinermann, *Crystal Night: 9–10 November 1938*, trans. Gilles Cremonesi (London, 1972).

28. Adam, "Wie spontan," 79. Ulrich vom Hassell, *Vom anderen Deutschland: Aus den nachgelassenen Tagebüchern 1938–1944* (Zurich, 1946), 39.

29. Robert Edwin Herzstein, *The War That Hitler Won: Goebbels and the Nazi Media Campaign* (New York, 1987), 61.

30. Alfred Rosenberg, *Das politische Tagebuch Alfred Rosenbergs 1934–1935, 1939–1940* (Munich, 1964), 81, cited by Herzstein, *War That Hitler Won*, 70.

31. Himmler's reference in his speech of 30 Jan. 1943, in NA RG 319, IRR 1903, Kaltenbrunner XE 000440.

32. Von Hassell, *Vom anderen Deutschland*, 49–50. Diary of Siegfried Kasche, NA RG 242, T-120/R 1026/4086. This conversation took place in Dec. 1941.

33. Uwe Dietrich Adam, *Judenpolitik in Dritten Reich* (Düsseldorf, 1972), 198.

34. Carl J. Burckhardt, *Mein Danziger Mission* (Munich, 1960), 230. Wolff to the Head of the SS Court, 22 Nov. 1938, NA RG 242, T-175/R 84/2609684. Jochen von Lang, *Der Adjutant, Karl Wolff: Der Mann zwischen Hitler und Himmler* (Munich, 1985), 107. Himmler's schedule, NA RG 242, T-581/R 38A/no frame nos.—see dates instead.

35. Adam, *Judenpolitik*, 208–9.

36. IMT 28, 499–540, 1816-PS.

37. Burckhardt, *Mein Danziger Mission*, 228. Gilbert to Secretary of State, 14 Dec. 1938, NA RG 59, Lot file 52D408, folder, Germany 1938.

38. Bormann Aktenvermerk für Pg. Friedrich und Pg. Dr. Klopfer, 14 Oct. 1942, Akten der Parteikanzlei, Institut für Zeitgeschichte microfiche 103/22534: "*der Reichsmarschall betonte, er hielte die vom Reichsführer SS Himmler unternommenen Schritte für durchaus richtig, aber in besonderen Fällen müssten eben Ausnahmen gemacht werden.*"

39. Riddleberger Memorandum regarding General Göring's Views, 11 Aug. 1938, in NA RG 59 CDF 711.62/163. Bormann quoted in Karl A. Schleunes, *The Twisted Road to Auschwitz: Nazi Policy Toward German Jews 1933–1939* (Urbana, Ill., 1970), 225.

40. IMT 28, 532–39, 1816-PS. Heydrich suggested the idea of a Reich Central Office for Jewish Emigration on 12 Nov., and by 22 Nov. there is mention of a plan to create it and to install Heydrich as its head. NA RG 238, Office of Chief of Counsel for War Crimes, Berlin Branch, BB 1961. I benefited from Robert Wolfe's analysis of this 12 Nov. meeting: "Nazi Paperwork and the Final Solution," paper delivered to the American Historical Association meeting, 30 Dec. 1983.

41. IMT 28, 538–39, 1816-PS.

42. Hugo Rothenberg's Report to the Brothers of B'nai B'rith Lodge 712, Copenhagen, Dec. 1938, copy graciously supplied by Bent Blüdnikow.

43. Richard Breitman and Alan M. Kraut, *American Refugee Policy and European Jewry, 1933–1945* (Bloomington, Ind., 1988), 56–62.

44. Alfred Kube, *Pour le Mérite und Hakenkreuz: Herman Göring im Dritten Reich* (Munich, 1986), 303–4.

45. Gilbert to Secretary of State, 14 Dec. 1938, NA RG 59, Lot file 52D408, box 4, folder, Germany 1938. Geist to Messersmith, 4 Jan. 1939, Messersmith Papers, folder 1122, University of Delaware. R. J. Overy, *Göring: The Iron Man* (London, 1984), 76–91, sees Göring less in conflict with Hitler than Kube (n. 44) does, but concedes that Göring wanted five more years before Germany entered war, and that his function was to help prevent Britain from entering the conflict.

46. Circular of the Foreign Ministry, 25 Jan. 1939, *Documents on German Foreign Policy*, series D, vol. 5, 931. Geist to Messersmith, 4 April 1939, Messersmith Papers, folder 1187.

47. Combs, *Voice of the SS*, 22. D'Alquen SS File, Berlin Document Center.

48. "Juden, was nun?" *Das Schwarze Korps*, 24 Nov. 1938.

49. Geist to Messersmith, 5 Dec. 1938, Messersmith Papers, folder 1087. Conti quoted in Robert N. Proctor, *Racial Hygiene: Medicine Under the Nazis* (Cambridge, Mass., 1988), 210.

50. Heydrich's topic and scheduled address on 24 Jan., NA RG 242, T-175/R 17/2520613. Himmler's notes, NA RG 242, T-175/R 94/2615243, which dates the address as 25 Jan. 1939. I have here borrowed some of the analysis of these notes done by Charles W. Sydnor, Jr., "Executive Instinct: Reinhard Heydrich and the Final Solution to the Jewish Question," paper presented to the American Historical Association Meeting, 30 Dec. 1987.

51. Gilbert to Secretary of State, 14 Dec. 1938, NA RG 59, Lot file 52D408, box 4,

Germany 1938. Geist to Messersmith, 4 Jan. 1939 and 4 April 1939, Messersmith Papers, folders 1122 and 1187.

52. Johannes Popitz, conversation with von Hassell, 17 Dec. 1938, Hassell, *Vom anderen Deutschland*, 38.

53. Conversation of Rolf Vogel with Schacht, 16 Jan. 1970, in Rolf Vogel, ed., *Ein Stempel hat gefehlt: Dokumente zur Emigration deutscher Juden* (Munich, 1977), 210. For the provisions of the Schacht plan, *Documents on German Foreign Policy*, ser. D, vol. 5, 911–13, 921–25; Henry L. Feingold, *The Politics of Rescue: The Roosevelt Administration and the Holocaust 1938–1945* (New Brunswick, N.J., 1970), 45–68.

54. Notes on German trip by Robert Yarnall, American Friends Service Committee, Refugee Service 1938, American Friends Service Committee Archive. Vogel, *Stempel*, 186–208. *Documents on German Foreign Policy*, ser. D, vol. 5, 912–13, 925.

55. Rublee to Secretary of State, 21 Jan. 1939, RG 59, CDF 840.48 Refugees/1328. On Himmler's attitude toward Schacht, see his 1936 statement that he wanted to have Schacht arrested for making a speech implicitly critical of the Nazi regime—Himmler discussed the matter with Hitler, 1 May 1936, NA RG 242, T-175/R 62/2578175; speech on 2578176–77. On the secret report, Gilbert to Secretary of State, 23 Jan. 1939, Confidential, NA RG 59, Lot file 52D408, box 5, folder, Germany 1939.

56. Geist to Messersmith, 22 Jan. 1939, Messersmith Papers, folder 1136. Rublee to Secretary of State, 21 Jan. 1939, NA RG 59, CDF 840.48 Refugees/1328

57. Gilbert to Hull, 3 Feb. 1939, *Foreign Relations of the United States*, 1939, II, 77–81. Hull to Myron Taylor and George Rublee, 8 Feb. 1939, NA RG 59, CDF 840.48 Refugees/1384. Interrogation of Helmuth Wohlthat, 29 Jan. 1948, NA RG 238, M-1019/R 80/789.

58. Geist to Messersmith, 4 April 1939, Messersmith Papers, folder 1139. Geist was friendly with Himmler's press secretary, Sturmbannführer Grau. See Geist to Messersmith, 22 Jan. 1939, Messersmith Papers, folder 1136.

59. *Documents on German Foreign Policy*, ser. D, vol. 5, 935.

60. Göring mentioned Hitler's interest in Madagascar during the meeting of 12 Nov. on the Jewish question, IMT 28, 539, 1816-PS.

61. Anordnung 1/39, 17 Jan. 1939, NA RG 238, NG-2091.

62. Geist to Messersmith, 22 Jan. 1939, Messersmith Papers, folder 1136. Myron Taylor's statement at a meeting in the White House, quoted in Jay Pierrepont Moffat Diary, 4 May 1939, Houghton Library, Harvard University. It is unclear precisely when Göring made his comment, but the most likely time would have been around the conclusion of the Wohlthat-Rublee agreement.

63. Pell to Secretary of State, 28 April 1939; note by Sir Herbert Emerson, 1 May 1939; Pell to Secretary of State, 18 May 1939, NA RG 59, Lot file 52D408, box 15, folder, Wohlthat–London. See also Naomi Shephard, *A Refuge from Darkness: Wilfrid Israel and the Rescue of the Jews* (New York, 1984), 160–65.

64. Those who believe that Hitler was already planning the Final Solution include: Eberhard Jäckel, *Hitler's Weltanschauung: A Blueprint for Power*, trans. Herbert Arnold (Middletown, Conn., 1972), 61; and Lucy S. Dawidowicz, *The War Against the Jews 1933–1945* (New York, 1976), 142, 147–48. In contrast, Uwe Dietrich Adam maintains that "it is hardly conceivable that anyone in the SS already thought about *Einsatzgruppen* and Auschwitz at this time. The SS and even Hitler himself probably still had no ideas about the extent, way, and means of such . . . a destruction." Adam, *Judenpolitik*, 236. Hans Mommsen has Hitler wrapped up in his own rhetoric: "anti-Semitic spared him the need to reflect on the true consequences of his prophecies of the 'destruction of the Jewish

race.' " Hans Mommsen, "The Realization of the Unthinkable: The Final Solution of the Jewish Question in the Third Reich," trans. and reprinted in Gerhard Hirschfeld, ed., *The Politics of Genocide: Jews and Soviet Prisoners of War in Nazi Germany* (London, 1986), 112. See p. 61 on advance planning of the speech.

65. Weinberg, *Foreign Policy*, II, 503, 513–15. Geist to Secretary of State, 13 April 1939, strictly confidential, NA RG 59 CDF 740.00/794 and President's Secretary's File, Confidential File, Franklin D. Roosevelt Library, Hyde Park, N.Y.

66. Max Domarus, *Hitler, Reden und Proklamationen 1932–1945* (Munich, 1965), II, 1, 1,047–67, quote on 1,058.

67. Quoted in Jäckel, *Hitler's Weltanschauung*, 60.

68. Jochen Thies, *Architekt der Weltherrschaft: Die Endziele Hitlers* (Düsseldorf, 1976), 110–13. Memorandum for Undersecretary Woermann on Goebbels's conference in the Propaganda Ministry, 20 March 1939, NA RG 238, T-1139/R 20/98, NG-1531.

69. Erzählungen und Aussprüche des Reichsführer SS beim Mittagessen, 9. Jan. 1939, NA RG 242, T-175/R 88/2611408.

70. Geist to Messersmith, 4 April 1939, Messersmith Papers, folder 1139. On Geist's direct contacts with Himmler and Heydrich, see his affidavit of 28 Aug. 1945, IMT 28, 242, 1759-PS.

71. See pp. 56–58. Robert Wolfe has made the point that the minutes of the 12 Nov. 1938 meeting reveal a good part of this same strategy. "Nazi Paperwork and the Final Solution," paper at the American Historical Association Meeting, 30 Dec. 1983.

72. Geist affidavit, 28 Aug. 1945, IMT 28, 250, 1759-PS.

73. Geist to Sec. State, 3 May 1939, NA RG 59 CDF 840.48 Refugees/1597. Welles to Miss Le Hand, 29 April 1939, with Myron Taylor's background memo for FDR, NA RG 59, Lot file 52D408, box 12, folder, Taylor, Myron C. FDR quoted in Jay Pierrepont Moffat Diary, 4 May 1939.

74. Yet historians have sometimes criticized Roosevelt not merely for failing to act to assist European Jews, but for indifference to their fate. David S. Wyman, *The Abandonment of the Jews* (New York, 1984), 311–13. Henry L. Feingold, *The Politics of Rescue: The Roosevelt Administration and the Holocaust* (New Brunswick, N.J., 1970), 68. Henry L. Feingold, "Courage First and Intelligence Second: The American Jewish Secular Elite, Roosevelt, and the Failure to Rescue," *American Jewish History* 72 (1983): 456.

CHAPTER 3: TANNENBERG

1. Interrogation of Erich von dem Bach-Zelewski, 9 Nov. 1945, NA RG 238, M-1270/ R 1/429–31. The idea of staging a Polish attack and using concentration-camp prisoners to provide casualties was apparently Heydrich's. Heinz Höhne, *The Order of the Death's Head: The Story of Hitler's SS*, trans. Richard Barry (New York, 1979), 294–300.

2. Charles W. Sydnor, Jr., *Soldiers of Destruction: The SS Death's Head Division 1933– 1945* (Princeton, 1977), 35; Rudolf Hoess, *Commandant of Auschwitz* (New York, 1961), 73–74, 77–79, cited by Sydnor, *Soldiers of Destruction*, 35n. See also Sydnor, *Soldiers of Destruction*, 38.

3. Sydnor, *Soldiers of Destruction*, 22.

4. Helmut Krausnick and Hans-Heinrich Wilhelm, *Die Truppe des Weltanschauungskrieges: Die Einsatzgruppen der Sicherheitspolizei und des SD 1938–1942* (Stuttgart, 1981), 34–41.

5. Ibid., 64, 40.

6. *"Reichsführer SS und Chef der Deutschen Polizei hat fernmündlich angeordnet, dass . . . für das Armeegebiet Ostpreussen der SS-Obergruppenführer Lorenz als Befehlshaber der Polizei eingesetzt wird mit den bekannten Aufgaben."* Daluege to Bomhard, 5 Sept. 1939, Udo von Woyrsch SS file, Berlin Document Center.

7. Krausnick and Wilhelm, *Truppe des Weltanschauungskrieges*, 51 and 51n.

8. Himmler Diaries, 6 Nov. 1921, Hoover Institution, Stanford University.

9. Himmler's schedule NA RG 242, T-581/R 38A, 26 Aug. 1939.

10. Otto Richard Tannenberg, *Gross-Deutschland: Die Arbeit des 20. Jahrhundert* (Leipzig, 1911), 18–19, 74.

11. Otto Dietrich, *Auf den Strassen des Sieges: Erlebnisse mit dem Führer in Polen* (Munich, 1939), 24–26. Walter Schellenberg, *Hitler's Secret Service* (New York, 1971), 65–66. Hinrichsen to Kranefuss, 5 Sept. 1939, NA RG 242, T-175/R 57/2572148. Willi Frischauer, *Himmler: The Evil Genius of the Third Reich* (London, 1953), 127.

12. Erich Kordt, *Wahn und Wirklichkeit* (Stuttgart, 1948), 219. Schellenberg, *Hitler's Secret Service*, 71–72, locates Wolff on Himmler's train, at least early on, but this is contradicted by Jochen von Lang, *Der Adjutant, Karl Wolff: Der Mann zwischen Himmler und Hitler* (Munich, 1985), 133, and by Dietrich, *Auf den Strassen*, 33. On Eicke, see Sydnor, *Soldiers of Destruction*, 38.

13. Krausnick and Wilhelm, *Truppe des Weltanschauungskrieges*, 42–62.

14. Ibid., 42: *"Die führende Bevölkerungsschicht in Polen soll so gut wie möglich unschädlich gemacht werden."* Heydrich went on to discuss the deportation of leaders to concentration camps in Germany—they could under no circumstances remain in Poland. NA RG 242, T-175/R 239/2728501. Helmuth Groscurth, *Tagebücher eines Abwehroffiziers 1938–1940: Mit weiteren Dokumenten zur Militäropposition gegen Hitler*, ed. Helmut Krausnick and Harold Deutsch (Stuttgart, 1970), 201–2, cited by Krausnick and Wilhelm, *Die Truppe des Weltanschauungskrieges*, 63.

15. This according to notes taken two days after the conference by Lieutenant Colonel Lahousen, who was present; reprinted in Groscurth, *Tagebücher*, 357.

16. Interrogation of Erwin Lahousen, 19 Sept. 1945, NA RG 238, M-1270/R 25, p. 10. Two years later Lahousen testified that Keitel had been the one to use the term "political housecleaning," but as if he was repeating Hitler's words, and Keitel had explained that it meant extermination of those groups responsible for the Polish will to resist: intelligentsia, clergy, nobility, and Jews. Interrogation of Erwin Lahousen, 17 April 1947, NA RG 238, M-1019/R 40/76–77.

17. Amtschefbesprechung, 14 Sept. 1939, NA RG 242, T-175/R 239/2728513. *The Halder Diaries: The Private War Journal of Colonel General Franz Halder*, ed. Arnold Lissance (Boulder, 1976), 10.

18. Himmler and Heydrich also both subsequently attributed the killings (Heydrich used the word "liquidations") in Poland to Hitler's decision. On Himmler's subsequent statement about Hitler's authorization, see esp. Himmler's speech of 13 March 1940 to the Army Oberbefehlshaber, 13 March 1940, NA RG 242, T-580/R 39/no frame nos., p. 3 of notes. Only Himmler's notes for this speech survive, but they are quite clear: "Execution of the leading figures of the opposition, very hard—but necessary. [I] myself was there. Not a wild action by subordinates [*Unterführer*] any more than it came from me. [I or he]—do(es) nothing that—doesn't know." One of the officers present, General Ulex, recalled Himmler actually saying, "I do nothing that the Führer doesn't know." See Helmut Krausnick, "Hitler und die Morde in Polen: Ein Beitrag zum Konflikt zwischen Heer und

SS um die Verwaltung der besetzten Gebiete," *Vierteljahrshefte für Zeitgeschichte* 11 (1963): 205n.

On Heydrich, see his Aktenvermerk of 2 July 1940, reprinted in Krausnick, "Hitler und die Morde," 204. There is also Heydrich's statement to his division heads on 14 Oct. 1939—after the war had ended—that liquidation of the Polish leadership must be carried out by 1 Nov. 1939, because martial law would terminate with the withdrawal of military control. Heydrich had asked Gauleiter Arthur Greiser to get Hitler to approve police use of martial law after 1 Nov. (and this was done, for executions continued). Amtschefbesprechung, 14 Oct. 1939, NA RG 242, T-175/R 239/2728537.

19. NA RG 238, NOKW-1621. Krausnick and Wilhelm, *Truppe des Weltanschauungskrieges*, 52–53.

20. Interrogation of Otto Woehler, 4 Nov. 1946, NA RG 238, M-1019/R 80/548–53.

21. Thus Brauchitsch met with Heydrich to request, among other things, "no overly rapid elimination of the Jews." He wanted the end of the military administration of Poland and the establishment of civilian authority first. Quartermaster General Wagner retreated even from that position. Aufzeichnung des Major Groscurth, "Mündliche Orientierung am 22.9. [1939]," reprinted in Groscurth, *Tagebücher*, 361. Krausnick and Wilhelm, *Truppe des Weltanschauungskrieges*, 63–82. Klaus-Jürgen Müller, *Das Heer und Hitler: Armee und nationalsozialistische Regime 1933–1940* (Stuttgart, 1969), 428–35.

22. Vermerk, 5 Oct. 1939, NA RG 242, T-175/R 239/2728534. Krausnick and Wilhelm, *Truppe des Weltanschauungskrieges*, 82–83.

23. Pancke to Hildebrandt, 8 Sept. 1939, NA RG 238, NO-1392.

24. Interrogation of Ernst Schaefer, 16 July 1945, NA RG 238, M-1270/R 27/186–90.

25. Ibid., 190. The second meeting after the declaration of war is referred to in Himmler's letter to Schaefer, 7 Sept. 1939, NA RG 242, T-84/R 257/6617472.

26. Himmler to Schaefer, 7 Sept. 1939, NA RG 242, T-84/R 257/6617472–73.

27. Canaris worked out the broader plans, which included Schaefer, and, one way or another, Himmler got hold of them. Interrogations of Schaefer, 31 March and 16 June 1947, NA RG 238, M-1019/R 62/613 and 673.

28. Himmler to Schaefer, 7 Sept. 1939, NA RG 242, T-84/R 257/6617472–74. Interrogations of Schaefer, 31 March and 16 June 1947 (see n. 27). Himmler's argument and the quotation are taken from Himmler's letter rather from Schaefer's recollections of the conversation, which are less extensive.

29. Copy in NA RG 242, T-175/R 426/2955875.

30. Schaefer, Bericht über den Stand des Tibet-Unternehmens an den Reichsführer, 12 Jan. 1940; Himmler to Schaefer, 11 March 1940, Himmler Collection, Hoover Institution, Stanford University, box 12, folder 332. Interrogation of Ernst Schaefer, 12 Feb. 1946, NA RG 238, M-1270/R 27/191–92.

31. Dietrich, *Auf den Strassen*, 75–77. Hitler's itinerary in NA RG 242, T-84/R 387/000485.

32. Frischauer, *Himmler*, 127.

33. Amtschefbesprechung, 14 Sept. 1939, NA RG 242, T-175/R 279/2728514. Several months later Martin Bormann confirmed this line of authority on the Jewish question, which shows that Heydrich was not simply inflating Himmler's importance. Notiz für Parteigenosse Friedrichs, 6 Dec. 1939, NA RG 242, T-81/R 676/5485594.

34. See pp. 34–35, 70–71.

35. Martin Broszat, *Nationalsozialistische Polenpolitik 1939–1945* (Stuttgart, 1961), 9–20.

36. *NCA*, V, 97–99, 3363-PS.

37. Richard C. Lukas, *The Forgotten Holocaust: The Poles Under German Occupation* (Lexington, Ky., 1986), 3. Martin Gilbert, *The Macmillan Atlas of the Holocaust* (New York, 1982), 33 (map 29).

38. See *Eichmann Interrogated: Transcripts from the Archives of the Israeli Police*, ed. Jochen von Lang and Claus Sibyll (New York, 1983), 92–93. Interrogation of Erich von dem Bach-Zelewski, 25 March 1946, NA RG 238, M-1270/R 1/486–87.

39. Harold C. Deutsch, *The Conspiracy Against Hitler in the Twilight War* (Minneapolis, 1968), 184.

40. Seyss-Inquart report, 20 Nov. 1939, in IMT 30, 95, 2278-PS. Comment about the Lodz ghetto by District Administration Uebelhoer, quoted in Raul Hilberg. *The Destruction of the European Jews* (Chicago, 1961); 2nd expanded ed., 3 vols. (New York, 1985), I, 222.

41. Arthur Greiser, Erich Koch, and Albert Forster were named civil commissars on 10 September. Hitler's schedule, NA RG 242, T-84/R 387/485.

42. Before the war Forster had been engaged in a long political battle with Arthur Greiser, who had presided over the Danzig Senate. After some delay, Himmler had sided with Greiser. When Hitler appointed Greiser as Gauleiter of the annexed portion of western Poland which became known as the Wartheland, he also appointed Forster as Gauleiter of Danzig–West Prussia. On the Forster-Greiser rivalry and Himmler's position, see Herbert S. Levine, *Hitler's Free City: A History of the Nazi Party in Danzig, 1925–39* (Chicago, 1973), 143–44. Robert Lewis Koehl, *RKFDV: German Resettlement and Population Policy, 1939–1945: A History of the Reich Commission for the Strengthening of Germandom* (Cambridge, Mass., 1957), 62–63.

43. Frank's appointment, which was not announced until October, was apparently made on 10 Sept. Hitler's schedule, NA RG 242, T-84/R 387/485.

44. On Hitler and Himmler at Zoppot, David Irving, *Hitler's War* (London, 1977), 20. On resettlement matters and the RSHA, Koehl, *RKFDV*, 49–50.

45. This was what Lammers told Walther Darré. Interrogation of Richard Walther Darré, 10 April 1947, NA RG 238, M-1019/R 12/533. This testimony seems highly likely, since the decree itself was not published. Secrecy was the order of the day. On Lammers's suggestion to postpone resettlement, see interrogation of Lammers, 8 Oct. 1947, NA RG 238, M-1019/R 40/300–7.

46. Lammers to Schwerin von Krosigk, 28 Sept. 1939, Confidential; Himmler to Lammers, 4 Oct. 1939 (referring to Lammers to Himmler, 29 Sept. 1939), NA RG 242, T-175/R 43/2554739–44. Lammers explained only part of the decree to Schwerin von Krosigk.

47. Darré to Lammers, 4 Oct. 1939, NA RG 238, T-1139/R 12/848–855, NG-444. Interrogation of Darré, 10 April 1947, NA RG 238, M-1019/R 12/533.

48. Darré's account may be slightly exaggerated. He was able to sit down with Himmler and rework a few sections of the decree. Still, Himmler not only got his way on the fundamental points, but was actually able to enhance his position during the conference with Darré. Koehl, *RKFDV*, 52–53.

49. Ibid., 53.

50. According to Hans Ehlich of the RSHA, Hitler's speech of 6 Oct. was the impulse for Himmler to establish the *Volksliste*. Interrogation of Hans Ehlich, 11 Sept. 1947, NA RG 238, M-1019/R 15/552.

51. Undated [early Oct.] guidelines, NA RG 238, NO-4059. Sources agree that Himmler intentionally chose the relatively weak Greifelt as his deputy for the RFV to be sure of having someone who would do his bidding. See, for example, interrogation of Otto Ohlendorf, 16 Oct. 1947, NA RG 238, M-1019/R 51/197; Koehl, *RKFDV*, 55.

52. Koehl, *RKFDV*, 54–56. But Koehl's dating of Himmler's trip to the South Tyrol is incorrect. He was actually gone 7–15 Oct. See Himmler's schedule in NA RG 242, T-581/R 38A.

53. Much later Eichmann claimed that he had been inspired by Adolf Böhm's book *Der Judenstaat* to try to bring about a Jewish state within Poland. Adolf Eichmann, *Ich Adolf Eichmann: Ein historischer Zeugenbericht* (Leoni am Starnberger See, 1980), 118–21. For a more likely reading of his situation and his motives, see Seev Goschen, "Eichmann und die Nisko-Aktion im Oktober 1939: Eine Fallstudie zur NS-Judenpolitik in der letzten Etappe vor der 'Endlösung,'" *Vierteljahrshefte für Zeitgeschichte* 29 (1981): 74–96; Jonny Moser, "Nisko, the First Experiment in Deportation," *Simon Wiesenthal Center Annual* 2 (1985): 1–30.

54. NA RG 242, T-581/R 38A, 16–17 Oct. 1939.

55. Besprechung des Führers mit Chef OKW über die künftige Gestaltung der polnischen Verhältnisse zu Deutschland, IMT 26, 378–79, 864-PS.

56. NA RG 242, T 581/R 38A, 19 Oct. 1939. Koehl, *RKFDV*, 57, 60–61. Aktennotiz für SS-Gruppenführer Wolff betr. Volksdeutsche Mittelstelle, n.d., NA RG 242, T-175/R 112/2637204.

57. Himmler, Zusammenarbeit der Behörden des Reichsführers SS mit der Haupttreuhandstelle Ost, 10 Nov. 1939, NA RG 238, NO-2676.

58. Goshen, "Eichmann und die Nisko-Aktion," 87–92. Moser, "Nisko," 12–19. Wilson to Secretary of State, 2 Dec. 1939, NA RG 59, Central Decimal file 862.4016/2153 (this dispatch relays information obtained by Jewish sources in Berlin from official German sources). Browning, "Nazi Resettlement Policy and the Search for a Solution to the Jewish Question," *German Studies Review* 9 (1986): 504–5.

59. Becker to Barth, 13 Nov. 1939, NA RG 238, T-301/R 10/1026, NI-1052.

60. Himmler's planned itinerary and entourage identified in NA RG 242, T-175/R 112/2637825–27. Itinerary confirmed, NA RG 242, T-581, R 38A, 24–30 Oct. 1939. On the executions, see interrogation of Joachim [Jochen] Peiper, 17 April 1947, NA RG 238, M-1019/R 52/186; Wolff's recollections in Lang, *Der Adjutant*, 138.

61. Alvensleben to Wolff, 12 Dec. 1939, NA RG 242, T-175/R 112/2636602–04. Interrogation of Ernst Schaefer, 16 July 1945, NA RG 238, M-1270/R 27/192.

62. Groscurth, *Tagebücher*, 232, 406–7, 407n.

63. See n. 60.

64. Lucjan Dobroszycki, ed., *The Chronicle of the Lodz Ghetto 1941–1944* (New Haven, 1984), xxx. Jacob Apenszlak, ed., *The Black Book of Polish Jewry: An Account of the Martyrdom of Polish Jewry Under the Nazi Occupation* (New York, 1943), 66, 71. Gilbert, *Macmillan Atlas*, 41.

65. Apenszlak, ed., *Black Book*, 32–33. Raul Hilberg et al., eds., *The Warsaw Diary of Adam Czerniakow: Prelude to Doom* (New York, 1982), 86.

66. S. Moldawer, quoted in Apenszlak, ed., *Black Book*, 93–94.

67. Anordnung I/II, 30 Oct. 1939, reprinted in Jüdisches Historische Institut Warschau, *Fascismus-Getto-Massenmord: Dokumentation über Ausrottung und Widerstand der Juden in Polen während des Zweiten Weltkrieges* (Berlin-Ost, 1960), 42–43.

68. Dobroszycki, ed., *Chronicle*, xxxiv–xxxv.

69. Militärgeschichtliches Forschungsamt, ed., *Das Deutsche Reich und der Zweite Weltkrieg, vol. II: Die Errichtung der Hegemonie auf dem europäischen Kontinent*, ed. Klaus A. Maier et al. (Stuttgart, 1979), 244–63. Albert Seaton, *The German Army 1933–45* (London, 1983), 120–24. H. R. Trevor-Roper, ed., *Blitzkrieg to Defeat: Hitler's War Directives 1939–1945* (New York, 1964), 18–21.

70. [Gero von Gaevernitz] Memorandum, 28 Dec. 1939, Leland Harrison Papers, box 28, G folder, Library of Congress. Gaevernitz had just returned from a five-week visit to Germany, and he had superb connections not only with leading businessmen, but also with Cabinet members and military officials. Among his best sources were individuals on Göring's staff. Thus, what he reported about Hitler's intentions should not be considered ordinary rumor or gossip. On Gaevernitz's value as a source of intelligence, see Walter Laqueur and Richard Breitman, *Breaking the Silence* (New York, 1986), 61–62, 71–72.

71. Schellenberg, *Hitler's Secret Service*, 89. Anton Hoch, "Das Attentat auf Hitler im Münchener Bürgerbräukeller 1939," *Vierteljahrshefte für Zeitgeschichte* 17 (1969): 383–413. Peter G. Hoffmann, *The History of the German Resistance 1933–1945* (Cambridge, Mass., 1977), 257–58.

72. In 1933 Himmler commented, referring to a book that he had read and liked, that the author must have been in contact with the British Secret Service. Gelesene Bücher, 1926–1934, #334, German Captured Document Collection, box 418, Library of Congress. In a 30 Jan. 1943 speech to the high officials of the RSHA, Himmler called the SD at least the equal of the British Secret Service. NA RG 319, IRR files, 1903 Ernst Kaltenbrunner, XE000440.

73. Schellenberg, *Hitler's Secret Service*, 89–105. Höhne, *The Order*, 324–27.

74. Aktenvermerk für Gruppenführer Wolff, 18 Nov. 1939, NA RG 242, T-175/R 112/2637233. Also Himmler's schedule, NA RG 242, T-581/R 38A, 18 Nov. 1939 (meeting with Trippel); 19 Nov. 1939 (Heydrich, Besichtigung v. Ostend).

75. IMT 26, 327–36, 789-PS.

76. Seaton, *German Army*, 124. Militärgeschichtliches Forschungsamt, *Das Deutsche Reich und der Zweite Weltkrieg*, II, 249.

77. IMT 26, 327–36, 789-PS.

CHAPTER 4: RACIAL PLANNING AND EUTHANASIA

1. Gross to Himmler, 2 Dec. 1939, NA RG 238, NO-1679. The report, without the covering letter, may be found in NA RG 242, T-74/R 9/380572ff.

2. The authors estimated a Jewish population of three million, another one million baptized (converted) Jews, and 1–1.5 million *Mischlinge* (half-breeds). NA RG 242, T-74/R 9/380580.

Otto Ohlendorf, one of the high officials in the RSHA and simultaneously an official in the Economics Ministry, later claimed that, just after the Polish campaign, he had submitted a proposal to define Jewish rights in Poland, which would have left the Jews in an inferior position but with some guarantees. Himmler and Heydrich, he said, had rejected the idea outright, and Himmler had asked for Ohlendorf's resignation. Once Ohlendorf was out of favor with Himmler, Heydrich, typically, wanted to keep Ohlendorf on, since Ohlendorf could no longer pose a threat to him, and Heydrich managed to do so. Interrogation of Ohlendorf, 23 June 1947, NA RG 238, M-1019/R 51/154.

This Ohlendorf testimony is self-serving, but it is consistent with other sources that maintain that Himmler and Ohlendorf did not get along. See, for instance, interrogation of Ernst Kaltenbrunner, 18 June 1945, NA RG 238, M-1270/R 25/0089.

3. Brandt to Race and Settlement Office, 11 Dec. 1939, and to RFSS [Reich Führer SS, Himmler], 5 Jan. 1940, NA RG 238, NO-1679. Gross's weakness, affidavit of Dr. Kurt Blome, 17 Jan. 1946, NO-1710. Blome also testified there that Himmler did not like Gross.

Reichsleitung, Rassenpolitisches Amt to Himmler, 13 April 1940; Himmler to Gross, 3 July 1940 (summaries only), log of Himmler's correspondence, NA RG 242, T-581, R42A. Greifelt to Himmler, 25 May 1940; Himmler to Greifelt, 28 May 1940 (summaries only), NA RG 242, T-581, R42A.

4. Rudolf Höss Aufzeichnungen, Institut für Zeitgeschichte, Munich, F 13/6, 344.

5. Pohl SS file, NA RG 238, NO-192. See also the consensus assessment of Pohl by a group of WVHA officials, NA RG 238, NO-1573.

6. Rudolf Höss affidavit, Nov. 1946, p. 7, NA RG 238, NO-3361.

7. Himmler to Pohl, 22 March 1942, NA RG 242, T-175/R 38/2548361. Pohl SS file, NA RG 238, NO-1573.

8. Notes of 5 Dec. 1939, NA RG 242, T-175/R 94/2615210.

9. See, for example, Degesch to K. L. Auschwitz, 2 Dec. 1941, NA RG 238, NI-14164.

10. The meeting with Pohl, which began at 3:00 p.m., went on longer than expected, and Himmler's adjutant had to move the appointment of a Fräulein Hohn from 4:00 p.m. to 5:00 p.m. The first six items on the agenda were checked off, but items 7 and 8 were crossed out. Did Himmler discuss the idea of gas chambers with Pohl and reject it—temporarily? Or did he simply fail to get to the matter? The latter is more likely. There are other cases in which Himmler crossed off only the final items of his agendas, but I have seen none where he crossed off early items. Himmler's schedule, NA RG 242, T-581, R 38A. Himmler's notes for meeting (see n. 8 above).

11. Himmler's schedule, NA RG 242, T-581/R 38A, 28–29 Nov. 1939.

12. Ernst Klee, *"Euthanasia" im NS-Staat: Die "Vernichtung lebensunwerten Lebens"* (Stuttgart, 1983), 95, 105. On 30 Nov. Schwede-Coburg came to Berlin for further discussions with Himmler. Himmler's schedule, NA RG 242, T-581, R 38A, 30 Nov. 1939.

13. Josef Radzicki and Jerzy Radzicki, "Verbrechen des Hitlerfaschistischen Sanitätsdienstes in der Irrenanstalt Obrzyce [German translation of Polish], Gutachten für die Staatsanwaltschaft bei dem Landgericht Hamburg zum Strafverfahren gegen Lensch und Andere wegen Mordes," Verfahren 147 Js 58/67, 30–31, cited but inaccurately summarized in Klee, *Euthanasia*, 105. I am grateful to Henry Friedlander for supplying me with a copy of this document.

14. Ibid., 62–63. Klee, *Euthanasia*, 105–6, 458. Also *Nationalsozialistische Massentötungen durch Giftgas*, ed. Eugen Kogon et al. (Frankfurt am Main, 1983), 62–65.

15. Himmler's notes for meeting with Hitler, NA RG 242, T-175/R 94/2615233.

16. Notiz für Pg. Friedrichs, 6 Dec. 1939, NA RG 242, T-81/R 676/5485594–95. The unnamed author quoted Dr. Hansen, who relayed Bormann's comment. All of this was in reaction to a proposal from the Propaganda Ministry to remove telephones from Jewish residences. Bormann was in effect telling others that Himmler was in charge.

17. Himmler's schedule, NA RG 242, T-581, R 38A, 12 Dec. 1939. NA RG 242, T-175/R 112/2637823. Dobroszycki, *Chronicle*, xxxv.

18. Klee, *Euthanasia*, 31.

19. The fundamental study here is Gisela Bock, *Zwangssterilisation im Nationalsozialismus: Studien zur Rassenpolitik und Frauenpolitik* (Opladen, 1986). See also Klee, *Euthanasia*, 36–37; Robert J. Lifton, *The Nazi Doctors: Medical Killing and the Psychology of Genocide* (New York, 1986), 22–29.

20. Testimony of Karl Brandt, U.S. Military Tribunal, Case 1, 2,482. I am grateful to Henry Friedlander for this reference. Klee, *Euthanasia*, 31. Alexander Mitscherlich and Fred Mielke, eds., *Medizin ohne Menschlichkeit* (Frankfurt, 1960), 184.

21. Klee, *Euthanasia*, 62–63, 279.

22. Ibid., 62. Viktor Brack, an official in the Führer Chancellery, tied this motive directly to Hitler. Brack affidavit, 14 Oct. 1946, NA RG 238, NO-426.

23. Friedrich Karl Kaul, *Die Psychiatrie im Strudel der "Euthanasia": Ein Bericht über die erste industriemässig durchgeführte Mordaktion des Naziregimes* (Frankfurt, 1979), 57–62. *Nationalsozialistische Massentötungen*, 29–32.

24. Copy of Hitler's letter, NA RG 238, NO-824. Karl Heinz Roth and Götz Aly, "Die Diskussion über die Legalisierung der nationalsozialistische Anstaltsmorde in den Jahren 1938–1941," *Recht und Psychiatrie* 1 (1983): 51–64, 2 (1984): 36–47. I am grateful to Henry Friedlander for these references. Klee, *Euthanasia*, 101. Lifton, *Nazi Doctors*, 63–64.

25. Lifton, *Nazi Doctors*, 71.

26. Sources disagree on exactly when Hitler signed the euthanasia authorization, but it may have been in early Oct. (see Klee, *Euthanasia*, 100), when Hitler and Himmler were both at the Kasino Hotel in Zoppot. On the Waffen-SS Sanitation Office, Bundesarchiv Koblenz, R 58/1059; reference from Henry Friedlander.

27. Lifton, *Nazi Doctors*, 71. On the origin of the gas vans, Christopher Browning, *Fateful Months: Essays on the Emergence of the Final Solution* (New York, 1985), 58–59, describes the KTI involvement but does not provide a date. But see *Nationalsozialistische Massentötungen*, 62–63, and pp. 88–89.

28. About a year later Himmler became quite upset when news of the euthanasia operations and the SS's participation began to leak to the German public. He also stressed to Nazi Party High Court chairman Walter Buch that the SS only helped with vehicles, etc.; the doctors gave the orders. Himmler to Brack, 19 Dec. 1940, and Himmler to Buch, 19 Dec. 1940, NA RG 238, NO-018 and NO-002.

29. This point has been made forcefully by Henry Friedlander, "Jüdische Anstalts-patienten im NS-Deutschland," in *Aktion T4 1939–1945: Die "Euthanasia"-Zentrale in der Tiergartenstrasse 4*, ed. Götz Aly (Berlin, 1987), 34. It will be the central theme of Friedlander's forthcoming study of the euthanasia program, to be published by Oxford University Press.

30. Eberhard Jäckel, *Hitler's Weltanschauung: A Blueprint for Power*, trans. Herbert Arnold (Middletown, Conn., 1972), 58–59. "Secularized Satan" from Yehuda Bauer, "Escape from the Holocaust in the Context of the Final Solution," paper delivered at conference on "Escape to Scandinavia," University of Minnesota, Minneapolis, 9 Nov. 1989.

31. See p. 74.

32. Himmler's schedule, NA RG 242, T-581/R 38A, 19–20 Dec. 1939. MacGregor Knox, *Mussolini Unleashed: Politics and Strategy in Fascist Italy's Last War* (Cambridge, 1982), 62, 67.

33. Himmler's brief notes of the meeting mix together his own comments with Mussolini's. Deciding who said what is not easy, but the notes still provide important insight into what occurred. NA RG 242, T-172/R 94/2615283.

34. Ibid. Knox, *Mussolini Unleashed*, 68.

35. Himmler's notes, NA RG 242, T-175/R 94/2615283. Knox, *Mussolini Unleashed*, 68.

36. Knox, *Mussolini Unleashed*, 68–69. Galeazzo Ciano, *The Ciano Diaries, 1939–1943* (Garden City, N.Y., 1947), 21 Dec. 1939, 376.

37. Schlegel affidavit, 3 June 1943, NA RG 238, NO-1074. This affidavit resulted from an investigation by SS prosecutor Konrad Morgen of alleged crimes at Soldau.

38. Ibid.

39. Ibid.

40. Pohl to Himmler, 17 Jan. 1940, in log of Himmler's correspondence, NA RG 242,

T-58/R 42A. This is a summary of Pohl's letter and Himmler's response; I was unable to locate the original letters, if they survive. Pohl reported that the Polish prison Wisnice-Wowj[?] was unsuitable.

Himmler or his staff wrote to Keppler on 22 Jan. 1940, and Keppler responded on 2 Feb. 1940, referring to the first letter and recommending against a phosphorus-mining site in the Government General. NA RG 238, T-1139/R 27/602, NG-2382.

41. *Auschwitz: Geschichte und Wirklichkeit des Vernichtungslagers* (Reinbek bei Hamburg, 1980), 15–16. *From the History of KL Auschwitz* (New York, 1982), I, 1–2.

42. Ulrich von Hassell, *Vom anderen Deutschland: Aus den nachgelassenen Tagebüchern 1938–1944* (Zurich, 1946), 118.

43. Christopher Browning, "Nazi Resettlement Policy and the Search for a Solution to the Jewish Question, 1939–1941," *German Studies Review* 9 (1986): 504–6, has stressed the priority given to the resettlement of ethnic Germans. His interpretation is quite correct, but he does not enumerate all the reasons for this immediate resettlement. In a late-Feb. 1940 speech to the party Reichsleiter and Gauleiter, Himmler pointed out that what he had done and what he was planning to do in 1940 was, by and large, dictated by outside events: the Führer's treaty with Estonia and Latvia calling for the transfer of the ethnic Germans before the Russians established garrisons there, and the agreement to accept ethnic Germans from Volhynia, Narev, and Galicia, which came under Russian control. In both cases, Germany faced tight deadlines, Himmler said, and if it failed to act, there was concern about what the Russians would do to the ethnic Germans. In other words, the priority given to the resettlement of ethnic Germans should not be used to imply a lack of interest in action on the Jewish question.

For the difficulties with the late-1939 deportations of Jews to Nisko, see Jonny Moser, "Nisko: The First Experiment in Deportation," *Simon Wiesenthal Center Annual* 2 (1985): esp. 18–19.

44. Hans Ehlich affidavit, 19 Sept. 1947, NA RG 238, NO-5179. Otto Hofmann affidavit, 9 June 1947, NA RG 238, NO-4699. Interrogation of Hans Doering, 26 Sept. 1947, NA RG 238, M-1019/R 13/1000–1001. Leo Reichert affidavit, 22 Oct. 1947, NA RG 238, NO-5483. Jacob Soluk affidavit, 7 Oct. 1947, NA RG 238, NO-5442. See Robert Lewis Koehl, *RKFDV: German Resettlement and Population Policy, 1939–1945: A History of the Reich Commission for the Strengthening of Germandom* (Cambridge, Mass., 1957), 60, 66–74.

45. Himmler's schedule, NA RG 242, T-581/R 38A: Backe, 3 Jan. 1940; Backe, Willikens, 9 Jan.; Greifelt, Meyer, 11 Jan.; Greifelt, 12 Jan.; Willikens, Greifelt, 13 Jan.; Göring (Stabsamt), 14 Jan.; Heydrich, Pancke, 19 Jan.; Stuckart, 20 Jan.; Behrens, Greifelt, Meyer, Holzschuher, 22 Jan.; Greifelt, 23 Jan.

46. Himmler's schedule, 15–30 Jan. 1940, NA RG 242, T-581/R 38A. Also for the trip, Brandt's office journal, NA RG 242, T-581/R 38A; and Himmler's itinerary, NA RG 242, T-175/R 112/2637820–22. Unless otherwise noted, all subsequent references to Himmler's movements during this trip come from these sources.

47. Interrogations of Ernst Schaefer, 1 April 1947, NA RG 238, M-1019/R 62/636–38; and 12 Feb. 1946, NA RG 238, M-1270/R 27/192.

48. Hanns Johst, *Ruf des Reiches—Echo des Volkes: Eine Ostfahrt* (Munich, 1941). For Brandt's comment, Brandt's office journal, NA RG 242, T-581/R 39A, 26 Jan. 1940.

49. Interrogation of Ernst Schaefer, 12 Feb. 1946, NA RG 238, M-1270/R 27/192. On the killings at Chełm-Lubielski, see the affidavits by one eyewitness and one near-eyewitness in Poland against Germany, charge 1273, roll 14/0506–0508, United Nations War Crimes Commission Records, United Nations Archive, New York.

50. Lammers to Himmler, 28 March 1940, referring to Himmler's letter to Lammers, 14 Jan. 1940, NA RG 238, T-1139/R 28/485, NG-2490.

51. All of this is based on what Himmler told Heydrich on 30 Jan. and what Heydrich reported to a high-level meeting on the same day. See Besprechung am 30. Jan. 1940, NA RG 238, NO-5322.

52. Himmler's schedule, NA RG 242, T-581/R 38A, 30 Jan. 1940.

53. Minutes of 30 Jan. 1940 meeting, NA RG 238, NO-5322.

54. Generaloberst Franz Halder, *Kriegstagebuch*, ed. Hans-Adolf Jacobsen (Stuttgart, 1962), I, 182. Brauchitsch, in fact, agreed to consider the idea, which was tested out on a much smaller scale.

55. Interrogation of Gerhard Maurer, 13 March 1947, NA RG 238, M-1019/R 45/166.

56. Minutes of 30 Jan. 1940 meeting, NA RG 238, NO-5322.

57. Helene Kraffuyk affidavit, 6 Sept. 1945, NA RG 238, M-1270/R 11/405. Interrogation of General Johannes Blaskowitz, 16 Aug. 1945, NA RG 238, M-1270/R 23/393.

58. Helene Kraffuyk affidavit, 6 Sept. 1945, NA RG 238, M-1270/R 11/404.

59. IMT 26, 207–39, 661-PS. Raul Hilberg, *The Destruction of the European Jews* (Chicago, 1961); 2nd expanded ed., 3 vols. (New York, 1985), I, 206, maintains that Frank probably wrote this memo. In any case, it was written for the Academy of German Law, of which Frank was president, and it was consistent with Frank's ideas.

60. Frank to Göring, 25 Jan. 1940, IMT 27, 200–5, 1375-PS.

61. IMT 36, 299–307, 305-EC.

62. Hilberg, *Destruction*, I, 207–8. Browning, "Nazi Resettlement Policy," 507–8.

63. NA RG 238, NO-5322. Higher SS and Police Leader Posen to Field Office for Resettlement of Poles and Jews, 29 Feb. 1940, NA RG 238, NO-5402.

64. Norman Davies, *God's Playground: A History of Poland* (New York, 1982), II, 495. I am grateful to James A. Malloy for this reference.

65. The stenographic record of Himmler's speech is reprinted in Bradley F. Smith and Agnes F. Peterson, *Heinrich Himmler: Geheimreden 1933–1945 und andere Ansprachen* (Frankfurt, 1974), 115–44. Himmler's notes for the speech, which contain a few details not in the speech itself, are in NA RG 242, T-580/R 37, no frames.

66. Aktenvermerk über die Sitzung des RVA in Warschau, 2 March 1940, NA RG 238, EC-300.

67. Frank's protest is cited and Göring's telegram is quoted in Reichsstatthalter in Vienna to Himmler, 9 May 1940, NA RG 238, 1941-PS. Frank's announcement on the Government General and the rights of Poles is referred to in Schmelt's Niederschrift über das Ergebnis der Besprechung am 4. April 1940 (Lodz), NA RG 242, T-175/R 128/2654346.

68. The information that Himmler had "recently" prohibited emigration of Jews from the Government General was revealed at a Berlin press conference on 27 March and was relayed immediately to Washington. Kirk to Secretary of State, 28 March 1940, NA RG 59, CDF 862.4016/2159, reprinted in John Mendelsohn, ed., *The Holocaust: Selected Documents in Eighteen Volumes* (New York, 1982), VIII, 30.

69. See p. 142.

70. Advance schedule, NA RG 242, T-175/R 112/2637799–804. Daily activities, NA RG 242, T-581/R 38A, 27–29 April.

71. Friedrich Schlegel testimony, 3 June 1943, NA RG 238, NO-1074; also M-895/R 10/1322–25. Rasch testimony, 16 June 1943, NA RG 238, NO-1073.

72. Rediess to Wolff, 7 Nov. 1940, Herbert Lange SS file, Berlin Document Center. Browning, *Fateful Months*, 3, 59. Gerald Fleming, *Hitler and the Final Solution* (Berkeley,

1984; German original, 1982), 21–22. The term "evacuation" is used to describe the Soldau operation in Koppe to Sporrenberg, 18 Oct. 1940, and Rediess to Wolff, 7 Nov. 1940, Lange SS file.

73. Koppe to Sporrenberg, 18 Oct. 1940, Lange SS file.

74. Ibid. Rediess to Wolff, 7 Nov. 1940, Lange SS file.

75. Rediess to Wolff, 22 Oct. 1940 (Auszug); Koppe to Wolff, 22 Feb. 1941, Lange SS file. Brandt's phone records for 20 and 22 July 1940 show that Koppe called to discuss Sonderkommando Lange on 20 and 22 July—about the time when the vacation would have been under consideration. NA RG 242, T-581/R 39A.

76. Advance schedule, 4–6 May 1940, NA RG 242, T-175/R 112/2637797–98. Daily activities, NA RG 242, T-581/R 38A.

77. Documents on the case in Globocnik SS file, Berlin Document Center.

78. On the early conflicts between Globocnik and Frank's subordinates, Philip Friedman, *Roads to Extinction: Essays on the Holocaust* (New York, 1980), 35–36. Krüger to Himmler, 20 June 1940; Himmler to Krüger, 9 July 1940, NA RG 242, T-175/R 84/2609849–51. Peter Black, "Terror's Cutting Edge: The Ethnic German Selbstschutz in District Lublin, 1939–1940," paper for the American Historical Association meeting, 30 Dec. 1989, stresses Globocnik's efforts to use Jews as forced laborers. Black provides a wealth of details about Globocnik's source of manpower, and new evidence of killings and other acts of violence.

79. Interrogation of George [sic] Johannsohn, 22 May 1945, Camp Forrest, Tenn., NA RG 153, entry 143, box 571, folder 19-121. Johannsohn, a German POW, was an eyewitness to the drownings.

80. See p. 75.

CHAPTER 5: RACIAL EDUCATION AND THE MILITARY

1. Interrogation of Johannes Blaskowitz, 16 Aug. 1945, NA RG 238, M-1270/R 23/391–92.

2. Helmut Krausnick and Hans-Heinrich Wilhelm, *Die Truppe des Weltanschauungskrieges: Die Einsatzgruppen der Sicherheitspolizei und des SD 1938–1942* (Stuttgart, 1981), 96–99.

3. Harold C. Deutsch, *The Conspiracy Against Hitler in the Twilight War* (Minneapolis, 1968), 186.

4. Himmler to Krüger, 29 Dec. 1939; [Brandt] to Heissmeyer, Heydrich, and Daluege, 3 Jan. 1940, NA RG 242, T-175/R 57/2572579. Himmler also criticized Krüger's excessive bureaucracy and threatened to intervene ruthlessly if there were further problems.

5. Klaus-Jürgen Müller, *Das Heer und Hitler: Armee und nationalsozialistische Regime 1933–1940* (Stuttgart, 1969), 441–42.

6. Ibid., 443–45. Himmler's schedule, NA RG 242, T-581/R 38A, 24 Jan. 1940.

7. See p. 78.

8. Müller, *Das Heer und Hitler*, 446–48. Himmler's schedule, NA RG 242, T-581/R 38A, 2 Feb. 1940.

9. Müller, *Das Heer und Hitler*, 374–77. Gerhard L. Weinberg, *The Foreign Policy of Hitler's Germany: Starting World War II, 1937–1939* (Chicago, 1980), 458–62, 513–15.

10. Müller, *Das Heer und Hitler*, 447, 449–50. Müller's account of the conversation

between Himmler and Tippelskirch is based on Tippelskirch's notes. The meeting between the two men is confirmed by Himmler's schedule, NA RG 242, T-581/R 38A, 20 Feb. 1940.

11. Müller, *Das Heer und Hitler*, 450, mentions an intervening meeting on 29 Feb. in which Göring supposedly announced that the highest goal in the East must be the strengthening of the German war potential. This is erroneous. Göring had made such a statement on 12 Feb.; the 29 Feb. meeting in which Himmler took part was the meeting of Reichsleiter and Gauleiter discussed above. Himmler was the main speaker. I found no evidence that Göring and Himmler met between 20 Feb. and Himmler's early-March decision to accept Brauchitsch's invitation.

12. IMT 31, 181–82, 2825-PS. Müller, *Das Heer und Hitler*, 459.

13. Bradley F. Smith and Agnes F. Peterson, *Heinrich Himmler: Geheimreden 1933–1945 und andere Ansprachen* (Frankfurt, 1974), 118–19.

14. Ibid., 119–21.

15. Interrogation of Hedwig Potthast, 22 May 1945, NA RG 238, M-1270/R 26/466.

16. Interrogation of Ernst Schaefer, 12 Feb. 1946, NA RG 238, M-1270/R 27/192.

17. *Hitler's Secret Conversations, 1941–1944* (New York, 1976), 286, 15 March 1942.

18. Müller, *Das Heer und Hitler*, 459–62.

19. Günter d'Alquen telephoned Himmler's office manager, Rudolf Brandt, on 10 Jan. to say that the armed forces were outraged over the order. Brandt's log, NA RG 242, T-581/R 39A.

20. Diktat des Nachsatzbefehls zum Befehl vom 28.10.39, Brandt's log, NA RG 242, T-581/R 38A, 14 Jan. 1940.

21. Müller, *Das Heer und Hitler*, 462–64.

22. Ibid., 465–67.

23. Ibid., 467–69.

24. Smith and Peterson, *Heinrich Himmler: Geheimreden*, 122–23.

25. Vortragsnotiz von Major Radke, 3 March 1940, reprinted in Müller, *Das Heer und Hitler*, 673–74. Himmler's 6 March inspection, Charles W. Sydnor, Jr., *Soldiers of Destruction: The SS Death's Head Division 1933–1945* (Princeton, 1977), 78.

26. Interrogation of Rudolf Brandt, 16 Dec. 1946, NA RG 238, M-1019/R 9/714.

27. Himmler's notes for the 13 March 1940 speech, NA RG 242, T-580/R 37/no frame nos.

28. This question bears directly on some of the historiographical disputes in recent years. See pp. 20–30.

29. See the discussion of Genghis Khan, pp. 39–43. See also Himmler's 5 April 1940 speech, pp. 113–14.

30. Walter Schellenberg, *Hitler's Secret Service* (New York, 1971), 109. On Hitler in 1941, see p. 179. On Hitler in 1942, Aktenvermerk über Besprechung des Führers mit Mussert, 10 Dec. 1942, Akten der Parteikanzlei, Institut für Zeitgeschichte microfiche 102/00764.

31. Müller, *Das Heer und Hitler*, 452n.

32. Himmler's notes, NA RG 242, T-580/R 37/no frame, p. 3 of speech. Ulex's recollection in Müller, *Das Heer und Hitler*, 451. About a month later Heydrich wrote a memo that established a direct connection between the SS's difficulties with the military in Poland and Heydrich's inability then to reveal that the orders to liquidate the Polish leadership came from Hitler. Helmut Krausnick, "Hitler und die Morde in Polen: Ein Beitrag zum Konflikt zwischen Heer und SS um die Verwaltung der besetzten Gebeite," *Vierteljahrshefte für Zeitgeschichte* 11 (1963): 196–208.

33. Detailed itinerary, 27–28 March 1940, NA RG 242, T-175/R 112/2637810–11. Speech notes, NA RG 242, T-580/R 37/no frame nos.

34. Himmler's schedule, NA RG 242, T-581/R 38A, 4–5 April 1940. Detailed itinerary, 4–7 April 1940, in NA RG 242, T-175/R 112/2637807–8.

35. NA RG 242, T-580/R 37/no frame nos.

36. Note that Himmler had briefed Greifelt orally, in a private meeting, on 10 April 1940. See Greifelt to Himmler, 15 April 1940, NA RG 242, T-175/R 128/2654343. See also Bach-Zelewski's description of Himmler's methods, interrogation of 30 Oct. 1945, NA RG 238, M-1270/R 1/420–21.

37. Interrogation of Ewald Loeser, 8 April 1947, NA RG 238, M-1019/R 43/93.

38. See the treatment in Sydnor, *Soldiers of Destruction*, 70–86.

39. Niederschrift über das Ergebnis der Besprechung vom 4 April; Greifelt to Himmler, 15 April 1940; Himmler to Greifelt and Krüger, May 1940 [day not listed], NA RG 242, T-175/R 128/2654341–48.

40. Berger to Himmler, 25 April 1940, NA RG 238, NO-1325.

41. Müller, *Das Heer und Hitler*, 452.

42. Kienitz for the Commanding General to Seventeenth Army Corps, 23 July 1940, NA RG 238, NOKW-3437.

CHAPTER 6: TO MADAGASCAR AND BACK

1. Helmut Krausnick and Hans-Heinrich Wilhelm, *Die Truppe des Weltanschauungskrieges: Die Einsatzgruppen der Sicherheitspolizei und des SD 1938–1942* (Stuttgart, 1981), 108.

2. *Das Deutsche Reich und der Zweite Weltkrieg*, vol. II: *Die Errichtung der Hegemonie auf dem europäischen Kontinent* (Stuttgart, 1979), 284. Jochen von Lang, *Der Adjutant, Karl Wolff: Der Mann zwischen Himmler und Hitler* (Munich, 1985), 153. Details on Felsennest from interrogation of Walter Warlimont on the Führer's headquarters, 24 Oct. 1945, NA RG 226, XL 28065.

3. Himmler's schedule, NA RG 242, T-581/R 38A.

4. Details in George H. Stein, *The Waffen-SS: Hitler's Elite Guard at War* (Ithaca, 1966), 61–67.

5. Generaloberst Franz Halder, *Kriegstagebuch*, ed. Hans-Adolf Jacobsen (Stuttgart, 1962), I, 302, 17 May 1940, cited by Krausnick and Wilhelm, *Truppe des Weltanschauungskrieges*, 108. Bormann's record of Hitler's schedule, however, lists 18 May as the date of the appointment. See NA RG 242, T-84/R 387/000494.

6. Baerwald to Pell, 23 May 1940, NA RG 59, lot file 52D408, box 1, American Jewish Joint Distribution Committee folder.

7. OKW racial guidelines in NA RG 238, T-1119/R 20/553, NOKW-1515. Brandt's office log, NA RG 242, T-581/R 39A, 23 May 1940.

8. Lang, *Der Adjutant*, 154–55.

9. Probably after Himmler's inspection tour in the Low Countries, but clearly before his meeting with the Führer on 22 May (otherwise Himmler could not have asked Hitler's reaction to the memo on the 22nd). Himmler's notes of 22 May 1940, NA RG 242, T-175/R 94/2615221.

10. Himmler's notes, 22 May 1940, NA RG 242, T-175/R 94/2615221.

11. Himmler not only jotted down the Führer's reaction at the meeting; three days

later he wrote out a longer note on what had taken place, what should now be done, and who should receive the report. Himmler's notes, 25 May 1940, NA RG 242, T-175/R 94/ 2615218. Himmler's memo for the files, 28 May 1940, NA RG 242, T-175/R 119/ 2645120–21.

12. Krüger was in Berlin on official business from 8 May to 10 May 1940. Krüger SS file, Berlin Document Center. Himmler met with Krüger at least once during that time, on the afternoon of 10 May. Himmler also met with RFV Deputy Greifelt on 9 May. Himmler's schedule, NA RG 242, T-581/R 38A.

13. Gross to Himmler, 2 Dec. 1939, NA RG 238, NO-1679.

14. Text reprinted in Helmut Krausnick, "Denkschrift Himmlers über die Behandlung der Fremdvölkischen im Osten (Mai 1940)," *Vierteljahrshefte für Zeitgeschichte* 5 (1957): 194–98. Original in NA RG 242, T-175/R 119/2645113ff, and NA RG 238, NO-1880–81.

15. See p. 113.

16. Himmler's memo for the files, NA RG 242, T-175/R 119/2645120. The memo was also allowed to go to various subordinates of Himmler—Heydrich, Greifelt, and relevant higher SS and police leaders.

17. See n. 14.

18. Werner Präg and Wolfgang Jacobmeyer, eds., *Das Diensttagebuch des deutschen Generalgouverneurs in Polen 1939–1945* (Stuttgart, 1975), 211–12, 30 May 1940.

19. See p. 101.

20. See p. 74.

21. Andreas Hillgruber, *Hitlers Strategie: Politik und Kriegführung 1940–1941* (Frankfurt am Main, 1965), 144–49. Klaus Hildebrand, *Vom Reich zum Weltreich: Hitler, NSDAP, und koloniale Frage 1919–1945* (Munich, 1969), 647–49.

22. Frank, *Diensttagebuch*, 205, 22 May 1940.

23. Mathias Beer, "Die Entwicklung der Gaswagen beim Mord an den Juden," *Vierteljahrshefte für Zeitgeschichte* 3 (1987): 406.

24. Gerhard L. Weinberg, *The World in the Balance: Behind the Scenes of World War II* (Hanover, N.H., 1981), 105–7. Hildebrand, *Vom Reich*, 644. Indicatively, Himmler was working out plans for a colonial police force more than a year earlier. See Leni Yahil, "Madagascar—Phantom of a Solution for the Jewish Question," in Bela Vago and George L. Mosse, eds., *Jews and Non-Jews in Eastern Europe 1918–1945* (New York, 1974), 324.

25. Krausnick, "Denkschrift," is convinced that Himmler's statement did not apply to the Jews. Christopher R. Browning, "Nazi Resettlement Policy and the Search for a Solution to the Jewish Question," *German Studies Review* 9 (1986): 510, implies that it did.

26. Gerald Reitlinger, *The Final Solution: The Attempt to Exterminate the Jews of Europe* (London, 1953), 76–79. Philip Friedman, *Roads to Extinction: Essays on the Holocaust* (New York: 1980), 49. Leni Yahil, "Madagascar," 315–34. In contrast, Christopher R. Browning, *The Final Solution and the German Foreign Office: A Study of Referat III D of Abteilung Deutschland* (New York, 1978), 38–43.

27. See minutes of 12 Nov. 1938 meeting on the Jewish question in International Military Tribunal, *Trial of the Major War Criminals* (Nuremberg, 1947), vol. 28, 539, 1816-PS.

28. Himmler's notes, 27 May 1940, NA RG 242, T-175/R 94/2615288.

29. See p. 97.

30. Yahil, "Madagascar," 319.

31. Francis R. Nicosia, *The Third Reich and the Palestine Question* (Austin, 1985), 165–66; Yahil, "Madagascar," esp. 315–18, 321–22, 329.

32. Stein, *Waffen-SS*, 76–77. Charles W. Sydnor, Jr., *Soldiers of Destruction: The SS Death's Head Division 1933–1945* (Princeton, 1977), 106–8.

33. Telephone call, Wolff to Rudolf Brandt, NA RG 242, T-581/R 39A, 29 May 1940. After an early-morning meeting with Brandt on 31 May, Himmler was apparently out of the office the rest of the day and the next one. Confirmation that Himmler inspected the division at Le Paradis, Eicke to Wolff, 4 June 1940, NA RG 242, T-175/R 107/2630062.

34. Eicke to Wolff, 4 June 1940, NA RG 242, T-175/R 107/2630062–63, cited by Stein, *Waffen-SS*, 78.

35. Stein, *Waffen-SS*, 78, notes that it was not the habit of the SS to refer to atrocities in writing. Sydnor, *Soldiers of Destruction*, 109n., suggests that the military documents dealing with the incident were destroyed and that Himmler protected Eicke against the army.

36. Weinberg, *World in the Balance*, 107–8.

37. Kurzer Überblick über die neu aufzunehmenden, vordringlichen Aufgaben des Ref. D III, NA RG 238, T-1139/R 56/1101, NG-5764.

38. Brandt's log, NA RG 242, T-581/R 39A, 16–17 June 1940. There is a picture of Hitler in Max Domarus, *Hitler, Reden und Proklamationen 1932–1945* (Munich, 1965), II, pt. 1, 1,528.

39. Galeazzo Ciano, *The Ciano Diaries 1939–1943* (Garden City, N.Y., 1947), 265–66; Paul Schmidt, *Hitler's Interpreter* (New York, 1951), 178; Hildebrand, *Vom Reich*, 751–52; all cited by Browning, "Nazi Resettlement Policy," 511.

40. Yahil, "Madagascar," 332n. We should not assume that Ribbentrop knew Hitler's mind, for there were other differences in their presentation of Germany's aims in the peace settlement too. See Hildebrand, *Vom Reich*, 650.

41. Schmidt, *Hitler's Interpreter*, 178.

42. Heydrich to Ribbentrop, 24 June 1940, NA RG 242, T-120/R 780/372047.

43. Bormann's notes on Hitler's schedule, NA RG 242, T-84/R 387/497.

44. Browning, *Final Solution*, 41. Brack later testified that Bouhler wanted to become police governor of Madagascar. Brack testimony in Nuremberg Military Tribunal, Case 1, Medical Case Trials, cited by Friedman, *Roads to Extinction*, 49.

45. Interrogation of Hermann von Stutterheim, 11 March 1947, NA RG 238, M-1019/R 72/774.

46. Quoted in Yahil, "Madagascar," 333n. Ribbentrop seems to have received the message earlier. Rademacher's superior, Martin Luther, passed along Ribbentrop's response: "The fundamental idea of preparing the deportation [*Abschiebung*] of the Jews recently approved. Proceed in closest cooperation with the office of the Reich Führer SS." Handwritten in margin of Rademacher memo, 3 June 1940, NA RG 238, T-1139/R 56/1101, NG-5764. It is not clear when Ribbentrop responded.

47. Browning, *Final Solution*, 38, describes the competition but leaves Hitler out of this picture.

48. This process is effectively described in ibid., 37–40.

49. Adolf Eichmann, *Ich Adolf Eichmann: Ein historischer Zeugenbericht*, ed. Rudolf Aschenauer (Leoni am Starnberger See, 1980), 170–71.

50. Andreas Hillgruber and Gerhard Hümmelchen, *Chronik des Zweiten Weltkrieges* (Frankfurt am Main, 1966), 15–16.

51. Brandt's log, NA RG 242, T-581/R 39A, 3 July 1940, quotes Müller as saying, "*Bezugnahme auf Unterredung mit RF, die andere Hälfte soll bleiben.*"

52. Another piece of evidence supporting the conclusion that the conversation dealt with Jewish policy is a subsequent well-placed intelligence report that reached Switzerland that only half the European Jews would be sent to Madagascar. See p. 135.

53. On Eichmann's statement, Rudolf Höss Aufzeichnungen, Institut für Zeitgeschichte F 13/6, 337.

54. Frank to Lammers, 25 June 1940, NA RG 238, T-1139/R 21/236, NG-1627.

55. Frank referred to this goal in a conference with Krüger, Greiser, and others on 31 July 1940. Präg and Jacobmeyer, eds., *Diensttagebuch*, 259–62.

56. Präg and Jacobmeyer, eds., *Diensttagebuch*, 248, 10 July 1940.

57. Abteilungsleitersitzung, 12 July 1940, and Frank's Ansprache, 25 July 1940, in Frank, *Diensttagebuch*, 252, 258, cited by Browning, "Nazi Resettlement Policy," 512.

58. Präg and Jacobmeyer, eds., *Diensttagebuch*, 258, 25 July 1940.

59. Ibid., 260–62, 31 July 1940.

60. Apparently an oral order, since no written order survives. Himmler had lunch with the Führer in Berlin on 8 July. Krüger met with Himmler later that afternoon and returned to Cracow by 10 July. Himmler's schedule, NA RG 242, T-581/R 38A. It is also possible that Frank met directly with Himmler afterward—there is reference in Brandt's log on 16 July to setting up such an appointment, but Himmler's incomplete appointment book does not actually list an appointment with Reich Minister Frank. Brandt's log and Himmler's schedule, NA RG 242, T-581/R 39A and 38A.

61. Himmler's guidelines, first draft 19 June and second draft 24 June 1940, NA RG 242, T-175/R 138/2665975–82 and 2665958–65.

62. Himmler's schedule, 26 July 1940, NA RG 242, T-581/R 38A.

63. Meeting and quote from Frank's Diensttagebuch, NA RG 242, T-992/R 2, 31 July 1940. Himmler's schedule, NA RG 242, T-581/R 38A, 25 July 1940.

64. Interrogation of Otto Abetz, 26 June 1947, NA RG 238, T-1139/R 22/735, NG-1838.

65. Luther to Rademacher, 15 Aug. 1940, streng vertraulich! NA RG 238, T-120/R 780/372049. *"Gelegentlich einer Besprechung mit Herrn Botschafter Abetz in Paris erzählte mir dieser, dass der Führer ihm bei seinem vor zirka 2 Wochen stattgefundenen Vortrag über Frankreich erzählt habe, dass er beabsichtige, nach dem Kriege sämtliche Juden aus Europa zu evakuieren."* This document at least confirms Abetz's postwar dating of the conversation and the general thrust of Hitler's remarks.

66. See Richard Breitman and Alan M. Kraut, *American Refugee Policy and European Jewry, 1933–1945* (Bloomington, Ind., 1988), esp. 119–25.

67. Militärgeschichtliches Forschungsamt, ed., *Das Deutsche Reich und der Zweite Weltkrieg*, vol. IV, *Der Angriff auf die Sowjetunion*, ed., Horst Boog et al. (Stuttgart, 1983), 202–16. Interrogation of Walter Warlimont, 24 July 1945, NA RG 238, M-1270/R 28/281. Testimony of Walter Warlimont (June–July 1948), *Trials of War Criminals Before the Nuremberg Military Tribunals* (Washington, D.C., 1951), X, 1022–23. H. R. Trevor-Roper, ed., *Blitzkrieg to Defeat: Hitler's War Directives 1939–1945* (New York, 1964), 49–52.

68. Himmler to Berger, 11 July 1940, NA RG 242, T-175/R 94/2626155, quoted in Stein, *Waffen-SS*, 98. Himmler to Krüger, 30 July 1940 (summary only), NA RG 242, T-581/R 42A.

69. See p. 96.

70. Background information on Dirlewanger in Dirlewanger SS file, Berlin Document Center. On the Führer Chancellery, see Brack to Berger, 17 May 1940, Dirlewanger SS file. On Berger, Berger to Himmler, 4 June 1940, NA RG 238, NO-2920. Berger originated the idea, according to SS judicial investigator Konrad Morgen, affidavit of 29 Dec. 1947, NA RG 238, NO-5742.

71. Interrogation of Karl Wolff, 12 April 1947, NA RG 238, M-1019/R 80/1029.

72. Interrogation of Berger, 3 Dec. 1946, NA RG 238, M-1019/R 6/423.

73. Brandt to SS Main Office, 17 June 1940, NA RG 238, NO-2920.

74. Interrogation of Berger, 3 Dec. 1946, NA RG 238, M-1019/R 6/424.

75. Raul Hilberg, *The Destruction of the European Jews* (Chicago, 1961); 2nd expanded ed., 3 vols. (New York, 1985), I, 252–54.

76. Globocnik to Chief SS Main Office, 5 Aug. 1941, Dirlewanger SS file.

77. Morgen affidavit, 28 Jan. 1947, NA RG 238, NO-1908. James J. Weingartner, "Law and Justice in the Nazi SS: The Case of Konrad Morgen," *Central European History* 16 (1983): 285.

78. Eichmann seems to have been the driving force. Dieter Wisliceny affidavit, 4 Feb. 1947, NA RG 319, IRR Adolf Eichmann, XE 004471. Wisliceny joined Eichmann's section in Aug. 1940. The twenty-seven-year-old Dannecker was another RSHA "expert." Michael R. Marrus and Robert O. Paxton, *Vichy France and the Jews* (New York, 1983), 5. Browning, *Final Solution*, 40.

79. Text of RSHA plan in NA RG 242, T-120/R 780/372056–71. See also the analysis by Browning, *Final Solution*, 40–41.

80. This is the judgment of Charles W. Sydnor, Jr., who is currently working on a biography of Heydrich. See "Heydrich and the Final Solution," his paper delivered at the American Historical Association meeting, 30 Dec. 1987.

81. Rabbi Max Nussbaum, who left Berlin on 1 Aug. 1940 and arrived in the United States several weeks later, passed on this information to Stephen Wise. Wise to Felix Frankfurter, 16 Sept. 1940, Stephen Wise Papers, box 109, American Jewish Historical Society, Waltham, Mass. Similarly, Adam Czerniakow, the head of the Jewish council in Warsaw, heard from an SD official that after the imminent end of the war the Jews would all go to Madagascar. Raul Hilberg, Stanislaw Staron, and Josef Kermisz, eds., *The Warsaw Diary of Adam Czerniakow* (New York, 1979), 169.

82. Even later Eichmann's powers were constrained. Kurt Lindow in the RSHA specified: "Actions taken against the Jews as a body could not come from Eichmann, but again from Himmler only." Interrogation of Lindow, 31 Oct. 1945, NA RG 238, M-1270/R 25/743.

83. Abetz to Ribbentrop, 20 Aug. 1940: Heydrich to Luther, 20 Sept. 1940, NA RG 238, T-1139/R 27/1123 and R 49/835–36, NG-2433 and NG-4893.

84. Stuckart express letter to Reich Finance Minister et al., 4 July 1940, NA RG 238, T-1139/R 16/708, NG-1141.

85. Along these lines, if on a slightly different point, see Weinberg, *World in the Balance*, 110.

86. Marrus and Paxton, *Vichy France*, 5.

87. Bericht über die Verschickung von Juden deutscher Staatsangehörigkeit nach Süd-frankreich, 30 Oct. 1940, NA RG 238, T-1139/R 50/20, NG-4933.

88. Marrus and Paxton, *Vichy France*, esp. 3–71.

89. Himmler's itinerary and appointments, NA RG 242, T-175/R 112/2637788-89. Kaul's discussion of Himmler's decision and the first stage of deportations referred to in Kaul to Greifelt, 27 May 1942, NA RG 238, NO-2247. For Lorraine, see p. 134 and n. 103 below. For Himmler's clear view at a later time, see Himmler to Lammers, 18 June 1942, NA RG 238, NO-2475.

90. "A Visitor's Sorrow and Pity Yield a Memorial," *New York Times*, 2 July 1989.

91. Bormann to Lammers, 21 Oct. 1940, Akten der Parteikanzlei, Institut für Zeitge-schichte microfiche 101/27369–371.

92. Vermerk über Besprechung, 4 Aug. 1942, NA RG 238, NO-5202. This document specifies that blacks, Jews, gypsies, foreigners, the *patois*-speaking population, "asocials," and the insane fell into the general categories Hitler had enumerated.

93. Besprechung zwischen Gauleiter Bürckel und Gruppenführer Berkelmann, Metz, 8 Oct. 1940, NA RG 238, Office of Chief of Counsel for War Crimes, Berlin Branch SS, box 23, 5054.

94. Conference with Scheel, Reichel, and Koch, Strasbourg, 2–3 Oct. 1940, NA RG 238, NO-5589.

95. See nn. 91 and 93.

96. Vermerk über Besprechung, 4 Aug. 1942, NA RG 238, NO-5202. Also IMT 38, 331, 114-R.

97. Bericht über die Verschickung . . . , 30 Oct. 1940, NA RG 238, T-1139/R 50/20–21, NG-4933.

98. On 1 Oct. 1940 Plötz, who was Heydrich's aide, spoke with Brandt of Himmler's office about investigations in Baden. Brandt's log, NA RG 242, T-581/R 39A. On Hitler's order, Chef der Sicherheitspolizei und des SD to Luther, 29 Oct. 1940, NA RG 238, T-1139/R 50/28, NG-4934.

99. Bericht über die Verschickung . . . , 30 Oct. 1940, Chef der Sicherheitspolizei und des SD to Luther, 29 Oct. 1940, NA RG 238, T-1139/R 50/28, NG-4934.

100. Eichmann interrogations, I, 141, 145, quoted by Browning, "Nazi Resettlement Policy," 513.

101. Parker Buhrman to American Legation, Bern, 3 Dec. 1940, NA RG 84, Basel Confidential file, 800.

102. Wisliceny affidavit, 4 Feb. 1947, NA RG 319, IRR Adolf Eichmann, XE 004471. Wisliceny mentions "Commissioners" sent starting in Aug. 1940 to France, Slovakia, Rumania, Croatia, Italy, and Bulgaria.

103. Conference with Scheel, Reichel, and Koch, 2–3 Oct. 1940, NA RG 238, NO-5589.

104. So Eichmann told Bernard Lösener in the Interior Ministry. Lösener, "Als Rassereferent im Reichsministerium des Innern," *Vierteljahrshefte für Zeitgeschichte* 9 (1961): 296, cited by Browning, *Final Solution*, 42.

105. Himmler's schedule, NA RG 242, T-581/R 38A, 8 Aug. 1940.

106. Himmler's schedule, NA RG 242, T-581/R 38A, 10 Aug. 1940. On Himmler's preference for individual meetings, see also interrogation of Hans Jüttner, 25 March 1948, NA RG 238, M 1019/R 32/832.

107. See p. 125.

108. Andreas Hillgruber, "Die ideologisch-dogmatische Grundlage der nationalsozialistischen Politik der Ausrottung der Juden in den besetzten Gebieten der Sowjetunion und ihre Durchführung 1941–1944," *German Studies Review* 2 (1979), 284.

109. Himmler's speech of 7 Sept. 1940, reprinted in IMT 29, 107–8, 1918-PS.

110. Brandt's log, NA RG 242, T-581/R 39A, 12 Aug. 1940.

111. Bach-Zelewski to Wolff, 13 Sept. 1940, Bach-Zelewski SS file, Berlin Document Center. This letter refers to the conference that Bach-Zelewski had with Himmler the previous day, but Himmler's appointment book indicates that the conference was on 11 Sept. NA RG 242, T-581/R 38A.

112. Himmler's itinerary, NA RG 242, T-175/R 112/2637776.

113. Pohl to Himmler, 4 Dec. 1940; Himmler to Pohl, 7 Dec. 1940 (summaries only), NA RG 242, T-581/R 42A.

114. Hilberg, *Destruction*, I, 252–55.

115. On conditions in the camps and forced-labor columns, ibid., I, 254–55.

116. Greifelt to Reich Interior Minister, 21 Aug. 1940, NA RG 238, T-1139/R 23/601–2, NG-1916.

117. Heydrich Aktennotiz, 11 Sept. 1940, Czechoslovakian State Archives. I am exceedingly grateful to Charles Sydnor, Jr., for supplying me with a copy of this document and giving me the benefit of his analysis. Himmler's general guidelines for a racial register, issued the next day, divided racial Germans into four groups, according to how actively they supported or opposed the German national cause. See excerpt in IMT 3, 586, 2916-PS. The full text of the decree is in NA RG 242, T-74/R 14/386017–21.

118. Ulrich von Hassell, *Vom anderen Deutschland: Aus den nachgelassenen Tagebüchern 1938–1944* (Zurich, 1946), 95. Interrogation of Konrad Morgen, 11 Oct. 1946, NA RG 238, M-1019/R 47/593, based on Morgen's conversation with Grawitz.

119. Leland Morris to Secretary of State, 8 Sept. 1941, with attached "Poland Under German Occupation," n.d. [Dec. 1940], see p. 52: copy in NA RG 226, plain number file 898. On Heydrich's prewar strategy and Geist's recognition of it, see pp. 64–65 of this book.

120. Henry Friedlander, "Jüdische Anstaltspatienten im NS-Deutschland," in *Aktion T4 1939–1945: Die "Euthanasia"-Zentrale in der Tiergartenstrasse 4*, ed. Götz Aly (Berlin, 1987), 39. In his forthcoming study to be published by Oxford University Press, Henry Friedlander has been able to trace some killings of Jews within the framework of the euthanasia program back to the spring of 1940. Ernst Klee, *"Euthanasia" in NS-Staat: Die "Vernichtung lebensunwerten Lebens"* (Stuttgart, 1983), 259.

121. Klee, *Euthanasia*, 260–61. Affidavit by Moritz Schnidtmann, 8 Nov. 1946, NA RG 238, NO-720. Himmler attended Chefbesprechungen at the Interior Ministry on 24 July and 6 Aug. 1940, an unusual move that may have been related. Himmler's schedules NA RG 242, T-581/R 38A.

122. Himmler's schedule, NA RG 242, T-581/R 38A.

123. Brack SS file, Berlin Document Center.

124. Himmler's schedule, NA RG 242, T-581/R 38A, 13–14 Dec. 1940.

125. Himmler to Brack, NA RG 238, NO-018; also quoted in Klee, *Euthanasia*, 291.

126. Klee, *Euthanasia*, 291–92. Klee maintains that the shutdown was probably in the works even before Himmler's letter. The timing, however, seems more than coincidental.

127. Up until the interrogation on the afternoon of 13 Sept. 1946 Brack had been denying participation in and knowledge of criminal activities. Interrogator Fred Rodell then showed Brack a portion of a document proposing the sterilization of the Jews and asked him whether he had ever seen it. Brack said no. Rodell then took the cover off the bottom of the document to reveal Brack's signature. Brack broke out in tears, admitted he had been lying, and asked Rodell to tear up the previous testimony; now, he promised, he would tell the truth. See interrogation, 13 Sept. 1946 (12:30–1:00), NA RG 238, M-1019/R 8/975–77. Much of what he said subsequently on that day, which included self-incriminating testimony, is supported by other sources.

128. Interrogation of Brack, 13 Sept. 1946 (1:00–3:30), NA RG 238, M-1019/R 8/981–82.

129. Brack to Himmler, 28 March 1941, NA RG 238, NO-203. Himmler's files from Hallein, 8 Nov. 1945, NA RG 226, XL34777, pp. 26–27. An extensive search has failed to turn up the original documents, dated 11 Nov. 1940.

130. Interrogation of Brack, 13 Sept. 1946, NA RG 238, M-1019/R 8/988.

131. Darré's article was excerpted in *Zeitschriftendienst*, 15 Nov. 1940, and *NS Landpost*, 22 Nov. 1940, NA RG 238, T-1139/R 18/1333ff, NG-1333.

132. Bormann's minutes, IMT 39, 425–29, 172-USSR. Frank, *Diensttagebuch*, 302, 6 Nov. 1940, cited by Browning, "Nazi Resettlement Policy," 514.

133. This decree, dated 25 Oct. 1940, is quoted in part of the General Government circular of 23 Nov. 1940, which is reprinted in Jüdisches Historische Institut Warschau, *Fascismus-Getto-Massenmord: Dokumentation über Ausrottung und Widerstand der Juden in Polen während des Zweiten Weltkrieges* (Berlin-Ost, 1960), 59.

134. Ibid.

135. Himmler's itinerary, NA RG 242, T-175/R 112/2637774–75.

136. See n. 133.

137. Reconstructed from Himmler's notes for speech, NA RG 242, T-580/R 37.

138. Frank, *Diensttagebuch*, 319, 11 Jan. 1941.

139. Frank, Diensttagebuch, 19 Dec. 1940 (not in edited, published version), NA RG 242, T-992/R 2/1158–59.

CHAPTER 7: TOWARD THE FINAL SOLUTION

1. *The Testament of Adolf Hitler: The Hitler-Bormann Documents, February–April 1945*, ed. François Genoid, tr. Col. R. H. Stevens (London, 1961), 63–66. For scholarly analyses of Hitler's decision to strike to the east, see Gerhard L. Weinberg, "Der deutsche Entschluss zum Angriff auf die Sowjetunion," *Vierteljahrshefte für Zeitgeschichte* 1 (1953): 301–18, and the recent synthesis by Jürgen Förster in Militärgeschichtliches Forschungsamt, ed., *Das Deutsche Reich und der Zweite Weltkrieg*, IV, *Der Angriff auf die Sowjetunion*, ed. Horst Boog et al. (Stuttgart, 1983), 3–18.

2. Eberhard Jäckel, *Hitler's Weltanschauung: A Blueprint for Power*, trans. Herbert Arnold (Middletown, Conn., 1972), 25–46.

3. H. R. Trevor-Roper, ed., *Blitzkrieg to Defeat: Hitler's War Directives 1939–1945* (New York, 1964), 49. Albert Seaton, *The German Army 1933–45* (London, 1983), 166.

4. Hitler, *Monologe im Führerhauptquartier 1941–1944: Die Aufzeichnungen Heinrich Heims*, ed. Werner Jochmann (Hamburg, 1980), 66.

5. Walter Warlimont, *Inside Hitler's Headquarters 1939–1945*, trans. R. H. Barry (London, 1964), 138.

6. Andreas Hillgruber, *Hitlers Strategie: Politik und Kriegführung 1940–1941* (Frankfurt am Main, 1965), 683. Notes for Himmler's speech, NA RG 242, T-175/R 112/2636892–96. Confirmation of speech, Himmler's schedule, NA RG 242, T-581/R 38A.

7. Himmler's schedule, NA RG 242, T-581/R 38A, 18 Dec. 1940.

8. For details of the reorganization, see George H. Stein, *The Waffen-SS: Hitler's Elite Guard at War* (Ithaca, 1966), 93–110.

9. Seyss-Inquart to Himmler, 27 Dec. 1940; Himmler to Seyss-Inquart, 7 Jan. 1941, NA RG 242, T-175/R 33/2541305–9.

10. On the history of Wewelsburg, see Heinz Höhne, *The Order of Death's Head: The Story of Hitler's SS*, trans. Richard Barry (New York, 1979), 173–74. There was a Wewelsburg concentration camp with about two thousand prisoners which supplied laborers for the renovation. See Albert Rzadkowski affidavit, 10 Sept. 1947, NA RG 238, NO-4967. On the decoration of Wewelsburg, NA RG 242, T-175/R 112/2637228-31. On the SS "school" cover, interrogation of Wilhelm Krause, Ernst Specht, and Albert Rzadkowski, 10 Sept. 1947, NA RG 238, M-1019/R 38/45–46.

11. Himmler's appointment book for 1941 has been lost. His movements and contacts

must be reconstructed from other, incomplete sources. According to Brandt's office log, Himmler did not meet with Brandt in his office for the customary handling of correspondence on 2–5 and 10–12 January. He could have been at Wewelsburg either time. NA RG 242, T-581/R 39A.

12. IMT 4, 482. Although this testimony is uncorroborated, roughly the same figure crops up in later documents. In November 1941 Hans Ehlich of the RSHA told Wetzel that the general planning for the East called for thirty-one million foreigners to be expelled, "*aussiedelt*," a term that sometimes meant "killed." See Wetzel, Stellungnahme und Gedanken zum Generalplan Ost des Reichsführers SS, 27 April 1942, NA RG 238, T-1139/R 26/1126, NG-2325. Another confirming detail—Himmler usually met at Wewelsburg with twelve senior SS officials. See Höhne, *The Order*, 172.

There is a high probability that Bach-Zelewski's statement is accurate—he had little to gain in 1946 by making Himmler's statement known, and such a directive also fits logically into the sequence of events.

13. Rosenberg, *Politisches Tagebuch*, quoted by Robert M. W. Kempner, *Eichmann und Komplizen* (Zurich, 1961), 97. Christian Streit, *Keine Kameraden: Die Wehrmacht und die sowjetischen Kriegsgefangenen, 1941–1945* (Stuttgart, 1978), 63–65.

14. On Heydrich's reputation, see, for example, interrogation of Martin Sandberger, 12 June 1947, NA RG 238, M-1019/R 61/752. On preparations for police action, Helmut Krausnick and Hans-Heinrich Wilhelm, *Die Truppe des Weltanschauungskrieges: Die Einsatzgruppen der Sicherheitspolizei und des SD 1938–1942* (Stuttgart, 1981), 141.

15. Bericht über den Einsatz des Sonderkommandos AA. in Holland, Belgien und Frankreich. 19 Dec. 1940, NA RG 238, T-1139/R 36/1163–66, NG-3515. This memo concludes with Künsberg's enthusiastic declaration: "*Wir sind wieder bereit!*" For details of Künsberg's unit's activity in the Soviet Union, after June 1941, NA RG 242, T-354/R 184.

16. Künsberg (Übernahme in die Waffen-SS, Stellung des Sonderkommandos), 24 Jan. 1941; Künsberg (Entscheidung des Gruf. Wolff mitgeteilt), 25 Jan. 1941; Künsberg (nochmalige Bitte, seine Angelegenheit dem RF vorzutragen), 25 Jan. 1941; Künsberg (Übernahme seines Sonderkommandos i. Waffen-SS), 26 Jan. 1941; Plötz (Brief an Künsberg), 27 Jan. 1941; all NA RG 242, T-581/R 39A.

17. Martin Luther of the Foreign Office wanted a copy of the Heydrich-Brauchitsch agreement to present to Foreign Minister Ribbentrop before any decision could be made. He was informed in early February that another meeting between Heydrich and Brauchitsch was still necessary; a formal agreement was not yet available. Künsberg Aufzeichnungen, 4 Feb. 1941 and 10 Feb. 1941, NA RG 238, T-1139/R 52/1100–101, NG-5225. Picot to Künsberg, 10 Feb. 1941, NA RG 238, M-946/R 1/113. On the negotiations' still being in progress, handwritten notation based on information from Plötz at end of Picot memorandum, Einbau des Sonderkommando AA in die SS, 10 Feb. 1941, NA RG 238, M-946/R 1/109.

18. Göring's comment to Thomas quoted by Streit, *Keine Kameraden*, 28 (see also 31–49). Helmut Krausnick, "Kommissarbefehl und 'Gerichtsbarkeitserlass Barbarossa' in neuer Sicht," *Vierteljahrshefte für Zeitgeschichte* 25 (1977): 685. See also Warlimont, *Inside Hitler's Headquarters*, 150–53. Other quotes in Krausnick and Wilhelm, *Truppe des Weltanschauungskrieges*, 116–17.

19. For a detailed analysis of the origins of the Commissar Order, see Krausnick, "Kommissarbefehl," 682–738.

20. On longstanding indoctrination of the military, see Omer Bartov, *The Eastern Front, 1941–45: German Troops and the Barbarisation of Warfare* (Oxford, 1985), 76–88. On the Wehrmachtführungsstab guidelines, Streit, *Keine Kameraden*, 49–50.

21. In early June Müller gave a presentation to the intelligence officers and military judges of the various armies, with the instruction to liquidate the "bearers of enemy attitudes." Krausnick, "Kommissarbefehl," 709–10; Streit, *Keine Kameraden*, 85. Bechler's testimony to the Russians, reported in *Freies Deutschland*, 19 Dec. 1943, summarized in NA RG 338, box 575, folder 21–9, is consistent, but more detailed and far-reaching. According to Bechler, Hitler originally wanted to liquidate all Russian officers, businessmen, engineers, etc., but eventually agreed to issue only the order to have the commissars killed.

A set of detailed military documents suggests that various military authorities also received prewar briefings about the deployment and planned actions of the *Einsatzgruppen* and police battalions. Einsatz von SS und Polizeikräften im rückw. Heeresgebiet, 11 June 1941; Kriegsgliederung der den Höh. SS und Pol. Führern bei den Befehlshabern des rück. Heeresgebiets unterstehenden Einsatzkräfte der Sicherheitspolizei und des SD; Anlagen; and SS, Pol. und Grenzsperre im Einsatzfall, 20 June 1941 (NA RG 242, T-501/R 7/117, 91, 87–88, 69–70 respectively).

22. OKH, Regelung des Einsatzes der Sicherheitspolizei und des SD im Verbande des Heeres, 26 March 1941, NA RG 238, NOKW-256. Walter Schellenberg, *Hitler's Secret Service* (New York, 1971), 210, has Müller conducting the negotiations with Wagner. Heydrich had been involved earlier, but Heydrich was not satisfied with this draft, so he could not have negotiated it. See n. 24 below.

23. Unfortunately, Himmler's instructions do not survive. That he wrote to Heydrich about the agreement is recorded in the log of his correspondence, Aktenvermerk über die Verständigung der Einsatzkommandos der Sicherheitspolizei, Himmler to Heydrich, 20 March 1941, NA RG 242, T-581/R 42A.

24. Wagner to Heydrich, 4 April 1941, NA RG 238, M-895/R 10/271, and Heydrich's handwritten reaction: "*Ich vermisse die Anordnungen f. das Gefechtsgebiet.*" This document is only slightly inconsistent with Schellenberg's claim that he was sent into the negotiations with Wagner in May 1941. See Schellenberg, *Hitler's Secret Service*, 209–10.

25. See pp. 106–10, 115.

26. *Trials of War Criminals Before the Nuremberg Military Tribunal*, vol. 10, 1,239–41, NOKW-2080. Krausnick and Wilhelm, *Truppe des Weltanschauungskrieges*, 129–30.

27. Krausnick and Wilhelm, *Truppe des Weltanschauungskrieges*, 143–48.

28. Testimony of Dr. Filbert in the prosecution indictment of Bruno Streckenbach, 30 June 1973, StA Hamburg, Az. 147 Js 31/67, cited and discussed by Krausnick and Wilhelm, *Truppe des Weltanschauungskrieges*, 141. Interrogation of Albert Hartl, 9 Jan. 1947, NA RG 238, M-1270/R 24/786–87, 839. Hartl was the Vatican expert within the RSHA in 1941. Although it is possible that the two witnesses recounted different meetings, Filbert spoke of a March or April session, and Hartl of a meeting two or three months before the invasion of the Soviet Union—virtually identical dates. Both men claimed that there was a small audience, both mentioned the announcement that Hitler had decided to invade the Soviet Union with three columns (north, center, and south), and both mention the discussion of the *Einsatzgruppen*. The biggest discrepancy is that Filbert has Heydrich speaking to the group, whereas Hartl says it was Müller. The discrepancy is more likely the result of a lapse of memory than of two such meetings. To my knowledge, Hartl's testimony has never before been cited in this context.

29. The rivalry between the RSHA and the Foreign Office over the Jewish question went back at least to mid-1940. A bit later Heydrich was specifically informed that Luther had been intriguing against him. See Berger to Himmler, 26 April 1941, NA RG 242, T-175/R 123/2648809.

30. Heydrich to Luther, 5 and 14 Feb. 1941, quoted in Michael R. Marrus and Robert O. Paxton, *Vichy France and the Jews* (New York, 1983), 10.

31. Bericht über die Besprechung betreffend Umsiedlung von Polen und Juden in das Generalgouvernement im Reichssicherheitshauptamt Berlin, 8 Jan. 1941, NA RG 242, T-992/R 5; Besprechung mit SS-Obergruppenführer Krüger und Oberlandrat Westerkamp, 11 Jan. 1941; Arbeitssitzung der Regierung des Generalgouvernements, 15 Jan. 1941, in Werner Präg and Wolfgang Jacobmeyer, eds., *Das Diensttagebuch des deutschen Generalgouverneurs in Polen 1939–1945* (Stuttgart, 1975), 318–21, 326–29. Heydrich memos establishing emigration centers in Danzig–West Prussia and Upper Silesia, 23 Jan. 1941 and 14 Feb. 1941, NA RG 242, T-175/R 426/2955265–66 and 2955402–3. More generally, Robert Lewis Koehl, *RKFDV: German Resettlement and Population Policy, 1939–1945: A History of the Reich Commission for the Strengthening of Germandom* (Cambridge, Mass., 1957), 117–24.

32. In the text I follow closely the source in the next note; it refers specifically to Jews from the Reich (and Bohemia-Moravia). It is likely, however, that the actual conception was to clear Jews from much of the continent, a fact which Eichmann had no need to reveal at the meeting.

33. Notiz. Betrifft: Evakuierung der Juden aus Berlin, 21 March 1941, NA RG 242, T-81/R 676/5485604–5. Responding to pressure from the Propaganda Ministry to remove the Jews from Berlin, Eichmann first reminded the others that the Führer had entrusted Heydrich with the final evacuation of the Jews (*endgültigen Judenevakuierung*). Then he explained that eight to ten weeks earlier Heydrich had made a proposal to the Führer (*einen Vorschlag vorgelegt*) that was not implemented only because the Government General was temporarily unable to take in one Jew or one Pole from the Old Reich. Eichmann exempted the Jews capable of labor, whose number, he said, was not great. Although his language was more restricted, Eichmann's comments were consistent with the idea of deporting most European Jews to the East.

34. Paul C. Squire interview with Dr. Carl J. Burckhardt, 7 Nov. 1942, NA RG 84, American Consulate Geneva, Confidential file 1942, 800. Harrison to Undersecretary of State, Personal, 23 Nov. 1942, NA RG 59, CDF 740.00116 E. W. 1939/653. Burckhardt was told independently by two Germans in whom he had unlimited confidence that they had both seen this order. The sources were said to be an official in the Foreign Office and an official in the War Ministry.

35. Brack to Himmler, 28 March 1941, NA RG 238, NO-203. Interrogation of Brack, 13 Sept. 1946, NA RG 238, M-1019/R 8/982–84.

36. Report on sterilization in Germany and occupied countries to be sent to the members of Committee I, United Nations War Crimes Commission, submitted by Dr. B. Ecer, written by Dr. Theo Lang (Lang Report), 10 May 1945, NA RG 59, Records of the Legal Advisor Relating to War Crimes, lot file no. 61D33, box 6, folder Commissioner's Despatches #147–278. On the sterilization law and resistance to its application, Gisela Bock, *Zwangssterilisation im Nationalsozialismus: Studien zur Rassenpolitik und Frauenpolitik* (Opladen, 1986), 178–298. Robert N. Proctor, *Racial Hygiene: Medicine Under the Nazis* (Cambridge, Mass., 1988), 106–7, 115–16, also notes problems with the use of the sterilization law.

37. Lang Report, 10 May 1945, NA RG 59, lot file no. 61D33, box 6, folder Commissioner's Despatches #147–278, and (Lang's) Auszug aus meinen früheren Ausführungen vom December 1941 und Januar 1942, NA RG 208, entry 367, box 294. For related activities that provide some supporting evidence, Bock, *Zwangssterilisation*, 440–46, 453–54.

38. Tiefenbacher to Brack, 12 May 1941, NA RG 238, NO-204. See also Grawitz to Himmler, 29 May 1941, NA RG 238, NO-1639.

39. Interrogation of Brack, 13 Sept. 1946, NA RG 238, M-1019/R 8/982–84.

40. Copy in NA RG 242, T-175/R 15/2518530–42, quote on 2518542.

41. Hitler actually issued the first threat to destroy the Jewish race in Europe in his speech of 30 Jan. 1939, but two years later he referred to his statement from his speech of 1 Sept. 1939, the day World War II began. The error indicates Hitler's deeply embedded belief that the war was inseparable from the war against Jewry. See Lucy S. Dawidowicz, *The War Against the Jews* (New York, 1973), 147–48.

42. Excerpt from speech in Max Domarus, *Hitler, Reden und Proklamationen 1932–1945* (Munich, 1965), II, pt. 2, 1,663–64.

43. Avner Less interrogation of Eichmann, 6 June 1960, reprinted in *Eichmann Interrogated: Transcripts from the Archives of the Israeli Police*, ed. Jochen von Lang and Claus Sibyll (New York, 1983), 98.

44. Präg and Jacobmeyer, eds., *Diensttagebuch*, 332–33, 17 March 1941. Arbeitssitzung, 25 March 1941, in ibid., 336–37. On Eichmann, see n. 33 above.

45. Background on Globocnik's ideas in Arbeitssitzung, 15 Jan. 1941, in Präg and Jacobmeyer, eds., *Diensttagebuch*, 328. Arbeitssitzung, 13 Dec. 1940, in ibid., 311. I could not find Krüger's letter of 2 April 1941, but Himmler's response of 19 April 1941 is in the Globocnik SS file, Berlin Document Center. One can see from this response that Krüger had written about Globocnik's plan.

46. See Wisliceny affidavit, 4 Feb. 1947, NA RG 319, IRR Adolf Eichmann, XE 004471. The photograph referred to in this document, showing Wisliceny's presentation to the Slovakian government on 3 Sept. 1940, is missing. Also Vermerk, 23 Jan. 1941, NA RG 242, T-175/R 253/2745449. On the Foreign Office and Heydrich, Luther to Killinger, 15 Oct. 1940, NA RG 242, T-120/R 4442/E086118 and E086040–41, cited by Christopher R. Browning, *The Final Solution and the German Foreign Office: A Study of Referat III D of Abteilung Deutschland* (New York, 1978), 48. Wisliceny, Bericht über die Besichtigung der oberschlesischen Judenlager, 12 July 1941, NA RG 242, T-175/R 584/000080–83.

47. *From the History of KL Auschwitz* (New York, 1982), I, 188, has Himmler, Bracht, Glücks, and Ernst-Heinrich Schmausser going to Auschwitz on 1 March 1941. This last name appears to be an error, since Schmausser was not appointed higher SS and police leader for the region until May 1941, and since Himmler attended a birthday party for Bach-Zelewski, Schmausser's predecessor, in Breslau on the evening of 1 March. Programm für Sonnabend, 1 March 1941, NA RG 242, T-580/R 37. On the earlier phase of Auschwitz, see pp. 93–94 above.

48. Einstufung der Konzentrationslager, 2 Jan. 1941, NA RG 238, NO-743. Glücks to Wander, SS Personalhauptamt, 14 Jan. 1941, Höss SS file, Berlin Document Center.

49. Otto Ambros affidavit, 29 April 1947, NA RG 238, T-301/R 79/554–55, NI-9542. See also Peter Hayes, *Industry and Ideology: I. G. Farben in the Nazi Era* (Cambridge, 1989), 349. In this connection, Dr. Hans Deichmann, who in 1940 was a young I. G. Farben employee, has a clear recollection of overhearing a lunchtime conversation between Georg von Schnitzler and Fritz terMeer, both members of the Farben executive board, in the late summer of 1940. At that time they were already considering a Farben plant at Auschwitz that would make use of concentration camp labor. Letters Deichmann to Walter Laqueur, 22 Nov. 1988, and to Breitman, 2 May 1989. Schnitzler was Deichmann's uncle.

From the History of KL Auschwitz, I, 187. Bevölkerungspolitische Massnahmen für das Buna-Werk Auschwitz in Ostoberschlesien, 18 Feb. 1941, NA RG 238, T-301/R 13/358,

NI-1240. On the Himmler-Ambros school connection, see interrogation of Walter Dürr-feld, 1 Nov. 1946, NA RG 238, M-1019/R 14/334; and interrogation of Heinrich Bütefisch, 7 Jan. 1947, NA RG 238, M-1019/R 10/696.

50. Interrogation of Höss, 14 May 1946, NA RG 238, M-1019/R 28/621. I. G. Farben's Ambros got a tour not long after Himmler did, and Ambros recalled the crematorium and the prisoners' badges. Ambros affidavit, 29 April 1947, NA RG 238, T-301/R 79/557–58, NI-9542.

51. Höss's postwar accounts are marred by inexact and inconsistent dating of events, but much of the substance of his testimony is corroborated by wartime documents. There is no question that Himmler visited Auschwitz on 1 March 1941. For confirmation of the total number of prisoners, see Besprechung mit den Lagerkommanden, 27 March 1941, NA RG 238, T-301/R 123/534, NI-15148. His recollection of the substance of Himmler's orders was good.

52. Höss's March 1947 testimony in his trial, reprinted in Jüdisches Historische Institut Warschau, *Fascismus-Getto-Massenmord: Dokumentation über Ausrottung und Widerstand der Juden in Polen während des Zweiten Weltkrieges* (Berlin-Ost, 1960), 247. Höss's affidavit of 14 March 1946, NA RG 238, NO-1210. On the order for the Farben factory, Wirth to Ambros, 4 March 1941, NA RG 238, T-301/R 135/361–62, NI-11086 (Staff Evidence Analysis only—original document missing). On Farben's knowledge of concentration-camp labor, Besprechung mit den Lagerkommandanten, 27 March 1941, NA RG 238, T-301/R 123/534, NI-15148: interrogation of Walter Dürrfeld, 1 Nov. 1946, NA RG 238, M-1019/R 14/339–42.

53. Program for 1 and 2 March 1941, NA RG 242, T-580/R 37/no frame nos. More detailed description of the whole process in Koehl, *RKFDV*, 104–7.

54. Program for 2 March 1941, NA RG 242, T-580/R 37A. Text of speech there as well.

55. Interrogation of Isaak Egon Ochshorn, 14 Sept. 1945, NA RG 238, NO-1934. Ochshorn testified that the Jew was in the infirmary "by accident." Discussion of a general prewar order not to treat Jews, affidavit of Gerhard Oskar Schiedlausky, 4 March 1947, NA RG 238, NO-2332. Himmler's new order also in interrogation of Ochshorn.

56. Schellenberg letter, 20 May 1941, NA RG 238, NG-3104.

57. Himmler's itinerary, NA RG 242, T-175/R 112/2637754. Description of the trip by adjutant Werner Grothmann, interrogation of 13 June 1945, NA RG 319, IRR Himmler, XE 000632.

58. Reinhard Bollmus, *Das Amt Rosenberg und seine Gegner* (Stuttgart, 1970), 19–26, 237–39. Also Robert Edwin Herzstein, *The War That Hitler Won: Goebbels and the Nazi Media Campaign* (New York, 1987), 157–66; Michael H. Kater, *The Nazi Party: A Social Profile of Members and Leaders, 1919–1945* (Cambridge, Mass., 1983), 186–87.

59. Himmler said that the Führer had given him this assurance in the Reich Chancellery, before leaving for his headquarters. Himmler to Bormann, 25 May 1941, NA RG 242, T-175/R 123/2648747. Hitler had left Berlin on 4 May. Hillgruber, *Hitlers Strategie*, 689.

60. Rosenberg to Himmler, 6 May 1941, NA RG 242, T-175/R 123/2648745. Quotation from Himmler to Bormann, 25 May 1941, NA RG 242, T-175/R 123/2648747–48. In this letter Himmler also asked Bormann to consult Hitler again.

61. Bormann to Lammers, 16 June 1941, NA RG 242, T-175/R 123/2648754–55.

62. For further details, see Krausnick and Wilhelm, *Truppe des Weltanschauungskrieges*, 138–39.

63. Rosenberg to Bormann, 3 Nov. 1940: Rosenberg to Bormann, 6 March 1941, Akten der Parteikanzlei, Institut für Zeitgeschichte microfiche 001/00189, 001/00067–68.

64. Text of speech in *Völkischer Beobachter*, 29 March 1941, reprinted and trans. in *NCA*, V, 554–57.

65. Fritz Hesse, *Hitler and the English*, trans. F. A. Voigt (London, 1954), 124–25.

66. Interrogation of Ohlendorf, 23 June 1947, NA RG 238, M-1019/R 51/156–57. Ohlendorf claimed that he was a casualty of Bormann's intervention, because he had a reputation as a member of an anthroposophical society. Heydrich supposedly offered him a new position as the leader of an *Einsatzgruppe*. See also Brandt's log (Suchanek, Wimmer, Vorgehen Astrologen-Aktion), NA RG 242, T-581/R 39A, 10 June 1941.

67. Itinerary in NA RG 242, T-175/ R 112/2637752–53.

68. Jacob Presser, *The Destruction of the Dutch Jews* (New York, 1969), 45–53.

69. IMT 15, 667.

70. Presser, *Destruction*, 53–54, 69–70.

71. Brandt's log, NA RG 242, T-175/R 39A, 6 June 1941. However, *The Chronicle of the Lodz Ghetto* has Himmler visiting on 7 June, the same day some shots were fired at a sentry booth and the population was forced to spend the day indoors. See Lucjan Dobroszycki, ed., *The Chronicle of the Lodz Ghetto 1941–1944* (New Haven, 1984), 59–60. It may be that the chroniclers found out about the visit only after it occurred. Brandt's log has Himmler flying back to Berlin on the evening of 6 June.

72. Christopher Browning, "Nazi Ghettoization Policy in Poland," *Central European History* 19 (1986): 349–51, 356. Isaiah Trunk, *Judenrat: The Jewish Councils in Eastern Europe under Nazi Occupation* (New York, 1972), 84.

73. Browning, "Nazi Ghettoization Policy," 355–60, 365–66, argues that food officials were unwilling to divert scarce supplies for Jews. On late 1941, see Christopher R. Browning, *Fateful Months: Essays on the Emergence of the Final Solution* (New York, 1985), 30.

74. Directive reprinted in Trevor-Roper, ed., *Blitzkrieg*, 78–82. "Confidence of a sleepwalker," phrase from Domarus, *Hitler, Reden*, I, 606.

75. For the 26 May assignment, see the reference in the Feldpostnummerverzeichnis of 30 June 1941, Himmler Collection, Hoover Institution, box 10, folder 322, Stanford University. Stein, *Waffen-SS*, 111–12, stresses the police regiments in the Kommandostab, composed largely of men over age forty-five, youths, and wounded war veterans. Yehoshua Büchler, "Kommandostab Reichsführer SS: Himmler's Personal Murder Brigades in 1941," *Holocaust and Genocide Studies* I (1986), 11–21, emphasizes the Waffen-SS brigades in the Kommandostab. My own impression, based on considerable reading in West German postwar trial records, is that both elements played a significant role in the killing of Jews. *Unsere Ehre heisst Treue: Kriegstagebuch des Kommandostabes Reichsführer SS: Tätigkeitsberichte der 1. und 2. SS-Inf. Brigade, der 1. SS-Kav.-Brigade und von Sonderkommandos der SS* (Vienna, 1965), 7–13, Himmler's statement on 13.

76. *Festgabe für Heinrich Himmler* (Darmstadt, 1941), copy in Hoover Institution Library.

77. Heydrich referred to his meeting on 17 June and his instructions in a memorandum on 29 June 1941. See Krausnick and Wilhelm, *Truppe des Weltanschauungskrieges*, 151, 151n. This evidence convincingly sustains the recollections of those who later testified that Heydrich gave a speech in the Prinz Albrechtstrasse. See, for example, interrogation of Walter Blume, 29 June 1947, NA RG 238, M-1019/R 7/848; it refutes the testimony of Martin Sandberger (interrogation of 23 May 1947, NA RG 238, M-1019/R 61/683–85) that Streckenbach gave the speech in Berlin. The confusion may have arisen because Streckenbach gave a speech at Pretzsch, which Sandberger later remembered (interrogation of 27 Feb. 1948, NA RG 238, M-1019/R 61/780–81). On this much-disputed question of Streckenbach's instructions, see Krausnick and Wilhelm, *Truppe des Weltanschauungskrieges*, 159–62; Helmut Krausnick, "Hitler und die Befehle an die Einsatzgruppen im Sommer 1941,"

and Alfred Streim, "Zur Eröffnung des allegemeinen Judenvernichtungsbefehls gegenüber den Einsatzgruppen," in Eberhard Jäckel and Jürgen Rohwer, eds., *Der Mord an den
Juden im Zweiten Weltkrieg* (Stuttgart, 1985), 91, 107–12. Sandberger, Blume, and Erwin
Schulz (on Schulz, interrogation of 9 April 1947, NA RG 238, M-1019/R 67/486–87) are
in general agreement about the size and composition of the group in Berlin.

78. Krausnick and Wilhelm, *Truppe des Weltanschauungskrieges*, 141, 146–49. Interrogation of Martin Sandberger, 27 May 1947, NA RG 238, M-1019/R 61/714–16.

79. See literature cited in n. 77. Also Browning, *Fateful Months*, 18–20.

80. Interrogation of Walter Blume, 29 June 1947, NA RG 238, M-1019/R 7/848.

81. Interrogation of Erich Naumann, 15 March 1948, NA RG 238, M-1019/R 49/484.

82. See p. 142 and n. 133 to chap. six.

83. See literature cited in n. 77 above. Also Browning, *Fateful Months*, 18.

84. Interrogation of Heinz Jost, 6 Jan. 1948, NA RG 238, M-1019/R 32/784.

85. What I have done here is to pick out an interesting piece of evidence thus far
unmentioned in the existing debate among historians. I have not tried to reproduce the
entire case. Interrogations of Sandberger, 23, 27 May, 1947, 4 June 1947, 27 Feb. 1948,
NA RG 238, M-1019/R 61/683–764, 780–81, esp. 764, 780–81. Karl Hennicke affidavit,
4 Sept. 1947, NA RG 238, NO-4999. For the broader debate, see Krausnick, "Hitler und
die Befehle," and Streim, "Zur Eröffnung," 88–119.

86. Interrogation of Sandberger, 27 May 1947, NA RG 238, M-1019/R 61/716.

87. Hanns Johst said in February 1940 that he remembered Himmler's admonition
months earlier to his men on the new border of the Reich: *"Bleibet hart! Werdet nicht brutal!"*
Aktenvermerk, 26 Feb. 1940, NA RG 242, T-175/R 88/2611403.

88. For the substance of the meeting between Himmler and Dwinger on 18 June, I
am entirely depending upon Dwinger's memoirs (see n. 93), which are by no means
completely reliable, but there is independent evidence of the meeting itself. Brandt's log
confirms that Dwinger spoke with him about Eastern problems and a "return conversation
with the Reich Führer," NA RG 242, T-581/R 39A, 18 June 1941. For Dwinger's own
later role, and his attempts after the war to put the best light on what he had done, see
David Dallin, *German Rule in Russia, 1941–1945: A Study of Occupation Policies* (Boulder,
1981), 512, 512n.

89. Information taken from Dwinger's SS file, Berlin Document Center. For Himmler's
agreement with Dwinger on agriculture, see Himmler to Dwinger, 15 April 1941, Dwinger
SS file.

90. Edwin Erich Dwinger, *Panzerführer: Tagebuchblätter vom Frankreichfeldzug* (Jena,
1941).

91. Edwin Erich Dwinger, *Der Tod in Polen: Die volksdeutsche Passion* (Jena, 1940), 31.

92. Himmler's notes, 22 May 1940, NA RG 242, T-175/R 94/2615221.

93. Edwin Erich Dwinger, *Die zwölf Gespräche, 1933–1945* (n.p., 1966), 21–22.

94. Himmler's Aktenvermerk, 21 June 1941, NA RG 242, T-175/R 106/2629109.

95. Gerhard Peters affidavit, NA RG 238, T-301/R 99/700, NI-12111.

CHAPTER 8: CLEANSING THE NEW EMPIRE

1. Earl F. Ziemke and Magna E. Bauer, *Moscow to Stalingrad: Decision in the East* (Washington, D.C., 1985), 7, 19–20.

2. See, for example, Francis Harry Hinsley et al., *British Intelligence in the Second World*

War (Cambridge, 1981), II, 67; Ziemke and Bauer, *Moscow to Stalingrad*, 3; Polish General (and Prime Minister) Sikorski's appraisal in David Engel, *In the Shadow of Auschwitz: The Polish Government-in-Exile and the Jews, 1939–1942* (Chapel Hill, N.C., 1987), 114–15.

3. The most detailed account is in Militärgeschichtliches Forschungsamt, ed., *Das Deutsche Reich und der Zweite Weltkrieg*, IV, *Der Angriff auf die Sowjetunion*, ed., Horst Boog et al. (Stuttgart, 1983), 451–86. See also Ziemke and Bauer, *Moscow to Stalingrad*, 3, 22–23; Amnon Sella, " 'Barbarossa': Surprise Attack and Communication," *Journal of Contemporary History* 13 (1978): 555–69.

4. Brandt's log, NA RG 242, T-581/R 39A.

5. *Justiz und NS-Verbrechen: Sammlung deutschen Strafurteilen nationalsozialistischen Tötungsverbrechen 1945–1966* (Amsterdam, 1979), XX, 304–5.

6. Interrogation of Kuno Wirsich, 13 Oct. 1947, NA RG 238, M-1019/R 80/159–60.

7. Helmut Krausnick and Hans-Heinrich Wilhelm, *Die Truppe des Weltanschauungskrieges: Die Einsatzgruppen der Sicherheitspolizei und des SD 1938–1942* (Stuttgart, 1981), 412–13. Meyer-Hetling to Himmler via Greifelt, 15 July 1941, NA RG 242, T-175/R 68/2585097.

8. Brandt's log, NA RG 242, T-581/R 39A, 25 June 1941. Walter Warlimont, *Inside Hitler's Headquarters 1939–1945*, trans. R. H. Barry (London, 1964), 173. Marianne Feuersenger, *Mein Kriegstagebuch: Zwischen Führerhauptquartier und Berliner Wirklichkeit* (Freiburg, 1982), 62.

9. Interrogation of Werner Grothmann, 13 June 1945, NA RG 319, IRR Himmler, XE 000632. R. Raiber, "The Führerhauptquartiere," *After the Battle* 19 (1977): 48.

10. See the numbers and judgment in George H. Stein, *The Waffen-SS: Hitler's Elite Guard at War* (Ithaca, 1966), 120, 289.

11. IMT 37, 687, 180-L. Lange quoted in Krausnick and Wilhelm, *Truppe des Weltanschauungskrieges*, 534–35.

12. Raul Hilberg, *The Destruction of the European Jews* (Chicago, 1961); 2nd enlarged ed., 3 vols. (New York, 1985), I, 292–94, 318, suggests this.

13. There is a substantial dispute among experts over whether the initial instructions (before the war) included the killing of all Jews—men, women, and children—or whether a subsequent order, sometime between early August and September, added women and children to the targets. See Eberhard Jäckel and Jürgen Rohwer, eds., *Der Mord an den Juden im Zweiten Weltkrieg* (Stuttgart, 1985), 88–124; Alfred Streim, "The Tasks of the SS Einsatzgruppen," *Simon Wiesenthal Center Annual* 4 (1987), 311–16; Helmut Krausnick and Alfred Streim in the Correspondence Section, *Simon Wiesenthal Center Annual* 6 (1988), 311–47. Eichmann's proposal of early 1941 (see p. 151) involved the killing of all Jews, and some Jewish women and children were killed from the beginning, which tips the argument toward Krausnick's view. Nonetheless, Streim is not wrong about an intensification of killing in August–September 1941. See pp. 192–205.

14. The RSHA compilation of reports begins with Sammelmeldung UdSSR #1, 23 June 1941, original copy (hitherto lost) in RG 238, Office of Chief of Counsel for War Crimes, box 14, SS 3574; afterward the title changed to Ereignismeldung UdSSR (hereafter EM). On the means of transmission, affidavit of Theodor Paeffgen, 16 Jan. 1946, NA RG 238, NO-5393; affidavit of Heinz Hermann Schubert, 4 Feb. 1947, NA RG 238, NO-2716; affidavit of Kurt Lindow, 21 July 1947, NA RG 238, NO-4327.

15. Examples of Heydrich's instructions in Krausnick and Wilhelm, *Truppe des Weltanschauungskrieges*, 534. Stahlecker's call to Himmler's office, Brandt's log, NA RG 242, T-581/R 39A, 29 June 1941.

16. Ruth Bettina Birn, *Die Höheren SS- und Polizeiführer: Himmlers Vertreter im Reich und*

in den besetzten Gebieten (Düsseldorf, 1986), esp. 172. Berger to Wolff, 11 July 1942, NA RG 238, NO-2410. Interrogation of Ohlendorf, 16 Oct. 1947, NA RG 238, M-1019/R 51/210. Yehoshua Büchler, "Kommandostab Reichsführer SS: Himmler's Personal Murder Brigades in 1941," *Holocaust and Genocide Studies* I (1986): 14–15.

17. Himmler's itinerary in NA RG 242, T-581/R 39A, 30 June 1941. Heydrich's presence in Krausnick and Wilhelm, *Truppe des Weltanschauungskrieges*, 534.

18. Krausnick and Wilhelm, *Truppe des Weltanschauungskrieges*, 534; EM #19, 11 July 1941, NA RG 242, T-175/R 233/2721470. On the units' functions in Grodno, testimony of Eliahu Jezierski in the Grodno trial in Cologne, reprinted in Serge Klarsfeld, ed., *Documents Concerning the Destruction of the Jews of Grodno 1941–1944* (New York, 1988), I, 110.

19. Interrogation of Bräutigam, 25 May 1948, NA RG 238, M-1019/R 9/86.

20. *Halder Diary*, vol. 3, 8, quoted in Ziemke and Bauer, *Moscow to Stalingrad*, 28.

21. See p. 149.

22. Christian Streit, *Keine Kameraden: Die Wehrmacht und die sowjetischen Kriegsgefangenen 1941–1945* (Stuttgart, 1978), 76–87. Militärgeschichtliches Forschungsamt, ed., *Das Deutsche Reich und der Zweite Weltkrieg*, IV, 440–47.

23. IMT 37, 672, 180-L.

24. Heydrich to Jeckeln, Bach, Prützmann, and Korsemann, 2 July 1941, Bundesarchiv Koblenz R 70 Sowjetunion/32, 266. Krausnick and Wilhelm, *Truppe des Weltanschauungskrieges*, 533–34, attribute this strategy to Heydrich, but do not deal with the issue of whether it was planned in advance. For discussion of the significance of the 2 July telegram's instructions regarding the Jews, Krausnick and Wilhelm, *Truppe des Weltanschauungskrieges*, 150–65; Helmut Krausnick, "Hitler und die Befehle an die Einsatzgruppen im Sommer 1941," in Jäckel and Rohwer, eds., *Der Mord an den Juden*, 90–96. Both are more convincing than Alfred Streim, "Zur Eröffnung des allgemeinen Judenvernichtungsbefehls gegenüber den Einsatzgruppen," in Jäckel and Rohwer, ed., *Der Mord an den Juden*, 112–15.

25. IMT 37, 677–78, quote on 682, 180-L. Krausnick and Wilhelm, *Truppe des Weltanschauungskrieges*, 173. On Norkus, Alois Wehner affidavit, 26 Aug. 1947, NA RG 238, NO-4847.

26. IMT 37, 683, 180-L.

27. EM #15, 7 July 1941, NA RG 242, T-175/R 233/2721440. Interrogation of Martin Sandberger, NA RG 238, M-1019/R 61/789.

28. IMT 37, 682–83, 180-L.

29. Ibid., 683, 180-L.

30. EM #14, 6 July 1941, NA RG 242, T-175/R 233/2721430. Gesamtaufstellung der im Bereich des EK. 3 bis zum 1. Dez. 1941 durchgeführten Exekutionen (Jäger Bericht), reprinted in Adalbert Rückerl, ed., *NS-Prozesse* (Karlsruhe, 1971), unpaginated facsimile appendix.

31. EM #17, 9 July 1941, NA RG 242, T-175/R 233/2721454–55. EM #21, 13 July 1941, NA RG 242, T-175/R 233/2721494.

32. EM #24, 16 July 1941, NA RG 242, T-175/R 233/2721537. One area where pogroms were effective was in the city of Lemberg (Lvov)—see p. 174 and n. 36 below. This was by no means the only such case, yet what is striking is that the commanders of the Nazi police units were far from satisfied with later Ukrainian (un)willingness to conduct pogroms. See, for example, EM #47, 9 Aug. 1941; EM #67, 29 Aug. 1941, NA RG 242, T-175/R 233/2721847 and 2722114.

33. Hilberg, *Destruction*, I, 328–31, discusses a variety of fictions used to justify killings.

34. Written statement by Erich von dem Bach-Zelewski, n.d. [1945]; interrogation of

Bach-Zelewski, 30 Oct. 1945, NA RG 238, M-1270/R 1/ 295–96 and 420–21. Bach-Zelewski described a meeting with Himmler at Himmler's headquarters days after the war began. However, contemporary sources put them together at the dinner in Białystok on 1 July, just after "looting" was discovered. Czechoslovakian Military Archive, Prague, A-2-1-3, Kr. 1, War Diary No. 1 of Police Battalion 322, and Kr. Varia, N. Police Regiment, Company Diary. I discount Bach's testimony where he claims that he was opposed to such executions, and that Himmler took jurisdiction away from him. Bach-Zelewski's diary, a copy of which may be found in the Zentrale Stelle der Landesjustizverwaltungen Ludwigsburg, Sammlung Verschiedenes, microfilm #329, is of no help in illuminating this issue, since Bach-Zelewski surrendered the original copy of only the second volume (1943–45). The first volume has apparently been altered to eliminate incriminating material, and, typically, there is no entry for the Himmler–Bach-Zelewski meeting or for the executions—even though Bach-Zelewski mentioned both of them while he was in American captivity just after the war.

35. Czechoslovakian Military Archive, "PZ," A-3-1-7, Nr. 1, and Zentrale Stelle Ludwigsburg, CSSR 397, excerpt quoted in Birn, *Die Höheren SS- und Polizeiführer*, 171n. Krausnick and Wilhelm, *Truppe des Weltanschauungskrieges*, 180–81. On Himmler's instructions, see pp. 220–21.

36. Erwin Schulz affidavit, 13 Aug. 1947, NA RG 238, NO-3644, refers to twenty-five hundred to three thousand killed. EM #24, 16 July 1941, T-175/R 233/2721538, cites an overall total of seven thousand shot by the police and one thousand beaten and jailed by the Ukrainians during the period 30 June–3 July.

37. Affidavit of Robert Barth, 12 Sept. 1947, RG 238, NO-4992. Also Ortskommandantur Ananiev/Staff of 836th Landesschützen Battalion to Korück 553 in Berezovka, 3 Sept. 1941, NA RG 238, NOKW-1702, cited by Hilberg, *Destruction*, II, 330. On the earlier Rumanian purge of Jassy, Martin Gilbert, *The Holocaust: The Jewish Tragedy* (London, 1986), 161–63.

38. Erwin Bingel affidavit, n.d., [1945], NA RG 238, NO-5301.

39. Hilberg, *Destruction*, I, 322–27.

40. This account is based on the collection of documents by Avraham Tory, later secretary of the Jewish council of elders in the Kowno ghetto: particularly "Massacre at the Seventh Fort" and "Total Massacre of Ghetto," exhibits at the trial *U.S.* v. *Kazys Palciauskas*, #81-547-Civ-T-GC, United States District Court, Middle District, Fla. (1983). I am indebted to Michael Wolf for this reference. Tory's collection has now been published as *Surviving the Holocaust: The Kovno Ghetto Diary* (Cambridge, Mass., 1990), 7–14, 23–26. Confirming evidence, report by Karl Jäger, 1 Dec. 1941, in Rückerl, *NS-Verbrechen*, appendix.

41. EM #143, 8 Dec. 1941, NA RG 242, T-175/R 234/2723365.

42. Büchler, "Kommandostab," 14–15.

43. Hilberg, *Destruction*, I, 304–7.

44. Christopher R. Browning, *The Final Solution and the German Foreign Office: A Study of Referat III D of Abteilung Deutschland* (New York, 1978), 52–53. Von Killinger to Abteilung Deutschland, 1 Sept. 1941, NA RG 238, T-1139/R 41/106, NG-3989.

45. EM #52, 14 Aug. 1941, NA RG 238, NO-4540. Erdmannsdorff Aufzeichnung, 15 Oct. 1941, NA RG 238, T-1139/R 41/107–8, NG-3989.

46. Himmler speech, T-175/R 109/2632686–90. For Sicily, Michael R. Marrus, *The Holocaust in History* (Hanover, 1987), 26.

47. Himmler's second speech, NA RG 242, T-175/R 109/2632683–85, quoted and trans. by Stein, *Waffen-SS*, 126–27.

48. Brandt's log entries, "Berger . . . Bildmappe gegen Bolschewismus," NA RG 242 T-581/R 39A, 14 July 1941. "Bei der Besprechung RFSS-Gruf Berger zugegen. Thema: Heft über den Kampf gegen Untermenschen," T-581/R 39A, 18 July 1941. Interrogation of Berger, 30 Oct. 1947, NA RG 238, M-1019/R 6/665. Brandt's log, "Eggers hat unmittelbaren Auftrage vom Führer, Durchsicht der Bildmappe gegen den Untermenschen," T-581/R 39A, 2 Oct. 1941. Interrogation of Günther d'Alquen, 16 Feb. 1948, NA RG 238, M-1019/R 2/438–40. For the publication itself, NA RG 238, NO-1805.

49. *Die Völker des Ostraumes: Die Bücherei des Ostraumes*, ed. Georg Leibbrandt (Berlin, 1942), 31.

50. Vertrauliche Information, 21 Feb. 1942, NA RG 238, 3244-PS.

51. Unterredung des Führers mit Marschall Kvaternik im Führerhauptquartier, 21 July 1941, reprinted in Andreas Hillgruber, ed., *Staatsmänner und Diplomaten bei Hitler: Vertrauliche Aufzeichnungen über Unterredungen mit Vertretern des Auslandes 1939–1941* (Frankfurt am Main, 1967), I, 610, 613–14.

52. "Der Sowjetmensch," *Völkischer Beobachter*, 19 July 1941, 1. On 1940, see pp. 112–13 above.

53. Quoted in Gilbert, *Holocaust*, 186.

54. According to Kajum Khan, the Soviet Union gained only loose control over Turkestan during the 1920s, and many Turkmen who became nominal communist officials remained loyal to their original cause. They were not liquidated until 1938. Interrogation of Prince Veli Kajum Khan, 27 Feb. 1947, NA RG 238, M-1019/R 33/222.

55. Interrogation of Kajum Khan, 27 Feb. 1947, NA RG 238, M-1019/R 33/220–39.

56. On the Asiatics, for example, EM #36 28 July 1941, NA RG 242, T-175/R 233/2721691; EM #128 9 Oct. 1941, NA RG 242, T-175/R 234/27222859. On Mogilev, testimony of Paul Popp, 26 June 1961, Hauptverhandlung Dr. Emil Schönpflug, Kreisgericht Wels (Austria), 11 Vr 767/60, Hv 33/61, 59. On Kiev, interrogations of Dr. Wilhelm Gustav Schüppe, April 1945, NA RG 153, entry 143, box 575, folder 21-11. I have adjusted downward the total number of fatalities listed in the document (130,000), because the latter is based on a misdating of the length of Schüppe's stay in Kiev.

57. See p.151.

58. Stein, *Waffen-SS*, 179–96. On the use of the Turkmen, see NA RG 242, T-354/R 161/3806724–7078.

59. Unless otherwise noted, the following discussion of the meeting of 16 July 1941 is drawn from Bormann's minutes in IMT 38, 86–94, 221-L.

60. David Dallin, *German Rule in Russia, 1941–1945: A Study of Occupation Policies* (Boulder, 1981), 127.

61. Lammers had shown some sympathy for Rosenberg's position in earlier Rosenberg-Himmler disputes. He had written to Himmler on 8 May 1941 to urge him to coordinate his activities with Rosenberg. See Himmler's response of 28 May 1941, NA RG 242, T-175/R 123/2648801.

62. Erlass des Führers über die polizeiliche Sicherung der neu besetzten Ostgebiete, copy in NA RG 238, T-1139/R 21/751, NG-1688: also in IMT 29, 236–37. For the background to the dispute between Rosenberg and Himmler over jurisdiction in the East, see Rosenberg to Lammers, 27 Aug. 1941, NA RG 238, NO-3726.

63. Dallin, *German Rule*, 127–28. Rosenberg to Lammers, 27 Aug. 1941, NA RG 238, NO-3726. Interrogation of Kuno Wirsich, 15 Oct. 1947, NA RG 238, M-1019/R 80/238.

64. Himmler's acknowledgment of Bormann's minutes, Himmler to Bormann, 22 July 1941, NA RG 242, T-175/R 123/2648662.

65. Berger to Himmler, 2 July 1941, NA RG 238, NO-029.

66. Himmler to Globocnik, 14 July 1941, Globocnik SS file, Berlin Document Center.

67. Appointment and Himmler's Vermerk, written in Lublin, 21 July 1941, both in Globocnik SS file.

68. Müller to Hofmann, 5 Oct. 1941, NA RG 238, NO-5875.

69. Baedeker, *Das Generalgouvernement* (Berlin, 1942), 135–36.

70. Vermerk, 21 July 1941, Globocnik SS file. Kleinmann to Himmler, 7 March 1942, Himmler Collection, Hoover Institution, Stanford University, box 11, folder 332.

71. Fähndrich (RFV) speech, 2 May 1941, at Interior Ministry, NA RG 238, NO-5006, p. 11. Himmler to Lorenz and Heydrich, 11 July 1941, NA RG 238, NO-4274.

72. B. K. Schultz to Hofmann, 4 Aug. 1941; Hofmann to Scholtz, 8 Aug. 1941, NA RG 238, Office of Chief of Counsel for War Crimes, Berlin Branch, box 27, SS-5735.

73. Aktenvermerk für Parteigenosse Friedrichs, 16 Aug. 1941, Akten der Parteikanzlei, Institut für Zeitgeschichte microfiche 117/08066.

74. Interrogation of Johann Sporrenberg, 2 Sept. 1945, Globocnik file, U.S. Army Intelligence and Security Command, obtained through Freedom of Information Act request. Interrogation of Kuno Wirsich, 13 Oct. 1947, NA RG 238, M-1019/R 80/197.

75. Brandt's log, NA RG 242, T-581/R 39A, 20 July 1941.

76. Müller to Hofmann, 5 Oct. 1941, NA RG 238, NO-5875.

77. The minutes of this meeting were taken by the Foreign Ministry's liaison to Hitler's headquarters, Ambassador Hewel. Parts of them are illegible, and one key page is entirely missing. Most of what can be read is reprinted by Hillgruber, ed., *Staatsmänner*, 609–15, esp. 611, 614. I also rely partly on the reading of Klaus Hildebrand, *The Third Reich* (London, 1984), 69.

78. Frank, Diensttagebuch, 22 July 1941 (not in published version), NA RG 242, T-992/R 5. This argument is similar to the point made, on the basis of different evidence, by Herman Graml, "Zur Genesis der 'Endlösung,'" in *Der Judenpogrom 1938: Von der "Reichskristallnacht" zum Völkermord*, ed. Walter H. Pehle (Frankfurt am Main, 1988), 173.

CHAPTER 9: HEYDRICH'S PLAN

1. Glücks to Wander, 14 Jan. 1941, Höss SS file, Berlin Document Center. Hoess [sic] affidavit, 14 March 1946, NA RG 238, NO-1210.

2. Höss Aufzeichnungen, Institut für Zeitgeschichte, F 13/5, 279. Abschrift der Beurteilungsnotiz anlässlich der Dienstreise des SS-Gruf. v. Herff durch das General Gouvernement im Mai 1943, Höss SS file.

3. Affidavit of 14 March 1946, NA RG 238, NO-1210. Rudolf Hoess, *Commandant of Auschwitz* (New York, 1961), 11.

4. Christopher R. Browning, *Fateful Months: Essays on the Emergence of the Final Solution* (New York, 1985), 23, reaches this conclusion as well.

5. "Vernichtungsstellen im Osten," in original German version of Höss's memoirs, Institut für Zeitgeschichte, F 13/5, 244.

6. Hoess, *Commandant of Auschwitz*, 173.

7. Various attempts to redate this meeting are off the mark. Höss could not have mistaken a summer-1942 meeting with Himmler for 1941—first, because Himmler's 1942 appointment book, which exists, contains no such entry, and, second, because Höss was already gassing Jews then.

It is most unlikely that Himmler set the Final Solution in motion before 22 June.

Organizing the strategy for the Waffen-SS and the *Einsatzgruppen* must have taken a considerable amount of Himmler's time, and he had to see how successful the initial attack against the U.S.S.R. would be. Himmler left the capital for East Prussia on 25 June and did not return until 13 July. On 15 July he went back to East Prussia. At most he went to Berlin for one brief visit during August, though we cannot be sure where he was on several days late that month.

Brandt was in Berlin on 3–4 Aug., returning to East Prussia on the 5th. Whether Himmler was with him is unclear. Wolff's telegram, sent from Himmler's train in East Prussia to Heydrich on 4 Aug. 1941, mentions that he had just obtained Himmler's agreement to a compromise with Foreign Minister Ribbentrop, who was also in East Prussia. The telegram at least suggests that Himmler was also in East Prussia on 4 Aug. NA RG 242, T-175/R 426/2970407. On 21, 22, and 24 Aug. Himmler did not appear for his customary sessions with Brandt at his field headquarters, but he may have been ill. See Brandt's telephone call with Baumert (Gesundheit RF), 21 Aug. 1941, NA RG 242, T-581/R 39A. Dates in September are too late for the meeting, since the first test gassing at Auschwitz occurred on 3 Sept. What is left is 13–15 July 1941.

8. Hoess, *Commandant of Auschwitz*, 173. IMT 11, 398. Also, for a shorter but entirely consistent version, Höss's private conversation with Nuremberg psychologist Gilbert, in G. M. Gilbert, *Nuremberg Diary* (New York, 1947), 149–50.

9. Höss affidavit, 14 March 1946, NA RG 238, NO-1210.

10. Hoess, *Commandant of Auschwitz*, 135.

11. Interrogation of Gerhard Maurer, 13 and 18 March 1947, NA RG 238, M-1019/R 45/167 and 194.

12. In *Fateful Months*, 23–26, Browning does as well as one can with Eichmann's contradictory accounts, but in my opinion errs by according Eichmann's version roughly equal weight with Höss's. Eichmann was trying to recapitulate events almost twenty years earlier, and trying to minimize his own role.

13. See pp. 185–87.

14. See p. 139.

15. Hoess, *Commandant of Auschwitz*, 174. Daluege telegram to Himmler, 28 July 1941, NA RG 242, T-175/R 112/2637751.

16. Prützmann to Himmler, 28 July 1941, NA RG 242, T-175/R 112/2637749. Itinerary in NA RG 242, T-175/R 112/2637747. At the 16 July meeting at Hitler's headquarters, Rosenberg had pressed hard for Hitler's approval of Lohse's appointment. Göring expressed opposition, Hitler a degree of skepticism. IMT 38, 90, L-221.

17. EM #53, 15 Aug. 1941, NA RG 238, NO-4539. Daluege's telegram to Himmler, 28 July 1941, NA RG 242, T-175/R 112/2637751.

18. EM #48, 10 Aug. 1941, NA RG 242, T-175/R 233/2721867.

19. Gabriel Ziwian's affidavit, 1 Oct. 1942, and his Report Concerning the Jews of Latvia, NA RG 84, American Consulate Geneva, Confidential file 1942, 800 (attached to Squire to Harrison, 29 Oct. 1942).

20. Minsk is indicated in the itinerary, but Brandt's log confirms the trip to Baranowicze, and Bach-Zelewski, who did not volunteer any information about a meeting with Himmler in Baranowicze at this time, nonetheless confirms that his office was in Baranowicze. Itinerary, NA RG 242, T-175/R 112/2637748; NA RG 242, T-581/R 39A, 31 July 1941. Interrogation of Bach-Zelewski, NA RG 238, M-1270/R 1/296. Conclusive evidence also in *Unsere Ehre heisst Treue: Kriegstagebuch des Kommandostabes Reichsführer SS: Tätigkeitsberichte der 1. und 2. SS-Inf. Brigade, der 1. SS-Kav.-Brigade und von Sonderkommandos der SS* (Vienna, 1965), 23.

21. Interrogation of Bach-Zelewski, 19 June 1947, NA RG 238, M-1019/R 4/133–36, 153. Bach-Zelewski's request for *Fronteneinsatz*, 18 March 1941, in log of Himmler's correspondence, NA RG 242, T-581/R 45A.

22. Kommandobefehl #19, NA RG 242, T-175/R 109/2632873. Himmler telegram to Bach-Zelewski, NA RG 242, T-175/R 109/2632872. *Unsere Ehre*, 20. Kommandosonderbefehl, 28 July 1941, NA RG 242, T-175/R 124/2598661–64.

23. Reitende Abteilung, SS-Kav. Rgt. 2, 1 Aug. 1941, NA RG 242, T-354/R 168/3818936. Interrogation of Bach-Zelewski, 19 June 1947, NA RG 238, M-1019/R 4/153. Bach-Zelewski to Wolff, 23 Aug. 1941, Bach-Zelewski SS file, Berlin Document Center.

24. Quote from interrogation of Bach-Zelewski, 19 June 1947, NA RG 238, M-1019/R 4/153. Bach-Zelewski to Wolff, 23 Aug. 1941, Bach-Zelewski SS file, Berlin Document Center.

25. Brandt's log, NA RG 242, T-581/R 39A, 31 July 1941. Heydrich's appointment with Göring, 6:15–7:15 p.m. (from Göring's appointment book) in Hermann Weiss, "Die Aufzeichnungen Hermann Görings im Institut für Zeitgeschichte," *Vierteljahrshefte für Zeitgeschichte* 31 (1983), 366.

26. Text from Raul Hilberg, ed., *Documents of Destruction: Germany and Jewry 1933–45* (London, 1972), 88–89; text also in NA RG 238, 710-PS.

27. Luther Aufzeichnung, 21 Aug. 1942, NA RG 238, NG-2586J, cited by Gerald Fleming, *Hitler and the Final Solution* (Berkeley, 1984; German original, 1982), 46n. Heydrich's statement came at the Wannsee Conference, according to Luther, who was present.

28. Göring to Himmler, 26 Aug. 1941, NA RG 238, NO-1019. That Göring was unhappy with Himmler's aggrandizement of the SS's economic activities in the East is obvious from this letter. Rosenberg also said to Lammers that Göring shared his views about the necessity of a unified administration in the East. See Rosenberg to Lammers, 27 Aug. 1941, NA RG 238, NO-3726. For Göring's statements on Jews, see Browning, *Fateful Months*, 22.

29. On Müller's message to the *Einsatzgruppen*, see Helmut Krausnick and Hans-Heinrich Wilhelm, *Die Truppe des Weltanschauungskrieges: Die Einsatzgruppen der Sicherheitspolizei und des SD 1938–1942* (Stuttgart, 1981), 540; Fleming, *Hitler and the Final Solution*, 73–74.

30. IMT 33, 197, 3839-PS.

31. Lohse's draft, NA RG 238, NO-4539.

32. Stahlecker to Lohse, 6 Aug. 1941, Latvian State Archives, Riga, discovered by Gerald Fleming and quoted extensively by Hermann Graml, "Zur Genesis der 'Endlösung,' " in *Der Judenpogrom 1938: Von der "Reichskristallnacht" zum Völkermord*, ed. Walter H. Pehle (Frankfurt am Main, 1988), 170.

33. NA RG 238, 1138-PS.

34. Himmler's itinerary, NA RG 242, T-175/R 112/2637745–46.

35. Shalom Cholawsky, "The Judenrat in Minsk," in Yisrael Gutman and Cynthia Haft, eds., *Patterns of Jewish Leadership in Nazi Europe 1933–1945: Proceedings of the Third Yad Vashem International Historical Conference* (Jerusalem, 1979), 115.

36. EM #17, 9 July 1941, T-175/R 233/2721450. Dorsch to Rosenberg, 10 July 1941, NA RG 238, 022-PS. EM #21, 13 July 1941, T-175/R 233/2721493. EM #32, 24 July 1941, NA RG 242, T-175/R 233/2721638. Hersh Smolar, *The Minsk Ghetto: Soviet-Jewish Partisans Against the Nazis* (New York, 1989), 15–16.

37. Cholawsky, "Judenrat," 115. Smolar, *Minsk Ghetto*, 17–21.

38. EM #33, 25 July 1941, NA RG 238, NO-4438.

39. Description of Minsk and the Lenin House in mid-August 1941 in "Sowjetische

Städte," *Völkischer Beobachter*, 14 Aug. 1941, 8. Himmler's lodging in the Lenin House according to Bach-Zelewski's account in "Leben eines SS-Generals," *Aufbau*, 23 Aug. 1946.

40. Bach-Zelewski statement, n.d. [1945], NA RG 238, M-1270/R 1/296. Bach-Zelewski's account presented in "Leben," and quoted by Raul Hilberg, *The Destruction of the European Jews* (Chicago, 1961); 2nd expanded ed., 3 vols. (New York, 1985), II, 332.

41. Testimony of Paul Dinter, 3 April and 15 April 1959, Hauptverhandlung Dr. Egon Schönpflug, Landgericht Wien (Austria), 9Vr $\frac{767/60}{11}$.

42. Bach-Zelewski's account presented in "Leben." Testimony of Paul Dinter, 3 April 1959, Hauptverhandlung Dr. Egon Schönpflug, Landgericht Wein, 9Vr $\frac{767/60}{11}$. Bradfisch quoted by Fleming, *Hitler and the Final Solution*, 51.

43. Bach-Zelewski, "Leben."

44. If Höss's meeting with Himmler was in mid-July, then the Höss-Eichmann meeting was in mid-August. In his testimony at Nuremberg, Höss testified that Eichmann had visited him about four weeks later. IMT 11, 396–422, cited by Browning, *Fateful Months*, 23. On one occasion Eichmann admitted that Heydrich informed him of the Führer's order two or three months after the invasion of the Soviet Union, or in any case in late summer. See Browning, *Fateful Months*, 24. Hoess, *Commandant of Auschwitz*, 174.

45. Hoess, *Commandant of Auschwitz*, 174–75. There is no entry for Höss in Himmler's correspondence log for 1941.

46. See pp. 88–89, 102–3.

47. Ernst Klee, *"Euthanasia" in NS-Staat: Die "Vernichtung lebensunswerten Lebens"* (Stuttgart, 1983), 334–35, 339–40. Henry Friedlander, "Das nationalsozialistische Euthanasieprogramm," in *Geschichte und Verantwortung*, ed. Aurelius Freytag, Boris Marte, and Thomas Stern (Vienna, 1988), 286. Friedlander's forthcoming study of the euthanasia program should have additional material on Hitler's termination of the euthanasia gassings.

48. Müller an die Staatspolizeileitstellen et al., 27 Aug. 1941, NA RG 242, T-175/R 426/2956026–27.

49. Henry Friedlander has stressed this point in conversations with me.

50. Werth (RF mit Plan Heydrich einverstanden), NA RG 242, T-581/R 39A.

51. Morgen affidavit, 13 July 1946, SS(A)-65, cited by Raul Hilberg, *The Destruction of the European Jews* (Chicago, 1961), 562. Interrogation of Morgen, NA RG 238, M-1019/R 47/590.

52. Quoted by Browning, *Fateful Months*, 26.

53. Gorgas affidavit, 23 Feb. 1947, NA RG 238, NO-3010.

54. Quoted by Yitzhak Arad, *Belzec, Sobibor, Treblinka: The Operation Reinhard Death Camps* (Bloomington, Ind., 1987), 17.

55. Brack to Himmler, 23 June 1942, NA RG 238, NO-205.

56. Schmitt to Himmler, 2 Sept. 1941; Himmler to Schmitt, 4 Sept. 1941, NA RG 242, T-581/R 45A; summaries only, log of Himmler's correspondence; the originals were apparently destroyed.

57. Interrogation of Waldemar Hoven, 16 Oct. 1946, NA RG 238, M-1019/R 29/445–47, 461. Hoven placed the transport of Jews in the summer or early fall of 1941. On the general transfer of concentration-camp prisoners to the euthanasia facilities (Aktion 14f13), Klee, *Euthanasia*, 345–55.

58. Interrogation of Hubert Karl, 21 May 1947, NA RG 238, M-1019/R 33/945. Brandt's log, NA RG 242, T-581/R 39A, 10 Sept. 1941. On Pohl, Kammler, and Vogel, see Hilberg, *Destruction* (1985 edition), III, 865–69. Vogel had been involved in developing plans for Auschwitz even earlier. See Himmler's correspondence log, Pohl to Himmler, 25 July 1941: "betr. Planning Auschwitz. Bericht des Stubaf. Vogel mit Plan übers.," NA RG 242,

T-581/45A. Wolfgang Scheffler has already pointed out that the plans for Maidanek and Birkenau were drawn up and implementation begun at the same time, Sept. 1941. Wolfgang Scheffler, "Chełmno, Sobibor, Belzec, und Maidanek," in Jäckel and Rohwer, eds., *Der Mord an den Juden*, 147. The same is true of Belzec. On the plans for Birkenau, see n. 74 below.

59. Czeslaw Rajca and Anna Wisniewska, *Maidanek Concentration Camp*, trans. Anna Zagorska (Lublin, 1983), esp. 11–13, 24, 81–82. Elizabeth B. White, "Majdanek: Cornerstone of Himmler's SS Empire in the East," paper presented at American Historical Association meeting, San Francisco, 30 Dec. 1989.

60. On Belzec, see Adalbert Rückerl, ed., *NS Vernichtungslager im Spiegel deutscher Strafprozesse* (Munich, 1978), 132–45; Hilberg, *Destruction*, III, 875–76. Brandt's daily log, with telephone calls 15 Oct., to Pohl, report on Globocnik; 17 Oct., to Pohl, report on Globocnik; 20 Oct., to Pohl, work with Globocnik, all NA RG 242, T-581/R 39A. On the nature of the cooperation and the textiles, interrogation of Georg Loerner, 20 Sept. 1947, NA RG 238, M-1019/R 42/946. Loerner dated these events "approximately 1941." Brandt's log notations (above) pin this down to Oct. 1941. Arad, *Belzec, Sobibor, Treblinka*, 24–25.

61. Arad, *Belzec, Sobibor, Treblinka*, 24–25, 17. Interrogation of Johann Sporrenberg, 2 Sept. 1945, Globocnik file, U.S. Army Intelligence and Security Command, obtained through Freedom of Information Act.

62. Commanding General, Eighth Service Command, ASF Dallas, to Provost Marshal, 21 May 1945, account of Willi Kempf, POW, NA RG 153, entry 143, box 571, folder 19–99.

63. Browning, *Fateful Months*, 60. *Nationalsozialistische Massentötungen durch Giftgas*, ed. Eugen Kogon et al. (Frankfurt am Main, 1983), 81–82. Zentrale Stelle der Justizverwaltungen Ludwigsburg, *Sammlung UdSSR*, no. 7, 19.

64. Browning, *Fateful Months*, 61–62.

65. Ibid., 62.

66. See p. 214.

67. See Höppner to Eichmann, 16 July 1941, reprinted in Lucjan Dobroszycki, ed., *The Chronicle of the Lodz Ghetto 1941–1944* (New Haven, 1984) lii–liii.

68. Hilberg, *Destruction*, I, 212–14.

69. Browning, *Fateful Months*, 30. Uwe Dietrich Adam, "The Gas Chambers," in François Furet, ed., *Unanswered Questions: Nazi Germany and the Genocide of the Jews* (New York, 1989), 142. There are slight variations on the date of the first gassings, but most sources favor 8 Dec.

70. Hoess, *Commandant of Auschwitz*, 175. Interrogation of Höss, 14 May 1946, NA RG 238, M-1019/R 28/63.

71. On Tesch and Stabenow, Gerhard Peters affidavit, NA RG 238, T-301/R 99/701, NI-12111. On Degesch, *8 Vorträge aus dem Arbeitsgebiet der Degesch* (n.p., 1942), 30, copy in NA RG 238, NI-9098. Interrogation of Höss, 14 May 1946, NA RG 238, M-1019/R 28/623–25.

72. Hoess, *Commandant of Auschwitz*, 173. See also Yehuda Bauer, "Auschwitz," in Jäckel and Rohwer, eds., *Der Mord an den Juden*, 167–68.

73. Hoess, *Commandant of Auschwitz*, 175. *From the History of KL Auschwitz* (New York, 1982), I, 190.

74. Heerdt-Lingler to Friedrich Boos, 27 June 1941, and to SS Haushalt und Bauten, Konzentrationslager Auschwitz, 1 July 1941, NA RG 238, NI-14159–60. Adam, "The Gas Chambers," in Furet, *Unanswered Questions*, 149.

75. Hilberg, *Destruction*, III, 886. Heerdt-Lingler to Friedrich Boos, 21 Nov. 1941, and to Degesch, 2 Dec. 1941, NA RG 238, NI-14163–64.

76. Interrogation of Bach-Zelewski, 19 June 1947, NA RG 238, M-1019/R 4/143–44.

77. Lammers to Gürtner, 7 June 1941, NA RG 238, T-1139/R 16/515, NG-1123.

78. Himmler to Greiser, 18 Sept. 1941, NA RG 242, T-175/R 54/2568695.

79. Hitler's whereabouts in Andreas Hillgruber, *Hitlers Strategie: Politik und Kriegführung 1940–1941* (Frankfurt am Main, 1965), 694. As it happens, Brandt's log is missing for 11–17 Sept., which makes it harder to place Himmler. But Himmler's notes list a conference with Pohl at the Führer's headquarters on 11 Sept., phone conversations from East Prussia on 16 Sept., and departure from Lötzen Airport in East Prussia on 18 Sept. See NA RG 242, T-175/R 94/2615287; T-84/R 26/no frame nos.; and T-175/R 112/2637724. He appears to have been in East Prussia for the entire period.

80. Bormann's list of Hitler's appointments, NA RG 242, T-84/R 387/515. Heydrich SS file, Berlin Document Center, promotion dated 27 Sept. 1941.

81. Arad, *Belzec, Sobibor, Treblinka*, 13. That "Operation Reinhard" was named after Heydrich has recently been contested by Uwe Dietrich Adam, who questioned the logic and noted the variant spelling "Reinhardt" in some of the documents. He suggested that it referred to State Secretary Reinhardt in the Finance Ministry. See Adam, "Gas Chambers," 144. The logic of naming the operation after Heydrich is clear—he had devised the original plan to concentrate the Jews along the eastern border of the Government General, and with his subordinates had developed the plan for the elimination of the Jews from the continent. Brandt, after all, wrote in his log that Himmler was in agreement with Heydrich's plan.

Himmler himself sometimes misspelled Heydrich's first name. See Richard Breitman and Shlomo Aronson, "Gaps in the Himmler Papers," in George O. Kent, ed., *Archives, Archivists, and Historians: Essays in Modern German History and Archival Policy* (Fairfax, Va., 1991).

82. Hitler's remarks in Adolf Hitler, *Monologe im Führerhauptquartier 1941–1944: Die Aufzeichnungen Heinrich Heims*, ed. Werner Jochmann (Hamburg, 1980), 68.

83. Albert Seaton, *The German Army 1933–45* (London, 1983), 178. Earl F. Ziemke and Magna E. Bauer, *Moscow to Stalingrad: Decision in the East* (Washington, D.C., 1985), 36–39. Militärgeschichtliches Forschungsamt, ed., *Das Deutsche Reich und der Zweite Weltkrieg*. IV, *Der Angriff auf die Sowjetunion*, ed., Horst Boog et al. (Stuttgart, 1983), 679.

84. Arno Mayer, *Why Did the Heavens Not Darken?: The "Final Solution" in History* (New York, 1988), 279, 289, 299. Martin Broszat, "Hitler und die Genesis der 'Endlösung': Aus Anlass der Thesen von David Irving," *Vierteljahrshefte für Zeitgeschichte* 25 (1977): 753n26. Uwe Dietrich Adam, *Judenpolitik im Dritten Reich* (Düsseldorf, 1972), 313–14. The seminal work in rebutting this view has been done by Christopher Browning, "Zur Genesis der 'Endlösung': Eine Antwort an Martin Broszat," *Vierteljahrshefte für Zeitgeschichte* 29 (1981), 97–109.

85. *"Für den Frieden ist Lublin als Standort für die Waffen-SS und Polizei zunächst in Aussicht genommen worden. Die Vorbereitungen für diese Baumassnahmen sind bereits von mir im Jahre 1941 für die Zeit nach dem Kriege zurückgestellt worden."* Himmler to Kleinmann, 14 April 1942, Himmler Collection, Hoover Institution, Stanford University, box 11, folder 332.

CHAPTER 10: RIVALS INTO COLLABORATORS

1. On 20 Sept. 1941 General von Roques announced that there was *no longer* any justification in the area of Rear Army Group North for unilateral arrests and mass executions on the part of non-German police officials or the native *Schutzmannschaften*. Arrests and executions could only be carried out by non-Germans at the express orders of a German office, especially the higher SS and police leader or the Security Police. Bundesarchiv-Militärarchiv Freiburg RH 2628545.

2. Himmler's itinerary, NA RG 242, T-175/R 112/2637724–27.

3. Kriegstagebuch Nr. 1 des SS- und Polizeistandortführers Libau, Bundesarchiv Koblenz, BA R 70 Sowjetunion/12, reprinted in Helmut Krausnick and Hans-Heinrich Wilhelm, *Die Truppe des Weltanschauungskrieges: Die Einsatzgruppen der Sicherheitspolizei und des SD 1938–1942* (Stuttgart, 1981), 571; SS Sturmbannführer With, Bericht für die Zeit 16–21 Mai, NA RG 242, T-175/R 66/2582809.

4. Krausnick and Wilhelm, *Truppe des Weltanschauungskrieges*, 571. EM #126, 29 Oct. 1941, NA RG 242, T-175/R 234/2723062. Kügler to Dietrich, 2 Oct. 1941, Bundesarchiv Koblenz R 70 Sowjetunion/20, in Krausnick and Wilhelm, *Truppe des Weltanschauungskrieges*, 574–75.

5. Interrogations of Lohse, 20 Oct. 1947 and 20 Nov. 1947, NA RG 238, M-1019/R 43/792–93 and 43/819. Lohse's provisional guidelines on the Jewish question had conceded superior jurisdiction to the Security Police.

6. Boenner draft, undated, to the Gebietskommissare, NA RG 238, 3658-PS.

7. Jäger Bericht, 1 Dec. 1941, reprinted in Adalbert Rückerl, ed., *NS-Prozesse* (Karlsruhe, 1971), unpaginated facsimile appendix.

8. Alois Wehner affidavit, 26 Aug. 1947, NA RG 238, NO-4847. On Schaulen, see Gewecke memos of 3 and 10 Sept. 1941, NA RG 238, 3661-PS and 3662-PS.

9. Interrogation of Bräutigam, 26 May 1948, NA RG 238, M-1019/R 9/92.

10. Wetzel referred to Lohse's report of 4 Oct. 1941, concerning the solution of the Jewish problem, in his own draft memo for Rosenberg, n.d. [October 1941], NA RG 238, NO-996–97; the original Lohse report apparently has not survived. Lohse's suggestions and comments can be inferred from Wetzel's response. See also p. 210.

11. NA RG 238, NO-365, quoted in Gerald Fleming, *Hitler and the Final Solution* (Berkeley, 1984; German original, 1982), 70–71.

12. NA RG 238, NO-997; the draft is marked: to be submitted again in four weeks.

13. Interrogation of Georg Leibbrandt, 24 Sept. 1947, NA RG 238, M-1019/R 41/598. Leibbrandt might have had reason to blame Wetzel, since he was trying to diminish his own responsibility, but Bräutigam's testimony is generally consistent. Interrogation of Bräutigam, 15 Jan. 1948, NA RG 238, M-1019/R 9/24–25.

14. Albert Seaton, *The German Army 1933–45* (London, 1983), 178. Koeppen's notes, NA RG 242, T-84/R387/770, cited by Timothy Patrick Mulligan, *The Politics of Illusion and Empire: German Occupation Policy in the Soviet Union, 1942–43* (New York, 1988), 11.

15. Widmann, misspelled "Dr. Wittmann," in NA RG 242, T-175/R 112/2637717. On Widmann's background and inventions, see Christopher R. Browning, *Fateful Months: Essays on the Emergence of the Final Solution* (New York, 1985), 58, 60–62. On the gassings in the East, at the asylum at Mogilev, *Nationalsozialistische Massentötungen durch Giftgas*, ed. Eugen Kogon et al. (Frankfurt am Main, 1983), 81–82. Less specific, but generally confirming the location and the general date, EM #108, 9 Oct. 1941, NA RG 242, T-175/R 234/2722861.

16. Again, this conclusion is based on Himmler's approval of the assignment of Son-

derführer to Friedrich Jeckeln, higher SS and police leader for the Ukraine, comparable to the assignment of men to Globocnik, at virtually the same time. See the log of Himmler's correspondence, summaries only, NA RG 242, T-581/R 45A, and p. 199 above.

17. In his 25 Oct. letter to Lohse, Wetzel gave Brack's expert opinion on precisely this point. See NA RG 238, NO-365, quoted in Fleming, *Hitler and the Final Solution*, 70–71.

18. Interrogation of Rudi Karl August Ferdinand Paltzo, 27–28 July 1965, Trial of Kuno Callsen, et al., Landgericht Darmstadt, copies from Zentrale Stelle der Justizverwaltungen Ludwigsburg, 207 ARZ 419/62, Sonderband: Vernehmungen, 1,489–90. Photocopies in my possession. Report by Captain Girus Koch, deputy of Reichsministerium für die besetzten Ostgebieten, 5 Oct. 1941, NA RG 238, 053-PS.

19. Interrogations of Julius Bauer, 2 Aug. 1965, and Rudi Paltzo, 27–28 July 1965, Callsen Trial, Ludwigsburg 207 AR-Z 419/62, 85–87 and 1,491–93. Photocopies in my possession.

20. Interrogation of Heinrich August Bernhard Huhn, 16 March 1966, Trial of Kuno Callsen et al., Ludwigsburg 207 AR-Z 419/62, photocopies in my possession. EM #106, 7 Oct. 1941, NA RG 242, T-175/R 234/2722806. Interrogation of Viktor Trill, 25 June 1960, Trial of Kuno Callsen, Ludwigsburg 207 AR-Z 419/62, 12–13, photocopies in my possession. Based on the course of events Trill described, Blobel's remarks to the drivers occurred on the evening of 29 Sept. after the first day's executions.

21. Interrogation of Huhn, 16 March 1966.

22. This description is based primarily on the highly detailed testimony in the interrogation of Viktor Trill, 25 June 1960. Other participants provide support for some particulars—see, for example, interrogation of Huhn, 16 March 1966; interrogation of Erich Otto Heidborn, 31 Jan. 1966, Callsen Trial, Ludwigsburg 207 AR-Z 419/62, 687–88.

23. EM #106, 7 Oct. 1941, NA RG 242, T-175/R 234/2722806.

24. Himmler's itinerary, NA RG 242, T-175/R 112/2637715–16. On Zhitomir, EM #27, 17 July 1941, and EM #106, 7 Oct. 1941, NA RG 242, T-175/R 233 and 234/2721571 and 2722808–9. On "Kiroffo," interrogation of Kurt Geissler, 27 Nov. 1941, NA RG 238, M-1019/R 20/815.

25. Interrogation of Heidborn, 31 Jan. 1966.

26. See interrogation of Ludwig Maurer, 13 Feb. 1964, Callsen Trial, Ludwigsburg 207 AR-Z 419/62, photocopy in my possession. Maurer testified that the killings went on for eight to fourteen days. Trill also testified in his interrogation (25 June 1960) that he had participated in further executions. EM #111, 12 Oct. 1941, NA RG 242, T-175/R 234/2722835, mentions that functionaries, saboteurs, and plunderers were executed at Babi Yar. Eyewitnesses, however, later testified that Soviet sailors were killed there. See the testimony of Natalija Tkatschenko and Nadjeshda Gorbatschew, 13 Feb. 1967, Callsen Trial, Ludwigsburg 207 AR-Z 419/62, photocopies in my possession. Other units carried out tens of thousands of executions at Babi Yar during the next two years. Soviet authorities now estimate the total killed there at well over one hundred thousand.

27. Reichenau's statement in NA RG 238, T-1139/R 4/396, NOKW-309.

28. Himmler's itinerary, NA RG 242, T-175/R 112/2637715–17. On Krivoi Rog, Lagebericht der Feldkommandantur 538, 14 Sept. 1941, *Sammlung UdSSR*, Ludwigsburg, no. 2, pt. III, 41, frame nos. 768–78.

29. Robert Barth affidavit, 12 Sept. 1947, NA RG 238, NO-4992. Ohlendorf testimony, 3 Jan. 1946, IMT 4, 318, 353. Interrogation of Barth, 14 Jan. 1948, NA RG 238, M-1019/R 5/231.

30. EM #107, NA RG 242, T-175/R 234/2722835.

31. Barth affidavits, 8 Oct. 1943 [sic; probably 8 Oct. 1946], NA RG 238, NO-3663; and 12 Sept. 1947, NA RG 238, NO-4992, listing the *Einsatzkommandos* and mentioning also that police battalions took part. Himmler's itinerary, NA RG 242, T-175/R 112/2637716, mentions Himmler's inspection of Police Battalion 311 at Cherson, which joined the *Einsatzkommandos* in the grisly work.

32. Blobel's testimony at the IMT, reprinted by *Nationalsozialistische Massentötungen*, 93. Interrogation of Josef Franz Suchanek, 30 Nov. 1965, Callsen Trial, Ludwigsburg 207 AR-Z 419/62, 1,878–91. Photocopies in my possession.

33. *Nationalsozialistische Massentötungen*, 93.

34. Interrogation of Julius Bauer, 2 Aug. 1965, Callsen Trial, ZSL 207 AR-Z 419/62, 88. Photocopies in my possession. Also Eugen Steimle affidavit, 14 Dec. 1945, NA RG 238, NO-3842; interrogation of Suchanek, 30 Nov. 1965.

35. Prützmann turned over his job to Jeckeln on 23 Oct. Brandt's log, NA RG 242, T-581/R 39A.

36. Andreas Hillgruber, *Hitlers Strategie: Politik und Kriegführung 1940–1941* (Frankfurt am Main, 1965), 694. Bormann's notes, T-84/R 387/515. The only detailed account of what the two men discussed on 2 Oct. is not completely reliable: Engel, *Heeresadjutant*, 111. Engel's diary was composed after the war, from notes, and contains some errors. He has Himmler present on 2 Oct. as well, and he lists the destinations of the transports of German Jews as Riga, Minsk, and *Reval*, not Kowno. Still, the thrust of the entry is confirmed by Heydrich's remarks in his Prague conference of 10 Oct. See pp. 214–15 and n. 37 below.

37. Notizen aus der Besprechung am 10.10.41 über die Lösung der Judenfragen, Czechoslovakian State Archives, Office of Reich Protector, I-365860, carton 390, cited by Miroslav Karny, "Zur Typologie des Theresienstadten Konzentrationslagers," *Judaica Bohemiae* 17 (1981), 7n. A copy of this document was graciously provided by Charles W. Sydnor, Jr.

38. Avner Less pretrial interrogation of Eichmann, 1 June 1960, Yad Vashem Archive, Jerusalem, T-37, VI, 26. I am grateful to Shlomo Aronson for supplying me with this information.

39. See, for example, Heydrich Fernschreiben, 9 Oct. 1941, NA RG 242, T-120/R 1026/406029–34.

40. Himmler's notes of phone conversations, 18 Oct. 1941, NA RG 242, T-84/R 25/no frame nos.

41. Rosenberg to Lammers, 14 Oct. 1941, NA RG 238, T-1139/R 21/717–18.

42. YIVO Institute for Jewish Research, Berlin Collection, Doc. Occ E 3–30.

43. NA RG 238, 3663-PS.

44. Adolf Hitler, *Monologe im Führerhauptquartier 1941–1944: Die Aufzeichnungen Heinrich Heims*, ed. Werner Jochmann (Hamburg, 1980), 44.

45. Lange to Lohse, 8 Nov. 1941, YIVO Institute for Jewish Research, Doc. Occ E 3–31.

46. In several interrogations Jeckeln later dated his meeting with Himmler variously as the 10th, 11th, or 12th. Jeckeln's testimony in Krausnick and Wilhelm, *Truppe des Weltanschauungskrieges*, 567. Interrogation of Lohse, 20 Oct. 1947, NA RG 238, M 1019/R 43/793.

47. Interrogations of Lohse, 20 Oct. and 20 Nov. 1947, NA RG 238, M-1019/R 43/792–93 and 819–20.

48. Niederschrift über die Chefbesprechung, 30 Oct. 1941, NA RG 238, 1539-PS. Himmler to Heydrich, 27 Oct. 1941, NA RG 242, T-175/R 123/2648539.

49. Carl to Kube, 30 Oct. 1941; Kube to Lohse, 1 Nov. 1941, forwarded to Rosenberg; Bigenwald to Marquart, 21 Nov. 1941, sent on to Heydrich, all in NA RG 238, 1104-PS, 2406-PS, 1104-PS.

50. Hersh Smolar, *The Minsk Ghetto: Soviet-Jewish Partisans Against the Nazis* (New York, 1989), 41–42. Shalom Cholawsky, "The Judenrat in Minsk," in Yisrael Gutman and Cynthia Haft, eds., *Patterns of Jewish Leadership in Nazi Europe 1933–1945: Proceedings of the Third Yad Vashem International Historical Conference* (Jerusalem, 1979), 118.

51. Himmler's Aktennotiz, 15 Nov. 1941, T-175/R 128/2654508; also NA RG 238, NO-5329. Text of the agreement, dated 19 Nov. 1941, in NA RG 242, T-454/R 100/887–88.

52. Browning, *Fateful Months*, 33. Recollections of Professor Widukind Lenz in Benno Müller-Hill, *Murderous Science: Elimination by Scientific Selection of Jews, Gypsies, and Others, Germany, 1933–1945* (Oxford, 1988), 110–11. Text of Rosenberg's speech (section on Jews) NA RG 242, T-77/R 1175/433.

53. NA RG 242, T-84/R 26.

54. NA RG 238, 709-PS.

55. On the process in the Riga ghetto, Ziwian affidavit, 1 Oct. 1942, NA RG 84, Geneva Confidential file 1942, 800, which, however, states there were eight thousand victims on 29–30 Nov. and sixteen thousand on 8–9 Dec., which actually should be reversed. A postwar German court concluded that at least fourteen thousand Jews of Riga were executed on 30 Nov., and a later scholarly study gives the figure as fifteen thousand (plus a thousand more German Jews). See Fleming, *Hitler and the Final Solution*, 76 and 76n.; Gertrude Schneider, *Journey into Terror: Story of the Riga Ghetto* (New York, 1979), 12–15. See also Krausnick and Wilhelm, *Truppe des Weltanschauungskrieges*, 565; Frida Michelson, *I Survived Rumbuli*, trans. Wolf Goodman (New York, 1979), 77–85. On the inclusion of the transport from Berlin, Martin Brozsat, "Hitler und die Genesis der 'Endlösung': Aus Anlass der Thesen von David Irving," *Vierteljahrshefte für Zeitgeschichte* 25 (1977): 760–61. Quotation from the eyewitness report reaching the Reich Interior Ministry, Lösener affidavit, 24 Feb. 1948, NA RG 238, T-1139/R 23/796, NG-1944-A. For a comparable description, the Riga Trial verdict of 1973, quoted by Fleming, *Hitler and the Final Solution*, 79.

56. Himmler's notes of telephone conversations, "Aufenthalt der über 60 Jahre alten Juden," 1 Nov. 1941, NA RG 242, T-84/R 26. On the policy of exempting decorated veterans, Fleming, *Hitler and the Final Solution*, 77.

57. Broszat, "Hitler und die Genesis," 760–61. Himmler-Heydrich phone conversation, NA RG 242, T-84/R 26, 30 Nov. 1941.

58. Broszat, "Hitler und die Genesis," 761. Krausnick and Wilhelm, *Truppe des Weltanschauungskrieges*, 548.

59. The background and evidence for this story have been uncovered and spelled out by Fleming, *Hitler and the Final Solution*, 80–89, quote on 85.

60. Himmler to all higher SS and police leaders and all SS and police leaders, 12 Dec. 1941, Latvian State Archives, Riga, Collection P-83, entry 1, file 80. Photocopy in my possession.

61. Hitler-Rosenberg conference, IMT 27, 270–73, 1517-PS. Rosenberg had more difficulty handling the portions of the speech on the other Eastern peoples, and in the end the speech had to be canceled. See David Dallin, *German Rule in Russia, 1941–1945: A Study of Occupation Policies* (Boulder, 1981), 130.

62. Ministry to Lohse, 18 Dec. 1941, NA RG 238, 3666-PS. Interrogations of Bräutigam, 25 and 26 May 1948, M-1019/ R 9/71 and 87.

63. IMT 15, 666.

64. See p. 157. For more details, Yeshayahu Jelinek, "Slovakia's Internal Policy and the Third Reich, August 1940–February 1941," *Central European History* 4 (1971), 242–70; and Yeshayahu Jelinek, "The 'Final Solution'—the Slovak Version," *East European Quarterly* 4 (1971): 431–41.

65. See the summary judgment in Christopher R. Browning, *The Final Solution and the German Foreign Office: A Study of Referat III D of Abteilung Deutschland* (New York, 1978), 21.

66. Ibid., 27–28.

67. Woermann to Abteilung Deutschland, 1 March 1941, NA RG 238, T-1139/R 20/9–10, NG-1515. The list of complaints against SS-Sturmbannführer Beisner, head of Einsatzkommando Agram, went back to June 1941. See Aufstellung über Schwierig-keiten . . . , 20 Sept. 1942, NA RG 238, T-1139/R 41/46, NG-3981. On Rumania, Browning, *Final Solution*, 52.

68. Browning, *Final Solution*, 52–55.

69. Wolff to Heydrich, 4 Aug. 1941, NA RG 242, T-175/R 426/2970407–10. Notes of Himmler's phone conversation with Wolff, 26 Sept. 1941, NA RG 242, T-84/R 26.

70. Browning, *Final Solution*, 57–64.

71. Vortragsnotiz, 8 Oct. 1941, NA RG 238, T-1139/R 49/126–27, NG–4846.

72. Browning, *Final Solution*, 66.

73. Ibid., 66–67, 72.

74. On the Slovaks and Hitler's pattern, Jelinek, "The 'Final Solution' " 432; also pp. 240–41 of this book. This meeting between Hitler and the three Slovak officials, which Jelinek dates as Nov. 1941 based on postwar testimony, probably occurred on 20 Oct., though Hitler did meet again with Tuka alone on 27 Nov. For the 20 Oct. meeting, Hillgruber, *Hitlers Strategie*, 695; also NA RG 242, T-84/R 387/516.

75. Luther Aufzeichnung, 21 Aug. 1942, NA RG 238, T-1139/R 29/582–83, NG-2586.

76. On the 27 Nov. meetings, see Empfänge beim Führer, 27 Nov. 1941, NA RG 242, T-175/R 112/2637237. On Haj Amin el-Husseini, Paul Otto Schmidt's minutes, 28 Nov. 1941, quoted by Fleming, *Hitler and the Final Solution*, 103–4.

77. Browning, *Final Solution*, 76–77.

78. Non-Biographical files, Berlin Document Center, RFSS, Ordner 8, SS 920. Helmut Müller to Hofmann, 15 Oct. 1941, NA RG 238, NO-5875.

79. SS- und Polizeiführer im Distrikt Galizien, *Lösung der Judenfrage in Galizien 1943 (Abschlussbericht)*, with cover letter, Hofmann to Krüger, 30 June 1943, Hoover Institution, Stanford University.

80. See p. 183.

81. Heydrich to Lammers, 18 Sept. 1941, and related documents, NA RG 238, T-1139/R 16/841–45, NG-1151. Himmler's telephone-conversation notes, NA RG 242, T-84/R 26, 23 Oct. 1941.

82. Lasch Nazi Party file, Berlin Document Center.

83. Jerzy Sawicki, *Vor dem polnischen Staatsanwalt* (Berlin, 1962), 198.

84. Handwritten notations on the cover letter, Heydrich to Lammers, 18 Sept. 1941, NA RG 238, T-1139/R 16/853, NG-1151.

85. Krüger to Himmler, 7 Nov. 1941, NA RG 242, T-175/R 123/2648581.

86. Raul Hilberg, *The Destruction of the European Jews* (Chicago, 1961); 2nd expanded ed., 3 vols. (New York, 1985), II, 482.

87. Frank speech of 16 Dec. 1941, in Werner Präg and Wolfgang Jacobmeyer, eds., *Das Diensttagebuch des deutschen Generalgouverneurs in Polen 1939–1945* (Stuttgart, 1975), 457.

88. Probably Heydrich, who was in Berlin at that time. Himmler's notes of the phone conversation with Heydrich, 2 Dec. 1941, simply say "conference with Stuckart." NA RG 242, T-84/R 26.

89. Lösener affidavit, 24 Feb. 1948, NA RG 238, T-1139/R 23/796, NG-1944-A. Also quoted by Fleming, *Hitler and the Final Solution*, 106–7.

CHAPTER 11: WANNSEE AND BEYOND

1. Günther Deschner, *Reinhard Heydrich: A Biography* (New York, 1981), 112–13.

2. Earl F. Ziemke and Magna E. Bauer, *Moscow to Stalingrad: Decision in the East* (Washington, D.C., 1985), 69–172.

3. Stahlecker Report of Feb. 1942, excerpt in IMT 30, 73–74, 77, 2273-PS.

4. Unless otherwise noted, the following account of the Wannsee Conference is from the official summary, NA RG 238, NG-2586, trans. in Raul Hilberg, ed., *Documents of Destruction: Germany and Jewry 1933–1945* (London, 1972), 89–99. Luther's mention of Hitler, Luther Aufzeichnung, 21 Aug. 1942, NA RG 238, NG-2586J, cited by Gerald Fleming, *Hitler and the Final Solution* (Berkeley, 1984; German original, 1982), 46n.

5. See p. 59.

6. See pp. 224 and 154.

7. On this point, see Yeshayahu Jelinek, "The 'Final Solution'—the Slovak Version," *East European Quarterly* 4 (1971): 431–32. See also, more generally, Yeshayahu Jelinek, "The Holocaust of Slovakian and Croatian Jewry from the Historiographic Viewpoint, Comparative Analysis," in Yisrael Gutman and Gideon Greiff, eds., *Historiography of the Holocaust Period: Proceedings of the Fifth Yad Vashem Historical Conference* (Jerusalem, 1988), 275–85.

8. On Himmler's attitude toward German blood in foreign races, see chapter four. For Himmler's plant-animal analogy, Himmler to Bormann, 22 May 1943, NA RG 242, T-175/R 83/2609253.

9. Lammers to the highest Reich officials, 20 July 1942, NA RG 238, T-1139/R 48/1096, NG-4819.

10. One example of the use of the term "Endlösung der Judenmischlingsfrage" in Hildebrandt to Brandt, 2 June 1943, and Brandt to Hildebrandt, 23 June 1943, NA RG 242, T-175/R 83/2609250–51.

11. Testimony of Adolf Eichmann at the Eichmann Trial, Jerusalem, 23, 26 June 1961, 24 July 1961, reprinted in Hilberg, *Documents of Destruction*, 101–5. Robert M. W. Kempner, *SS im Kreuzverhör: Die Elite, die Europa in Scherben brach* (Hamburg, 1987), 236.

12. Eichmann testimony in Hilberg, *Documents of Destruction*, 101–4.

13. Himmler's notes of phone conversations, 21 and 25 Jan. 1942, NA RG 242, T-84/R 26/no frame nos.

14. Himmler to Glücks, 26 Jan. 1942, and Himmler to Heydrich, 27 Jan. 1942, NA RG 242, T-580/R 69/no frame nos. See the excellent analysis by Ulrich Herbert, "Arbeit and Vernichtung: Ökonomisches Interesse und Primat der Weltanschauung im Nationalsozialismus," in Dan Diner, ed., *Ist der Nationalsozialismus Geschichte?: Zu Historisierung und Historikerstreit* (Frankfurt am Main, 1988), espec. 213–21.

15. Himmler to Glücks, 26 Jan. 1942, and Himmler to Heydrich, 27 Jan. 1942, NA RG 242, T-580/R 69/no frame nos.

16. Himmler to Rosenberg, 29 Jan. 1942, Eichmann Trial, Document #1088, copy in Institut für Zeitgeschichte, Munich; copy, without cover letter, in IMT 25, 302–6, 212-PS. See also Eberhard Jäckel and Jürgen Rohwer, eds., *Der Mord an den Juden im Zweiten Weltkrieg* (Stuttgart, 1985), 93–94.

17. Hitler's speech in the Sportpalast on 30 Jan. 1942, reprinted in Max Domarus, *Hitler, Reden und Proklamationen 1932–1945* (Munich, 1965), II, 1,828–29; Adolf Hitler, *Monologe im Führerhauptquartier 1941–1944: Die Aufzeichnungen Heinrich Heims*, ed. Werner Jochmann (Hamburg, 1980), 293, 2 Feb. 1942.

18. Berger to Himmler, 10 April 1942, NA RG 242, T-175/R 127/2649922.

19. This account is based on Himmler's detailed memorandum written just after the meeting. NA RG 242, T-175/R 125/2649954–56. However, a persistent Frank did not give up the battle. Five days later he tried to recoup some lost ground with a letter to Lammers, which was quickly sent on to Himmler. NA RG 242, T-175/R 125/2649950–3. And Globocnik never did get appointed as regional governor, partly because of Krüger's lack of assertiveness. See Himmler to Krüger, 15 May 1942, Krüger SS file, Berlin Document Center.

20. *Reichsgesetzblatt*, 1942, pt. 1, 242.

21. Yitzhak Arad, *Belzec, Sobibor, Treblinka: The Operation Reinhard Death Camps* (Bloomington, Ind., 1987), 46.

22. Brandt's log, NA RG 242, T-581/R 40A, 17 July 1942. Hoess, *Commandant of Auschwitz* (New York, 1961), 197–98. *From the History of KL Auschwitz* (New York, 1982), I, 192–93.

23. Hoess, *Commandant of Auschwitz*, 198.

24. Höss later repeated to Eichmann Himmler's comment about the coming generation. See *Eichmann Interrogated: Transcripts from the Archives of the Israeli Police*, ed. Jochen von Lang and Claus Sibyll (New York, 1983), 83.

25. Hoess, *Commandant of Auschwitz*, 200–1. Confirmation that Himmler promoted Höss that day—and thus partial confirmation for Höss's account generally—in I. G. Farben, Wochenbericht für die Zeit 13–20 July 1942, NA RG 238, NI-14551. For contemporary evidence of the plans for expansion of Auschwitz (and evidence that Alfred Speer was directly involved), see Pohl to Himmler, 16 Sept. 1942, NA RG 242, T-175/R 19/2522807.

26. Himmler's schedule, NA RG 242, T-581/R 39A, 18 July 1942.

27. The written form, dated 18 July 1942, that the men were supposed to sign has survived and is reprinted in Yitzhak Arad, Yisrael Gutman, and Abraham Margaliot, *Documents on the Holocaust: Selected Sources on the Destruction of the Jews of Germany, Austria, Poland, and the Soviet Union* (Jerusalem, 1981), 274–75; an excerpt is quoted here.

28. Testimony of Kurt Gerstein, 26 April 1945, reprinted in *Vierteljahrshefte für Zeitgeschichte* 1 (1953): 188. For reasons explained in n. 38 below, though there are minor errors in Gerstein's dates, his testimony seems accurate.

29. Himmler's schedule, NA RG 242, T-581/R 39A, 18–20 July 1942.

30. Miriam Novitch, *Sobibor: Martyrdom and Revolt—Documents and Testimonies* (New York, 1980), 34–35. Description of the normal process from Arad, *Belzec, Sobibor, Treblinka*, 76–77.

31. Arad, *Belzec, Sobibor, Treblinka*, 76–78. On Himmler's group, Novitch, *Sobibor*, 35.

32. Himmler to Krüger, 19 July 1942, NA RG 238, NO-5574, quoted by Arad, *Belzec, Sobibor, Treblinka*, 47.

33. On the start of deportations to Treblinka, Arad, *Belzec, Sobibor, Treblinka*, 60–61, 392. Quote from Globocnik to Wolff, 22 July 1942, Globocnik SS file, Berlin Document Center.

34. Rudolf Höss Aufzeichnungen, Institut für Zeitgeschichte F 13/6, 364.

35. For the date of Himmler's flight, see Himmler's schedule, 24 July 1942, NA RG 242, T-581/R 39A. On Himmler's headquarters and Dr. Thomas's orders, testimony of Dr. Franz Razesberger, 18 July 1961, Landgericht Wien, Hauptverhandlung Razesberger, 20 Vr. 5774/60, Hv 21/61, 155–58. Photocopies in my possession. Order for the liquidation of Jews in Vinnitsa, An die Aussendienststelle d. Sipo u. d. SD in Winniza: Juden und Ukrainer in den Sicherungsobjekten, in Central Archive of the October Revolution, Kiev, Collection 3676 (Einsatzstab Rosenberg), entry 4, file 116, p. 56.

36. Testimony of Dr. Franz Razesberger, 18 July 1961, 158–62. Himmler's schedule for 25 July 1942 confirms that Razesberger was at this dinner. NA RG 242, T-581/R 39A.

37. Himmler to Berger, 26 July 1942, reprinted in Jüdisches Historische Institut Warschau, *Fascismus-Getto-Massenmord: Dokumentation über Ausrottung und Widerstand der Juden in Polen während des Zweiten Weltkrieges* (Berlin-Ost, 1960), 296.

38. Brandt's memo, 21 Aug. 1942, NA RG 242, T-175/R 88/2611400. Himmler's schedule also confirms Himmler's presence in Lublin. NA RG 242, T-581/R 40A, 21 Aug. 1942. Gerstein's account, reconstructed on 26 April 1945, reprinted in *Vierteljahrshefte für Zeitgeschichte* 1 (1953): 185–93, contains two types of inaccuracies. First, he erred slightly on the dates of his trip to Lublin, and therefore of Himmler's visit to Lublin. Second, he of course could only repeat what Globocnik had told him, and Globocnik had a habit of inflating his own role. See Rudolf Höss Aufzeichnungen, Institut für Zeitgeschichte, F 13/6, 360–61. So it is not surprising that Globocnik invented Hitler's presence, a claim that no other documentation supports, and which contradicted Hitler's tendency to avoid the appearance of direct association with the killing.

Based on the available contemporary documentation, the accurate dates are as follows: Himmler's trip to Lublin, 21 Aug.; Gerstein's trip with Günther and Pfannenstiel, 22 Aug.; Gerstein's meeting with Swedish diplomat Göran von Otter, late 22 Aug. On the last, see the new evidence in Steven Koblik, *The Stones Cry Out: Sweden's Response to the Persecution of the Jews, 1933–1945* (New York, 1988), 58.

39. Wehrwirtschaftsrüstungsamt, Rüstungsinspektion Ukraine, Tätigkeit für die Zeit vom 1.9.42–15.9.42, NA RG 242, T-77/R 1093/1044–46. On Himmler's order to liquidate the Jews of Pinsk, NA RG 238, NO-2027. There were parallel decisions at this time, temporarily exempting some Jews working on military contracts but ordering the extermination of most, in other areas as well. See, for example, Herbert, "Arbeit und Vernichtung," 221.

40. Gespräch des Reichsführer-SS am Mittagessen am 13 Sept. 1942, NA RG 242, T-175/R 88/2611398.

41. I am here following the careful account in Hannu Rautkallio, *Finland and the Holocaust: The Rescue of Finland's Jews* (New York, 1987), 168. The limited information in Himmler's appointment book, NA RG 242, T-581, R 39A, and R 40A is consistent with Rautkallio's account, and contradicts on matters of detail the various accounts by Felix Kersten.

42. Himmler's agenda notes for meeting with Hitler, 22 Sept. 1942, NA RG 242, T-175/R 94/2615170. On the preliminary preparations, Rinteln to Luther, 19 Aug. and 28 Aug. 1942, NA RG 238, T-1139/R 41/76–79, NG-3985.

43. Bracht to Himmler, 17 Sept. 1942, and Himmler to Bracht, 23 Sept. 1942, NA RG 242, T-175/R 58/2573260–64.

44. Luther explained that Ribbentrop had said that either Hitler or Ribbentrop would have to discuss the Italian Jews with Mussolini or Ciano. Luther to Weizsäcker, 24 Sept. 1942, NA RG 238, T-1139/R 55/1016, NG-5631.

45. Himmler's Niederschrift über meinen Empfang beim Duce . . . , 11 Oct. 1942, NA RG 242, T-175/R 69/2585529–34.

46. For discussion of the documentation of this meeting, and for more details of the meeting, see Richard Breitman, "Auschwitz and the Archives," *Central European History* 18 (1985): 381–82.

47. *"Ich habe den Führer wegen der Loslösung von Juden gegen Devisen gefragt. Er hat mir Vollmacht gegeben, derartige Fälle zu genehmigen, wenn sie wirklich in namhaften Umfang Devisen von auswärts hereinbringen."* Himmler's memo for the files, NA RG 242, T-580/R 39/no frame nos. See also Himmler's notes made at the meeting, NA RG 242, T-175/R 94/ 2615065.

48. On Korherr's prior work, see his brief description in Besprechung Dr. Korherr-Gruf. Berger vom 28.7.1942, NA RG 242, T-175/R 68/2584564. Himmler's authorization of Korherr to work on the Final Solution, Himmler to RSHA, 18 Jan. 1943, NA RG 238, NO-4790.

49. Korherr's reports in NA RG 238, NO-5193 and 5194, cover letter, NO-5195. Himmler's correction of wording in Brandt to Korherr, 20 April 1943, NA RG 238, NO-5196. Raul Hilberg, *The Destruction of the European Jews* (Chicago, 1961), 2nd expanded ed., 3 vols. (New York, 1985), I, 322–23, reviews the whole range of Nazi terms that veiled the realities.

50. The "official" version of the speech, published in IMT 29, 110–73, 1919-PS, does not contain this section, or a number of others, because, after recording his speeches, Himmler would have an exact transcript made, then edit it. One has to go to the recording to get the exact speech that Himmler gave. The recording is available in the National Archives, Motion Picture, Sound, and Video Branch.

51. IMT 29, 115, 1919-PS.

52. Again, this is not in the printed text. See n. 50.

EPILOGUE: HIMMLER IN RETROSPECT

1. *Topographie des Terrors: Gestapo, SS und Reichssicherheitshauptamt auf dem "Prinz Albrecht-Gelände"—Eine Dokumentation* (Berlin, 1987), 12.

2. Ernst Nolte, "Between Myth and Revisionism," in H. W. Koch, ed., *Aspects of the Third Reich* (London, 1985), 27, has cited Weizmann's statement as an influence upon Hitler. For a sound critique of Nolte's argument, see Jürgen Kocka, "Hitler sollte nicht durch Stalin und Pol Pot verdrängt werden," in *"Historikerstreit": Die Dokumentation der Kontroverse um die Einzigartigkeit der nationalsozialistischen Judenvernichtung* (Munich, 1987), 132–42, esp. 142.

3. Nolte's discussion of Hitler's reaction to Asiatic deeds, "Vergangenheit, die nicht vergehen will: Eine Rede, die geschrieben, aber nicht gehalten werden konnte," in *Historikerstreit*, 44–45.

4. See p. 144.

5. Here I am in general agreement with Christopher R. Browning, *Fateful Months: Essays on the Emergence of the Final Solution* (New York, 1985), 32.

6. Christian Streit, *Keine Kameraden: Die Wehrmacht und die sowjetischen Kriegsgefangenen 1941–1945* (Stuttgart, 1978). Omer Bartov, *The Eastern Front 1941–1945: German Troops and the Barbarization of Warfare* (Oxford, 1985).

7. For a sample, Alan D. Beyerchen, *Scientists Under Hitler: Politics and the Physics Com-*

munity in the Third Reich (New Haven, 1979); Friedrich Karl Kaul, *Die Psychiatrie im Strudel der "Euthanasia": Ein Bericht über die erste industriemässig durchgeführte Mordaktion des Naziregimes* (Frankfurt, 1979); Robert J. Lifton, *The Nazi Doctors: Medical Killing and the Psychology of Genocide* (New York, 1986); Geoffrey Cocks, *Psychotherapy in the Third Reich: the Göring Institute* (New York, 1985); Robert N. Proctor, *Racial Hygiene: Medicine Under the Nazis* (Cambridge, 1988); Michael Kater, *Doctors Under Hitler* (Chapel Hill, N.C., 1989); Konrad Jarausch, *The Unfree Professions: German Lawyers, Teachers, and Engineers, 1900–1950* (New York, 1990); Claudia Koonz, "Genocide and Eugenics: Ministers, Priests, and Parishioners," paper presented at Northwestern University conference "Lessons and Legacies: The Meaning of the Holocaust in a Changing World," 12 Nov. 1989; Götz Aly and Susanne Heim, "The Economics of the Final Solution: A Case Study from the Government General," *Simon Wiesenthal Center Annual* 5 (1988): 3–48.

GLOSSARY OF TITLES
AND SPECIAL TERMS

Abwehr The central German military intelligence organization, headed by Admiral Wilhelm Canaris, an enemy of Himmler's.

Einsatzgruppen Battalion-sized, mobile, armed units of police, primarily Security Police and SD officials, which were used to attack and execute perceived enemies in conquered territories. Once these units or parts of them became stationary, they were formally designated as Security Police and headed by a Security Police commander.

Einsatzkommando Company-sized component of the *Einsatzgruppen*.

Final Solution Short version of Nazi term "Final Solution of the Jewish Question," a euphemism for the program to exterminate European Jewry. See extended discussion in Introduction.

Führer Chancellery Adolf Hitler's personal chancellery, an extended staff that handled his personal affairs, interests, and a number of specially assigned policies.

Gauleiter Supreme territorial or regional party authority (-ies) (the term is both singular and plural). The Nazi Party divided Germany and some annexed territories into geographical units called *Gaue*, headed by Gauleiter.

Government General of Poland, or Government General The Nazi-ruled state in central and eastern Poland. Headed by Governor Hans Frank, one of Himmler's antagonists.

Higher SS and Police Leader(s) (*Höhere SS- und Polizeiführer*) Supreme territorial/regional commander(s) for all SS officers as well as for police officers within the territory or region. Directly responsible to Himmler for the implementation of policies related to the security of the state and the investigation and treatment of dangerous elements within the realm(s).

Holocaust Postwar term for the Nazi murder of some six million Jews. Sometimes includes other victims as well. See extended discussion in Introduction.

Kristallnacht Literally, "night of broken glass." Name for the organized pogrom that began on Nov. 9–10, 1938. See extended discussion in chapter two.

Local SS and Police Leader (*SS- und Polizeistandortführer*) Local commander for all SS officers and police officers within a district, usually a city.

Order Police (*Ordnungspolizei*) Separate from the Gestapo and Criminal Police. Included the remaining city and rural policemen (*Schutzpolizei* and *Gendarmerie*) who handled matters such as traffic, patrols, and routine police business. Battalions of Order Police, however, functioned like the *Einsatzgruppen*—they carried out mass killings—in the Soviet Union and in Poland. Headed by Kurt Daluege, Himmler's longtime friend and Reinhard Heydrich's rival.

Ostland Reich Commissariat Ostland, the Nazi administrative unit comprising the conquered territories of Estonia, Latvia, Lithuania, and Byelorussia. The other Reich Commissariat in the Soviet Union was the Ukraine.

Party Chancellery The supreme administrative organ of the Nazi Party. Headed first by Rudolf Hess and then by Martin Bormann.

Reich Chancellor Hitler's formal title as head of government, but less common than, and subordinate to, his title of Führer.

Reich Chancellery Both a building and an office—the chancellor's extended staff, composed mostly of experienced civil servants familiar with government practices and procedures.

Reich Führer SS (*Reichsführer SS*) Reich Leader of the *Schutzstaffel* or SS—namely, Heinrich Himmler, who from 1936 on also added to his title "Chief of the German Police."

Reich Ministry for the Occupied Eastern Territories The government ministry nominally responsible for policy and civil administration in the conquered areas of the Soviet Union. Headed by Alfred Rosenberg, this ministry lacked jurisdiction over the SS and police and the policies they carried out.

Reichsleiter Member(s) of an executive board of the Nazi Party. (The term is both singular and plural.)

RFV (*Reichskommissariat für die Festigung des deutschen Volkes*) Reich Commissariat for the Strengthening of the German People. Designed to promote and extend settlement by those of German blood. Headed by Heinrich Himmler. See extended discussion in chapter three.

RSHA (*Reichssicherheitshauptamt*) Reich Security Main Office, created in September 1939. A combined government-SS organization incorporating major nonmilitary offices responsible for intelligence work, security, and criminal police work. Included the political police (Gestapo), criminal police, and the SS Security Service or SD, among other branches. Formally responsible to Himmler, but run by Reinhard Heydrich.

SA (*Sturmabteilung*)   The first Nazi paramilitary organization, formed to help protect meetings of the party and disrupt those of opponents. Grew into a large but undisciplined force under Ernst Röhm, who, along with a number of other SA officials, was liquidated on 30 June 1934 by Himmler's men. Himmler continued to distrust and dislike the SA thereafter.

SD (*Sicherheitsdienst*)   Security Service, the intelligence branch of the SS. Heavily involved in researching and later implementing the campaigns against Nazi Germany's ideological and racial enemies.

Security Police (*Sicherheitspolizei*)   A fusion of the various state political police and criminal police forces. Responsible for dealing with actual and potential enemies of the Nazi regime and the German *Volk*. Even though the Security Police were part of the government, not the SS, they were closely linked to the SD.

Sonderkommandos   A subdivision of the *Einsatzgruppen*, generally smaller than an *Einsatzkommando*, but also a more general term for special commando units assigned particular functions.

SS (*Schutzstaffel*)   The elite Nazi organization run by Heinrich Himmler. See extended discussion in chapter one.

SS and Police Leader(s) (*SS- und Polizeiführer*)   Subterritorial commander(s) for all SS and police authorities within the area. Subordinate to higher SS and police leader(s) and to Himmler.

Third Reich   Literally, "Third Nation or Empire." The Nazi term for the Nazi regime. The First Reich was supposed to have been the Holy Roman Empire from Charlemagne to Frederick II; the Second Reich was Germany under the Hohenzollern Emperors Wilhelm I and II, 1871–1918.

Volksdeutsche Mittelstelle   Ethnic German Liaison Office. Handled some aspects of the relationship of Nazi Germany to ethnic Germans in a number of other European countries, but it had competition from other government and party agencies. Not originally part of the SS, although Himmler gained effective control of it before the beginning of World War II.

Wartheland or Warthegau   Territory in western Poland annexed by Germany after its conquest of Poland. Does not include Polish Silesia, which was also annexed but was incorporated into German Silesia. Also excludes parts of Poland incorporated into East Prussia. The extermination camp at Chełmno was in the Wartheland.

WVHA (*Wirtschaftsverwaltungshauptamt*)   Economic-Administrative Main Office of the SS. Formally established in early 1942, but management of most SS construction and economic activities was unified in the hands of Oswald Pohl well before then. The WVHA oversaw the economic activities at the concentration and extermination camps.

Glossary

SS Ranks	Western Military Equivalent
Oberstgruppenführer	General
Obergruppenführer	Lieutenant General
Gruppenführer	Major General
Brigadeführer	Brigadier General
Oberführer	between Brigadier General and Colonel
Standartenführer	Colonel
Obersturmbannführer	Lieutenant Colonel
Sturmbannführer	Major
Hauptsturmführer	Captain
Obersturmführer	First Lieutenant
Untersturmführer	Second Lieutenant
Sturmscharführer	Master Sergeant
Hauptscharführer	Technical Sergeant
Oberscharführer	Staff Sergeant
Scharführer	Sergeant
Unterscharführer	Corporal
Rottenführer	Private First Class
Sturmann	Private
SS-Mann	no equivalent

ARCHIVAL COLLECTIONS

What follows is a list of the major archives and collections that I personally visited and used. See also Acknowledgments and Notes for other sources.

United States National Archives (abbreviated NA in Notes)
  Captured German Records, Record Group 242 (RG 242)
    Microfilm Series T-74, T-77, T-78, T-81, T-84, T-120, T-175, T-354, T-501, T-580, T-581, T-992.
  Diplomatic Records, RG 59
    Intergovernmental Committee on Refugees, Lot File 52D408
    Central Decimal File
  Diplomatic Post Records (Washington National Records Center), RG 84
  Records of the Office of the Judge Advocate General (Army) (Washington National Records Center), RG 153
  Records of the War Department General and Special Staffs (Washington National Records Center), RG 165
  Office of War Information Records (Washington National Records Center), RG 208
  Office of Strategic Services Records, RG 226
    Plain number file
    Entry 171
  War Crimes, RG 238
    Office of Chief of Counsel, Administrative Records and Berlin Branch Records
    NI series (microfilm T-301)
    NO series
    NG series (microfilm T-1139)
    PS series
    EC series
    NOKW series
    Pretrial interrogations, Microfilm series M-1019
    Pretrial interrogations, Microfilm series M-1270
  Records of the Army Staff, RG 319
    Investigative Repository Records (IRR)

U.S. Army Intelligence and Security Command, Ft. Meade, Maryland, Intelligence
Records (similar to IRR Records above)
Records of the U.S. Army Commands (Washington National Records Center), RG 338

Franklin D. Roosevelt Presidential Library
President's Secretary's File

American Friends Service Committee, Philadelphia
Refugee Service Records

American Jewish Historical Society, Waltham, Massachusetts
Stephen S. Wise Papers

Houghton Library, Harvard University
Jay Pierrepont Moffat Diaries

Library of Congress, Manuscript Division
German Captured Document Collection
Leland H. Harrison Papers

Stanford University, Hoover Institution
Himmler Collection

University of Delaware
George S. Messersmith Papers

United Nations War Crimes Commission Records, United Nations Archive, New York

Institut für Zeitgeschichte, Munich
Akten der Parteikanzlei (microfiche)
Rudolf Höss Aufzeichnungen
Günter d'Alquen Unterredung
Felix Kersten Sammlung
Karl Wolff Sammlung
Eichmann Prozess

Berlin Document Center
SS Files
Non-Biographic Collection

Central State Archives of the October Revolution of the Ukrainian SSR, Kiev
Collection 3676 (Einsatzstab Rosenberg), Entry 4
Collection 4620, Entry 3

INDEX